Organisations at work

Organisations at work
Second edition

M R Frampton
Vice-Principal, Richmond upon Thames Tertiary College

R T Norrie
Head of Department, Business Studies and Management, Merton College

A J Rees
Principal Lecturer, Head of School of Business, Office and Pre-vocational Studies, Gloucestershire
College of Arts and Technology

B Williams
Senior Lecturer, Organisation Studies and Business Planning, Hammersmith and West London College

PITMAN PUBLISHING
128 Long Acre, London WC2E 9AN

A Division of Longman Group UK Limited

© M R Frampton, R T Norrie, A J Rees, B Williams 1988

First published in Great Britain in Thomas Nelson & Son Ltd 1983
Second edition published in Great Britain by Pitman Publishing 1988
Reprinted 1989, 1990

British Library Cataloguing in Publication Data

Organisations at work. — 2nd ed.
  1. Organization
  I. Frampton, M.R.   II. Frampton, M.R.
  Organisations at work
  302.3'5'0941   HM131

ISBN 0 273 02646 1

Printed and bound in Singapore

Contents

Part I: An organisation in its environment – accountability

Preface

This book is designed principally for use with the BTEC National Diploma and Certificate Core Modules 'The Organisation in its Environment'.

The book takes account of the BTEC National Business and Finance, Public Administration, Distribution and Leisure Core Themes – Money, Technology and Change. The theme of change is crucial to this book. In this second edition, which has been extensively rewritten, the impact of change on people and organisations is continually highlighted.

Although the book is designed primarily for BTEC National and takes account of the division of The Organisation in its Environment Core into Year 1 and Year 2 (Chapters 1–27 deal primarily with Year 1, Chapters 28 onwards with Year 2), nonetheless the book will be of assistance to students on many other courses, e.g. BTEC Higher, Banking Courses, RSA Integrated Certificates, Advanced Level GCSE Business Studies and any course which requires a broad knowledge of organisations and the business environment.

The introduction sets the scene with the types of organisation and environmental influences evident in a typical High Street. This will strike an initial chord of familiarity for the student. The organisations in the High Street are subsequently used as an illustrative device in ensuing chapters, so that a continuing theme emerges through the book. Actual examples and information are widely included so that the book gives a clear insight into the business environment in the UK, the EEC and internationally.

An integrated approach is adopted, considering relevant themes from economic, legal, governmental, organisational and technological angles. A particular aspect of this new edition is a detailed case-study analysing the growth of and change in one of the High Street organisations.

The book has been written by college staff who have all been involved in the development and teaching of the revised BTEC National Curriculum framework. Throughout the text a questioning approach is adopted and readers are asked to relate the material to their own experience. In addition the authors, without being prescriptive, have included some assignment ideas which lecturers may adapt to their own teaching needs and there is an indication of the Business-related Skills covered by these suggested assignments. Given that the new BTEC scheme is student-centred, the aim of this textbook is to give an overview and a framework for activity based learning.

March 1987   M R Frampton
                  R T Norrie
                  A J Rees
                  R B Williams

Acknowledgements

The authors' thanks are due to Christopher Townsend and Janice Lambert for their contribution to the early stages of the compilation of this book.

Thanks are also due to the following for permission to reproduce tables, graphs and illustrations as credited in the text:

Allied Lyons
Amersham
Associated British Ports
Austin Rover
Bank of England
British Aerospace
British Petroleum
British Telecom
Burger King
Central Electricity Generating Board
Commission of the European Communities
Department of Trade and Industry
Illustrated London News
Investors in Industry plc
J Sainsbury plc
Lloyd's of London
Marks and Spencer
National Westminster Bank
Pilkington
The Controller of Her Majesty's Stationery Office
The Guardian
The Independent
The Post Office
The Stateman's Yearbook (pub. MacMillan)
The Stock Exchange
Times Books Ltd
Times Newspapers Ltd
Wimpy

PART A

THE CHANGING BUSINESS ENVIRONMENT

When you have read this part you should be able to:
- Appreciate the variety of services that are available throughout the country concentrated in your local High Street.
- Understand the meaning of the business environment.
- Understand the nature and interrelationship of the main environmental influences on organisations.
- Appreciate the need for organisations to adapt to environmental influences.
- Be aware of the nature of new technology.
- Illustrate and describe the impact of new technology in different industries.

1 The High Street

This book is concerned with helping you to learn about the various aspects making up the environment in which organisations exist. Our environment is the business world. It is a place constantly changing as economic, political, social and natural factors have an impact on commerce and industrial production; other elements affecting the conduct of business include legal, technological, and demographic factors. It is the place where you, your parents, your friends and others go shopping. It may be the workplace where, in exchange for contributing to an organisation's business, we receive a wage or salary; when we are at work we are **producers**, when we spend our income on goods and services we are **consumers**. The market-place, also part of our environment consists of specialists, in so far as the production of different sorts of goods and services is usually in the hands of different and separate organisations. Essentially then, organisations serve the community by meeting its needs, and as these needs change so organisations adapt.

Think of your own local High Street. Consider the different stores, shops, offices and government agencies there. You may well recall a department store, a record or clothes shop, a bank, a restaurant or the Town Hall where elected councillors decide how to allocate resources to meet local requirements. An important theme in this book is the **interdependence of organisations** and the way in which their activities integrate to produce the modern business environment.

By looking at the drawing of Sunhampton High Street (Fig. 1.1) explain how the different organisations rely on each other.

Sunhampton

The various activities undertaken by organisations, both privately owned or in the public sector, provide for the prosperity of the nation. Success in the private sector is measured by growth in profit and the ability to remain in an environment of competition. Growth may be achieved through an increase in an organisation's product base or by taking over other organisations so as to create a larger unit. If you examine some of the UK's largest companies you will find that they have become conglomerates through the acquisition of smaller organisations. Equally, of course,

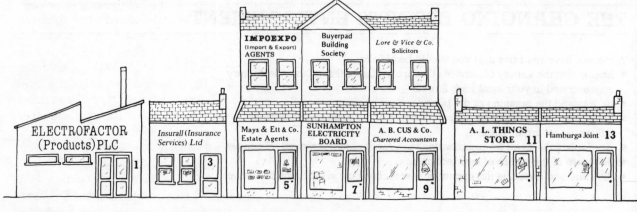

SUNHAMPTON HIGH STREET

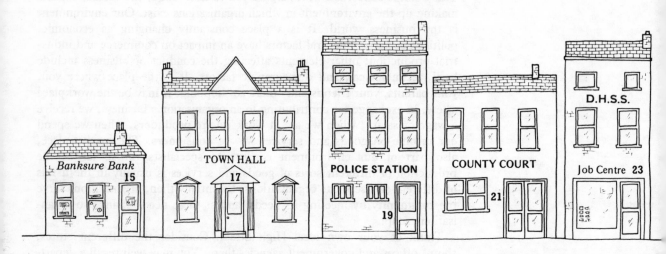

Fig. 1.1
Organisations in Sunhampton High
Street, Sunhamptonshire

organisations may fail. In 1984 there were 8229 bankruptcies of which a third were made up of builders, shops, hotels and catering.

While most organisations can carry on their activities in any commercial situation, the location of others is determined by geographical factors. This would apply in the case of a coal mine, a sand quarry, a uranium mine, a fish farm or a forest. Similarly, the location of an airline, a vehicle manufacturer or a computer factory will be decided by such matters as appropriate sites, the nearness of collaborative suppliers and the availability of skilled workers.

While we will be able to look at a great variety of organisations it is not possible in one book to study all of them in detail. We will however examine the general rules that relate to the different types of organisations, both public and private, and so construct a view of the business environment. We may appreciate the many factors at work here by focusing on an imaginary town. It is called Sunhampton, in the county of Sunhamptonshire.

The town

Sunhampton is some 40 miles from London in the South-east of England. Its location has attracted a number of commercial and industrial concerns which have sought a less expensive situation. The town was expanded as one of the post-war New Towns. In 1901 the population was 13 052; it rose to 96 175 in 1974 but dropped 1.8 per cent to 94 444 in 1981, and yet again to 93 594 in 1986. The town's wealth has been made mostly from light mechanical, electrical and now electronic engineering; but a significant service industry has also developed based on insurance, banking and other financial services. Some London financial organisations have moved their administrative offices to the town so as to benefit from lower costs. People from areas badly affected by unemployment, such as the North, Scotland and Wales and the large cities throughout Britain, have settled here attracted by jobs in the new industries and commercial enterprises. Others have come from the Irish Republic and British Commonwealth countries.

Conditions in the South-east are such that it is the most prosperous region in the country and as a result it is populated by 30 per cent of the UK total. In this region the average weekly wage in April 1985 was £214 for men, £141 for women, compared with £190 for men in Scotland and £122 for women in Northern Ireland. Unemployment levels, as in East

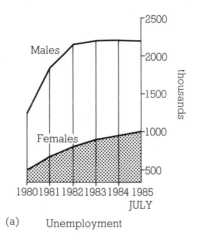

(a)   Unemployment

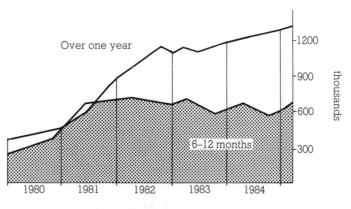

Fig. 1.2
Unemployment Statistics
Source: Department of Employment   (b)   Long term unemployment

Anglia and the East Midlands region, are lower than average. Against a national average of 13.5 per cent in October 1985 (an increase from 5.8 per cent in 1977), unemployment was 9.9 per cent in the South-east, 19 per cent in the North, 18.8 per cent in Strathclyde and 15.5 per cent in the West Midlands. The effect of the economic recession and the decline of the heavy industries left nearly half the heads of households in the North unemployed in 1984. By 1985 more than half the unemployed men in Northern Ireland, the West Midlands and the North-west had been in that state for a year (see Fig. 1.2).

The differences in affluence between the North and the South became more marked with the decline of manufacturing based industries, a trend which economists expect to continue. Indeed, in the South-east more than a fifth of the heads of households are in managerial or professional occupations. If you study Fig. 1.3 you will be able to see those activities which are expanding and those which are diminishing. The old industries tend to be more labour intensive whereas the newer, expanding industries do not always require such a large labour force, particularly with the adoption of more automation and information technology. We will consider this latter factor later in Chapter 3. Another change in the pattern of employment is in the greater use of temporary and part-time staff, such that of the 1 million jobs created since 1983, 589 000 went to female part-timers.

You will have noticed that the areas of anticipated growth are in distribution, financial and business services, leisure and tourism. Also expected to develop are small businesses, with self-employment accounting for

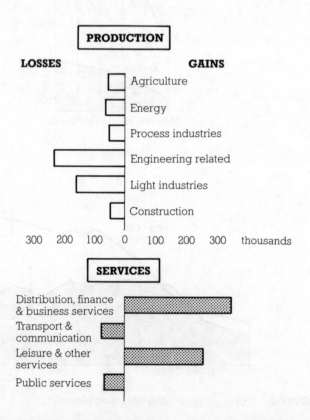

Fig. 1.3
The shifting job pattern to 1990

488 000 jobs since 1983, mostly as a result of government initiatives aimed at encouraging unemployed persons to start their own businesses.

It is worth making the point that the regional economic differences seen here need to be balanced by the fact that wealth is unevenly distributed, so that disparities also arise out of differences in wealth which exist in all parts of the country.

Sunhampton High Street

With this background in mind let us look closely at the main commercial area in the town – the High Street. Here there are hairdressers, dry-cleaners, motor repair and petrol stations, bakers and a cinema. The appearance of supermarkets and self-service shops demonstrates post-war affluence on the one hand and increasing organisational efficiency on the other. The national chain-stores and fast-food outlets have developed at the expense of the small independent shopkeeper. While more efficient use of resources has lowered prices, higher rents and local rate charges demand much better use of shopping floorspace. To get around this, many new out-of-town megastores are being built, selling everything from a bag of flour to a three-piece suite (see Chapter 45).

Looking down the High Street there is a company called **Electrofactor (Products) plc**, employing 395 people most of whom are skilled electrical and electronic engineers and the rest various support staff. Making a wide variety of consumer durable items the company has begun to make use of micro-chip circuits. The company draws its customers from all over the country, and Sunhampton's proximity to London offers access to export markets and imports of micro-chips from the Far East. Lower rates, rents and labour costs than those in the capital city made Sunhampton a sensible site for the company's head offices. Another advantage was the availability of skilled labour (see Table 1.1) and the research facilities of Sunhampton University which has established industry-linked programmes, in this case concerned with the application of computers for communication. Although the company has fared well in the economic environment its need for labour is not great as many of its processes are highly automated. The inflation rate (based on the rise in retail prices) of 2.8 per cent in the summer of 1986 (Fig. 1.4) gave the company a competitive advantage in enabling it to keep its costs down and to keep its prices steady. Of the 25 staff taken on since 1981 most have been employed to enhance the marketing push and customer support service. The company has recently reached agreement with the General Manufacturing Union whereby older, less skilled workers are able to take early retirement.

Employment

Employment opportunities in the town continue to decline, although, as we have seen, conditions are far worse in other regions of the country. Nevertheless, 14 per cent of the workforce (including school-leavers) was out of work in 1981, with some 5000 jobs lost in manufacturing, over 500 in construction, 300 in the public utility industry and 1500 in the service industries. In 1974 some 2250 people were unemployed, of whom 40 per cent were unskilled; between 1974 and 1979 nearly 5000 jobs were lost owing to the economic recession affecting British industry. Sunhampton Careers Office now estimate that only 18 per cent of school-leavers entered

Table 1.1
Distribution of labour – Sunhampton

Occupation	Approx. numbers
Agriculture	200
Food, drink and tobacco	1 300
Chemical and allied industry	1 500
Metal manufacture	20
Mechanical engineering	15 500
Instrument engineering	400
Electrical engineering	14 500
Vehicles	80
Textiles	150
Leather, leather goods and fur	400
Clothing, footwear	2 600
Bricks, pottery, glass, cement	800
Timber, furniture	1 500
Paper, printing and publishing	2 000
Construction	2 500
Gas, electricity and water	800
Transport	1 800
Insurance, banking, finance and business services	10 000
Professional and scientific services	1 000
Public administration	1 000
	58 050

Comparison of output	Sunhampton	UK
All manufacturing industry	70.2%	38%
Construction	4.3%	5.7%
Gas, water, electricity, transport	4.5%	9%
All service industry	20.7%	43.9%
Agriculture	0.3%	3.4%

manufacturing trades in 1986 as against 60 per cent in 1950. On a national basis 40 per cent of those leaving school without qualifications have not found a job a year later, compared with only 10 per cent of those who have at least one graded examination pass. Generally, those with some GCSE or equivalent passes tend to stay on for further education. The low rate of school-leavers seeking full-time education in the UK is in stark contrast to that of its international competitors for example in USA 75 per cent of youngsters remain in full-time education. As regards training and retraining for new skills British companies committed only 0.15 per cent of turnover to training compared with between 1 and 2 per cent in other countries.

Tackling these problems is **Sunhampton Job Centre**, which is controlled by the government Department of Employment, and is charged with matching available job vacancies with those seeking work. This task is not easy as for the last four years the number of jobs has fallen in the area. Instead the Centre's officers are concerned with placing 16 and 17 year old school-leavers on the two-year Youth Training Scheme (YTS), arranging training for adults wishing to learn new skills under the Job Training

Fig. 1.4
Retail prices and average earnings
Source: Department of Employment

Retail prices and average earnings   % changes on a year earlier

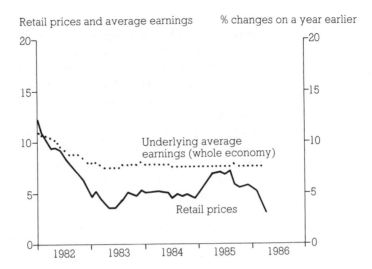

Scheme, and the Community Programme to train long-term unemployed people aged 18 or over. At the end of 1987 the government announced its intention to combine these two latter adult training schemes. For unemployed people able to put up £1000 to start their own business, the Enterprise Allowance Scheme pays an allowance of £40 per week for 12 months. Nationally in 1986, nearly three-quarters of those leaving school at 16 were a year later either in work or in YTS. This scheme provides entrants with a weekly allowance when they are taken on by employers who provide a combination of work experience and off-the-job training usually undertaken by a local college, here by Sunhampton Technical College. The Job Centre is rather conveniently placed in the premises occupied by the local branch of the Department of Health and Social Security from which State welfare benefits are calculated and paid.

Can you draw up a list of the reasons explaining the fall in Britain's manufacturing output in the last few years?

In Sunhampton, small business units and small factories, usually on industrial estates, have been more common than large enterprises; although small businesses are more vulnerable to the vagaries of changes in the economy. The clothing, footwear, printing and publishing, furniture and domestic appliance industries have been particularly badly hit by the recession and now find it hard to compete with cheaper, and often better quality imported goods. The financial weaknesses of some local businesses are well known to the firm of chartered accountants, **A.B. Cus & Co**, some of whose clients have recently had to cease trading. On the other hand, some new small businesses have been successfully established to service a factory opened in Closetown by the newly 'privatised' British Telecom. In some parts of the country, central government regional grants have encouraged some businesses to locate in specific areas.

What advantages occur to you as arising from the various government initiatives with regards to employment?

Overseas trade

Electrofactors is a direct importer of supplies from abroad as well as an exporter, so the company will be more than interested in the relative exchange rates of currencies (see Fig. 1.5). After all, its wages, rates, taxes and outgoings have to be paid in pounds sterling while other costs and some of its income is based on foreign currencies.

Despite your having read about the loss of jobs in manufacturing, the companies themselves survive for the most part but with a smaller workforce. Britain is essentially a manufacturing nation, supported by a strong financial services market including banking and insurance. Manufactured goods and specialised financial services are exported all over the world because Britain is a major exporting nation with nearly 30 per cent of total production sold to other countries (three times the percentage of USA and twice that of Japan). Unlike these last two countries – USA having vast natural resources, and both USA and Japan with huge home markets – Britain lacks the conditions necessary to support its population of 56 million without extensive international trade. Thus this country's well-being may be judged by the success of organisations like Electrofactors in exporting its products to other nations. A way of assessing the relative standing of trading nations is to look at the value of its own currency set against others using, as an agreed convention, the US dollar ($).

The price of exports and imports is affected by the changes which occur all the time in the exchange rate of currencies. No doubt you will have noticed the effect of currency exchange rates when taking foreign money abroad for your holidays.

These fluctuations affect the value of the pound which then affects the price of goods and raw materials imported by British companies as well as the price of Britain's exports. **Impoexpo Agents** in Sunhampton are well aware of this, in its business of arranging international deals for the sale of British goods abroad and the import of items into the UK. A rise in the value of the pound against the US dollar will mean that purchasers abroad will have to pay more for British goods and services. Conversely, a drop

Fig. 1.5
Sterling exchange rate index,
(a) against a basket of currencies,
(b) against the US dollar

(a) Sterling Exchange Rates

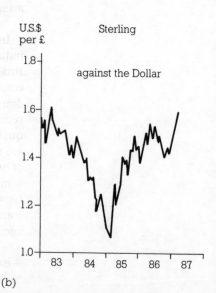

(b)

in the value of the pound means that our manufacturers will have to pay more for their raw materials.

Look around your home and note the country of origin of your food and manufactured products. What percentage come from other countries?

As regards this country's economic standing, you can examine Fig. 1.6 which sets out some additional indicators of performance.

The way in which we saw proof that the West's financial markets are interlinked, and based on investors' confidence in the financial markets was seen in the New York Stock Market crash of 19th October 1987 ('Black Monday' – the worst fall in share prices ever recorded). The crash reverberated around the world markets wiping billions off company share values as the panic of investors spread. Within a week more than £102 bn was knocked off the stock values in London. The US$ sank in value as it exchanged at over $1.8 to each £1.

Banking and finance

At the centre of the financial markets is the banking system, made up of commercial banks and the Bank of England. In Sunhampton High Street, is **Banksure Bank plc**, a branch of one of the 12 or so major commercial groups, playing an important role in the business community. Together with the branches of other banks it receives the deposits of organisations and individuals. An example of these deposits is the salary which is often paid directly into a bank account. From this householders with a mortgage pay their monthly repayment of a long-term loan usually arranged with building societies such as Buyerpad. However, although not previously a feature of bank business, the provision of bank mortgages has, since 1981, grown considerably.

You should note that the level of interest charged on loans will have an effect on whether, and the extent to which, people and organisations borrow. If the interest we have to pay is too high we may decide not to buy a hi-fi, video or car on credit, or take out a mortgage on a house. Similarly, organisations may find that borrowing money to buy new machinery or premises is unwise if the rate of interest charged by banks would make repayments too costly (for full explanation of this issue see Chapter 18).

The sale and purchase of homes may also involve Sunhampton Town Council by virtue of the Housing Acts 1985 and 1986, which give council tenants the legal right to buy their own homes.

Part of the business community is **Insurall (Insurance Services) Ltd**, which arranges insurance policy cover sometimes through Lloyds of London (see Chapter 7). Among the company's clients seeking insurance protection are home buyers who are usually obliged to take out a policy as a condition of being granted a mortgage. Life assurance, vehicle insurance, holiday cover and building policies make up the typical business of Insurall.

To what extent is it an advantage to Britain to have high or low interest rates?

Getting together people looking for premises with those offering to sell, is the business of **Mays and Ett & Co**, one of Sunhampton's leading estate agent partnerships, with a number of offices in Sunhampton as well as in

1 Money

Sterling M3 and M0 — % changes on a year earlier

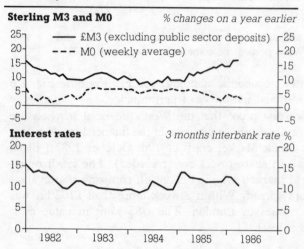

Interest rates — 3 months interbank rate %

2 Output

Gross domestic product — Quarterly average estimate 1980 = 100

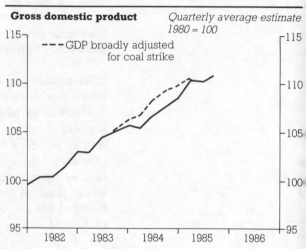

3 Balance of payments

Current balances — £ billion per quarter

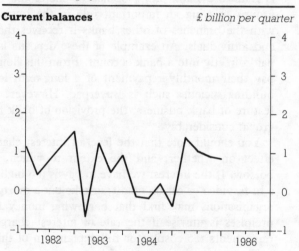

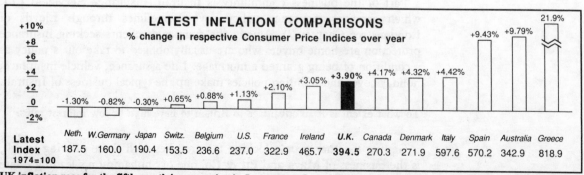

	Neth.	W.Germany	Japan	Switz.	Belgium	U.S.	France	Ireland	U.K.	Canada	Denmark	Italy	Spain	Australia	Greece
% change	-1.30%	-0.82%	-0.30%	+0.65%	+0.88%	+1.13%	+2.10%	+3.05%	+3.90%	+4.17%	+4.32%	+4.42%	+9.43%	+9.79%	21.9%
Latest Index 1974=100	187.5	160.0	190.4	153.5	236.6	237.0	322.9	465.7	394.5	270.3	271.9	597.6	570.2	342.9	818.9

LATEST INFLATION COMPARISONS — % change in respective Consumer Price Indices over year

UK inflation rose for the fifth month in succession in January, up from 3.7 per cent to 3.9 per cent, its highest level in 10 months

Fig. 1.6
Economic indicators in 1987
Sources: 1–3 HM Stationery Office;
4–7 *The Independent*

5

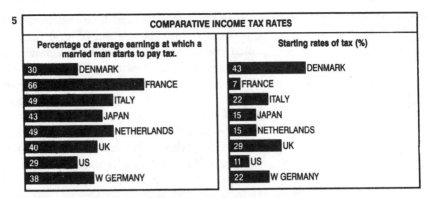

6

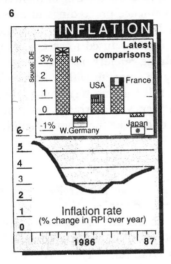

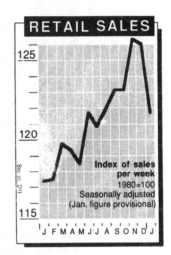

7

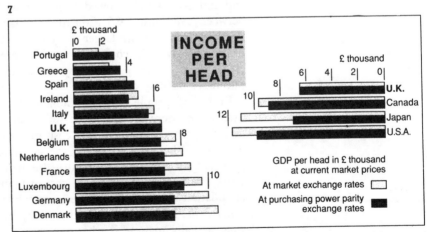

Closetown. Owing to a lowering of lending rates in 1985 and 1986 Mays and Ett have recorded an increased demand for properties, and this has led to high house prices in the area.

The offices of **Lore & Vice & Co**, solicitors, are just along from Mays and Ett, and next door to the **Sunhampton Electricity Board** showroom. Many residents have consulted the firm's partners, Ms R. Vice and Mr O.

Lore in the matter of their house purchase. Much of their business indeed, is concerned with the transfer of legal title in a home to a buyer, a process called **conveyancing**. It will be understood then that solicitors have been worried about the government's proposals announced in 1985 to end their monopoly in conveyancing. Licensed conveyancers are now able to do this work, and as the law is changed further, banks and building societies may also be able to compete with solicitors. Lore & Vice carry out many other tasks and number among their clients some of the larger local organisations for whom they act as legal advisers. They also advise people charged with criminal offences, draw up wills, advise on divorce, and, amongst other things represent clients in certain law courts (see Chapter 14 for a detailed discussion). One of their clients, Mrs Watt, was counselled this year to commence proceedings in **Sunhampton County Court** against the Electricity Board. The dispute concerned a faulty electric deep freezer for which the Board refused to accept responsibility. From January 1987, **Buyerpad Building Society** has been able, under the Building Societies Act 1986, not only to compete with solicitors in respect of conveyancing, but also to offer a full banking service including issuing cheque books, and to take on estate agency and arrange insurance cover. However, societies are more likely to undertake these latter facilities only in connection with house buying.

Retailing

A.L. Things is a large self-service store retailing foodstuffs, clothes and certain consumer durables. While the store's business in recent years showed a drop in the sale of more expensive items, probably as a result of greater unemployment in Sunhampton and lower income rises in 1986 there was a surge in retail sales. This was revealed by the Department of Trade and Industry which showed there was a 22 per cent rise in sales volume between 1980 and 1986. Contributory factors to this increased consumer spending may be the larger number of cut-price sales by shops and the dramatic growth in consumer credit. Here the wide availability of plastic credit cards, many provided by stores, has enabled card-holders to make purchases on easy credit.

Certainly, people always complain that prices are forever rising. When prices rise there is said to be **inflation**. If the price of raw materials to manufacturers goes up, the cost of making the finished product will increase. When passed on to the consumer more money is required to purchase the same items. In turn this will lead to those employed seeking a pay rise to keep up with the cost of living. At the close of 1986 the rate of inflation was just over 3 per cent while the average wage increase was 4 per cent. Of course, while there may be an apparent increase in wages, what actually matters is what one can buy with the money. It is easier to be a millionaire in Italy where the value of £1 is 1950 lire (the equivalent of £1000 in the bank would be 1 950 000 lire!). Economists therefore refer to **real income** as representing what money will buy. Thus, you will have heard older people talk of 'the good old days' when a house cost £2000, a full meal cost a shilling (5p) and a bus ride one penny (less than ½p). However, an examination may very well show that a bus ride or a meal today takes the same percentage of income as it did in the time recalled.

Think of a few items which you buy regularly. How has their price altered over the last year?

Since it was opened in 1981 in the High Street. **Hamburga Joint** has been doing a roaring trade in its fast-food business. Hardly a shopping centre in this country is without such a retailing outlet, and indeed the standardised shop fittings are in evidence throughout the western world. The Sunhampton unit is in fact 'franchised' by a parent company based in the USA, whereby the company livery and food concept is hired out to individuals who work independently rather than as employees. The franchise holder, Mr S. Ami, and his 10 employees (half of whom are part-time) are kept busy during the day and at night, attracting mostly a young clientele. It has to be admitted that there was a fight in the school holidays one night, when a plate glass window was cracked, and two people were arrested by the police. In court they were both fined for causing a public disturbance and criminal damage.

Can you list the advantages as well as the disadvantages of franchising as a way of going into business?

Local government

Sunhampton Town Hall is its civic centre containing local government administrative offices, where a wide range of employees carry out their duties. In the last two years the council has put some of its public services out to tender, so now rubbish collection, street cleaning and the provision of school meals is done by private contractors. This has been done despite opposition from council workers previously directly employed on these duties. This policy has been encouraged by the Conservative Government which in July 1986 reported that 16 per cent of councils were privatising some of their services compared with 11 per cent in 1984.

In order to meet the costs of carrying out the duties laid down by the law, the council has power to collect local rates charged upon business premises and private dwellings. Local authorities also rely on central government grants, although these were reduced in 1981 in line with the government's desire to reduce public spending. What is significantly different about Sunhampton Town Council as compared with the other organisations in the High Street is that the policy and direction of the authority is determined by councillors who are elected by local residents in the four electoral wards (see Fig. 1.7).

To what factors would you attribute the recent rise in burglaries in Sunhampton complained of by Sunhamptonshire's Chief Constable at a recent civic dinner?

Although we have seen how the severe economic depression has affected the Sunhampton community in the late 70s and early 80s, there was in this period a significant bright spot. That was the wealth generated by the exploitation of oilfields in the North Sea, particularly by way of oil revenue tax (see Fig. 1.8). It was the existence of this source of revenue which led Josephine Reddyspeke, MP for Sunhampton, to declare in a speech in 1986 in the House of Commons that the government was wasting this money on paying for a high level of unemployment rather than investing in new

Fig. 1.7
Sunhampton and Closetown

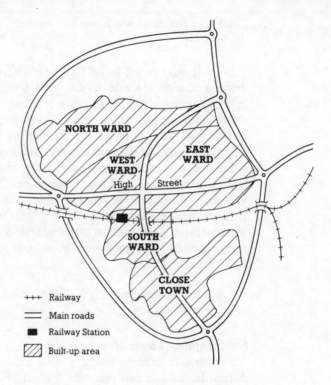

NORTH WARD

WEST WARD

EAST WARD

High   Street

SOUTH WARD

CLOSE TOWN

+++ Railway

= Main roads

■ Railway Station

▨ Built-up area

industry and for improving the country's ancient sewage system. Moreover, she added, she feared for the state of our nation when in the not too distant future the North Sea oil ran dry.

What today are: (i) the exchange rate of the pound against the US dollar, (ii) the level of unemployment in the UK, and (iii) the base rate of one of the major banks?

Can we at this stage say what we understand by the terms 'organisation' and 'environment'? An 'organisation' may be defined as a group of people involved in a common activity. We shall concentrate on those organisations operating in the business world, such as those we have commented on in Sunhampton High Street. The business 'environment' is made up of all the forces that are to be found outside the organisation, affecting its operations and behaviour. We have referred in this introductory chapter to a number of elements, economic, political and legal, which together make up the business environment. You will have seen too, how many of these elements change, and so our environment is not stagnant at all, but is continually altered by change. We will next examine in greater detail the business environment, and also look at some of the effects of the impact of change.

2 The business environment

In Chapter 1 we referred to the environment of business in general and to Sunhampton in particular. In this chapter we shall explore the nature of these environmental forces in more detail, showing how their interwoven effects can influence the actions of organisations.

Fig. 1.8
Oil extraction platform in the North Sea

Economic influences

Economic problems

* See Chapters 36 and 39 for a fuller
discussion of inflation and
unemployment.

We referred in Chapter 1 to major economic problems like inflation and unemployment, which have afflicted many economies in recent years. Such problems can exert an impact on both individuals and organisations.

Inflation*, when prices in general rise, means that the cost of living increases. The pounds we earn do not buy so many goods and services. Inflation also affects decisions by organisations. For example, costs of component parts and raw materials rise, making budgeting and future planning difficult.

Unemployment* obviously affects financially those people, and their families, who are unfortunate enough to lose their jobs, and the young unemployed who find it difficult to get a job for the first time. In addition, people who are unemployed receive a lower income and consequently they spend less. This causes a fall in sales for many organisations. Furthermore, the government will have to pay out more in unemployment benefits, which means that it will have to raise more revenue or reduce its expenditure in other fields.

Although economic problems such as these are most familiar to us, there is a more fundamental economic problem from which all others emanate. That is the root economic problem of **scarcity**. There are simply not enough resources to satisfy all the wants of individuals, firms and governments. Resources of all types, be they raw materials, manufactured goods or whatever, are limited in supply; they are **scarce**. If we could satisfy all the wants of everybody, we should not have economic problems.

As economic forces alter, so organisations need to respond to them and change. If the raw materials or component parts needed by an organisation cost more, then that business will react and change its policies.

Take a business organisation of your choice. How do you think it would react to rising costs? Before reading on, consider changes it might make and compare your thoughts with the suggestions below.

It would raise the price of the goods or services it sells in order to cover the higher costs and maintain profit levels. However it might need to be cautious in such a change. By how much may buyers of the product reduce their purchases in the face of a price rise? What might be the reaction of other competitor firms who are also facing the same cost increases? By how much may they change their prices?

If the rise in costs is large, then the organisation might seriously consider alternative methods of producing the goods or service. It could perhaps alter the type of technology it uses in order to find a cheaper method of production. For example, the large oil price rises of the 1970s gave more impetus to research into alternative energy forms like solar energy. Many householders and organisations began using the relatively cheaper gas central heating rather than oil-fired heating.

There was a substantial fall in the price of oil in 1986. If oil prices remained at a lower level, what effects do you think might ensue?

Any changes in the level of sales of an organisation clearly have an impact on the number and type of workers it needs to employ.

Consider some business organisations in your area which have recently made workers redundant, or alternatively others which have increased their labour force. Why do you think they changed their employment levels?

A likely cause could be a change in their volume of sales and output so that the size of their existing workforce was inappropriate. It is also possible that they might have changed their methods of production by substituting new technology for part of their labour force.

Later in this book you will learn more about the decisions that organisations make as a result of changes in economic factors – decisions such as changing their prices or methods of operation, and the consequences such changes have.

Remember, though, that economic problems relate basically to that issue of scarcity. As a consequence, certain decisions have to be made in a society.

Because of this inability to satisfy all our wants, we have to make choices. Out of your limited income you decide the spread of goods and services you acquire according to your needs and what yields you most satisfaction (or **utility**).

By the same token, a company is unlikely to be able to open up more factories and pay workers large wage rises and give higher dividends to shareholders. It would not have the funds at its disposal. Thus organisations have to make choices about the way they deploy their resources.

Similarly, a government does not have limitless resources at its disposal. A major expansion in government expenditure would cause great problems because of the difficulty of raising the necessary funds. Thus governments have to choose their priorities for expenditure. For example, how much should be spent on defence, hospitals or roads in relation to education, social security or grants to private industry? Any government must reconcile such conflicting needs.

When individuals, organisations or governments acquire goods and services, a money cost is likely to be paid – the price charged. However, there is also a more fundamental 'cost' in pursuing a particular course of action. This is called the **opportunity cost**, and it arises out of that basic economic problem of scarcity.

If Electrofactor (Products) plc of Sunhampton, for example, chooses to invest heavily in new machinery, it cannot spend that money on, say, new lorries for its transport fleet. If you buy a pair of jeans, that means you cannot buy some new records or whatever alternative you might have considered. A decision by the government to spend more on defence means that other sectors of government spending, e.g. hospitals or roads, cannot benefit from those resources.

Thus, the opportunity cost of the most desired use of resources is the benefits foregone of the next best alternative. Because we cannot have all we want, some sacrifices have to be made.

Given this basic problem of scarcity, certain decisions have to be made in a society:

- *What* range of goods and services are to be produced?
- *How* are they to be produced?
- *Where* are they to be produced?
- *For whom* are they to be produced, and how will the people who produce them be rewarded?

Different countries, with different types of economic and political systems, tackle those problems in different ways. In the UK economy we have privately owned as well as government organisations which supply goods and services. In some countries the influence of the State is far stronger, in others it is much weaker.

We shall consider how these questions are tackled in different types of economic systems.

There are three types of economic structure that we shall describe:

- the market economy
- the planned economy
- the mixed economy

The key differences between them relate to the ownership of resources, the manner in which prices are determined, and how resources are allocated to their various uses.

The relationship between political, economic and legal systems

We must remember that different kinds of States have different kinds of economic policy and that the nature of the economic solution will often be linked to the nature of the political and legal systems. A **mixed economy** (discussed later in this chapter), such as we have in the UK, is often associated with the type of political system called **parliamentary democracy**, in which the electors choose from different political parties their representatives in Parliament, the chief law-making body in the State. It is usually said that in a democratic State like the UK, government rests on **consensus** (agreement), in the sense that the government and its policy are ultimately determined by public opinion. A government would be very unwise to ignore public opinion. In a democracy a government can be voted out of office at a General Election (which in the UK must take place at least every five years) and can be replaced by a government of a different party. In a totalitarian, one-party, State that cannot happen.

Democracy is a difficult word to define. Technically, it means government by the people for the people – everyone should have the opportunity of participating in government even if, as in our system, most people can probably do so only at a General Election. The word is taken from the Greek word *demos*, meaning 'people'. However, many States which the West would not describe as democratic, e.g. East Germany, which is a one-party communist State, call themselves democratic. It is a word which is used and misused by governments to serve their own ends. The word we would use to describe States like East Germany and the USSR is **totalitarian**, i.e. States where there are no rival parties representing different shades of political opinion; instead there is only one, the governing party. The kind of economy which we tend to associate with a one-party communist State is a **planned economy** (discussed later in this chapter)

Fig. 2.1
The Houses of Parliament

where the State owns the means of production, and centralised planning determines the allocation of resources and the determination of prices.

The kind of **law** that we would expect to find in a country with a parliamentary democracy would be different from the kind of law which we would expect to find in a communist State. In the UK for example, we have a good deal of law about private ownership. We should not find such law in a communist State like the USSR which has a planned economy and, to a large extent, State ownership of the factors of production. Property is owned in common, not by private individuals. One result of this is that fraud in communist countries may be a capital criminal offence (i.e. one punishable by death). The only capital offence in the UK is treason. In a communist State fraud means, in a sense, undermining the State by stealing from it and thus can be equated with treason in a country like the UK. In a democratic State we would expect to find laws about freedom of speech, freedom of association, e.g. to join a trade union, freedom to express political views and to criticise the government. We might not find such laws in a totalitarian State, or we might find in such States that there is a gap between law and practice. We have only to read the writings of famous Russian dissidents like Solzhenitsyn and Bukovsky or to look at events in Poland in 1981–2 to be reminded of this.

The conclusion that we draw is that certain types of economy tend to be linked with certain types of political and legal systems.

The market economy

In a pure market economy the government would play no role in the economic system. There would be private ownership of the means of production. Goods and services would be produced with the aim of maximising profits by firms. There would be competition between firms as they competed for the patronage of customers.

Prices of goods and services would be determined by the interplay of the forces of demand (on the consumer side) and supply (on the selling side). If people wanted to buy more of a particular product, the price would rise. Similarly if firms had unsold goods, they would need to lower the price to expand sales.

More resources in the economy, like labour, land and machines, would be acquired by the expanding organisations, those facing growing demand. Other organisations which were less efficient or those which faced a fall in demand because a more attractive substitute was being offered by competitors, would be forced to cut back their level of output and would need fewer productive resources. For the successful, profits and wages increase, for the others they fall.

This interaction of supply and demand to determine prices and allocate resources in known as the **market mechanism** or **price mechanism**. In the pure form of the market economy, the market mechanism alone regulates business activity, and the government is not involved.

Can you think of a country which has adopted this type of economy?

It is very difficult to find a perfect example. Perhaps the best approximation is Taiwan or Hong Kong. However, even in these countries there is some, albeit small, degree of government involvement, e.g. taxation to help in the financing of expenditure on roads or the police.

Thus a pure market economy can be considered as one end of a spectrum of economic structures, rather than being a model any country would completely follow in reality. How does the planned type of economy compare and contrast?

The planned economy

This economic system would be set within a communist type of political system. In a fully planned economy, the State owns all the means of production. All organisations are State-run.

Centralised planning, not the market mechanism, is the means by which resources are allocated to their various uses and prices are determined. For example, in the USSR the central planning agency, known as Gosplan, considers the many interrelationships between industries and sets output targets for each one. These data are then broken down into targets for each factory or other production unit.

The interlinking of industries is very important in this planning process. For example, if it is desired to increase the level of output of lorries and vans, it is necessary to increase the output of tyres and other motor components. The planning agency should ensure that ready supplies of necessary resources, including labour, are available. Thus, the planned output of one industry often depends upon the availability of supplies from other industries. If an output target is not met by one factory, that can seriously jeopardise the ability of others to meet their targets if they are short of inputs as a result.

Both the range and prices of goods and services are likewise set by the central planning body. Such prices do not change in direct response to demand and supply forces, but are held constant often for long periods of time. For example, the rises in food prices in China in 1980 were the first for 30 years. The decisions of what to produce are made by State bodies in their estimation of their society's needs. Like prices of goods and services, wage levels are controlled by the State.

Russia and China have been been quoted as illustrating features of the planned economy. However, as with the pure form of the market economy, it is difficult to suggest a valid example of a completely planned economy. In Russia, a significant proportion of agricultural output is produced on privately run plots of land. Since 1980 in China, there has been some government encouragement for workers to buy up factories and make production and pricing decisions themselves. The policy of liberalisation of the USSR economy introduced by President Gorbachev (this is known as 'perestroika') is a further trend towards relaxing the rigours of central-ised planning.

If a purely planned economy is at the other end of the spectrum from the market economy, what lies in between? No doubt you have deduced it is the **mixed economy**.

The mixed economy

In such an economy both the market mechanism and government involve-ment are active in determining prices and allocating resources. In the UK we have taxes like VAT which affect the price level of goods and services. There are nationalised industries such as coal or electricity. Governments have intervened in private sector activity by methods such as the provision of grants to contribute to the cost of investment by firms in areas of high unemployment.

Side by side with government involvement operate the market forces of demand and supply. They are also important in setting prices and influencing which enterprises expand or contract. Therefore the allocation of resources also involves the market mechanism.

We explained earlier that pure forms of the free market or planned economies are unlikely to exist. What we have in the world are some economies which tend towards one extreme or the other, while many lie in the middle range of the mixed economy span. This would be true of most Western European countries like the UK, West Germany and the Netherlands. The USA have relatively less State involvement.

The plans of the Conservative Government which was first elected in 1979 included a greater play for market forces and less involvement on the part of the State. To those ends the government sold shares to private buyers in organisations such as British Aerospace, Cable and Wireless, Britoil, British Telecom, British Airways, British Airports Authority and British Gas, which were previously nationalised.

The public sector

The public sector covers activity operated by various State bodies, which include the central government departments, the local authorities and the nationalised industries.

Certain central government departments are ultimately responsible for services such as the State school system and the National Health Service. However, local authorities and area health authorities are respectively responsible for the implementation of these services in their part of the country.

Besides education, the local authorities offer services of council housing and parks, for example. The nationalised industries include State-owned producers like the Electricity Council, British Steel and the Post Office. In line with the Conservative Party's policy to reduce State ownership, the government, following its re-election in 1987, announced proposals to pass to private ownership the Electricity Generating Board, the Water Boards, and at the close of 1987 added British Steel to its privatisation list.

The prime objectives of the public sector are less profit-orientated than the private sector. Essentially, the major aim is to provide an efficient and satisfactory level of service or supply and quality of goods. However, in recent years financial targets and constraints have become more a feature of public sector operations. As will be explained in Chapter 8, targets have been set for some nationalised industries to make a predefined rate of return on funds invested. Tighter limits have been set on the supply of government money to the nationalised industries. Furthermore, cash limits on expenditure have been imposed by the Treasury, laying bounds that government departments are not to exceed. Local authorities have also faced tighter control of their expenditure through changes in the methods by which central government supplies funds to local government.

Altogether total public sector expenditure in 1985/6 amounted to 45 per cent of the **Gross Domestic Product** of the UK (the overall value of income, output and expenditure in the country as a whole).

As was mentioned earlier in this chapter, the policies of the 1979 Conservative Government have attempted to reduce the size of the public sector by the policy of 'privatisation' and by restraining the growth of public expenditure. Thus, the size and role of the public sector are by no means constant. Changes in government, reflecting variations in political, economic and social viewpoints and policies, bring differing approaches to the scale and operations of the public and private sectors.

The private sector

* These organisations are considered in detail in Chapter 5.

Organisations which are privately owned lie in the private sector. This includes the various sole traders, partnerships, companies, clubs, societies and charities with which we regularly come into contact as workers, customers or members.*

Organisations as small as your local fish-and-chip shop or as big as ICI are all part of the private sector. Over half of the UK Gross National Product (55 per cent in fact) was contributed by the private sector in 1985.

The prime aim of most private sector productive organisations is to make the highest profit for the owners of the organisations. Those who manage them are likely to make decisions on product lines, pricing, location and methods of production with the overriding objective of improving efficiency and maximising profit.

In constrast, bodies like clubs, societies and charities, though privately run, are not formed to make profits, but to enhance interest and enjoyment in a particular field, or to channel funds towards a worthy cause. Your local swimming club or amateur dramatic society does not aim to maximise profits. Charities like Oxfam hope to raise as much money as they can for the relief of hunger in the less developed countries. Even so, for the most part, private sector organisations are run with profit in mind.

Some degree of overlap exists between the private and public sectors. The shares of some companies are owned both by the State and by private investors. For example, until 1987, 32 per cent of British Petroleum (BP) shares were State-owned, but the government announced its intention to sell these, and over 99 per cent of shares in Austin Rover Group (ARG) are owned by the State. Such organisations as ARG straddle both sectors, but are still registered as companies so that in essence their base is in the private sector.

Public and private sector organisations in our mixed economy exist in a fluid business environment. They are both subject to changes, especially in the legal, political and economic climate. In this book we shall explore further features of the mixed economy, describe the details of that environment, and consider the impact of environmental change on organisations.

In Chapter 26 for example, we shall consider further the merits and demerits of the price mechanism. In Chapter 19 we shall examine certain legal forces which restrain the free use of economic resources, such as the Health and Safety at Work Act. In Chapter 20 laws which influence an organisation's behaviour in a market will be described, such as the Trade Descriptions Act. The operation of policies to combat major problems like inflation will be considered in Chapter 41.

Later in this chapter you will discover the nature of political and governmental forces which can affect the behaviour of organisations. You will see that the type of economic structure of a country to a large part reflects the type of political system it adopts.

These important forces of law, government and economics are closely intertwined. This will be a central theme throughout this book.

What expansions or reductions in the size of the public sector have happened recently? Why do you think these changes have occurred?

The influence of the law

Status and rules of behaviour

Let us look now at those rules in society which have the nature of law, and which play an important part in the business environment. Legal rules, for example, set out the rights and duties of buyers and sellers, describe the legal relationship between workers and employers and regulate the conduct of business organisations. Moreover these laws are not generally set once and for all time. Like the other factors influencing industry and commerce, laws change to reflect different conditions and the needs of a changing society. Thus the laws which govern us today in a technological age, are different from those in existence at the start of the British Industrial Revolution in the nineteenth century, and then again from those of the agricultural society of medieval times. Of course there must be a process by which new laws can be created and we will examine this presently. For the moment let us view some examples of laws.

In Chapter 1 you will have read of the various types of organisations in Sunhampton High Street. These organisations exist only by virtue of laws which allow for their creation. Thus the principal law on the procedures to be followed for the creation of a new company, and for the conduct of all existing companies, is the Companies Act 1985. Parliament passed the Local Government Act in 1972, which governs the status and principal powers of our local councils. Some organisations have come into being through particular legislation, whereby previously privately owned businesses have been purchased by the State. This process of nationalisation has produced **public corporations**. The Coal Industry Nationalisation Act 1946 set up what is now called British Coal; the electricity industry controlled by the Central Electricity Generating Board was nationalised by the Electricity Act 1947; the railways, controlled by the British Railways Board (now British Rail), was nationalised by the Transport Act 1947; and the British Steel Corporation (now British Steel) was established originally by the Iron and Steel Act 1967. A full discussion of this topic will be seen in Chapter 8.

Laws also serve us by seeking to influence our behaviour when we enter negotiations with others. This may be in respect of seeking to rent or buy a car, or buying a bus or train ticket, or ordering a restaurant meal, or purchasing clothes. What the law does here is to recognise legal rights and duties on both the purchaser and the vendor. Certainly the absence of such laws, combined with the desire to cheat, would make market operations difficult and fraught with dangers for the honest buyer and seller. As you will see in Chapter 30, many of these rules are set out in the Sale of Goods Act 1979. It is this law which sets out your legal rights if shoes bought by you fall apart, or if a music cassette is faulty on first playing.

What is the influence of law when we take up a job? Employment legislation is essentially protective and has been introduced to prevent a history of abuses in a relationship which is based on people selling their labour in exchange for payment. Parliament has stepped in to impose laws governing the relationship between employees and their employers. Together with Acts of Parliament, the legal principles laid down by judges in their decisions in court cases tell us the rights and duties of each party. Individual rights such as periods of notice to end employment, entitlement of women to return to work following pregnancy, and a right not to be unfairly dismissed are to be found principally in the Employment Protection (Consolidation) Act 1978. Similarly, as we will soon discuss, discrimination based on race or sex is governed by the Race Relations Act 1976 and the Sex Discrimination Act 1975 respectively.

What is the 'law of the land'?

The law we shall be referring to is that which applies to England, Wales and Northern Ireland. Scotland, although part of the UK, has a separate system of law, influenced by the principles common to European countries, which have their origins in the ancient Roman law. Although there are two legal systems in the UK, there is only one Parliament and one government.

It will help your understanding of English law to appreciate the long history of its development. We may conveniently take as our starting point the Norman Conquest in 1066. This event was to lead to the establishment of a central and strong system of government, supported by the custom and practice of the King's law courts which modelled a system of law common to the whole of England. Parliament was not then the body that it is today, and so the role of the King's judges as lawmakers was of great importance and was to lay the foundation of the present system. That is why today there are two major sources of law: **Common Law**, the law declared by judges in case decisions, and **Statute Law**, the law made by Parliament.

Many of the legal influences we have mentioned refer to laws made by Parliament, consisting of the House of Lords and the House of Commons. Over a hundred Acts of Parliament, as these laws are called, are passed every year, and many of those Acts give power to government Ministers to make regulations which have the force of law. Every year more than 2000 regulations become law. The origin of this type of law of the land is again bound up with history. The Norman kings ruled by issuing royal proclamations which had the force of law throughout the land. These were later known as **statutes** and were made by the kings but with the help of a body which is now the House of Lords, but was then called the King's Council. It was not until after the dispute between King Charles I and the Parliamentary forces led by Oliver Cromwell that Parliament became supreme. After this Civil War in the seventeenth century, Parliament (the word comes from the French verb *parler*, to talk) became the initiator of legislation.

Legislation refers to the process whereby the democratically elected House of Commons, together with the non-elected House of Lords (consisting mostly of hereditary peers, who by reason of inheriting a title have a right to sit in the Lords) draft Acts of Parliament. Most of these Acts start life as a government proposal (called a **Public Bill**) which is discussed in both chambers of Parliament and is voted on at each of the stages of its passage through Parliament. Bills may originate from members of the House and are called **Private Members' Bills**, while outside organisations

Fig. 2.2
First page of an Act of
Parliament

ELIZABETH II

Companies Act 1985

1985 CHAPTER 6

An Act to consolidate the greater part of the Companies
Acts. [11th March 1985]

BE IT ENACTED by the Queen's most Excellent Majesty, by and
with the advice and consent of the Lords Spiritual and
Temporal, and Commons, in this present Parliament
assembled, and by the authority of the same, as follows:—

PART I

FORMATION AND REGISTRATION OF COMPANIES;
JURIDICAL STATUS AND MEMBERSHIP

CHAPTER I

COMPANY FORMATION

Memorandum of association

1.—(1) Any two or more persons associated for a lawful Mode of
purpose may, by subscribing their names to a memorandum of forming
association and otherwise complying with the requirements of incorporated
this Act in respect of registration, form an incorporated company, company.
with or without limited liability.

(2) A company so formed may be either—

    (*a*) a company having the liability of its members limited
        by the memorandum to the amount, if any, unpaid on

such as local authorities and nationalised corporations may draft their
proposals for legislative changes in the form of **Private Bills**.

Once passed by both chambers of the House, the bill must receive the
agreement of the Monarch, but this **Royal Assent** is now a mere formality.

Having received the Assent the bill becomes an Act of Parliament and its provisions form part of the law of the land.

To give you an idea of the variety of subject matter of these laws, let us record that in December 1986 Royal Assent was given to the following legislative proposals: Education Act (No 2);* European Communities (Amendment) Act; Family Law Act; Financial Services Act; Housing and Planning Act; National Health Service (Amendment) Act; Parliamentary Constituencies Act; Public Order Act; Public Trustee and Administration of Funds Act; Rate Support Grants Act; Salmon Act; Sex Discrimination Act.

Secondary legislation

The process by which bills become Acts of Parliament is usually very slow, consisting as it does of debates and consideration by committees of the Houses. In order to deal with the many problems that arise in a highly complex society like ours it has become necessary to have extremely varied and detailed legislation. It would not be feasible for Parliament to give adequate time to every regulation made by the government, and this is recognised by Parliament itself. In recent times it has become the practice for Acts to give additional or subsidiary powers to Ministers of the Crown to issue regulations which, after approval by Parliament, have the force of law. Such delegated legislation is known as **statutory instruments** and forms one of the newest sources of law. We have commented that some 2000 statutory instruments are brought into effect every year.

A typical statutory instrument was the one issued in December 1979, concerned with ordering persons to install and use Vehicle Recording Equipment (known by its opponents as the 'spy in the cab') in commercial vehicles. The equipment records the length of the journey and the time taken. One of the aims of the Minister of Transport in issuing these regulations is to regulate the number of continuous driving hours by a driver, with a view to ensuring road safety. The regulations tell us that the Minister is able to issue this statutory instrument '. . . in exercise of the powers conferred by . . . the Transport Act 1968'.

European Community law

There is, however, another reference in these regulations which brings us to another important source of law, the European Economic Community Council Regulation No 1463/70. A regulation made outside the UK can be given effect in British law because this is permitted by the European Communities Act 1972. That Act gave legal effect to the provisions of the Treaty of Rome signed by the then Prime Minister, Edward Heath. Under this European Economic Community Treaty, the UK was admitted to membership of the EEC. We will see in Chapter 12 that the result of our membership was the recognition of Community law as being superior to British law in cases of conflict. Moreover, the institutions of the EEC are able to make laws which are applicable to all 12 member States. Along with the UK, the original group of six member countries, was joined by Eire and Denmark, followed by Greece in 1981 and Spain and Portugal in 1986.

What are these institutions which have had such a tremendous influence on the business environment since the UK became a member State in January 1973? The Treaty of Rome was originally signed in 1957 by France, Italy, West Germany, Luxembourg, Belgium and the Netherlands under the influence of the beliefs of European politicians Jean Monnet and

Fig. 2.3
The European Commission Building, Brussels, by courtesy of The Commission of the European Communities

Robert Schuman that European wars could be ended if all the European countries shared their resources and acted as a unified economic entity. Under the EEC Treaty the first step to achieve this was for all member States to allow the free movement of goods between themselves, as well as the free movement of persons, services and capital. Further, the EEC Treaty provides for the maintenance of economic policies common to all member States on such matters as agriculture, transport and rules of competition among commercial and industrial organisations within the Community. It also seeks common policies on social matters and external trade and to bring the laws of the separate States into harmony. (Hence the statutory instrument we were examining.) The institutions consist of the European Commission, which is the watchdog of the Treaty; the Council of European Ministers (which issued the 'spy in the cab' regulation); and the European Parliament (which unlike our own Parliament is only there to be consulted and not to legislate). In order to deal with any disputes, and to provide a definitive statement as to the meaning of a particular community law, the Treaty created a Court of Justice, which meets in Luxembourg.

An example of the influence wielded by these institutions may be seen in the decision in 1981 by the European Council of Ministers to cease government subsidies to national steel producers by 1985. The purpose of this measure is to allow for fair competition between the various steel-making organisations in the Community and it will have, therefore, a fundamental effect on the operations of British Steel.

Similarly the European Court of Justice upheld, in 1986, a fine on Austin Rover for trying to block imports of cheap Metro cars from the continent in contravention of the Community's competition laws. However getting total agreement to competition in relation to air fares, which are at present fixed at a European-wide level, was not possible when the proposal was rejected by some transport ministers at a European Council meeting at the end of 1986.

You may be wondering, having read this far, how anyone in the business environment can possibly know of all the laws which affect them. Surely one would be able to plead ignorance of the law? In fact it is a basic principle of law that ignorance of the law is no defence. We are thus assumed to have knowledge of every law that affects us.

The application of this principle was felt by the Chief Housing Surveyor of the Taff-Ely Borough Council in 1980. The council, as the Surveyor's employer, was successfully sued by a Mrs Clarke, who received £5000 damages, when she suffered an injury after rotten floorboards of her sister's council home gave way. The fact that the Surveyor and the council were 'blissfully unaware' of the legal duty imposed on the council by the Defective Premises Act 1972 could not excuse it from its duty (Clarke *v.* Taff-Ely Borough Council, 1980).

Do judges make law?

The dispute we have just seen was resolved in a court of law with each party presenting their version of the facts and the judge making a decision by interpreting the law authoritatively. The function of judges of interpreting Acts and declaring the law is exercised by close examination of the relevant law to a case and by applying legal principles to the facts.

The decisions of judges must contain their reasons (known by lawyers as the *ratio decidendi*) for arriving at a judgement. It has become the practice of judges also to review relevant decisions made in past cases and to use the legal principles contained in the *ratio* employed by those judges. This practice of following the reasonings of past recorded cases is enshrined in the doctrine of **judicial precedent**. We have previously observed that before Parliament became firmly established as the legislator, much of English law was to be found in legal judgements known as **case law**. Certainly before the nineteenth century, when the House of Commons and Cabinet government became powerful and the Industrial Revolution wrought such changes in social conditions, the court decisions were a major source of law. In the nineteenth century we note the beginning of a far more active role undertaken by Parliament to make law. This resulted in a considerable increase in statute law with the consequence that the judges' role as interpreters of Acts became more and more important.

The doctrine of judicial precedent functions through an elaborate system of courts. Courts, which may be civil or criminal (see Chapter 14), and judges are arranged in order of seniority. The most senior courts (see Fig. 2.4) are the House of Lords Judicial Committee and the Courts of Appeal, which may hear appeals against decisions of judges in the lower courts. The consequence of this structure (known as the 'hierarchy' of the courts) is that decisions made by judges in superior courts do not merely provide a guideline to lower court judges. They, in fact, provide a superior authority that *must* be followed by the lower courts. That is why most cases referred to in this book will be decisions by either the House of Lords or the Courts of Appeal.

The importance of this for the business environment, apart from the

Fig. 2.4
The English Courts in order of
importance

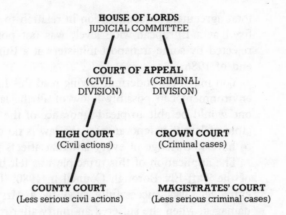

HOUSE OF LORDS
JUDICIAL COMMITTEE

COURT OF APPEAL
(CIVIL   (CRIMINAL
DIVISION)   DIVISION)

HIGH COURT   **CROWN COURT**
(Civil actions)   (Criminal cases)

COUNTY COURT   **MAGISTRATES' COURT**
(Less serious civil actions)   (Less serious criminal cases)

courts' function in resolving disputes between participants in our environment, is that some laws have been made by the judges and not by Parliament. Indeed, there are many areas of law where Parliament has not created an Act, and so we need to know the cases in order to know the law.

Let us illustrate our point by explaining an area of law which is the pure creation of judges. It is known as the **tort** (meaning a civil rather than a criminal wrong) of negligence. If a person is bound to take account of another's interest or safety but despite such a duty fails to take care, and another person is consequently injured, the injured person may sue the other for the lack of care. As an example, a driver on the road owes other road users a duty to be careful; if he is not careful and a pedestrian is injured, not only is a possible crime committed (e.g. 'driving recklessly') but the pedestrian may sue the driver for tortious **negligence** and claim damages.

This type of action is known as a **civil action** and must be brought before the civil courts. A civil action arises between private persons or organisations whenever a private right is breached. Examples of civil rights include those arising under the law of contract; rights not to suffer assault and battery or damage to goods or land; the rights of shareholders to expect directors of companies to carry out their duties; and the right not to suffer from another's careless acts. Together with many other rights which we

Fig. 2.5
An employer held liable in
negligence to workers affected by
PVC poisoning

PVC FIRM TO PAY £½m DAMAGES

A plastics plant, where workers suffered health disorders, including sex problems, after being exposed to poisonous fumes, yesterday agreed to pay nearly £500,000 in damages.

The money is shared among 15 workers who brought claims against Vinatex Ltd, of Staveley, near Chesterfield. All but one of the men settled out of court while the case was proceeding.

Mr Justice Woolf was told that the men were all exposed to fumes from vinyl chloride, used in the making of PVC, while they were working at the plant in the early 1970s.

Some of the men became impotent, and others suffered bone disease, breathlessness, aching joints, stomach disorders, clubbing of the fingers and headaches.

Mr Christopher Rose, Q.C., for the men, said the long-term effects of the disease were still unknown.

Some of the men were unable to work at all. Others had taken light jobs with a drop in pay.

shall be considering in succeeding chapters, this field of law is called **civil law**. In essence, a person who claims that his or her rights have been infringed may pursue an action before the civil courts and seek, very often, a payment of compensation known as 'damages' from the wrongdoer.

The case of Donoghue v. Stevenson

Let us illustrate the significance of case law on the business environment by looking at the case illustrated in Fig. 2.6. The case was brought, originally before the Scottish courts, by a woman who became ill through drinking the contents of a bottle of ginger-beer bought for her by a friend and which contained a decomposed snail. She could not sue the shopkeeper because she had not bought the ginger-beer herself and so had made no contract with him, so she sued the manufacturers. There was no Act of Parliament she could rely upon to base her claim. However, after the judges have considered previous judgements together with all the facts in a case, they may lay down legal principles in general terms. This is what the House of Lords did in its judgement in Donoghue's case. It declared that persons owe each other a duty of care and if that is not observed and someone else is injured they may be liable in the tort of negligence.

---

562   HOUSE OF LORDS   [1932]

[HOUSE OF LORDS.]

H. L. (Sc.)* M'ALISTER (or DONOGHUE) (PAUPER) . APPELLANT ;
1932   AND
May 26.   STEVENSON . . . . RESPONDENT.

Negligence—Liability of Manufacturer to ultimate Consumer—Article of Food —Defect likely to cause Injury to Health.

By Scots and English law alike the manufacturer of an article of food, medicine or the like, sold by him to a distributor in circumstances which prevent the distributor or the ultimate purchaser or consumer from discovering by inspection any defect, is under a legal duty to the ultimate purchaser or consumer to take reasonable care that the article is free from defect likely to cause injury to health :—

So *held*, by Lord Atkin, Lord Thankerton and Lord Macmillan ; Lord Buckmaster and Lord Tomlin dissenting.

George v. Skivington (1869) L. R. 5 Ex. 1 approved.

Dicta of Brett M.R. in *Heaven v. Pender* (1883) 11 Q. B. D. 503, 509–11 considered.

Mullen v. Barr & Co., Ld., and *M'Gowan v. Barr & Co., Ld.,* 1929 S. C. 461 overruled.

APPEAL against an interlocutor of the Second Division of the Court of Session in Scotland recalling an interlocutor of the Lord Ordinary (Lord Moncrieff).

By an action brought in the Court of Session the appellant, who was a shop assistant, sought to recover damages from the respondent, who was a manufacturer of aerated waters, for injuries she suffered as a result of consuming part of the contents of a bottle of ginger-beer which had been manufactured by the respondent, and which contained the decomposed remains of a snail. The appellant by her condescendence averred that the bottle of ginger-beer was purchased for the appellant by a friend in a café at Paisley, which was occupied by one Minchella ; that the bottle was made of dark opaque glass and that the appellant had no reason to suspect that it contained anything but pure ginger-beer ; that the said Minchella poured some of the ginger-beer out into a tumbler, and that the appellant drank some of the contents of the tumbler ; that her friend was then proceeding to pour the remainder of the contents of the bottle into the tumbler when a snail, which

* *Present :* LORD BUCKMASTER, LORD ATKIN, LORD TOMLIN, LORD THANKERTON, and LORD MACMILLAN.

Fig. 2.6
The first page of the report on Donoghue *v.* Stevenson

This decision, like the judgements made almost daily by superior courts, laid down the law. Since this case in 1932 many thousands of actions have been brought by private individuals and organisations using the principles in the case of Donoghue *v*. Stevenson. Of course, these cases could not be used as law if they were not recorded, and so lawyers use Law Reports, containing judgements for hundreds of years, to find out what the law is on this or that matter.

The law of contract

This is another very important branch of the Law. Like negligence it is an area which judges have developed through their decision making. We saw that in Donoghue *v*. Stevenson there could be no action against the café owner because Donoghue had not herself bought the ginger-beer from him, i.e. there was no contract of sale between them, and so the action had to be founded in negligence. However a vast number of business and other relationships are 'underpinned' by the law of contract – sale, credit, employment, etc. We shall be describing the law of contract in some detail in later chapters. What we have to keep in our minds is that any organisation in its relationships with employees, suppliers and customers and in its acquisition of resources is bound to take note of contract law, which will impose on it both rights and duties.

Criminal law

If an organisation in the business environment finds it necessary to resort to the law, it will usually be involved with the civil law. It may have to bring a civil action against another organisation or individual over some dispute which cannot be otherwise resolved. As we have said, civil law is concerned with the rights, duties and obligations between private individuals, be they persons or organisations. In contrast, the **criminal law** is concerned with those wrongs that are regarded as being against the community as a whole. As such the State itself, on behalf of us all, may take legal action against individuals or organisations. This is known as a **prosecution**. Often, you will be able to recognise that a dispute concerns the criminal law because the police are involved. We have seen that in civil cases the recognition by a court that one of the parties in the dispute is in the wrong may be by the award of damages. The position is different if a criminal court finds an accused guilty of committing the crime as charged. In this event the accused will be punished by the imposition of a fine and/or imprisonment or some other form of punishment. Unlike damages which are payable to the victorious party, a fine is payable to the State.

As with civil wrongs, some criminal wrongs were created by judges in their case decisions. These, you will remember, we refer to as the Common Law. However, most crimes are defined by Acts of Parliament. Examples include the Theft Acts 1968 and 1978, the Criminal Damage Act 1971, the Offences Against the Person Act 1861, the Forgery and Counterfeiting Act 1981 and the various crimes created by the Companies Acts 1985. The last legislation creates crimes often referred to as 'regulatory offences'. These have the character of not carrying the same moral reprehensibility as crimes such as murder, rape, grievous bodily harm, burglary and theft. Apart from company legislation you will find regulatory offences created by the Health and Safety at Work Act 1974, the Food and Drugs Act 1955, the Licensing

Fig. 2.7
Police

Act 1964, the Road Traffic Act 1972 and the Rivers (Prevention of Pollution) Act 1951.

You will not, however, be able to consider an Act itself as saying the final word on the meaning of the law. We must very often examine how the judges have **interpreted** the Act, when cases come before the courts involving the particular statute. Finally, we should note that if an organisation is found guilty of a crime it can only be punished by a fine – it can hardly be sentenced to a term of imprisonment.

Can you remember any recent Acts of Parliament or decisions by judges reported in the news? What were they about?

Can you identify any effects that the UK's membership of the EEC has had on the business environment other than those mentioned on pages 27–9?

Can you distinguish between civil law and criminal law, and describe the role of the judges and law courts?

Other influences

By far the major influences affecting the behaviour of organisations are economic, legal and governmental. Much of this book concentrates on describing and analysing these forces and their impact upon organisations. However, that is not to ignore other forces which also play a part in the business environment, such as social, technological, demographic and natural forces.

Social forces

These forces generate changes in the attitudes and behaviour of particular groups in society or of society as a whole. They may exert important influences on organisations, often manifested in economic, political or legal forms.

The impact on organisations of social change can be felt in changes in demand for goods and services. If social patterns change, needs and tastes may vary both in quantity and type. This can be seen in terms of changing fashions and symbols of social groups. Styles of clothes for young people continually change. For example, from Teddy Boys to Mods and Rockers and Punks, clothes have formed an important link in the mutual identity of such groups. Many clothing retailers and manufacturers alter their product lines to satisfy such changing tastes, and can on occasion stimulate such fashions by successful advertising and marketing strategies.

Think back a few years. Has the style of clothes and footwear you buy altered? How much are you influenced by social trends in fashion?

Sometimes there may be a fundamental change in attitude among people which then acts as a social force having effect on organisations. For example, the drive of the Health Education Council (a government body) to make people realise the dangers of smoking cigarettes, combined with increasing taxation imposed by the government on cigarettes, must affect the organisations that manufacture cigarettes. If the anti-smoking campaign is successful, fewer young people will take up the habit and many smokers will try to reduce their cigarette consumption or cut it out altogether. This will have the effect of reducing demand for cigarettes, which will cause cigarette manufacturers to reduce their production. Fewer employees as a consequence will be needed in the production of cigarettes. This is, in fact, what has happened in recent times.

In order to meet this changed climate of opinion about cigarette smoking, many of the manufacturers have diversified their interests. In other words, they have chosen not to rely only on cigarette manufacturing for their business, and have widened the types of business in which they are concerned. For example, Imperial Tobacco, the producer of Embassy and John Player cigarettes, diversified, and the Imperial Group now owns Courage and John Smith's beers, Hofmeister and Kronenbourg lager, Golden Wonder crisps, Anchor hotels, Happy Eater restaurants, Finlays newsagents, Ross frozen foods, Youngs seafoods and HP tinned foods and sauces. The Imperial Group itself became part of a larger conglomerate when it was taken over by Hanson Trust.

A further example of a change in social attitudes which could affect business organisations relates to Sunday trading. It appears that relatively more people now regard it acceptable that shops are allowed to open Sundays rather than stay closed on the grounds of religious observance. In Scotland it is permissible for shops to open seven days a week, although in 1986 Parliament narrowly rejected such a move for the rest of the UK.

As there has been a trend towards a shorter working week, the opportunities for leisure have grown. A number of organisations in both the private and public sectors have acted to meet changing demand. This is manifested, for example, in the provision of bingo or snooker halls by the private sector, while many local councils have built sports centres offering a variety of sporting facilities to local residents.

Note, though, that as social habits change, organisations need to react. As shown in Fig. 2.8, cinema attendance dropped initially due to competition from television. However, in recent years the cinema has been further affected by the growing popularity of watching video films at home. Increasingly, film companies rely on income from sales of video cassettes rather than revenue from cinema-goers.

Another social change in recent years shows up in the market for alcoholic drink. There has been a decline in sales of beer in contrast to growth in sales of lager and wine. This partly reflects the greater numbers of people going abroad for holidays leading to a broadening of tastes, as well as a relative fall in the price of wine compared with other alcoholic drinks. Clearly this change affects the orders that public houses and off-licences would place with breweries and wine suppliers.

Greater foreign travel by UK residents has also broadened attitudes to food. In recent years there has been growth in the number of restaurants

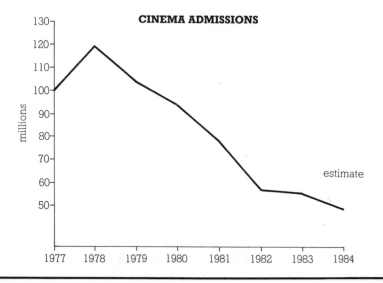

Fig. 2.8
Cinema admissions from 1977–84

and take-aways specialising in foreign foods like pizza or kebab. Such increasing variety of foods also relates to the ethnic mix of the UK population, reflecting immigration into this country.

We mentioned earlier that social forces can bring about changes in the law, as well as having an economic or political impact. An important example of this in recent years has been the changing status of women in our society.

The more equal treatment and status of women has been the aim of pressure groups in a number of countries. The force of the argument induced governments to make changes in the law to bring about a more equal treatment of men and women in a number of situations.

Organisations must now take heed of the Equal Opportunities Commission and observe the Equal Pay Act. The Commission considers complaints that women have been unfairly discriminated against in employment because of their sex, while the Equal Pay Act states that employers must make the same rate of pay to both men and women who are employed on similar work.

Demographic influences

Demographic influences relate to changes in the size and structure of the population. Such changes can affect organisations because:

- people are buyers of goods and services (consumers)
- people are workers

Thus changes in market size due to population trends can be a significant feature affecting the planning of organisations in both the public and the private sectors. Furthermore, demographic influences on the availability of labour can influence the location of an organisation or its method of operation.

We shall next consider examples of demographic features and how they affect organisations.

Birth rate and death rate

The total size of the country's population can change in two ways:

- by natural changes (births and deaths)
- by immigration and emigration

Natural change is often measured by comparing the crude birth rate and the crude death rate. They are expressed as a rate per thousand of the population.

$$\text{Crude birth rate} = \frac{\text{Number of births}}{\text{Number of thousands in the total population}}$$

For example in country X there were 4 000 000 people in the total population at the start of 1986. During that year there were 100 000 births.

$$\text{Crude birth rate} = \frac{100\ 000}{4000} = 25 \text{ per thousand}$$

This means that for every thousand people in the population at the start of 1986, 25 babies were born.

The crude death rate is calculated in a similar fashion.

$$\text{Crude death rate} = \frac{\text{Number of deaths}}{\text{Number of thousands in the total population}}$$

For example in the same country X there were 60 000 deaths during 1986.

$$\text{Crude death rate} = \frac{60\ 000}{4000} = 15 \text{ per thousand}$$

Hence, with a birth rate of 25 per thousand and a death rate of 15 per thousand, there was natural growth in the population of 10 per thousand.

Whether the population actually fell or grew during 1986 would also depend on net immigration into and out of country X.

Trends in UK population size

The dramatic take-off in UK population growth coincided with the Industrial Revolution, as can be seen in Fig. 2.9. The birth rate rose steeply in the latter half of the eighteenth century, and this, allied with a falling death rate in the nineteenth century, led to a large increase in population size. The population more than doubled from 1801, the year of the first official census, to 1851. The rate of growth was still high in the second half of the nineteenth century. Thus clearly the supply of labour was growing, as was the number of consumers.

In the current century, the birth rate has fallen while the death rate has stabilised in the post-World War 2 period. Figure 2.9 shows that population growth has slowed considerably after the 1960s, a feature common to many industrialised countries. In fact, in the late 1970s the UK population even began to fall very slightly.

Compare the trend of birth and death rates in recent years shown in Table 2.1.

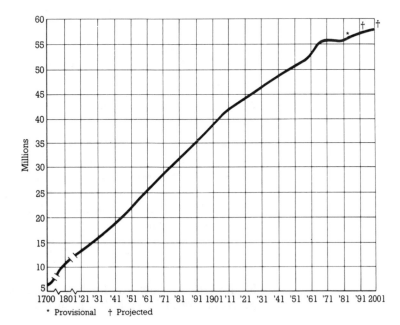

Fig. 2.9
UK population, 1700–2001

Table 2.1
UK crude birth and death rates (per thousand)

Year	1961	1966	1971	1976	1981	1982	1983	1984	1985
Birth rate	17.9	17.9	16.1	12.0	13.0	12.8	12.8	12.9	13.3
Death rate	12.0	11.8	11.5	12.1	11.7	11.8	11.7	11.4	11.8

Sources: *Annual Abstract of Statistics* 1980 Tables 2.24 and 2.32 (derived) and *Population Trends* Winter 1986 Table 9.

From the mid-1960s to the late 1970s there was a fall in the birth rate, whereas the death rate, though showing slight decline, was relatively stable. Total population statistics for recent years showed a slight fall in the late 1970s but a slow growth subsequently (see Table 2.2).

Table 2.2
UK population (thousands)

Year	1971	1974	1977	1980	1983	1984	1985
Population	55 907	56 224	56 179	56 314	56 350	56 460	56 618

Source: *Monthly Digest of Statistics*, November 1986 Table 2.1

The fall in the late 1970s was due to the natural change evident in Table 2.1, that the birth rate had fallen below the death rate. Also there had been more emigration than immigration, adding to the slight decline. The projections for population shown in Fig. 2.9 are based on mid-1983 estimates of future trends in births and deaths allied with a net outflow in migration of 27 000 each year. Such projections are revised as trends in births, deaths and migration vary.

Causes of the fall in the birth rate

Why did the birth rate decline from the mid-1960s? A number of factors are significant.

1 There is a link between greater affluence, as has occurred for much of the post-war period, and a decline in the birth rate – a feature common to many countries.

2 Some young couples prefer to buy consumer goods, e.g. colour TVs or freezers, rather than spend their income on bringing up children.

3 Conversely from the mid-1970s a different influence appeared. There has been some degree of industrial depression and, because of pressures on incomes, this tends to cause a fall in the birth rate. More mouths to feed mean incomes have to be stretched further and so some families may have fewer children. This relationship has been evident in periods of depression in the past, e.g. the 1930s.

4 Greater awareness and use of contraception, especially the contraceptive pill.

5 The 1967 Abortion Act legalises abortions if there is a serious risk to the pregnant woman or child before or after birth.

6 The changing role of women in society has been an important factor. The participation of women in the labour force has increased as women have become less housebound. A less domestic-based existence has contributed to fall in the birth rate. The average family size has fallen.

The death rate has stabilised, despite medical improvements. The incidence of deaths from previously serious illnesses like TB has declined, but more deaths are caused by 'diseases of affluence'. Significant increases have taken place in deaths caused by cancer and by heart disease. The influence of tobacco, unhealthy diet and lack of exercise are important in such cases.

It is noticeable that in the late 1970s the birth rate rose once more, though stabilising in the 1980s. Possibly this could be explained in that some couples were starting families after postponing child-rearing in the early years of marriage. Another influence on the upturn in the birth rate was a rise in the number of women of child-bearing age (the 15–44 age group).

Effects of changes in population size

A growing population logically means more mouths to feed but also more hands for work – more consumers and more workers. Conversely, a falling population will lead to fewer consumers and a smaller labour force.

Is changing population size good or bad for a country? The answer to this question must be qualified by a consideration of the resources, income and wealth in that country. A country with a large population does not automatically have a higher standard of living than a country with a smaller population.

Effects of recent changes in the UK population

What were the effects of the significant fall in the birth rate from the mid-1960s to the late 1970s?

The fall in the birth rate

The fall in the birth rate has influenced planning in some areas of the social services, e.g. education. Because of falling school rolls, the government has decided to reduce recruitment of teachers and has closed down a number of colleges of education, where teachers are trained.

These measures stand in contrast to earlier plans to cope with the sudden bulge in post-war births, which necessitated greater school facilities.

However, demographic change is by no means the only factor that is important in such planning. Some critics argued that instead of cutbacks, the government could have maintained expenditure on education, to reduce class sizes and improve the quality of teaching. The 1979 Conservative Government's decision to cut educational expenditure was based not only on demographic factors, but also on a desire to reduce public expenditure. This, it was argued, would help to reduce inflation and make more resources available for use in the private sector of the economy.

By the same token, the Robbins Report of 1963, which laid plans for the expansion of Higher Education in the UK, recognised the population 'bulge' in the number of young people in their late teens and early twenties, and also expressed a desire to expand university and polytechnic courses to accommodate not only higher numbers of young people, but also a greater proportion of that age group than in the past.

The fall in the birth rate from the mid-1960s to the late 1970s also influenced planning in council house building. Because of falling family size, more council houses and flats with one or two bedrooms have been built instead of dwellings with more bedrooms.

In the private sector it would seem logical to deduce that demand for baby products would decline. Up to a point this has occurred. However, one should remember that although family size has fallen, family incomes have risen. Expenditure on children's goods has not changed as much as one might think. Mothercare Ltd adapted to the changing pattern of birth rate by broadening their range of products. Originally the company specialised in babywear and related products for the very young. However, in the face of possible falls in demand the company decided to extend its product lines to include goods for older children also. 'Mothercare goes up to ten' was the advertising slogan adopted. The company has become increasingly successful and profitable by this change in strategy.

The fall in the birth rate will also affect organisations by changes in the supply of labour. As was mentioned earlier in this chapter, the reduction in birth rate has been paralleled by greater female participation in the working population. However, the longer-term effects of the fall in births will be seen in the late 1980s when relatively fewer young people enter the labour force. In a period when unemployment is likely to rise, this is probably no bad thing.

An ageing population

Through this century there have been changes in the age structure, the proportion of the population in various age groups, as shown in Fig. 2.10. It can be seen that there has been a growing tendency for a larger proportion of people to be in the elderly age group: there is an ageing population. This is due to:

1 Longer life expectancy with improved health and diet.

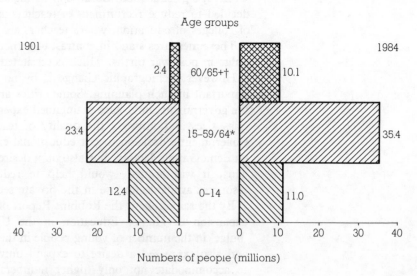

Fig. 2.10
The age structure of the UK populations, 1901 and 1984
Source: *Annual Abstract of Statistics* 1986, Tables 2.3 and 2.4

* 15–59 for women, 15–64 for men
† 60 and over for women, 65 and over for men.

2 The falling birth rate, ensuring a larger proportion of people in older age bands.

What are the effects of an ageing population?

1 Relatively more planning has to be done, particularly in the field of social services, e.g. more old people's homes, more medical staff specialising in geriatrics, greater provision for old age pension payments.

2 There will be a relatively greater demand for the types of commodity that older people are likely to need, e.g. styles of clothing suited to the old, package holidays for the aged. Private sector organisations need to react accordingly by supplying greater quantities.

3 There is a heavier burden on the workforce to provide the tax and National Insurance contributions which help to finance social services for the elderly. It has meant that the smaller percentage of the population in work has to support a larger dependent population at both the young and the old ends of the age spectrum. Sizeable tax and National Insurance deductions from incomes can create a disincentive to work, leading to slower expansion in the economy.

In their planning, some organisations use a more detailed breakdown of the age structure. Consideration of the trends in age structure into narrower age bands, e.g. 15–19, 20–24, 25–29 years, etc. could be made. This would be particularly useful for organisations whose goods or services are geared towards specific age bands, e.g. holidays or clothing for young people.

A large firm which sets up in a particular area of a country is likely to consider the age structure and (un)employment levels of the region when probing the possibilities of hiring a labour force.

These illustrations of demographic change show how this influence can affect organisations' planning and decisions.

What influence might other kinds of population change, like immigration and emigration to and from the UK, or the geographical migration of people within this country, have on UK organisations in both the public and private sectors?

Natural forces

Changes in the natural environment can also affect the operations of organisations. Again, the impact of such changes is often felt through economic forces and modifications in the law.

For example, the weather obviously has effects on organisations. Good weather is important to farmers to enhance the supply and quality of crops. Severe snow can inhibit the transportation of goods and make it difficult for people to get to work so that output is restricted. In less developed countries in the tropics, the effects of weather can be even more extreme. Floods or hurricanes can ruin crops, causing further hunger problems and reducing food export earnings, as happened to the sugar crop of St Lucia in the West Indies in 1980.

A hot summer will cause increases in demand for ice creams and cold drinks, to the delight of organisations selling them. Prices may rise as a result of the greater demand. A higher price was also the outcome of the restricted supply of coffee when the crop in Brazil was damaged by frost

.in the middle 1970s. Suppliers of products like Nescafé and Maxwell House raised their prices in consequence.

Pressure groups stressing concern for the preservation of the natural environment and the pleasure and livelihoods of people and organisations in areas under threat, have influenced governments in passing laws in that field.

Firms risk prosecution if their method of production involves the disposal of harmful effluent into the air or rivers. Such controls include the designation of smokeless zones, the Control of Pollution Act 1974 and specific local by-laws. Thus the production techniques of organisations need to be chosen not only on pure cost grounds, but also with heed to the relevant environmental legislation.

The Merchant Shipping Oil Pollution Act of 1971 was passed as a direct response to the problems caused by the wreck of the *Torrey Canyon* oil tanker in 1967, when large volumes of oil were washed up on coastlines in South-west England. Not only was there an expensive 'mopping-up' operation, but sea birds were killed and the affected areas suffered from a reduction in the numbers of holiday makers. Restaurants, hotels and boarding houses faced reduced revenue and profits. You may recall a similar instance of oil spillage affecting the tourist trade in Brittany in 1980.

So natural forces also play their part in the business environment, their impact often having very direct consequences on the supply or demand facing organisations, and on their methods of production.

Conclusion

In this chapter we have talked about the way in which political, economic, social and other forces in the environment all have an impact on the organisation. Let us look at one example to illustrate this point.

If we take an organisation like a road haulage firm we can see how it is affected by a whole range of forces within the environment. The way in which such an organisation is formed, its relationships with customers, employees, suppliers, etc. are all underpinned by the **law**. In addition to the national law of the UK, EEC law may have a special impact on the firm by making transport laws directly affecting member States, e.g. the introduction of the tachograph, 'the spy in the cab', referred to earlier in this chapter. EEC regulations about the permitted size of heavy lorries will also obviously have an effect.

The firm will inevitably be influenced by **economic factors**, e.g. the effects of the recession, inflation, possible government investment in railways rather than roads, the 'privatisation' of the public road haulage sector under a Conservative Government, increases in the price of petrol and derv.

Social factors, such as increasing pressure from society to preserve the environment and to protect villages and old buildings from the effects of heavy lorries, may affect the road haulage business. Routes may have to be changed to avoid small villages or the centre of cities like York, whose cathedral is suffering from the vibration caused by heavy lorries. If the firm is forced to take longer routes, costs will inevitably rise.

Demographic factors, relating to the birth and death rate and the level of population are important factors. For example, the lower stable birth rate has led to a reduced need for school places, while greater longevity has created a large population of older people.

Natural forces – heavy snow, flooding, etc. – will obviously have a considerable impact on a road haulage business. The firm may be so badly affected by a long spell of bad weather that it may be put out of business.

Thus we can see – and this point will be made throughout the book – that an organisation cannot function in isolation but is affected by the totality of forces which go to make up its environment.

3 The impact of change

One of the most fundamental changes in the 1980s to affect organisations and the way they function is the increased use of information technology, based on advanced computers. Today, miniaturisation of the integrated circuit upon which computers rely, means that the capacity of older equipment (large enough to fill a room) is now equalled by desk-top machines. Moreover, the greatly reduced size of computers and the efficient production of silicon chips (containing the circuit) has allowed prices which make computers widely accessible (see Fig. 3.1). For evidence of the growth of computer ownership you need only note that a larger proportion of homes in the UK have computers than in any other country.

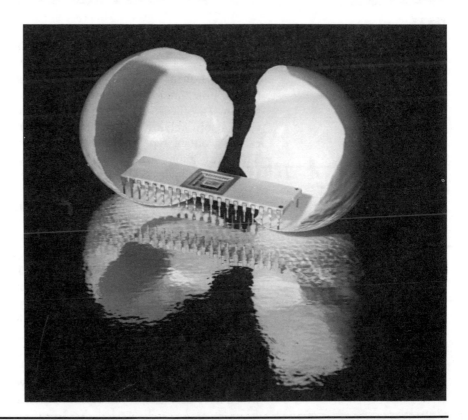

Fig. 3.1
Silicon chip

Fig. 3.2
Robot on the automatic direct
glazing system of Austin Rover

It is the workplace that best illustrates the impact of computers. In the manufacture of motor cars, for instance, conveyor-belt tasks like spot welding, fitment attachment and painting are now done by mechanical robots programmed to repeat a procedure previously undertaken by a person. In offices, 100 years after the invention of the typewriter, many clerical jobs relying on the storage and retrieval of information and the carrying out of repetitive functions are now widely done on a computer. The most common form of this technology consists of a monitor screen, a typewriter-style keyboard, a printer and a computer disc-drive (see Fig. 3.3). Programs, which may be set to allow functions such as typing, filing of information, accounting and stock-control, are fixed on a disc similar to a small flexible music disc. Placed in the disc drive, the computer reads the information off the disc, which can also be used for storage of new information created by the person operating the system, who uses the screen to view operations. For example, a letter could be typed, checked for errors on the screen, and only then copied on paper by the printer.

Can you list examples of the impact of computer technology in your own experience?

In order to assess the changes brought about by the application of the latest advances in this high technology we will examine a few industries which have been transformed. Let us look at your daily paper. Traditionally

Fig. 3.3
Small desk-top computers have created a technological revolution in the commercial and industrial world. The computer in the picture can be operated by touching the screen.

the process of preparing an edition started with the journalists typing their copy, then the hand setting of each letter in metal for every article, the processing of photographs, the composition of the separate items on a page on a semi-cylindrical metal plate, the fixing of this to the printer roller, followed by printing and the distribution. The new method, widely adopted by 1986, involves a high level of automation. The journalist feeds articles into a computer, the computer sets the type and produces a printing plate, photographs are processed and added to the plate, a computer-controlled printer rolls off copies, followed by distribution. Because all information is stored in the computer, all editing and copy examination can be effected by calling it up on a screen (see Fig. 3.4). In this example the separate functions have been halved, and of those remaining many are carried out by computer.

However, the process has dispensed with a large number of manual tasks and there has not been a widespread acceptance of the adoption of such automation. Printing workers and their trade unions, have in some cases

Fig. 3.4
Use of a computer in editing and
page layout
Source: The *Independent*

refused to agree to the new methods. In the face of such opposition some proprietors have relocated their offices from the 80-year London home for newspapers, Fleet Street. *The Times* is now printed at Wapping, and in 1986 the *Daily Telegraph* announced it would also transfer to London's dockland; the *Observer* to Battersea; the *Financial Times* to the Blackwall Tunnel; and the *Mirror* Group to Watford. The choice of some of these locations may have been influenced by their being Enterprise Zones (e.g. London Docklands) offering various financial inducements to new industry.

Your local supermarket may very well be another example of this technology revolution (see Fig. 3.5). Most people are now familiar with the **bar codes** to be seen on the packaging of items. These contain information about the particular thing including a price code, which can be read by a laser scanner operated by the cashier. Each item is recorded by a computer, which stores information and can notify the supermarket's warehouse when items need to be restocked. The supermarket can therefore know instantly what stock sells best and so learn customers' preferences. Indeed, the warehouse itself might be computerised to the extent that it is controlled by computers with the stacking and removal from shelves being done by programmed robots.

At the cash till a so far little used possibility exists, in what is known as 'electronic funds at the point of sale' (EFTPOS). A customer would hand the cashier a plastic card which once fed through the till would be read by

Fig. 3.5
Using bar codes at the Supermarket
check-out by courtesy of J
Sainsbury plc

a computer and issue instructions to the customer's bank or building society
to debit the account and transfer the grocery costs directly into the supermarket's bank account. Actual money would not handled.

This non-cash transaction is also seen at the centre of home-shopping
opportunities envisaged by the use of a special service provided by British
Telecom called 'Prestel'. Specially adapted units can link the telephone to
a television screen so that information can be 'dialled up', an item can be
selected, ordered, debited or invoiced and finally arrangements made for
delivery.

What factors might influence the continued existence of the High Street despite
the possibility of home shopping?

The opportunities offered by such innovations based on national and
international communications are continually being exploited to allow infor-

mation to be rapidly transferred. No better illustration of this need can be provided than in the international market in company shares, currencies and raw material commodities. You may have learnt from the media that these items are not so much bought by people who actually want them as they are by people and institutions who **deal** in them with a view to making a profit when they are eventually bought by those intending to own them. Thus is the price set for a company share, our foreign currency for a holiday and even a cup of tea. As we will see later, this dealing is centred in the City of London and on 27 October 1986 the Stock Exchange underwent a so-called *Big Bang*, involving the change from face-to-face dealing between 'jobbers' and 'brokers' on the floor of the Exchange to an abolition of this distinction and the introduction of a computer-based system called Stock Exchange Automated Quotation system (SEAQ). The system collects and displays the information needed to trade in stocks and shares.

Nor are other traditional professions unaffected by this revolution. Lawyers are beginning to use the huge information storage capacity of computers to keep a record of changes in the law, as well as to be able to call up fixed clauses and standard forms when producing legal documents like wills and leases. Doctors and hospitals are now able to use specially designed computer programes as tools in the diagnosis of ailments. Posted mail, still massively used by industry, alongside message transmission services such as Telex could be replaced to some extent by the advent of **electronic mail**. For example, British Telecom offers Telecom Gold, by which a computer linked to the telephone can send and receive messages electronically. Now ready for greater commercial exploitation, is the use of satellite communication. In 1986 small home receiver dishes became available to make possible the receipt of television broadcasts planned to be beamed via space satellites. In 1987 the government is considering to whom it should grant a British licence to operate these new satellite operations, and some stations in USA already plan international broadcasting.

Such a growth of computer technology does pose certain problems. We have seen that there are repercussions on people's jobs: in June 1986 the Policy Studies Institute reported a survey showing 80 000 jobs lost since 1984 because of use by manufacturers of micro-chips in products and processes. Another survey carried out by Manpower employment agency revealed that 80 per cent of office workers were dissatisfied with computers mostly because they felt inadequately trained.

As with much human innovation there has been the accompanying chance to perpetrate new crimes. Computer software is unlawfully copied in breach of the 1985 Copyright (Computer Software) Amendment Act. Fraud has been committed by employees and outsiders who have broken into bank and insurance company computer systems – one person in USA instructing a computer to transfer millions of dollars into a Swiss bank account. Further abuses may result from incorrect computer files being kept on individuals. For this reason the Data Protection Act 1984 attempts to limit the data that is kept on individuals, and the length of time that the data is kept, as well as giving the right for persons to see their file on the payment of a fee.

What other problems can you think of which might arise from the wider use of computers?

Can you describe a computer chip? What is its significance?

What is EFTPOS?

How does the Data Protection Act 1984 seek to protect privacy?

Summary, Part A

1 The fundamental economic problem is scarcity, that resources are limited in supply.

2 As a result people and organisations must make choices of how to deploy resources.

3 When resources are used for a particular purpose, there is an opportunity cost, namely the benefits foregone of the next best alternative.

4 Societies must make decisions about what to produce, and about how, where and for whom this production should take place.

5 Answers to these questions vary according to the type of economy, be it a market, planned or mixed economy.

6 The key distinction between these types of economy lies in the relative importance of the market mechanism and State involvement.

7 A mixed economy like the UK contains a public and a private sector.

8 Organisations exist in a legal framework which influences directly and indirectly the participants in the business environment, and often lays down how an organisation may come into being.

9 English law is made up from various sources including Acts of Parliament, Statutory Instruments, EEC regulations and Case Law.

10 The role of the judges is of particular importance in the legal environment, for through their judgements they declare and interpret the law.

11 Law is divided into civil wrongs heard before civil courts and crimes heard before the criminal courts.

12 The size of a country's population can alter by variation in births, deaths, immigration and emigration.

13 In recent years the UK population size has been stable, reflecting the decline in the birth rate from the mid-1960s to the late 1970s.

14 The UK has tended to experience an ageing population – a greater percentage of people in the older age groups.

15 Trends in the birth rate, death rate, age structure, balance of migration and geographical distribution of population exert effects upon organisations as regards supplies of labour and patterns of consumption.

16 Social forces generate changes in attitudes and behaviour in society.

17 Social, demographic and natural factors, often manifested in economic, legal or political forces, influence the behaviour of organisations.

18 The discovery and wider use of the micro-chip has created new opportunities to automate production.

19 The adoption of computerised systems has transformed certain industries and commercial undertakings.

Assignments, Part A

1 Your High Street

Visit your own local High Street. Make a list of 20 different types of organisations located there, categorising them according to the nature of the goods or services which they supply.

2 Sunhampton

Look back at Chapter 1 for the picture of Sunhampton and its High Street. Take the following organisations:

Insurall (Insurance Services) Ltd
Buyerpad Building Society
Banksure Bank plc
The Town Hall

and, for each organisation, give *two* examples of possible changes in the environment which would affect it.

3 The Business Environment

The following organisations are in Sunhampton High Street:

Electrofactor (Products) plc
A. L. Things
Lore & Vice & Co
A. B. Cus & Co
Sunhampton Electricity Board
Hamburga Joint

Which of the following changes would affect which organisation in the list given above? Explain *how* the change would affect the organisation.
a An EEC regulation is passed laying down rules about the weight of portions of meat served in restaurants.
b Questions have recently been asked in Parliament about the operation of nationalised industries. A proposal has been made that the Monopolies and Mergers Commission should investigate the gas and electricity industries.
c Because of the recession there is a considerable drop in expenditure on household goods and clothes.
d Under international pressure the government has withdrawn import controls on Japanese technical and electrical equipment.
e The government, in renewed efforts to cut public expenditure, has abolished a legal aid scheme whereby people could get cheap legal advice from solicitors.
f The EEC has issued a Directive on Company Law which will lead to changes in the law about the auditing of companies' accounts.
g The Secretary of State for the Environment has given permission for the construction of a hypermarket just outside Sunhampton.
h The local authority has made a decision to 'pedestrianise' Sunhampton High Street.

4 Computerisation

Select either an office environment or a factory, and assess the impact of the introduction of computerisation, over, say the last 10 years. Identify the type of equipment now used and that which it replaces. Prepare a chart fixing the introduction of various computer-based processes. On the chart detail the effects on the staff, the premises, work procedures, clients and other factors which you may think important. Try to get the help of a local company, or if you are at work ask your employer to help you.

Skills
Identifying and tackling problems, information gathering, learning and studying, communicating.

PART B

BUSINESS ORGANISATIONS

When you have read this part you should be able to:
- Appreciate the principal reasons why people associate in organisations.
- Distinguish different types of organisations in terms of their function and purpose.
- Understand the different legal forms of organisations.
- Consider some of the legal, social and economic consequences of choice between forms of business units.
- Be aware of the nature of governmental organisations.
- Outline the ways in which the business environment is regulated.
- Appreciate the role of the courts and legal personnel.

4 The need for organisations

Organisations of many different kinds serve the great variety of our needs in society. Every day you come into contact with organisations, some large, some small, in both the public and the private sectors. You have direct involvement with organisations as a consumer, as an employee or perhaps as a student at college. In Part B we set out to describe the structure of organisations, the reasons why some organisations function on a large scale while others remain small, and the differences and similarities between the various types. You will be able to see why certain organisations have to be set up in a form laid down by the law and the limitations that the law places on their powers to do things. We must also examine those characteristics which are shared by all organisations and, indeed, consider why organisations are necessary.

What is an organisation?

We have already agreed that an organisation consists of a group of people involved in a common activity. Furthermore, though the activity may be different in each organisation, all organisations share a number of common characteristics:

    a each has a set of objectives – either implicit (i.e. understood by members) or explicit, and written down;

    b each has a task or tasks designed to meet its objectives;

    c each uses people to undertake the tasks;

    d each needs to co-ordinate people and tasks, usually by arranging staff in a hierarchy consisting of managers at the top, foremen/supervisors in the middle and workers at the bottom;

    e all exist within the wider environment of the world outside, while simultaneously creating their own internal environment.

This can be shown clearly in pictorial form (Fig. 4.1).

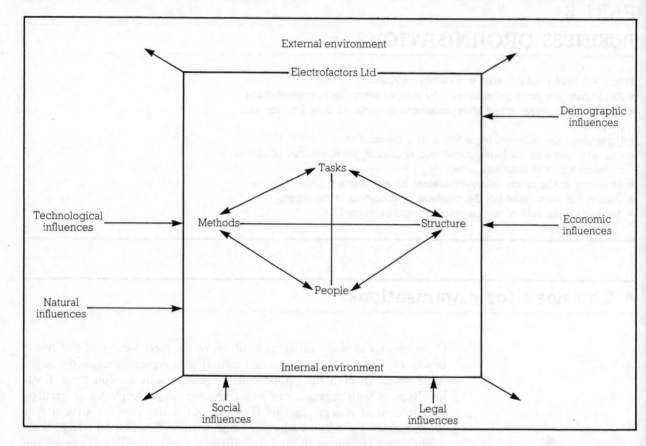

Fig. 4.1
Organisational environments

Here we have Electrofactor (Products) plc firmly placed within its environment with social, legal, economic, natural, demographic, political and technological influences feeding into it, while inside the company we can see the four important variables common to all organisations – tasks, people to carry out the tasks, methods of achieving the tasks, and a structure to co-ordinate them – all interlinked, all interactive.

The need for organisations

Organisations exist because they can fulfil needs more efficiently than when an individual attempts to cater for his/her requirements in isolation, and without assistance from others.

The primary reason for this can be attributed to an organisation's ability to employ the techniques of **specialisation** and the **division of labour** in the productive processes.

Specialisation

This is perhaps the oldest organisational device, and it occurs when organisations or individual workers concentrate on a limited type of activity. One manifestation of this is to be found in the division between managers and managed, where the specialisation is vertical; it also occurs horizontally when some engineers specialise in production while others are maintenance engineers (Figs 4.2 and 4.3).

Through specialisation, workers are able to build up a far greater level of skill and knowledge than if they had attempted to become Jacks of all trades. This technique is used extensively in organisations as diverse as local

Fig. 4.2
Vertical specialisation

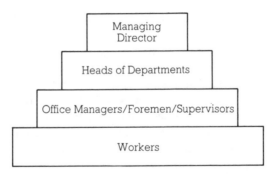

Fig. 4.3
Examples of horizontal specialisation
(a) at management level, (b) at
worker level

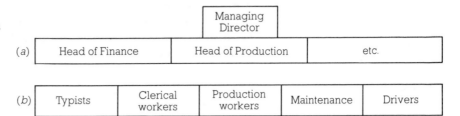

authorities, banks and the motor industry. Other examples of specialisation, on an individual level, occur through choice of career, e.g. doctors, teachers, lawyers, etc.

The advantage of arranging an organisation in this way lies in the fact that, by concentrating on one type or aspect of production, it is possible to become much more efficient. By concentrating its expertise into a limited range of activities, the organisation plans and arranges its production to achieve the most efficient use of resources. A key aspect of specialisation involves what is known as the division of labour.

The division of labour

The specialisation of labour developed as industrialisation advanced and bigger organisations became more common in both the manufacturing and the service sectors. Serving bigger markets, these organisations employ a large labour force and utilise the division of labour. The use of mass production techniques in the manufacture of cars, which was pioneered by Henry Ford for his 'Model T', illustrates the use of the division of labour. Here the production process is broken down into a large number of separate tasks and each worker is required to specialise in only one small aspect of the total process.

From the point of view of the manufacturer, the use of this type of technique has a number of significant benefits. Firstly, breaking the production processes down into a series of relatively simple tasks enables the manufacturer to employ highly specific equipment, such as power wrenches, which in turn speeds up the manufacturing operation. Secondly, the organisation is able to employ semi-skilled labour and save the money it would have to pay for the training and hire of more skilled operatives. Thirdly, since the workers are each responsible for only one simple aspect of the total production process they are soon able to develop a high level of expertise and are able to increase greatly their output per hour. The manufacturer is thus in a position to build and supply far more cars, and at a lower cost, than if specialisation and the division of labour had not been employed to such an extent.

One of the earliest proponents of the division of labour was an American, F. W. Taylor, who was a manager at a large American steelworks in the 1880s, and his writings were probably familiar to Henry Ford. Taylor believed that workers were influenced by money, and that if they were paid a fair day's wage then they, in turn, would deliver a fair day's work. He recommended that wages should be paid according to an 'incentive piece-rate' which means that the harder a worker works, the more he/she will produce, and thus the more he/she will be paid.

However, in order to make this easier and fairer, Taylor suggested that work should be scientifically designed, and that managers should ensure that all workers would undertake the same task in the same 'one best way', or in other words in the way designed by management with maximum efficiency and output in mind.

Work study

This is the name given to the technique devised by Taylor, whereby managers establish the best way to carry out a job. The general principles are as follows:

a Study the performance of 10–15 workers:
 • in different establishments,
 • in different parts of the country,
 • who are particularly skilful in carrying out the task to be analysed.
b Study the operations/motions which each worker uses in doing the job, and the tools each one uses.
c Study with a stop-watch the time it takes to make each movement and then choose the fastest way of carrying out each movement.
d Eliminate false movements, slow movements, useless movements.
e Combine the quickest and best movements into one sequence, using the best tools.

Once the survey has been completed, the correct tools and the best, quickest way of completing the work identified, Taylor suggested that this best way should be taught to the supervisor who would, in turn, teach it to each worker.

Consider a task which you do on your course, or at work or even at home and carry out your own work study survey to consider if it could be done more effectively.

It is, to a large extent, this principle which underpins much of the production methods in the motor industry since it lends itself very well to a production line approach.

Specialisation and the division of labour also become more important devices as an organisation grows: if we consider the origins of Electrofactor (Products) plc, when James Dodd did repairs, modified spare parts, etc. all from his garage workshop, we can see that James was indeed a Jack of all trades. As the business grew, however, and he began to employ more staff then, inevitably, he began to specialise, delegating other tasks to his employees.

While specialisation and division of labour are essential to the well-being of all organisations if they are to fulfil their needs more efficiently, it is important to note that an excessive use of these techniques means that each worker may be restricted to a boring and repetitive job which provides very little satisfaction; furthermore, Taylor's view that people are motivated by money is only partly true, since many people need to feel that they are more than just one of the factors of production.

Too much specialisation can lead to de-skilling: a worker in the textile industry who can only sew buttonholes, however skilfully, is less skilled than a tailor who can produce a whole suit. Industrial psychologists cite over-specialisation as a major cause of absenteeism, high labour turnover and unofficial strikes.

Some companies, notably Volvo at its Kalmar plant in Sweden, have introduced a modified form of the division of labour to try and overcome some of the problems of over-specialisation. They use team production techniques, where a group of workers is responsible for producing a car from start to finish; this allows more autonomy to the workers who can control the work-flow to some extent, while they benefit from job rotation, which means that the work they do is more varied. Volvo has found that output per worker compares favourably with other plants using more traditional division of labour methods. It has certainly had a positive effect on absenteeism, staff turnover and strikes, all of which have declined while the quality of the work has improved. It is thought that these benefits are due to greater job satisfaction and pride felt by individuals in a job well done; as each car is completed, each member of the team can see the results of their labour and can feel a sense of achievement and satisfaction.

Modern industrialised economies make great use of specialisation and the division of labour; they are the means whereby organisations control the tasks and the methods in which the tasks are delivered. For organisations to gain the full benefits of these techniques they also use another organisational device known as **the hierarchy** which underpins and defines the organisation's internal structure.

The hierarchy

Hierarchies are found in the private and public sectors of the economy. Consequently, the internal structure and organisation of a nationalised industry is broadly similar to that of any large-scale private sector firm.

The term hierarchy refers to the distribution of *authority, responsibility* and *accountability* within the organisation. In general, organisation structures tend to be pyramidal, where most of the authority is to be found at the top and we often speak of the **pyramid of power** (Fig. 4.4).

Authority: the right to exercise powers such as hiring and firing, buying and selling, planning, and decision making on behalf of the organisation.
Responsibility (for): the allocation of tasks to individuals and groups within the organisations.
Accountability (to): the need for individuals to explain and justify any failure to fulfil their responsibilities to their superiors in the hierarchy.

The pyramid of power is the result of the division of labour vertically and is an attempt, once again, to ensure efficient use of resources: organis-

Fig. 4.4

The pyramid of power. Authority
vested in the top (senior
management); responsibility
delegated to middle management;
all members of the organisation are
accountable for carrying out their
task efficiently.

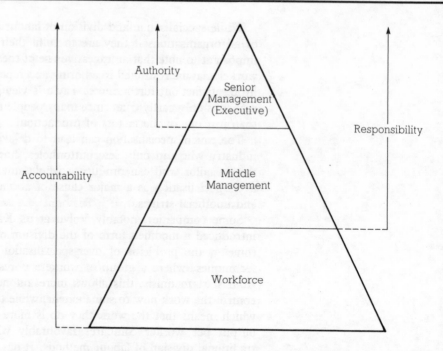

isations are also divided horizontally into specialised departments according
to function, and we can see how this works if we consider the structure of
Electrofactor (Products) Ltd in 1960, shortly after they became a limited
company.

Within each department, there are levels of authority, responsibility and
accountability, as there are with the Board and the Managing Director.

The Board will decide overall company policy (and, be accountable to
the shareholders), while the Managing Director has responsibility for the
running of the company and is thus accountable to Board members for the
implementation of policy.

Fig. 4.5

Organisational structure,
Electrofactor (Products) Ltd in 1960

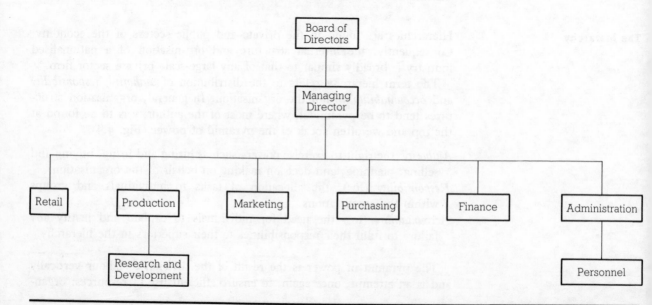

The specialisation of functions in this large organisation has meant a division into a number of departments. Each department head is responsible for the smooth running of his/her department and has authority to make decisions as problems arise, and each head is directly accountable to the Managing Director. Within each department, some authority is delegated to senior staff, e.g. supervisors in the production department, or buyers in the purchasing department; such employees are accountable to their department heads.

One interesting factor in the division by function as practised by Electrofactor (Products) Ltd in 1960 is the fact that the company clearly did not feel the need to establish either a separate Research and Development (R and D) Department or a Personnel Department. These functions will be carried out by members of, respectively, the Production Department and the Administration Department. This practice is by no means uncommon while a company is growing, though inevitably as the importance of product development grows, most companies establish an R and D Department. Similarly, as the numbers of staff increases and employment and industrial relations legislation becomes more complex, it makes sense to set up a separate Personnel Department.

By 1986, therefore, the internal structure of Electrofactor (Products) plc will have changed (Fig. 4.6).

What are the functions of these departments?

Purchasing: the acquisition of raw materials or components necessary in the production process.

Production: the operations at the factory of making, in this case, electrical goods, ensuring that the required volume and quality of production is promptly made to meet delivery schedules.

Marketing: responsibility for advertising, customer relations and selling the goods. There may be area sales managers responsible for sales in different parts of the country or overseas.

Personnel: responsible for activities like the employment of staff, training programmes to improve employee performance, and industrial relations with worker representatives.

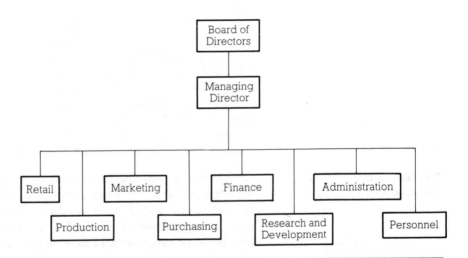

Fig. 4.6
Organisational structure,
Electrofactor (Products) in 1986

Accounting: monitoring the cash flow of the company and preparing information for the budgets for departments.

General administration: the day-to-day administration of the company offices, involving mail, the typing pool and telephonists.

Research and development (R and D): investigation into new product lines and variants on existing products.

Most, if not all, of these departments are likely to be found in many large organisations; they are not peculiar to Electrofactor (Products) plc.

Consider the structure of an organisation to which you belong; your workplace, college or a club of which you are a member. Can you identify any of the features of specialisation, division of labour, etc?

Before we move on from our consideration of organisation structure, it may be useful to look at the origins of hierarchic arrangements. The basis is military, with its concept of a direct, unbroken line of delegated authority from the top to the bottom of the hierarchy. This is known as **line structure** and, in theory, provides a basis for the authority relationship between superior and subordinate; people in authority are, therefore, often called **line managers** because their authority is derived from their position in the line.

In practice, however, line structure only works in small organisations where managers are responsible for a whole range of issues; each departmental manager would be responsible for staffing, purchasing, accounts, etc. within his/her department. In a large organisation like Electrofactor (Products) plc which is organised by function, this approach would be wasteful, and ignores the existence of the Personnel, Purchasing and Finance Departments. Nevertheless, line manager is still a useful term, and is widely used.

There is a further useful distinction to be made between the different types of department within an organisation. For example, the Production and Marketing Departments are known as *primary* or *line* departments; these are, in other words, the departments which have primary responsibility for meeting the organisations's objectives (which are usually about the maximisation of profit and growth). The other departments are known as *secondary* or *staff* departments, and their function is to service the needs of the line departments, by providing help and advice; for example, the Personnel Department would deal with staffing issues for all departments, while the Finance Departments would deal with the company's finances and provide advice to the other departments.

Since most departments are, in fact, inter-dependent it is no longer desirable, or even useful, to discuss any difference in status between line and staff departments. Many large organisations are, nevertheless, arranged to some extent on line and staff principles.

The significance of large organisations

We have suggested that the extent of division of labour and specialised departmental structure is dependent on the size of the organisation and thus the size of the market it serves. As in other Western industrialised countries, large organisations in the UK are few in number, but they account for very large proportions of total output and employment. The many sole traders, partnerships and small companies contribute correspondingly small proportions.

In 1975, the 4 per cent of organisations in manufacturing industry in the UK which were biggest in size contributed 83 per cent to total output and 75 per cent of employment in that sector. Similar pictures are evident in retailing and construction.

Which are these significant large organisations? Tables 4.1 and 4.2 give details of those with the biggest turnover (value of sales) and the largest number of employees.

As you can see, the large oil producers are the biggest revenue earners in the UK. Note also the importance of the big nationalised and recently privatised industries in terms of both turnover and employment.

Small businesses

Despite the overwhelming significance of large business organisations, we should not ignore the growing numbers of small businesses which have developed in recent years.

Between 1980 and 1983 there was a net increase in the number of companies by 120 000, the vast majority of which were small businesses. There were approximately 1.4 million small businesses in 1984, employing a quarter of the nation's workforce. The encouragement of small businesses has been an important theme of the policies of the Conservative Government headed by Mrs Thatcher. In Chapter 35 we review some of the approaches the government has used.

Table 4.1

Top ten industrial organisations in the UK at the end of 1984 by value of turnover.

	Turnover (£m)
1 BP	44 059
2 Shell Transport and Trading	29 522
3 BAT Industries	14 426
4 ICI	9 909
5 Shell UK	9 608
6 BNOC	9 562
7 Electricity Council	9 562
8 Esso UK	7 565
9 British Telecom	6 876
10 British Gas	6 392

Source: *Times 1000*

Table 4.2

Biggest industrial employers in the UK, 1984

	Numbers of employees
1 British Telecom	245 000
2 National Coal Board	243 000
3 BAT Industries	213 000
4 British Rail	207 000
5 Post Office	202 000

Source: *Times 1000*

Objectives of businesses

We have stated the likely major objective of organisations in the private sector is to maximise profits. While this is commonly the guiding principle, other objectives might be set as a performance target for the future.

For instance, the Marketing Department might set sales targets for the coming year or perhaps few years. Such targets could be framed in a number of ways:

- a target for absolute growth of sales (e.g. to sell 800 000 of the product next year);
- a target for percentage growth of sales (e.g. to increase sales by 5 per cent per annum);
- to increase market share. This means that the organisation would seek to attain a certain percentage of sales in the whole market, in competition with other suppliers (e.g. to acquire at least 18 per cent market share).

If such targets were not achieved then doubtless there would be consideration of what went wrong, and policy and planning could be adjusted accordingly in the future.

Objectives of nationalised industries are generally set by the government in financial terms, that a certain percentage surplus (or profit) should be earned on capital employed. Thus a profit target could be expected, but this would not accord with that of maximum profit since nationalised industries, as will be explained in Chapter 8 have social and other economic objectives beyond that of pure profitability.

Consider the organisation in which you may work or study. What are its objectives?
What are your own personal objectives in your job or in your studies?

5 How organisations are formed

How are organisations formed and what are the legal constraints on what they may do?

You will remember from having read about our model town, that we saw different types of business units, each composed of individuals displaying a variety of skills. Each organisation specialised in one aspect or another of a service for which there was a demand in the community. The High Street also alters in line with changes occurring in the environment. It is now quite common to see computer shops; most small grocers have disappeared as their business has been taken by supermarket chains; building societies offer services once the preserve of banks; gas showrooms are now controlled by a large private company (prior to 1986 they were part of a nationalised corporation). You have read of public companies like Electrofactor (Products) plc, Banksure Bank plc, as well as private companies such as Insurall (Insurance Services) Ltd and A.L. Things. Professional services are available from the partnerships of Lore & Vice & Co and the accountants A.B. Cus & Co Sunhampton Electricity Board represents a nationalised industry, the Sunhampton Job Centre is a central government body, and local government can be seen in the shape of Sunhampton Town Hall.

Why are organisations of different types? Is there a particular reason to explain why some are partnerships, while others are private or public companies; some run by the government, others by local councils? The reason is that each type of organisation fits into an overall pattern which by virtue of our history and economic system serves a society which is based on a mixture of free enterprise and government control. We will see that English law provides a structure which can be used by individuals to form a legally recognised business unit. Once formed, regulations exist to ensure that an organisation's conduct is within certain limits. There are by the same token certain activities which may not be undertaken by private persons, such as: maintaining the armed forces, collecting income tax, policing and running the court system. In each case the nature of the

Fig. 5.1

Different types of business units and other organisations

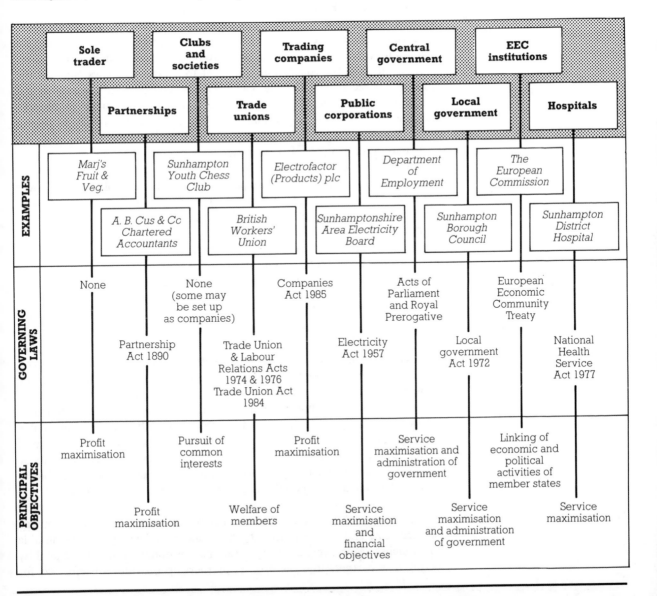

	Sole trader	Partnerships	Clubs and societies	Trade unions	Trading companies	Public corporations	Central government	Local government	EEC institutions	Hospitals
EXAMPLES	Marj's Fruit & Veg.	A. B. Cus & Co Chartered Accountants	Sunhampton Youth Chess Club	British Workers' Union	Electrofactor (Products) plc	Sunhamptonshire Area Electricity Board	Department of Employment	Sunhampton Borough Council	The European Commission	Sunhampton District Hospital
GOVERNING LAWS	None	Partnership Act 1890	None (some may be set up as companies)	Trade Union & Labour Relations Acts 1974 & 1976 Trade Union Act 1984	Companies Act 1985	Electricity Act 1957	Acts of Parliament and Royal Prerogative	Local government Act 1972	European Economic Community Treaty	National Health Service Act 1977
PRINCIPAL OBJECTIVES	Profit maximisation	Profit maximisation	Pursuit of common interests	Welfare of members	Profit maximisation	Service maximisation and financial objectives	Service maximisation and administration of government	Service maximisation and administration of government	Linking of economic and political activities of member states	Service maximisation

organisation will suit the intended function, and we will begin to examine this now.

Sole traders

We may start by looking at the basic business unit, the **sole trader**, who is a single person conducting business on his or her own account. As such a sole trader is not an 'organisation', although others may be employed to further the interests of the business. Outside the professions, for which specialist training is necessary, a person setting up 'shop' as a sole trader need not conform to any particular formality. One consequence, however, is that instead of paying income tax and social security contributions at the employed person's rate, a sole trader is taxed as a self-employed worker.

We come into almost daily contact with sole traders, like the local fruit and vegetable retailer, the domestic window cleaner and the interior decorator.

While it is true that any person may establish a sole trader business without having to comply with any particular registration procedure, there are certain legal restrictions. For instance it is illegal to practise as a medical practitioner, dentist or solicitor without proper qualifications. Of course, once in business the sole trader is subject to a variety of laws, such as the Consumer Credit Act 1974, the Sale of Goods Act 1979 and the Health and Safety at Work Act 1974. A building contractor will have to observe building and planning regulations (see Chapter 17), and a café proprietor must comply with public health and hygiene regulations.

A particular feature of a sole trader is that in law no separation is recognised between the trader's business and personal property such as a house and its contents. As a consequence, if the business collapses and there are insufficient assets to meet debts, the trader's personal property may also have to be made available to his or her creditors (see the section on bankruptcy proceedings in Chapter 20). Thus, in law, the individual and his or her business are regarded as one. However, while a sole trader might have to be a Jack of all trades, doing most of the jobs necessary to conduct the business, there are certain advantages. A sole trader has control over the business and is the only decision maker and profit earner.

Against such advantages as may be drawn from having total control over the running of the business, the sole trader has certain burdens. Very often there are long hours of work. You will have noticed this perhaps in your local High Street – it is the small stores that stay open late and even open on Sundays in contrast to the large chain-stores. Problems arise over the taking of holidays or becoming ill, either of which will disrupt business. Many sole traders cannot afford to close their business to take a holiday.

Owing to the fact that the individual trader is wholly and personally liable for business debts, the capacity to obtain credit is limited to the value of his or her personal assets. As a result these business concerns tend to be relatively small and employ a modest workforce, and so are not able to exploit the benefits of specialisation and the division of labour fully.

Partnerships

An association of individuals called a **partnership** does offer the advantage of small size and, to some extent, the economic advantages of being able to specialise. Moreover, such organisations can obtain additional capital by taking new partners into the firm. A partnership provides a useful way for two or more persons to associate in order to exploit their expertise, and also to share any liabilities.

The organisation is one recognised by the law as set out in the Partnership Act 1890, which describes a partnership as being 'the relation which subsists between persons carrying on a business with a view to profit'. However, the partnership need not be created formally, although in practice partners often make out a written agreement called a Deed of Partnership. Once the partnership has been formed, the partners are collectively regarded as a 'firm', and their name as the 'firm name'. Property brought into or acquired in the course of business, including business goodwill, is regarded as partnership property. Partners are entitled to share in the profits of their firm but are liable to contribute towards any losses. Should any of the partners commit a wrongful act in the ordinary course of the firm's business the other partners may also be held liable. Similarly an act of a partner in the course of business binds the firm and the co-partners.

Usually the law limits the number of persons able to form a partnership to 20, requiring larger groups to exist as a company under the Companies Act 1985 (see later). The exceptions are in relation to certain professions such as solicitors, accountants and stockbrokers which can exist only as partnerships and in this case partnerships may exceed twenty. Architects, estate agents and surveyors are also allowed to form partnerships in excess of 20.

Partnerships share one characteristic with a sole trader, and that is that despite being able to be sued in the firm's name, the firm is not regarded as being a separate thing, separate from the partners themselves. Thus, the partners not only risk the jointly owned business assets, but also their personal property, should there be insufficient assets to meet the claims of the firm's creditors.

An opportunity does exist for a person to invest in a partnership but to take no active part in the running of the business, i.e. to become a 'sleeping partner'. This type of partner may limit liability to the amount invested in the firm, but he or she must register under the Limited Partnership Act 1907.

Clubs and societies

The pursuit of some economic gain does not represent the sole reason for people associating with others, as we can see in the institution of marriage. The purpose of associating with others may be to pursue a common interest such as model railway building, playing cards or tennis, or swimming. In the business environment there are associations which pursue commercial interests, as illustrated by the Association of British Travel Agents and the Association of British Chambers of Commerce, as well as trade unions and employers' associations (e.g. the Engineering Employers Federation).

Unless the club, society or association is organised as a public or private company, which we shall examine later, it may not be sued as such. This is because in legal terms a club or society is regarded as consisting of individuals who will each be regarded as liable if the club defaults in the payment of a debt. If a rugby club's secretary ordered 20 crates of beer, but the supplier was not paid, the supplier could not sue the club. This is because, not having been formally created or registered in law, the club is no more than a convenient name used by a group of individuals with a common interest. Our supplier's only resort is to sue either the club secretary or *all* the club members. If the latter course is chosen, the supplier is allowed by the court's rules to bring a representative action, i.e. to sue just one member who represents the rest. That member may seek contribution from the others if the court orders payment of the club's debts.

As a club or society is just a 'convenient name', it is unable to enter into contracts to own land or to lease premises. In order to avoid having every member's name on a contract or the title deeds to land, this can be done in the name of one or two of the members on behalf of the others. In the case of the organisation's premises, these members would hold the title to the land in their own name as 'trustees'. Even though the title will register their names as the owners, they do not hold it for their own exclusive benefit, but only on behalf of all the members.

Let us take stock of what we have said so far. Like the sole trader, organisations of partners, clubs, societies and associations share a common disadvantage in that the individuals, not the organisations, will be personally liable for any debts arising in the course of business. A person, though sometimes only if over 18 years old (see Chapter 30), can enter into a contract and may be sued for breaches. An organisation, however, can only share these characteristics if granted such recognition by the law. Similarly an organisation cannot hold the title to land unless it has a special status. How then, do organisations obtain this status and what types of organisations are they?

Trade unions

Some trade unions have over one million members, and the prospect of holding all those members personally liable at law for any wrongs that might be committed is unrealistic. Yet trade unions are essentially associations of individuals who come together for a common purpose, mainly to use their collective strength in order to negotiate terms and conditions of employment with employers. It would be unrealistic for such an important association not to be able to enter into contracts or to sue for breaches of contract. That is why the Trade Union and Labour Relations Act 1974 grants to trade unions the right to sue and be sued and also to enter into contracts. So, while still basically remaining associations, trade unions are given a special status.

The history of the growth of trade unions is of immense importance, and their existence has exerted a great influence on the business environment. Originally unions were regarded as unlawful as being conspiracies aimed at restraining trade, in that any collective action taken by workers against their employer would breach employment contracts and prevent employers from conducting their business. However, over the years unions became recognised as pursuing lawful aims. Yet, in undertaking actions against employers such as strikes, they could not help but damage the economic interests of their employers. For this they could be sued, and this raised the dilemma that, although their aims were recognised as lawful, any steps they took to place pressure on employers exposed them to legal action. Taken to its natural conclusion, trade unions could have been sued out of existence. Parliament, at first in 1906, but now in the Trade Union and Labour Relations Act 1974, has therefore granted trade unions a certain immunity from legal action. This immunity can only be claimed if the wrongful acts (e.g. breaching contracts) arise in the course of industrial action 'in contemplation or furtherance of a trade dispute'. The Employment Act 1982 states that the dispute must be one only between workers and their employer, and relate to such matters as pay and conditions of employment. Thus actions resulting from inter-union squabbles, protests against government policies and demonstrations against apartheid in South Africa would not be regarded as 'trade disputes'.

These special immunities available to trade union organisations recognise their unique role of giving collective effect to the interests of individual employees. Typical actions likely to occur when there is an industrial dispute are withdrawal of labour and picketing an employer's premises to persuade employees and others not to enter while a strike is on. Obviously, an employer's business will be disrupted: employment contracts will be breached, as will contracts with suppliers and customers. In these circumstances when is an employer prevented from seeking compensation from the trade union involved for losses incurred? Firstly, the trade union is granted immunity if, according to the Trade Union Act 1984, it has obtained a majority of those employees involved in favour of the action, by holding a secret ballot not more than four weeks before the action begins. Secondly, the action must, as you have just read above, be in furtherance of a 'trade dispute'. Thirdly, it is lawful (under the Employment Act 1980) generally, for workers to picket at their place of work where the pickets are in dispute with their employer. An accompanying union official would also be protected. Immunity from legal action is limited to picketing for the purpose only of peacefully obtaining or communicating information, or peacefully persuading any person to work or abstain from working (Trade Union and Labour Relations Act 1974 and Employment Act 1980). Not subject to immunity are any crimes which might be committed by pickets as obstruction to the highway and criminal assault or damage. Subject to certain limited exceptions, secondary action, whereby disruptive activity is aimed at parties not directly part of the 'trade dispute', is made unlawful (Employment Act 1980).

Decide whether an employer could sue a trade union which calls a strike without having taken a ballot, whose pickets use force to prevent deliveries being made, and who call a strike in sympathy with another unconnected industrial dispute.

We know that trade unions are *unincorporated* associations and so lack 'legal personality'. Yet the law allows unions to sue and be sued in their own name. In one respect we have noted that if union industrial action occurs outside of the immunities just discussed, a union may be sued by an employer. However, the Employment Act 1982 states that any award made by a court must not exceed the following amounts: £10 000 if the union has less than 5000 members; up to £250 000 for unions with 100 000 members or more. A formality (per Trade Union and Labour Relations Act 1974) open to a trade union is to apply from the Certification Officer for a certificate that the organisation is an independent trade union. This means that it is not one paid for and controlled by an employer, as a 'staff association' might be. Every major union is now registered. In this way a trade union does have a separateness from the individual members, and so is a special sort of unincorporated association.

Also special, is the provision in the Employment Act 1980 permitting the Certification Officer to pay from public funds the costs incurred by an independent union in relation to holding secret ballots. The Trade Union Act 1984 further provides that the union executive must be subject to election by secret ballot at least every 5 years; and that a union having a political fund must ballot its members on maintaining it every 10 years. 'Closed shop' agreements, whereby employees have to belong to a particular union, must generally, under the Employment Act 1982, be approved in a ballot by not less than 80 per cent of the membership.

These legislative measures combined with the changes we have observed in the economy, have, between 1980 and 1986, created a different atmosphere for the trade union movement. Following the year-long miners' strike in 1984/5 when the National Union of Mineworkers returned to work having to give up its opposition to pit closures, strikes have tended to be shorter and an overall decline in actions was recorded. The trade union movement is now also becoming more white-collar based, and is experiencing a decline of membership in manufacturing.

Another change is the pursuance by some employers of no-strike agreements. At present the police and the armed services are not permitted to go on strike; and at the time of writing the government's 1984 trade union ban at the Government Communications Head Quarters (secret service listening post) awaits a decision by the European Commission of Human Rights. This will rule on the admissibility of the union's case that the Government was in breach of the right to 'free association' for the 7000 staff. No-strike agreements are becoming more of a feature for new plants built by Japanese companies. Companies like Toshiba and Sanyo have found one of the large unions, the Electrical, Electronic, Telecommunications and Plumbing Union, prepared to work within such agreements. Disputes arising are dealt with by each side agreeing to go to arbitration (known as pendulum arbitration) which can result in only one winner, and does not allow for compromise arrangements. The reader will appreciate that the context in which trade union organisations have been described can change further as conditions alter, not least by a change of government. In this respect, the main opposition Labour Party promised in 1986 that if returned to power at a general election it would replace the Acts of 1980, 1982 and 1984 above discussed.

Trading companies

An association of individuals which has no separate legal existence from its members cannot for that reason own property, make contracts or sue in its own name. This is a severe disadvantage for an enterprise which seeks a larger scale of production of goods and services and wishes to achieve a target of greater profits.

In order to grow larger, a business organisation needs to attract more capital by increasing its membership, and it must be able to continue in business after the death of its founder members. The logos in Fig. 5.2 belong to companies that have grown and developed long after their original entrepreneurs have died. The law provides for a process known as **incorporation**, by which an organisation can become registered as a legal

Fig. 5.2
Some well-known British trading
companies

'person', having much the same standing in certain respects as an ordinary adult individual. Those who wish to form such a company, either private or public, must register it as laid down in the Companies Act 1985. Once registered, the organisation becomes an *incorporated* body which has its own entity or separate legal existence.

Let us illustrate this last point by examining the case of Salomon *v.* Salomon and Co Ltd (1897).

Mr Salomon was a sole trader, making boots and shoes. He sold his business to a company which he formed under the statute which corresponded to the Companies Act 1985. In exchange he and his family received shares in the company and he lent it £10 000 for which he received a document termed a **debenture** (i.e. proof of the debt). Mr Salomon was employed by the company as Managing Director. The advantage to him was that if the company failed only its assets could be used to meet outstanding debts. As a shareholder, Mr Salomon's liability was limited to the amount of shares he had invested in the business (hence the term *limited* company). That meant that his personal property, his home and personal belongings, would not be available to creditors, in contrast to the position when he was a sole trader. Owing to economic depression, the company fared badly and was eventually bankrupted. At this point Mr Salomon claimed to be an ordinary creditor, and demanded to be paid on his debentures. The liquidator of the company was unwilling to pay Mr Salomon, and claimed that Mr Salomon and the company were one and the same person. The court disagreed. It gave judgement in favour of Mr Salomon, holding that once the company was formed it was a separate legal person from its creator and he was entitled to have his loan repaid.

Fig. 5.3
Sole trader becomes incorporated
company

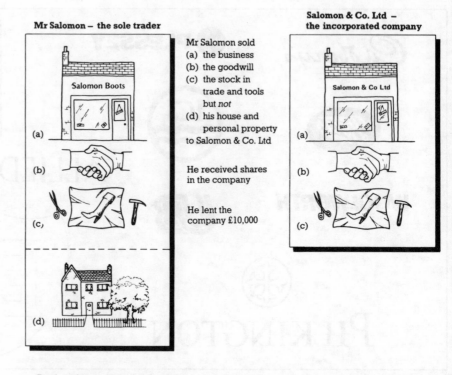

Mr Salomon – the sole trader

Mr Salomon sold
(a) the business
(b) the goodwill
(c) the stock in
    trade and tools
    but *not*
(d) his house and
    personal property
to Salomon & Co. Ltd

He received shares
in the company

He lent the
company £10,000

**Salomon & Co. Ltd –
the incorporated company**

In legal terms a body which becomes incorporated is said to have **legal personality**. Of course a corporation is only an artificial 'person', but certain consequences follow from incorporation apart from those we have already mentioned. Thus, once an organisation is incorporated it may sue and be sued in its own name, and as a 'person' it may make contracts, own land and carry on any authorised activities.

Differences between private and public companies

We are most likely to have heard of public companies because they issue shares which are traded on the Stock Exchange, with the daily prices quoted in newspapers and in radio broadcasts. There are about 6000 public companies, as against 900 000 registered companies in total, and around 2000 of these dominate our domestic industry. Some of the largest companies, like British Petroleum plc, Imperial Chemical Industries plc or Allied Lyons plc, operate on a multinational basis with branches in other countries. It will be obvious that most registered companies exist as private companies, with those that wish to grow through large capital acquisitions, 'going public' (issuing shares to the general public). It would be true to say that most large companies started off as small businesses. Most of the latter do not seek incorporation but carry on as partnerships or sole traders. We must begin our examination of the different forms of company and the process of incorporation.

Public companies

The Companies Act 1985 defines (s1. [3]) a public company as a one limited by shares or limited by guarantee and having a share capital whose memorandum (see below) states that it is to be a public company, and which has complied with the provisions for registration of such a company. It must have a minimum share capital of £50 000. The distinctive feature

Fig. 5.4
Marks and Spencer have grown from their original market stall in Leeds in 1884.
This shop is the Marks & Spencer in Newmarket in 1895.

of limited liability is that the extent of a shareholder's liability in a company, should it be wound up, is the sum of shares invested in it. Unlike a sole trader, a shareholder will not have to risk losing private possessions as it is the company, with its own legal personality, which is finally responsible for 'its' acts. A public company is one able to issue its shares to the public.

Alternatively, a public company may be limited 'by guarantee', where members are liable for the amount (say, £5) which they undertake to contribute in the event of winding-up. The Associated Examining Board, the Business and Technician Education Council and the Institute of Legal Executives are companies limited by guarantee. As you will notice, these companies tend to be for educational and charitable (see below) purposes.

Private companies

Under the Companies Act the definition of a private company is simply that it is a company which is not a public company. Apart from this not very

Fig. 5.5
The Sainsbury branch in the foreground was the company's first shop in Islington which opened in 1882

helpful description, the 1985 Act states (in s. 81) that a private company which attempts to offer its shares to the general public commits a criminal offence. Private companies are the most numerous of incorporated organisations, often being small family concerns issuing shares among relatives. The procedures for the running of such companies are simpler and cheaper than for public companies. In addition, they need not give so much publicity to their affairs. As in public companies, shareholders in private companies enjoy limited liability.

The requirement to produce public accounts is a particular feature of incorporated companies. The amount of information to be contained in the accounts is, however, determined (per Companies Act 1985) by the size of the company. Thus a small company with no more than 50 employees, or a turnover of up to £1.4 m, is exempted from the full disclosures applying to a large company having over 250 staff and whose turnover exceeds £5.75 m. In the middle are medium size companies with no more than 250 employees and a turnover not more than £5.75 m.

Other differences are that public companies must have at least two directors whereas private companies may have only one.

Unlimited companies

Although rare, there are companies with legal personality, yet where members' liability is unlimited in the event of the company being wound up. A good example are the insurance underwriting syndicates at Lloyd's of London (discussed below).

What are the requirements for the formation of companies?

There must be at least *two* members to form either a public or a private company. The words 'public limited company' (or plc) must follow the name of a public company. A *private* company's name must end with the word 'Limited' (Ltd). For Welsh companies these appellations are 'cwmni cyfyngedig cyhoeddus' (ccc) and 'cyfyngedig' (cyf), respectively. An offence is committed by persons or organisations which wrongly adopt these descriptions.

Company name

Persons forming a company will have to choose a name, but the proposed name must not be misleading, or resemble the name of another company, or suggest connection with the monarchy (by using the term Royal). There is also a restriction on the use of 'National', 'International' or 'Imperial'. The words 'bank', 'building society' and 'co-operative' are only available to organisations subject to the Banking Act, the Building Societies Acts and the Industrial and Providential Societies Acts (discussed later). The name adopted must be approved by the government Department of Trade. The name and status (plc or Ltd) must appear on all prospectuses, letter paper, bill heads and other official publications issued by the company. The law also requires the names of the directors of the company, the company registration number and the company's registered office to appear on company letters. The company's name must also be affixed outside any premises where its business is carried on.

The Registrar of Companies, whose job it is to maintain a register of all companies incorporated under the Companies Acts, keeps a file of certain documents pertaining to companies which are available to the general public for inspection. These documents are the Memorandum of Association and the Articles of Association.

Memorandum of Association

The **Memorandum of Association** is a particularly important document for any person wishing to deal with a registered company. This is because it sets out the sort of business which the company is empowered to carry out. The *objects* of a company are chosen by the promoters of the organisation, and once chosen there is no reason why they cannot be extended or changed; but the company must do this by calling a special meeting which has to agree to the change, and the change must then be registered with the Registrar of Companies. However the general rule is that a company has no authority to act beyond the powers set out in its objects clause. Such an act would be *ultra vires* (beyond its powers) and might be void.

The 1985 Companies Act includes a model of a Memorandum of a public limited company. The name of the company is the first item. After the name is the company's status, followed by a declaration that it is a public company. Next, the promoters must state whether the registered office is to be in England, Wales or Scotland. The fourth clause is the important 'objects clause' which sets out the company's powers. A company must conduct its business within the terms of this clause. Clause 5 is the declaration that the members' liability is limited to the amount of shares in which they invest. The company's share capital is stated as being £50 000 divided into £1 shares. Finally the subscribers, of whom there must be at least two, must be named and state their addresses and occupations with the number of shares they have taken. The document must be signed and witnessed.

Companies must act within their powers

Usually, the promoters of a company will draft an objects clause in wide terms in order to allow the company greater flexibility in its business. The 1985 Companies Act does permit the alteration of a company's objects clause, but it can only be altered within the terms of the Act and by special resolution of the shareholders.

A company which acts beyond its powers ceases to have authority. Thus, suppose the directors of the Western Steam Packet Company decided to run a pig-breeding factory. The company's Memorandum of Association might not be interpreted to include this purpose. If that were so a supplier of pigs to the company who was unaware of the company's stated objects might be unable to enforce the contract.

This principle was established in the case of Ashbury Railway Carriage and Iron Company *v.* Riche (1875). It was decided that Ashbury could not be held to a contract to finance a railway in Belgium. This was due to the fact that the company was incorporated only to manufacture and sell railway carriages and not to finance a railway.

* Now in Companies Act 1985

This harsh rule has been modified by the European Communities Act 1972 (Section 9)* which provides that any transaction decided upon by a company's directors will be taken to be within a company's powers (even though it may be technically *ultra vires*), but only in favour of someone dealing with the company in *good faith*. If the supplier of pigs in our example was well aware that the Western Steam Packet Company was acting outside its powers, Section 9 would be of no assistance because the supplier was not then acting in good faith and it might not be possible to force the company to pay for the pigs.

Companies foresee these difficulties, and so their objects clauses are, in practice, very widely drawn to include almost every conceivable activity to be carried on by the company.

Articles of Association

Promoters of an organisation which they wish to register as a company must also provide a document termed the **Articles of Association**. This document lays down the rules for the internal management of the company. In the case of a public limited company a model set of articles is produced in Table A in the first schedule of the Companies Act 1985. If a company limited by shares does not include articles, the Table A format applies automatically. There is no compulsion to use these articles however, and so many promoters draw up their own set or modify those in Table A. The Articles are concerned with: the manner in which shares may be transferred; the holding of general company meetings; the directors' powers of management; and, among other things, the payment of dividends.

The directors of a company are expected to manage the company so as to benefit the company. They must act with such care as is reasonable in a person with their experience and knowledge, and they must be reasonably diligent in managing the company's affairs. Very often the articles will empower the directors to appoint one of their number to the office of Managing Director. Certain powers of a company can only be exercised at meetings of the members of the company, e.g. the power to alter the objects clause. Directors give account of the company's performance at an annual general meeting, which the company is required to call in each calendar year.

Commencing business

We may call these organisations 'registered companies' because before they can exist to carry on their business, they must be registered with the Registrar of Companies. The Registrar must be satisfied that the requirements of the Companies Acts have been complied with by those seeking registration. In the case of a public limited company, the proposed name must be followed by that title, there must be at least two members, and the amount of share capital must not be less than the authorised minimum. At the time of writing the minimum is £50 000. Once the Registrar considers that all statutory requirements have been fulfilled a Certificate of Incorporation is issued. This has the effect of creating the company. A private company can thereafter commence business.

Commencement of business for a newly incorporated public company is, in contrast, delayed. A public company can neither commence business nor borrow money until the Registrar is satisfied, for example, that the nominal value of its shares is not less than the authorised minimum (Companies Act 1985). If satisfied the Registrar will issue a **Certificate to do Business**. This certificate confirms that the company is allowed to trade.

Files of registered companies are kept at the Companies Registration Office at Maindy in Cardiff, Wales. The company must send to the Registrar an annual return containing information about its capital liability, members and directors and, as the files are open to inspection by the general public on payment of a small fee, a notion may be obtained of a particular company's power and its financial resources.

6 Specially registered companies

A company registered under the Companies Act 1985 may be created for a whole variety of purposes. For instance the British Petroleum company trades in oil and allied products; the Thorn-EMI company produces televisions, electronic equipment and music records; the Raleigh Industries company manufactures pedal bicycles; and the Tesco company manages a supermarket chain.

Registered companies may commence business once properly registered under the Companies legislation. Certain types of business undertaken by companies are regarded as being of such a nature that the public require extra protection, and the companies are subject to special regulations, e.g. banks and insurance companies. Yet again there are other organisations whose formation and creation arises out of quite separate laws from those on which we have so far commented. In this respect we will study building societies, chartered corporations, charities and co-operatives.

Banking organisations

Banks occupy the centre of the British financial system by providing a safe place for the deposit of our money as well as arranging loans for people and organisations. Offering such services is not, though, open to ordinary organisations, for we will see that there must be recognition and licensing under the law, and disclosure obligations to the Bank of England, which has wide supervisory powers over the banking system.

The Bank of England

The Bank was established under public ownership by the Bank of England Act 1946. It is the focus of the British banking system, and through various committees it maintains consultation with the government Treasury Department. It is now the only bank empowered to issue bank notes, which are legal tender by the Currency and Bank Notes Acts 1929, 1939 and 1954. Administration of the Bank is carried out by a Governor, Deputy Governor and 16 directors appointed by the Crown, assisted by full- and part-time executive directors. As the central bank it acts as banker to the British Government by holding the Exchequer account. Together with the Treasury, the Bank exercises considerable powers of control over the commercial banks.*

* For a fuller discussion, see Chapter 41, pp. 370–72

The Banking Act 1979

The Banking Act of 1979 brought the United Kingdom into line with other member states of the European Community by introducing a statutory authorisation system for 'deposit-taking' institutions.

Now, only those institutions authorised by the Bank of England may legally carry on a deposit taking business. Under the 1979 Act the institution must be either a 'recognised bank' or a 'licensed deposit taking institution'. The effect of this provision is to make the deposit taking activities of such groups as savings clubs, retail co-operative societies and charities unlawful unless the Treasury declares them exempt under the Act.

The Act demands that there be at least *two* individuals to direct the business, which must be either a partnership or a corporate institution. Every director and manager of a licensed institution must be a 'fit and proper person' to hold that position, and the business must be carried out with care.

As far as setting up a new licensed institution is concerned, it must have net assets of not less than £250 000 at the time when it is granted a licence, while a new recognised bank needs assets of £5 m if it intends to provide a wide range of banking facilities.

The Banking Act 1987 updated the 1979 Act. Under the Act there will be a new Board of Banking Supervision to provide independent advice to the Bank of England. The present two-tier system of supervision for licensed deposit takers and banks will be replaced by a single set for all deposit taking bodies. There will also be increased powers for the Bank of England to obtain information from banks and to be advised about particularly large lendings to single customers. The aim of this legislative change is to increase the protection for bank depositors.

Clearing Banks

The major banking companies have branches in almost every High Street, and are termed 'clearing banks'. Their prime object is to collect sums of money deposited by people and organisations and to lend it out again at a rate of interest to those needing finance for personal or commercial, industrial or agricultural purposes. Since it is common practice, especially for those employed in 'white collar' occupations, to receive wages or salary through direct transfer to a personal bank account, this is the most common form of deposit. Banks also make a charge for services such as overdraft facilities and payment of regular debts by way of 'standing order'. A feature of clearing banks is that customers can be issued with cheque books and often a cheque guarantee card limited to a given amount (£50 at present).

Having once existed as an institution which under special legislation was charged with taking deposits of savings for a modest rate of interest, the Trustee Savings Bank became a public company in 1986. By passing the Trustee Savings Banks Act 1985 the Government acquired the power to offer the bank for sale by a share issue, with the proceeds going to the newly created bank. Under the 1985 legislation the TSB joined the ranks of clearing banks.

Fig. 6.1
Clearing banks

Saving Banks

The National Savings Bank (governed by an Act of 1971) has had a long history as the Post Office Savings Bank, and has been granted statutory authority to receive money on current account. The Post Office also operates the National Giro system, by which its members' debits and credits are entered on its records without the need to write a cheque.

Merchant Banks

A merchant bank is a commercial bank which channels finance for large businesses of a type with which the particular bank specialises. Some, for example, specialise in lending money for overseas trade or to foreign municipalities. Members of the public are not normally invited to open accounts, nor do merchant banks ordinarily issue cheque books to their clients.

Following the restructuring in October 1986 of the financial market centred on the Stock Exchange (the 'Big Bang', see Chapter 7), share dealing is no longer restricted to stockbrokers and jobbers. The Big Bang saw the merging of the deal professions of brokers and jobbers and they are now known as 'market makers'. Other institutions such as banks are now also able to become market makers, e.g. Barclays Bank owns Barclays de Zoëte Wett. A further development in recent years has been the role of merchant banks in financing and helping to organise the takeover bids that were a particular feature of 1986 (discussed fully below).

Building societies

Rather than needing Companies Act incorporation, building societies are able to register their rules with the Registrar of Friendly Societies in accordance with the Building Societies Act 1962. The Registrar (whose functions in respect of building societies will be taken over by the Building Societies Commission in 1987), on being satisfied that the rules comply with the Act's requirements, issues a Certificate of Incorporation. By this, a society becomes a corporate body under its registered name and having perpetual succession. The minimum number of members required to establish a society is ten. Shareholders in a building society receive interest on the money they have invested and do not, as in public companies, stand to participate in profits by way of a dividend.

Building societies are a peculiarly British invention and their role has been to provide finance to persons wishing to borrow on mortgage the wherewithal to buy a home. Indeed, this source of finance, together with the tax allowances available on the interest charged on loans, has enabled over 60 per cent of families to own their homes. We saw in Chapter 1 that banks have for some years begun competing by also offering home loans. In what became known as the 'Little Bang'; the Building Societies Act 1986 empowered building societies, as from 1 January 1987, to offer many new financial services. Under the 1986 Act societies may: issue cheque books and cheque guarantee cards; provide personal unsecured loans; provide foreign exchange; engage in estate agency, surveying, and conveyancing; manage unit trusts; and provide insurance broking services. From the total of 153 societies only about 50 will be able to offer some of the services, because the Act requires an asset base of over £100 m. Societies will be able to operate in Europe in 1988, and they will be able to convert their mutual status to public limited companies.

Can you name 6 building societies? What new services do they now offer apart from home loan activities?

Insurance companies

Insurance services also receive special attention aimed at ensuring that there is sufficient protection for the public. Those wishing to carry on business as insurers for motor vehicle, personal accident or property insurance, need the authorisation of the Secretary of State who is given wide powers of regulation and investigation under the Insurance Companies Act 1982. Members of Lloyd's, friendly societies, and trade unions carrying on insurance as part of their activities, are excluded from the Act. The Act applies to companies wherever they may be located provided they carry on business in the UK.

The Secretary of State for Trade and Industry controls entry into the insurance business by ensuring that the company's assets are sufficient, and that the management of the company and its directors are fit and proper persons to conduct the company. If need be, the Secretary may intervene in the affairs of an insurance company and exercise such powers as are necessary to protect policy holders against the risk of the company being unable to meet its liabilities. Further regulations require the Secretary to be satisfied that a company has an adequate margin of insolvency. This shows you the concern about protecting the public in a matter over which many of us have no choice but to take up: for instance, we may be required by a lender to take out a mortgage life protection policy, and the law demands that road drivers take out compulsory third-party insurance. Procedures to compensate policyholders whose insurance company cannot meet its liabilities are provided by the Policyholders Protection Act 1975.

Unit trust companies

Persons wishing to save money and possibly earn interest on their savings have a number of opportunities. These include buying government issued National Savings Certificates, opening a bank deposit account, taking out life assurance policies which mature if the policyholder survives to retirement age, opening a building society savings account, and buying company shares and so hope to receive annual dividends as well as perhaps having an appreciating asset. An alternative is offered by unit trust companies, which either invest lump sums or monthly payments from investors in a very wide spread of investments throughout the world. The companies essentially act as investment managers and so make decisions on behalf of their clients as to where to invest the total funds, and so obtain the best returns. We will discuss the nature of the protection offered by the **Financial Services Act 1986** in Chapter 13.

Are you able to distinguish between banks, building societies and insurance companies?

Corporations created by Royal Charter

Some organisations have obtained the right of incorporation by praying for the grant of a charter by petitioning the Crown. If a petition is granted the promoters become 'one body corporate and politic by the name of . . . and by that name shall and may sue or be sued, plead and be impleaded in all courts whether of law or equity, and shall have perpetual succession and a common seal'. Under the Chartered Companies Act 1837 and 1884 the Royal Prerogative was extended so that the Crown could grant charters for a limited period and extend them. Thus the BBC (British Broadcasting Corporation) charter was at first granted for ten years and has been prolonged from time to time. However, this form of incorporation is unlikely to occur often in future because the registration procedure under the Companies legislation is simpler, although a recent example is the Chartered Institute of Bankers (1987).

Charities

Charitable organisations hold funds in order to benefit a purpose defined as charitable. The purpose must be one which relieves poverty, advances education or religion or otherwise benefits the community. Recognition as a lawful charity is dependent on registration with the Charities Commission and compliance with the Charities Act 1960.

The Commission was established in 1853 and was reconstituted by the 1960 statute. It is charged with the general function of promoting the effective use of charitable resources. To this end the Commission may take responsibility for the investment of a charity's funds and may rationalise existing charities. The Commission maintains a register of charities, and registration confirms the charitable status of an organisation.

Co-operatives

Everyone is familiar with the local 'Co-op' shop, whether it be a grocer, a butcher, a store or a supermarket. The organisation is a prime example of the type of business organisation known as a co-operative. There are two types of co-operatives: **consumer co-operatives** whereby goods are bought in bulk at a discount and then sold cheaply to the members; and **producer co-operatives** whereby goods or services are produced by organisations in which the employees are the shareholders.

The Co-op shops in your High Street combine both of these types. They sell goods produced by other manufacturers as well as their own branded goods.

Co-operative societies exist to advance the interests of their members, whether they be consumers, farmers or industrial workers. Both types, producers of goods and retailers, are generally registered under the Industrial and Provident Societies Act 1965. Such societies' rules must include open membership, thus allowing membership to employees over 18 years old usually with one year's employment with the society; democratic control; limited return on capital; distribution of profits in proportion to members' involvement in the society; and the use of surpluses for social and educational purposes.

What are the origins of the co-operative society? Co-operative societies saw their beginnings in the early period of the nineteenth-century Industrial Revolution.

The present day movement owes its principles and its model to the Rochdale Society and Equitable Pioneers, formed in 1844. From that time societies were formed as agricultural federations, to run corn mills, bakeries, wholesale units and retail outlets. Today, societies involved with the manufacture of goods are to be found mostly in the clothing, shoe-making and printing industries.

However, the most prominent aspect of co-operative societies is their retail outlet system, consisting of small shops, supermarkets, stores and superstores. There are 180 retail societies, including the Invicta, South Suburban, Great Lancastrian, Sittingbourne and Royal Arsenal Co-operatives and the South East Co-operative Retail Services. The co-operatives' turnover is large, for example, the last named has a turnover of £8000 m per year. The societies created the Co-operative Wholesale Society (CWS) which, like each society, is separately registered and inde-pendent. The CWS is the manufacturer and wholesaler for the retail soci-eties. Together, the separate societies count as one of the largest retailers in the UK (see Ch. 29).

Because of hostility experienced by the early societies, the interests of the Co-operative Movement have gone beyond the provision of services and goods. The advancement of social conditions and education are also their objects, and indeed the Movement established a political party in 1917, although today its political activity is the sponsoring of Labour MPs.

Apart from these activities the movement has formed the Co-op Bank and the Co-operative Insurance Service. The controlling body of the movement is the Co-operative Union, whose Executive is responsible to the Co-operative Congress (the Movement's annual 'parliament'). The sources of capital for the societies are loans, principally from employees' pension funds, reinvested surpluses from members' shares, and profits retained after meeting interest payments and dividends. Another characteristic is the importance of the democratic voice of their members, which sometimes directs the societies to retain small unprofitable outlets. Despite this, competition from groups such as Tesco, Asda, Argyll and Sainsbury's have caused the Co-op to focus on larger supermarkets and stores.

Other types of worker co-operatives

In the period 1974–5 there were some prominent examples of businesses which closed down, but where the workers wished to manage affairs for themselves. In Liverpool the workers of a Thorn Company (now Thorn-EMI) took over the running of the Kirkby Manufacturing and Engineering Company business. In Glasgow the *Scottish Daily Express* was run by workers as the *Scottish Daily News*, and the Norton-Villiers-Triumph motorcycle plant outside Coventry was run by the Triumph Meriden workers. Each organisation was registered as a company under the Companies Acts, and received financial help from the then Labour Govern-ment in the sums of £1.8 m, £1.75 m and £5 m respectively. None of these three now survive. Having already failed under private ownership, their chances of success were remote at the outset, and their dependence on government funding gave them an unstable base. Now, under the Co-operative Development Agency (set up in 1978), advice can be given to those wishing to create co-operative organisations. Examples here are co-operatives in retail and catering, serving the growing health-food market.

Choice of form for a business unit

We have described key features of various types of business organisation in the private sector. What factors are important in influencing the form of business unit selected?

Very important are the nature and size of the market and the finance available. If the market is small, perhaps for a specialised product or purely localised, or if little finance is forthcoming, then inevitably the business unit will be small. The simplest form of unit, the sole trader, would be possible, or maybe a partnership or small private company. Remember that the protection of limited liability would be only gained with company status.

However, for bigger markets or where expensive high technology methods of production are needed, a large private company or a public company is suitable. It is easier to raise funds by the issue of more shares or large bank borrowing where a sizeable and potentially profitable market is beckoning.

One should not forget the objectives that owners of businesses set themselves. Although the sole trader's business might be small in size and facing only a small market, that might be all the owner wants. The ability to organise and run a small business can be within the compass of one individual, and can provide the satisfaction and level of financial rewards required. If greater profit and a larger scale of operation were important, a change in the legal status of the organisation to a partnership or company would probably be needed. This could mean that the former sole trader would lose the full measure of control that previously existed, although profits could be greater.

While emphasising the significance of large organisations in this chapter, we should not lose sight of the fact that there are still many small firms in operation. Their survival is explained by:

a the objectives of the owner(s) to maintain control, which they might lose if the organisation grew in size;
b small, localised markets, e.g. newsagent, fish-and-chip shop;
c specialised markets, where mass production is not possible since goods or services are designed to fit individual customer needs, e.g. custom-built cars, or clothing made and designed to individual taste.

Those wishing to start their own business may seek advice from a small business advisory service operated by their own council (see Chapter 18).

7 Financial institutions

Many have heard of expressions like 'the City', or 'the square mile' which denote that part of the City of London which serves as the financial services centre for this country and, indeed, in some respects as the central market in the world. The City operates under a Royal Charter, and has an annually elected Lord Mayor of London who acts as ambassador for the business community. Here all the major British financial companies are situated together with foreign companies from all over the world. The City shares with Wall Street, USA and Tokyo, Japan a pre-eminence in the financial markets of the world, although all western countries have their own financial centres. We have already mentioned some of the principal institutions: the Bank of England, the Stock Exchange and Lloyd's of London.

The Stock Exchange

Remembering what has already been said about the Stock Exchange you will know that only a minority of all companies are actually registered. This is in part due to the rule that a company must have a total capitalisation of more than £700 000 for full listing. Medium-sized companies which wish to offer shares to the public can now seek to join an intermediate stage called the *Unlisted Securities Market*. If such a company performs well it may be able then to transfer to a full Stock Exchange listing. To serve new companies with at least one year's trading behind them, the Stock Exchange opened the *Third Market* in 1987, by far the riskiest of all the share investments.

The function of the stock market is to provide a second-hand market where shares are traded between investors. This facilitates companies raising funds by new issues of shares to outside investors. Similarly investors wishing to sell their shares have access to a market of buyers. Local authorities issue stocks on the stock market, and the government does the same by issuing stocks (often called 'gilts'). The origin of the market was in the London coffee house meetings of traders in Threadneedle Street in the eighteenth century. Today's Stock Exchange has centres in London, as well as Belfast, Birmingham, Bristol, Dublin, Glasgow, Leeds, Liverpool, Manchester and Newcastle.

On 27 October 1986, the so-called '*Big Bang*' heralded the ending of various restrictive practices. Firstly, stockbrokers were allowed to merge with other bodies and have joined with merchant banks, clearing banks, insurance companies and other financial groups. Foreign companies were also permitted to enter the market as members. Another change was that the traditional division between brokers and jobbers was abolished, so that

Fig. 7.1
The London Stock Exchange

the only class of member is the broker/dealer. So as further to allow more competition the previous minimum commission charged to clients was ended. Finally, the system of quoting share and stock prices was computerised and so electronic dealing introduced. The computer stores records of trading and prices which are available for later inspection and so ensures that all deals are carried out fairly. It will now be possible for a single company to carry out previously separated functions such as broking, jobbing, unit trust management, as well as fund management, and this could create a conflict of interests with one part of the company advising a client to invest in another part of the same group.

It is interesting to note that one of the factors claimed to have contributed to the 'Black Monday' October 1987 crash (see p. 9) was the automatic selling programmed into computers used in stock exchanges.

Lloyd's insurance market

The most important insurance market in the world is Lloyd's of London which very often has to meet the claims of policyholders suffering from damage caused by typhoons in Florida, aeroplane crashes in Japan, sinking of merchant ships on the high seas, the payment of awards to asbestosis sufferers by mine companies in USA and the misplacing of satellites in space. Starting in 1688 in Edward Lloyd's coffee house, it acquired corporate status in the Lloyd's Act 1871. Lloyd's is made up of 23 000 members who have to show they have at least £100 000 in wealth to become a member. You already know that they have unlimited liability, and members trust their money to be managed by professional underwriters, who undertake percentages of risk on subjects offered by brokers for insurance. The market is ruled, since the Lloyd's Act 1982, by a committee of 28, and headed by a Chief Executive who is drawn from the business community to ensure that the interests of the outside members are

Fig. 7.2
Lloyds' Underwriting Room showing
Caller's Rostrum

protected. As a reaction to instances of fraud on Lloyd's members (one syndicate lost £130m in 1983 when their agents absconded) the government-appointed Neill Committee recommended in 1987 that further protections be introduced by Lloyd's for members, and that there should be an appointment of an ombudsman to investigate complaints. The government gave the ruling council one year to implement the 70 key recommendations made by Sir Robert Neill, the alternative to which could be legislative intervention.

8 Nationalised industries

The creation of public corporations as a means of nationalisation has been a particular feature of post-war economic development in the UK. The organisations created have a legal entity together with corporate rights and responsibilities often derived from statute. We have noted already the nationalisation in 1946 of the Bank of England, which had been privately owned until then. In fact, during World War 2 a number of major industries had been brought under government control. These industries were concerned with energy production and communication. This control of these key industries was combined with the political ideal of bringing certain areas under social rather than private control to give an impetus to nationalisation.

The Transport Act 1947 originally brought transport undertakings ranging from docks and road transport to railways under the control of a Transport Commission. After the Transport Acts 1962 and 1968 the British Rail Board, the National Bus Company and the British Transport Docks Board (the latter now returned to private control) were formed. What is now British Airways was formed originally by reorganising certain airlines under public control by the Air Corporations Act 1949.

As regards energy production, the coal industry was brought under the control of the National Coal Board by the Coal Industry Nationalisation Act 1946. The electricity supply was nationalised by the Electricity Act 1947, and the gas industry by the Gas Act 1948, represented by the Central Electricity Generating Board and the British Gas Corporation respectively.

Legislation was later introduced to bring under public ownership certain industries whose continued existence or profitability was uncertain. Thus British Shipbuilders was created as a public corporation. Even the Post Office, long established as a government department with its own Minister, was transformed into a public corporation by the Post Office Act 1969, and its telecommunications business has now been privatised as British Telecom plc.

Although public corporations are independent and are not government departments, the management boards are usually appointed by a designated Minister. The Minister is, in turn, answerable in Parliament for their affairs. These corporations are not staffed by civil servants, and so their personnel have no special status.

A public corporation combines public ownership with commercial management. While the aim to provide a good service to customers is

Fig. 8.1
Some public corporations

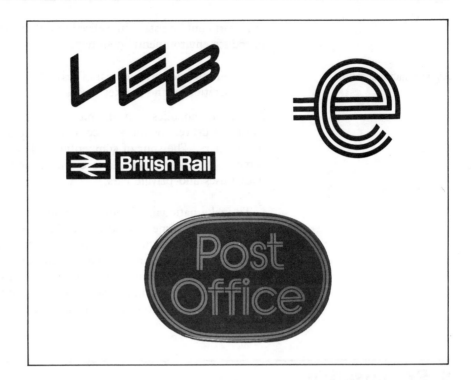

primary, since 1978 public corporations have been set targets by governments to make a surplus (or profit) on capital employed. For example British Gas was then expected to make an average 9 per cent surplus on net assets. The financial target for the Electricity Council was a 1.8 per cent surplus on net assets over the same period. The targets however, are *not* set so high that the organisations are expected to *maximise* profits, as is more likely in the private sector.

Arguments for and against nationalisation

For nationalisation

1 Socialist thinking suggests it is important that vital industries are owned by the State, rather than being left in private hands where sectional rather than national interests would prevail.

2 With a larger public sector, government planning of the economy is made easier. Needs of particular industries can be more readily interrelated, e.g. ensuring sufficient output of steel to meet needs in the ship-building industry.

* See further, Chapter 25, pp. 245–6.

3 By concentrating production in the hands of one organisation, the benefits of large-scale production can be reaped. Costs per unit of output should be lower.*

4 Unnecessary duplication of resources can be avoided. For example, if there were five organisations supplying electricity rather than just one, there would be additional power stations, power cables and administration which could be regarded as a waste of resources.

5 'Unprofitable' output can be permitted for social or economic reasons, e.g. supplying electricity to outlying regions. Private organisations would be less keen to use resources for such purposes. As a nationalised industry, rail

transport could be state-subsidised to reduce traffic congestion on roads and to reduce environmental pollution.

Against nationalisation

1 State industries are a denial of private ownership and enterprise, and the free operation of the market mechanism.

2 State monopolies can inhibit competition, breeding inefficiency and causing a dearer, poorer service to consumers, who have little or no choice of suppliers. The spur of competition is less apparent. (Note, though, that some public corporations do face competition. British Rail is in competition with buses and private cars.)

To make nationalised industries more answerable to consumer views and criticisms, consumer councils have been established. The pattern was set after the nationalisation of the coal industry when the 1946 Act set up the Industrial Coal Consumers' Council. Since that time various other consumer councils have been established, for example for users of electricity and the postal services. Consumer views on the quality of product or service and its price are put to the senior management of the public corporation.

9 Privatisation

The Conservative Government elected originally in 1979 favoured the arguments against nationalisation, and embarked on a policy to remove from public corporations their nationalised status. This process, termed 'privatisation', was planned in such a way that the general public would be encouraged to buy shares directly. The aim is to transfer some £21bn of State-owned assets to the private sector, and by widening the ownership of shares to ordinary members of the public, to create what the government has called 'popular capitalism'. Starting in 1979, a stream of companies has been privatised, including: the government's interest in British Petroleum, British Aerospace, Cable and Wireless, Britoil and Enterprise Oil, Jaguar Motors, British Telecom, British Gas, British Airways, Rolls Royce and the British Airports Authority (see Table 9.1). Under consideration for privatisation are British Shipbuilders, British Steel, the Central Electricity Generating Board, the Water Authorities, and there have been suggestions that British Coal might also be sold. Such is the preference for organisations to be controlled in the private sector that the government announced in 1986 that 20 city technology colleges would be created financed entirely by private capital.

Behind these moves is a belief that private ownership is a more effective means of running organisations profitably and that the introduction of competition is beneficial to consumers. In pursuance of this, the Transport Act 1985 saw the deregulation of the public bus service commencing in October 1986. Under the Act the state-run national bus service is to be broken up and sold off as smaller units, as would large local authority monopoly services; any operator with a licence is able to offer a service and

PRIVATIZED COMPANIES — A GOOD INVESTMENT?

Company	issue date	sale price	*£500 invested now worth	percentage (loss) gain	
British Aerospace	Feb 81	150p	£1,885	277	
	May 85	375p	£755	51	
British Petroleum	Oct 79	363p	£765	53	
	Sep 83	435p	£630	26	
Cable & Wireless	Oct 81	168p	£2,165	333	
	Dec 83	275p	£1,325	165	
	Dec 85	587p	£620	24	
Amersham	Feb 82	142p	£1,300	160	
Britoil	Nov 82	215p	£395	(21)	
	Aug 85	185p	£460	(8)	
Associated British Ports	Feb 83	112p	£2,635	427	
	Apr 84	270p	£1,095	119	
Enterprise Oil	Jun 84	185p	£390	(22)	
Jaguar	Jul 84	165p	£1,360	172	
British Telecom	Nov 84	130p	£960	92	
Total: £500 on all issues		£7,500	£16,740	123	

*£500 has been taken as a notional investment. With some issues, this amount would not have been available, depending on how shares were allocated

Fig. 9.1
Some of the companies privatised since 1979

compete. The Rover Group (formerly British Leyland), in preparing the way to be privatised completely, has sold off its Unipart subsidiary, Leyland Bus, ISTEL (a computer subsidiary), Leyland Trucks (to the Dutch DAF company), and is disposing of its foreign holdings. We have already noted that local councils are encouraged to offer certain of their services, e.g. rubbish collection, out to tender, as are hospital authorities for their cleaning services.

Privatising previous public monopolies has not always achieved competition, as can be seen with British Gas which remains a monopoly supplier. British Telecom, however, faces competition from Mercury, a company which, in May 1986, opened a national telephone network using optical fibre cables.

Given the choice, the Government decided in 1986 to grant authority to a private consortium to build the Channel Tunnel rather than to do so as a government enterprise. The company, called Eurotunnel, will construct a rail tunnel as an Anglo-French venture. An Act of Parliament permitted the Channel consortium to raise capital for its operations, the company issuing shares to the public in November 1987. It should be noted that the French Government also in this period set out upon a path of privatisation, a programme involving 65 companies, possibly raising £30bn when they are sold by 1989.

The sale of shares in nationalised corporations was planned in such a way as to make their purchases possible by ordinary consumers who would not normally invest in shares. Such has been the success of this policy, particularly after the sale of British Gas, that the number of small shareholders has increased dramatically. Research undertaken in 1987 by the *Observer* showed that 23 per cent of the adult population, or 9.4 million people (4 million in 1979), owned shares, many for the first time.

Despite the extent of privatisation, Britain's remaining nationalised industries gave employment to 1 038 976 workers and had a joint turnover of £32.2bn in early 1987.

What are the advantages and disadvantages of privatising public corporations?

Table 9.1
Privatisation of government assets

Organisation	Date issued	Share price (p)
British Aerospace	Feb 1981	150
	May 1985	375
British Petroleum	Oct 1979	363
	Sep 1983	435
Cable & Wireless	Oct 1981	168
	Dec 1983	275
	Dec 1985	587
Amersham	Feb 1982	142
Britoil	Nov 1982	215
	Aug 1985	185
Associated British Ports	Feb 1983	112
	Apr 1984	270
Enterprise Oil	Jun 1984	185
Jaguar Motors	Jul 1984	165
British Telecom	Nov 1984	130
British Gas	Nov 1986	135
British Airways	Jan 1987	125

What is the quoted market price for any of these shares today?

10 Central government

Unlike the other organisations which we have looked at which have a fixed and determined composition from their inception, the British Government is formed after a General Election (held at least every 5 years) by the political party obtaining the largest number of votes or possibly by a coalition of parties able to command a majority of MPs' support. The leader of the majority party or coalition is called by the Queen to act as her Prime Minister. The Prime Minister then appoints Ministers from among her/his colleagues, with responsibility as the political heads of government departments. These departments represent the areas of government concern in the administration of the country; they take responsibility for implementing the policies of the government of the day with regard to trade, industry, consumer affairs, employment, education, social services, environment and defence, among others. The Prime Minister is also responsible for appointing the Cabinet, which is the central policy-making body of the government and consists of those Ministers whose areas of responsibility are thought to be particularly important. It usually has about 20 members.

THE CABINET
Prime Minister, First Lord of the Treasury and Minister for the Civil Service: The Rt. Hon. Margaret Thatcher MP
Lord President of the Council and Leader of the House of Lords: Rt. Hon. Viscount Whitelaw CH MC
Lord Chancellor Rt. Hon. Lord Mackay
Secretary of State for Foreign and Commonwealth Affairs: Rt. Hon. Sir Geoffrey Howe QC MP
Chancellor of the Exchequer: Rt. Hon. Nigel Lawson MP
Secretary of State for the Home Department: Rt. Hon. Douglas Hurd CBE MP
Secretary of State for Energy: Rt. Hon. Cecil Parkinson MP
Secretary of State for Defence: Rt. Hon. George Younger MP
Secretary of State for Wales: Rt. Hon. Peter Walker MP
Lord Privy Seal and Leader of the House of Commons: Rt. Hon. John Wakeham MP
Secretary of State for Social Services: Rt. Hon. John Moore MP
Chancellor of the Duchy of Lancaster: Rt. Hon. Kenneth Clarke MP
Secretary of State for Northern Ireland: Rt. Hon. Tom King MP
Minister of Agriculture, Fisheries and Food: Rt. Hon. John MacGregor MP
Secretary of State for the Environment: Rt. Hon. Nicholas Ridley MP
Secretary of State for Employment: Rt. Hon. Norman Fowler MP
Secretary of State for Education and Science: Rt. Hon. Kenneth Baker MP
Paymaster General and Minister for Employment: Rt. Hon. Peter Brooke MP
Chief Secretary to the Treasury: Rt. Hon. John Major MP
Secretary to the State for Scotland: Rt. Hon. Malcolm Rifkin QC MP
Secretary of State for Trade and Industry: Rt. Hon. Lord Young of Graffham MP
Secretary of State for Transport: Rt. Hon. Paul Channon MP

DEPARTMENTS
Department of State
Defence
Education and Science
Employment
Energy
Environment
Foreign and Commonwealth Affairs
Health and Social Security
Law Officers' Department
Lord Advocate's Department
Lord Chancellor
Management and Personnel Office
Northern Ireland Office
Privy Council Office
Scottish Office
Trade and Industry
Transport
Treasury
Government Whips, House of Lords
Welsh Office

Fig. 10.1
The British Government after the June 1987 general election: Ministerial Posts and Departments

The government (see Fig. 10.1) is the Executive, but answerable to Parliament. So as to ensure this, by constitutional convention, the Prime Minister is always a member of the House of Commons, as are usually the government Ministers (although sometimes a Minister may be appointed from the unelected House of Lords). Policies are agreed upon at Cabinet meetings comprising senior Ministers and chaired by the Prime Minister. Detailed work, such as deciding cuts in government expenditure or the handling of a national strike, is carried out by Cabinet committees made up of a few Ministers who then report to the full Cabinet. The Cabinet and Ministers are served in the first place by senior civil servants, who assist in giving effect to government policy and may also give advice to Ministers. Recently, it has become customary to use outside political advisers, and in 1986 some 22, on 5-year contracts, were employed in various Ministers' offices.

Government departments have to be staffed on a permanent basis, but a government's life is limited to five years at most. They are therefore staffed by civil servants, who are the government's employees. It should be noted that their employment continues despite a change of government because theirs is not a political appointment.

Some government offices have been established by way of the **Royal Prerogative**, which is the ancient right of the Crown to rule and make law. Such a post is that of the Lord Chancellor, who is the government's 'Minister of Justice'. However, most government posts have been established by legislation. The Minister is regarded as occupying a post as a 'corporation sole', that is a body having perpetual existence (although it may be brought to an end by statute). Legally, this recognises that the office and the person occupying it have a separate existence. Generally all acts of the department are carried out in the Minister's name and not in the name of the department. Thus if you or I wished to sue a government department we should bring our action against the Minister.

Other 'corporations sole' include bishops and the Crown itself. The corporation sole that the King or Queen represents does not die, so when the holder dies the call has been traditionally: 'The King is dead, long live the King.'

Government-controlled organisations

Hospital provision will serve as an example of a government-controlled organisation.

The provision of hospitals had been the province of religious bodies until the Poor Law system, in 1834, was widened to include caring for the health of the poor. Central control of public health was undertaken by the Board of Health in 1848, then by the Local Government Board from 1871, until the appointment of a Minister of Health in 1919. Private charities had been responsible for establishing a number of private hospitals. In 1929, the Local Government Act gave local authorities the responsibility of taking over the poor law infirmaries. In the meantime the new medical professions began to come under the supervision of new statutory registration bodies.

The establishment of a comprehensive national health service took place in 1946 under the National Health Act 1946. By this statute the Minister of Health became responsible for supervising the personal health service, hospitals and the appointment of medical practitioners. Now the governing

Fig. 10.2
Central government budgeting

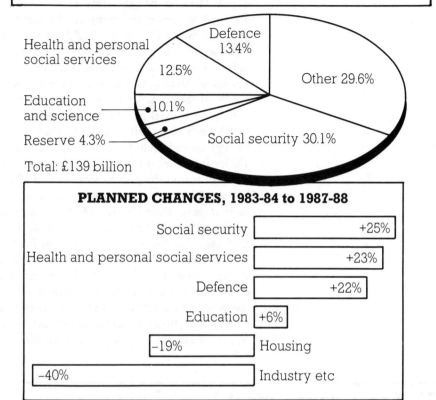

SHARES IN PUBLIC SPENDING YEARS 1986-87

Defence 13.4%

Health and personal social services 12.5%

Other 29.6%

Education and science 10.1%

Reserve 4.3%

Social security 30.1%

Total: £139 billion

PLANNED CHANGES, 1983-84 to 1987-88

Social security	+25%
Health and personal social services	+23%
Defence	+22%
Education	+6%
−19%	Housing
−40%	Industry etc

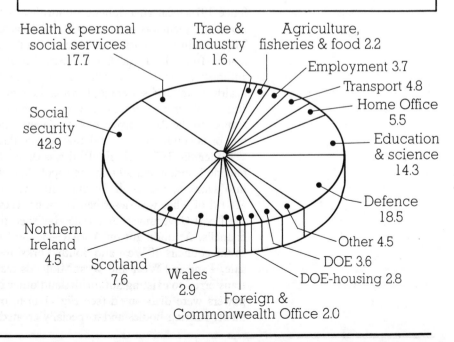

Department budgets 1986/87 £ billion

Health & personal social services 17.7

Trade & Industry 1.6

Agriculture, fisheries & food 2.2

Employment 3.7

Transport 4.8

Home Office 5.5

Social security 42.9

Education & science 14.3

Defence 18.5

Northern Ireland 4.5

Scotland 7.6

Wales 2.9

Foreign & Commonwealth Office 2.0

Other 4.5

DOE 3.6

DOE-housing 2.8

law is the National Health Service Act 1977, and the responsible Minister is the Secretary of State for Social Services.

The Minister has the duty to promote a comprehensive health service designed to secure and improve the health of citizens. The 1986/7 budget set aside was £17.7bn for health and personal social services, while the social security figure was £42.9bn, totalling 30 per cent of the Government's overall budget. The organisations created by the law are given 'body corporate' status, and include 14 regional health authorities, 200 district health authorities, and local family practitioner committees, the latter dealing with local general practitioners, dentists and pharmacists. District health authority chairmen are appointed by Ministers, and their members by regions and include doctors, nurses, local councillors and lay members. Theirs is the legal duty to run the service for the district. Since 1985, as a way of introducing an element of cost efficiency, each administrative level is headed by general managers, with a salary topped up only if they achieve their targets. Patients are able to raise complaints about the service with local community health councils, made up of volunteers, and these may then take the complaints up with the health authorities.

In November 1987 the government introduced in a White Paper its intention to end free dental check-ups and free sight tests and to make higher charges for treatment. Exemptions for children, pregnant mothers and the poor would remain. It also proposes to introduce competition amongst generall practitioners and to allow them to advertise. GPs will be expected to play a greater role in primary health care.

11 Local government

Since 1974 local government authorities (with the exception of the City of London which was created by Royal Charter) have been statutory bodies. They obtain their corporate status and authority to carry out their functions mainly from the Local Government Act 1972. The legislation sets out an authority's functions which, according to the 1972 Act, include: public health, water and sewerage, town and country planning, education, housing and social service provision. A local authority has widely expressed powers, subject to the Act's provisions, to do anything 'which is calculated to facilitate or is conducive or incidental to, the discharge of any of its functions'.

Under the 1972 Act, England was divided into six metropolitan counties outside London and 39 non-metropolitan counties, and the counties divided into districts, 342 in all. In line with the government's election promise to get rid of what was described as an unnecessary layer of local government the Local Government Act 1985 abolished the English metropolitan county councils. At midnight on April 1986, the Greater London Council, as well as the councils of West and South Yorkshire, Greater Manchester, Merseyside, Tyne and Wear and West Midlands ceased to exist. Their powers were transferred to existing authorities and other bodies. For instance, the GLC's powers were distributed (see Fig 11.1) to other boroughs, central government, existing bodies and a specially created London Residuary Body. The

Local government   93

Fig. 11.1
The effect of the Local Government
Act 1985 on the responsibilities of
the Metropolitan authorities

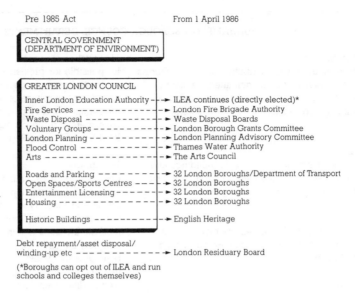

Pre 1985 Act   From 1 April 1986

CENTRAL GOVERNMENT
(DEPARTMENT OF ENVIRONMENT)

GREATER LONDON COUNCIL
Inner London Education Authority --|-→ ILEA continues (directly elected)*
Fire Services -------------|-► London Fire Brigade Authority
Waste Disposal -----------|-► Waste Disposal Boards
Voluntary Groups ---------|-► London Borough Grants Committee
London Planning ---------|-► London Planning Advisory Committee
Flood Control ----------|-► Thames Water Authority
Arts ----------------|-►The Arts Council

Roads and Parking -------|-► 32 London Boroughs/Department of Transport
Open Spaces/Sports Centres ---|-► 32 London Boroughs
Entertainment Licensing ------|-► 32 London Boroughs
Housing --------------|-► 32 London Boroughs

Historic Buildings ---------|-► English Heritage

Debt repayment/asset disposal/
winding-up etc -----------→ London Residuary Board

(*Boroughs can opt out of ILEA and run
schools and colleges themselves)

capital's bus and train service was transferred to a new body, London Regional Transport. Wales is divided into 8 counties with 37 districts. The main divisions of local government in Scotland are called regions, of which there are nine, divided into 53 districts, and there are three separate organisations for the island areas of Orkney, Shetland and the Western isles.

In contrast to the members of the boards of trading companies and public corporations, local government councillors are elected for a period of four years. Their decisions are made on the council or its committees by voting on resolutions and are carried out by officials who correspond to the central government's Civil Service. Finance is obtained through local taxation by imposing a rate on the occupier of premises in proportion to the net annual value of the property. The rates do not provide sufficient revenue for local authorities to carry out their functions, and so grants are received from the national Exchequer. The central government funding enables the government through the responsible Minister, the Secretary of State for the Environment, to exercise control over local authority spending. Indeed the Local Government Planning and Land Act 1981 enables the Minister to penalise an authority which overspends by reducing its grant.

Councillors who delay setting a rate through wilful misconduct may be subjected to disqualification from holding office for five years and fined up to £2000 under the Local Government Finance Act 1982. In order to deal with councils which refused to fix rates as a protest against being deprived of central government grants because they were regarded as having spent beyond government-set limits, the Local Government Act 1986 requires councils to set a rate on or before April. It also prohibits political publicity. Greater public access to council meetings, documents and reports is granted by the Local Government (Access to Information) Act 1985. Finally, local authority spending is monitored by the Audit Commission which publishes reports on its investigations.

Local authority corporations are bound to act within their powers, in the same way as trading companies and nationalised industries. When a local authority which had power to build wash-houses for citizens to wash their

SUNHAMPTON BOROUGH COUNCIL DEPARTMENTS

1. Administrative Services
Responsible for preparing and distributing agendas, reports and minutes of the council and its committees; electoral registration; registration of births, deaths and marriages; letting town hall premises for functions; the council's printing.

2. Architectural
Responsible for the design for new council buildings and overseeing their construction; improvement and conversion of old buildings; advice on improvement grants.

3. Baths
Responsible for 2 indoor baths and an open-air pool at Sunhampton Fields; public laundry facilities; warm baths; showers and turkish baths.

4. Building Works
Responsible for maintaining council housing and other council-owned properties.

5. Cleansing and Transport
Responsible for refuse collection; street sweeping; gully clearing; snow clearing; taking away abandoned vehicles; controlling street markets; providing dustbins; public conveniences; the council's transport fleet; approving refuse storage arrangements (particularly in new and converted properties).

6 Directorate of Recreation
Responsible for developing all types of leisure-time activities and opportunities; co-ordinating the work of the Baths, Libraries and Parks and Recreation Departments.

7. Engineering and Surveying
Responsible for the borough's roads; road safety; street lighting; sewers; drains, hoarding, scaffolds, skips, etc; parking control zones; cemeteries and crematorium.

8. Environmental Health
Responsible for enforcing the law on housing conditions; food hygiene; conditions in offices, shops and factories; air and noise pollution; control of pests; defective drains; registration, licensing and public control functions.

9. Finance
Responsible for financial guidance to the council and all its committees and departments; control of the council's budget.

10. Housing
Responsible for management of all council-owned housing; rehousing people from property which the council has bought for improvement or redevelopment; housing people from the waiting list; accommodating homeless families; giving rent rebates and rent allowances.

11. Legal
Responsible for provision of the council's legal services; contracts for works, goods and services; mailing of compulsory purchase orders; enforcement of planning and road traffic legislation; court action to protect tenants, consumers and the council's interests; maintenance of the local Land Charges Register.

12. Libraries
Responsible for providing books, newspapers, periodicals and general information; books for the blind published in Braille and Moon type; talking books for registered blind persons; large print books suitable for partially sighted readers; a record lending service – in three branch libraries; a mobile library, which visits nine sites in the borough each week; a visiting service for housebound readers; literacy schemes for people with reading and writing difficulties; local history collections and publications – at two libraries.

13. Parks and Recreation
Responsible for play, sport, community recreation and recreation projects; the maintenance and use of parks and smaller open spaces; the support and provision of services to voluntary organisations.

14. Personnel
Responsible for formulation and control of staffing policy and advice on, and monitoring of, all staff matters.

15. Policy and Programme Planning
Responsible for preparing the council's Programme Plan in conjunction with other departments; co-ordinating Partnership matters; monitoring performance and achievement; policy analysis and other studies; co-ordination of research and intelligence.

16. Planning
Responsible for advising the council on all aspects of the Planning Acts; preparation of the borough development plan; dealing with planning applications and permissions; giving licences for the erection of temporary structures and permission for the display of advertising signs; preservation of trees; major road improvements and traffic management; planning of open spaces.

17. Social Services
Responsible for ten local area offices, staffed by social workers and in some cases community workers, each team under the direction of an area team leader. Most of the department's services are provided from area offices.

Also responsible for four teams of hospital social workers; two specialist teams of occupational therapists and physiotherapists; social workers for handicapped children and for the blind and deaf; a Family Advice Centre; residential homes for children, the mentally and physically *cont'd*

handicapped and the elderly; day centres for the under fives, the elderly and the handicapped; meals-on-wheels; home helps; assisted holidays; concessionary fares for the handicapped; aids to mobility and home adaptations; the adoption and fostering of children, standards of childminding, private fostering and private day nurseries.

18. Technical Services

Responsible for the council's building programmes; implementation of the council's industrial policy; co-ordination of the work of the Architectural, Engineers, Planning and Valuation Departments.

19. Valuation

Responsible for buying property for the council, either by agreement or under Compulsory Purchase Orders; leasing or letting all council-owned non-residential property. (Residential property is let by the Housing Department.)

Fig. 11.2

clothes attempted to establish a laundry staffed by council employees, a legal action was commenced. The authority was declared to be acting *ultra vires* (beyond its powers) and was therefore prevented from building the laundry (Attorney General *v.* Fulham Corporation 1921). At the end of 1981 the House of Lords declared that the then Greater London Council was *ultra vires* the provisions of the Transport (London) Act 1969 when it raised a supplementary rate from London ratepayers to finance the cost of reducing fares by 25 per cent (R. *v.* GLC 1981). Having no such power the GLC had to repay the unlawfully collected rates. In order to acquire increased powers an authority must seek Parliament's consent by presenting a Private Bill, as did the West Midlands County Council in 1976 to enable it to run municipal shops – a proposal which was eventually rejected.

The decisions about what a local council does, i.e. its policy, are made by council meetings of which the most important is the full council meeting. However, most decisions are made by about a dozen committees and sub-committees of the council. Of course, we may raise local issues with our local councillor, who may bring the matter before the council if it is of general interest, or otherwise take it up with the appropriate council department. It is these departments, run by public authority employees and carrying out the day-to-day work of the council, with which we are more likely to come into contact.

In 1974 Parliament established 5 Commissioners for Local Adminis-tration (ombudsmen) to cover Britain. They may receive complaints about maladministration only when someone has referred a complaint through a local councillor. Their only power is to submit a report of the complaint to the authority, be it a council or other body such as a water board. Although usually councils do try to deal with cases of injustice, the ombudsman has no power to force the authority to put the matter right.

To what extent should central government interfere with local authority financial arrangements?

12 The European economic community

You will recall that in Chapter 2 we discussed the EEC as a crucially important influence on the business environment in the United Kingdom. Through the various policies adopted by the EEC, which are then implemented in all the member States, we are all affected. The best known of these policies is the Common Agricultural Policy, which seeks to achieve more efficient production, fair returns for farmers, stable markets and regular supplies of produce at reasonable prices. Membership of the Community requires the acceptance of removing barriers to trade, including trade in farm produce. This has the effect of exposing the less efficient farmers, who in many cases enjoy national subsidies, to competition from farmers in the other member States. Each year therefore the Council of Ministers, formed of the Agriculture Ministers of the 12 member States, sets a *common* target price on a proposal from the Commission (the watchdog of the Community Treaties) for various agricultural products. Once this is done, there will be a disparity between the different member States' agricultural producers as the value of their national currencies fluctuates according to the performance of their economies. Until all the member States rationalise their agricultural production so that only those most efficient at producing Community food do so, the Community buys surplus output from farms. This arrangement has avoided shortages of agricultural produce in the European Community but in turn has led to surplus production – the accumulation of wine and milk 'lakes' and butter, grain and beef 'mountains'. EEC Agricultural Ministers have attempted to reduce these stockpiles by allocating production quotas to individual farmers, for example dairy farmers, with the aim of leading to a reduction in surplus products.

The European Economic Community: structure and institutions

When the EEC was set up in 1957 by the **Treaty of Rome**, there were at first 6 Member States – France, West Germany, Italy, the Netherlands, Belgium and Luxembourg. The UK, Denmark and the Republic of Ireland joined in 1973, Greece joined in 1981, and Spain and Portugal in 1986. Total Community population is now 320 million. The 4 main institutions of the EEC are:

- the European Commission,
- the Council of Ministers,
- the European Parliament,
- the European Court of Justice.

The Commission

The Commission is at the centre of the EEC legal and administrative machine. It is not the supreme decision-making body (that is the Council), but it develops policy and drafts legislation (principally Regulations and Directives). There are 17 Commissioners, two each from France, West Germany, Italy, the UK and Spain, and one each from Belgium, Luxembourg, the Netherlands, Ireland, Denmark, Greece and Portugal. They are appointed by agreement between member States but must act independently as Europeans, not as their country's delegates. A Commissioner, when appointed, takes an oath of independence.

When the Commission has drafted legislation it makes proposals to the Council, which then approves or rejects the draft legislation. The Commission is accountable only to the European Parliament, which in theory has the power to dismiss it on a motion of censure passed by a two-thirds majority.

The European Commission

1 The Commission draws up a *proposal* for a new law

The European Parliament

2 The Council, formed of appropriate Ministers of member States considers the proposal

3 The Council submits the proposal to Parliament where it is considered by one of its committees

4 After the committee stage a report is made to a plenary session of Parliament for debate. The Commissioner who drafted the proposal may be asked to reply to the debate. Following a vote Parliament sends its opinion to the Council

5 When agreement is reached on the proposal, it is adopted and published

Council attended by Ministers of member govts. according to subject under discussion

Commission appointed by member governments for 4-year term

Parliament directly elected by voters of member States

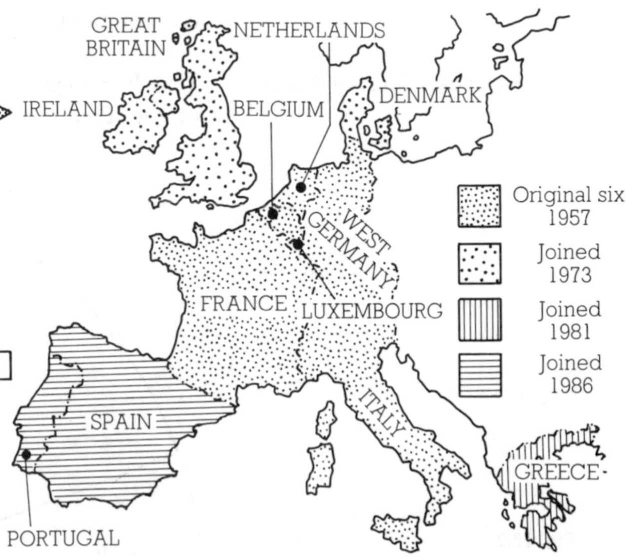

6 Regulations
These Community laws apply directly to all the member States just as national laws do

Directives
These direct member States on the object to achieve but leave it to the national governments to make it law by their own measures

The European Court of Justice

Judges appointed by member States for 6-year term

Deals with disputes arising out of the treaties or Community law

GREAT BRITAIN — NETHERLANDS — DENMARK — IRELAND — BELGIUM — WEST GERMANY — FRANCE — LUXEMBOURG — SPAIN — ITALY — GREECE — PORTUGAL

Original six 1957
Joined 1973
Joined 1981
Joined 1986

Fig. 12.1 The structure and institutions of the EEC

The Council of Ministers

The Council of Ministers is the highest decision-making body of the Community. It is made up of the appropriate representatives of the 12 member States. The Foreign Ministers are generally present for major decisions, but otherwise the composition of the Council varies according to the subject under discussion. If, for example, fishing rights were being discussed the Ministers responsible for fisheries would be present. The Ministers are assisted by permanent national staffs based in Brussels.

The Council makes decisions and legislates on the basis of proposals from the Commission. Some decisions must be made unanimously but others can be made by a majority. The Presidency of the Council changes every 6 months – whichever country has its representative as President controls the Agenda.

The European Parliament

The European Parliament is now a democratically elected body consisting of 518 members (MEPs), 81 elected by the UK, but it has few formal powers and cannot make law in the way that the UK Parliament does. It only has power to advise – the Commission and the Council are obliged to consult the Parliament but do not have to follow its advice. The process of consultation takes place through Parliamentary committees. However, the Parliament can, in theory, dismiss the Commission on a motion of censure. It has also developed the power to debate and question the EEC's budget and expenditure.

The European Communities (Amendment) Act 1986

This Act gave legal effect in Britain, to a Community law agreed between member states bringing about certain changes. Firstly, the Council is to extend its use of majority voting in respect of advancing policies to ensure freedom of movement within the Community of persons, goods, services and capital. Secondly, the European Parliament is given greater powers in certain circumstances to go beyond its 'advisory and supervisory' role and use a legislative procedure. Finally, the Community is given particular powers so as to be able to act in respect of health and safety at work and environmental matters.

The European Court of Justice

The European Court of Justice (ECJ) derives its powers from Article 164 of the Treaty of Rome. Its main task is to interpret and apply EEC law.

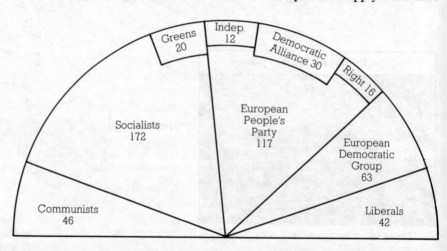

Fig. 12.2
Political composition of the European Parliament

Fig. 12.3
The European Court of Justice,
Luxembourg

Actions can be brought before the Court by member States, by the Council, by the Commission and by individuals. If the Court finds that the internal law of a member State (which we call 'municipal' law) is in conflict with EEC law, then the EEC law overrides the municipal law and the EEC law must be applied and implemented by the national court. In the very famous case of Costa *v.* Enel 1964 the Court held that the Treaty of Rome 'has created its own legal system which on the entry into force of the Treaty became an integral part of the legal systems of the member States and which their courts are bound to apply'.

Some cases brought before the Court are in fact 'references' from national courts asking the EEC Court whether their national law is in conflict with EEC law. The Court gives a ruling and refers the case back to the national court. United Kingdom courts have, for example, referred equal pay and sex discrimination cases to the European Court asking for rulings on the meaning and effect of Article 119 of the Treaty of Rome (on Equality of Treatment) and the EEC Directives on Equal Pay and Equal Treatment.

Sanctions

Supposing the member States ignore EEC law – what sanctions can be enforced against them? The Treaty of Rome contains no specific mention of enforcement procedures against member States – it merely says that member States must take the measures necessary to carry out the judgement of the European Court. Enforcement of a judgement is in practice achieved by the Commission, acting jointly with the Council, who put political and economic pressure on the member State. This happened in the case of the UK's refusal to obey an EEC Regulation making compulsory the use of the tachograph (the 'spy in the cab' which records mileage, speeds, etc. of commercial vehicles). Eventually the Commission took the UK to the EEC Court, the Court decided that the UK was in breach of the law, the Commission applied pressure behind the scenes, and ultimately the UK obeyed the law.

Differences between the ECJ and UK courts

We must not think of the ECJ as being a court like the UK courts. A judgement of the ECJ does not set a precedent, i.e. the Court does not bind itself as to future judgements. Also, its most important task is not to decide disputes between individuals but to interpret the Treaty of Rome, the founding treaty of the EEC. It is the only court which can do so. The ECJ does not enforce its judgements in the way that national courts do. It simply gives a ruling as to what the law is and as to whether a body is acting according to the law. The member State is under a treaty obligation to observe that law. The real sanctions are political and economic, not legal. The EEC was formed for the member States' self-interest, both political and economic. It is therefore in their own interest to obey EEC law.

The judges who sit in the Court are eminent lawyers (they may be academic lawyers, not practitioners) from each member State. Normally all the judges sit together and give one judgement. Court documents will be translated into the languages of the Community. In practice this is very difficult because different legal concepts, not merely language, must be translated. This causes particular problems for the UK which has a Common Law system quite unlike the codified systems of the other member States.

The nature of EEC law

You will remember that we said in Chapter 2 that not all law which applies in England and Wales is made here. Since the UK became a member of the EEC in 1973 some of our law is made by the EEC. It is therefore not only English judges and the English Parliament which make law but also EEC organisations. To this extent we can therefore no longer say that Parliament is *sovereign*. The UK Parliament is no longer the only ultimate law-making body in the UK.

Articles of the Treaty of Rome

The Treaty is of course binding on member States and creates rights and duties in international law. In addition the European Court of Justice has held that certain Articles of the Treaty are directly applicable in that they confer *individual* rights and duties which can be sued on in national courts. An example of this is Article 119 on equal treatment, which in a series of cases involving a Belgian air stewardess, Defrenne *v.* Sabena, was held to be directly applicable. Article 119 lays down that 'Each member State shall . . . ensure and . . . maintain the application of the principle that men and women shall receive equal pay for equal work'. (It is interesting to note that the inclusion of Article 119 was at the insistence of France for economic rather than philanthropic reasons, to ensure that free competition was not distorted by the employment of women at lower rates than those of men for doing the same work.) For discussion of Equal Value provisions in relation to sex discrimination, see Chapter 19, p. 186.

Regulations

Regulations are law as made and are directly applicable. They do not need to be ratified or confirmed by the national legislatures. An individual or an organisation may bring an action on this law in the national courts.

Directives

Directives are binding instructions to member States. They do not, generally speaking, confer individual rights and duties, i.e. they are not directly applicable. The member State must take steps to implement a directive.

The UK normally does so by means of statutory instruments.

The validity of Regulations and Directives can be questioned before the European Court and can be quashed (annulled) by the Court if they have not been properly made because the body concerned has acted *ultra vires* – beyond its powers.

The impact of EEC law

No business organisation can stand aloof from EEC law. We have already seen some examples of the impact of Community law on the business environment in Chapter 2 and again in Part B in our discussion of business organisations. In relation to consumer protection, we will discuss the EEC Directive on Product Liability in Chapter 31. There are many other examples of the impact of EEC law – in the fields of employment, energy, insurance, taxation, transport, weights and measures and competition law (which directly affects business organisations by making unlawful all agreements between organisations which might limit trade between member States).

The Community has developed an environmental policy, concerning itself with problems like those of marine and river pollution, air pollution, noise pollution, packaging and labelling of dangerous substances, control of chemical substances in foodstuffs intended for human consumption, storage and disposal of radioactive waste, and protection of wildlife. We mention in Chapter 44 ways in which special agencies like the European Social Fund are concerned with educational and social problems. Many of the EEC policies have been translated into law.

The EEC has had an effect which cannot be ignored.

13 Regulation of the business environment

Freedom of competition

We have been considering the complex of private and public organisations, commercial institutions, and policy making bodies both national and European. These all play a part in the commercial activities of organisations which survive or fail in an environment based on competition. The effect of competition is regarded as being beneficial in so far as it may encourage organisations to produce more efficiently and so offer their products to consumers at keener prices. It follows that practices such as agreements between suppliers and retailers to restrict the price at which goods may be resold, or a manufacturer refusing to supply a retailer who does not agree to maintain a price, are anti-competitive. To deal with this, the Restrictive Trade Practices Act 1976 makes void such trade restrictions as being contrary to the public interest, unless the issue has been brought to the attention of the Restrictive Practices Court which accepts that the restriction is reasonable. All restrictive agreements must be registered with the Director General of Fair Trading. Similarly the fixing of a minimum resale price is void under the Resale Prices Act 1976 unless otherwise agreed to by the same court.

The threat of a reference to the Restrictive Practices Court by the Director General, caused the Cement Makers' Federation to abolish its 53-

year-old price-fixing cartel in February 1987. The absence of the cartel, dominated by three companies holding 96 per cent of the market, will lead to competition in the pricing of cement products.

There exists also a general procedure for supervising anti-competitive practices, described by the Competition Act 1980 as products which have the effect of distorting or preventing competition in the supply of goods and services. Preliminary investigations are undertaken by the Director General of Fair Trading, who may then make a reference for full investigation to the Monopolies and Mergers Commission. This may be followed by an order prohibiting the practice in question. For example the Director General referred the practice of brewers managing public houses selling only their own beers to the Commission in 1986 as being an anti-competitive practice, and a report is expected in 1988. An earlier investigation resulted in the Commission ordering the travel trade to allow more competition so that now agents may offer customers a holiday for a lower price than that quoted in a brochure. Restrictive trade practices between companies in European member States may be invalidated as contrary to Article 85 of the Treaty of Rome.

Monopoly regulation

The Fair Trading Act 1973 sets out rules over monopoly situations, described as the control of 25 per cent of all goods and services in the UK by one person or group. Monitoring this is the Director General of Fair Trading, who may make references for investigation to the Monopolies and Mergers Commission. The latter prepares its report for submission to the Secretary of State, who may make appropriate orders.

As regards company takeovers and mergers, further regulations aim at avoiding the creation of monopolies thereby. The City has its own self-regulatory system, the City Takeover Panel, setting down the manner in which takeovers should proceed. However, the Director General has a duty to advise the Secretary of State of concern about a takeover bid, but it is up to the latter to decide whether to request the Monopolies and Mergers Commission to investigate. The final decision on what to do after the Commission has come to its conclusions is with the Minister. Thus in 1986 a merger was allowed between British Telecom and Mintel while the GEC merger with Plessey was not allowed.

Investor protection

Investors, whether they be individuals or large investment companies such as pension funds, enter an intrinsically risky market when buying shares, for the price of shares can increase or fall. On top of this is the opportunity for fraud, through the manipulation of takeover bids to inflate shares or the setting up of false companies or the absconding with company funds. This added, and perhaps avoidable risk, is dealt with in a number of ways. The Financial Services Act 1986 set up a statutory body, the Securities and Investments Board (SIB), to act as a watch-dog over investment businesses, the membership of the SIB being authorised by the Secretary of State. Only organisations regarded as fit and proper by the Secretary of State may conduct an investment business. The SIB will oversee a number of industry-specific self-regulatory bodies (SRO) which will be expected to keep their own house in order. For instance, the Stock Exchange, as an SRO, must regulate dealers in stocks and shares, as must similar SROs for unit trusts, commodity brokers and so on. An Investment Ombudsman will deal with complaints from investors and there is a compensation scheme (much on the lines of the one that exists if a holiday company becomes bankrupt when compensation comes from a fund maintained by all holiday companies). The fund will be created by a levy on individual firms, and investors with valid claims will be eligible to receive 100 per cent of losses up to £30 000 and 90 per cent of losses on a further £20 000.

As regards company fraud it is an offence for a company to buy its own shares, and it is illegal for persons with inside knowledge of impending company moves to exploit that position in order to make a profit. The Company Securities (Insider Dealing) Act 1985, makes punishable with a maximum of two years in prison for an act of one who, say, knowing as an insider that a takeover bid is planned, buys shares in the target company ahead of publication of this intention. The sentence is to increase to 7 years' imprisonment. The Secretary of State for Trade and Industry may also order government inspectors to investigate any instance of company fraud, or misgivings about conduct in company takeovers, the finding of which may lead to criminal prosecution.

Certainly, the effectiveness of the self-regulation and existing statutory framework for company takeovers came into question in the aftermath of one of the largest British company takeovers in 1986. A government investigation was undertaken of the methods employed when Guinness took over the Distillers company in 1986, after allegations of insider dealing, and the apparent purchase by Guinness, through nominees, of its own shares as a way of attracting Distillers' shareholders to vote in favour of the takeover. The government announced in 1987 that it would review the working of the self-regulatory system of the Takeover Panel and would be prepared to introduce legislation to replace that system.

Commercial ombudsmen

There has been great interest in the appointment of industry-specific persons to handle complaints of dissatisfied complainants to financial institutions. The Building Societies Act 1986 created the building societies ombudsman recognised by all societies as having authority in disputes, as well as setting up a compensation system for which the Building Societies Investor Protection Board has responsibility. In early 1986 a banking ombudsman commenced the task of receiving complaints from bank customers and is authorised to make awards of up to £50 000. The insurance ombudsman was established in 1981 and is able to investigate complaints, but only of participating insurance companies.

Consumer protection

The major part of our discussion of consumer protection will be in Part F, The Market. For the purposes of our present review of organisations we should note that there exist many consumer councils representing the interests of users of certain public utilities such as the Post Office, electricity boards, and local bus and train operations. This has been continued beyond privatisation, so that British Telecom is 'watched over' by Oftel, a government body headed by an independent Director General, with the task of looking after consumers' interests.

How far is a self-regulation system a satisfactory means of protecting the investor?

14 Legal institutions

Making use of the law

In almost every matter we have so far considered disputes may arise, not least because the business environment has participants with competing aims. Consumers, as we all know well because we are consumers, want goods and services at a quality and in a state which best meets what they can afford. If organisations produce goods and services which are defective, consumers can rely on the protective laws (see Chapters 30 and 31) to give them a right of action against those at fault. For example the Sale of Goods Act 1979 entitles the consumer to goods of such quality that they are reasonably fit for the purpose for which they are bought. The right is against the retailer from whom the goods were purchased, and often a dispute between a retailer and a customer will be resolved by exchanging the item or returning the customer's money. However, if the retailer refuses to recognise the customer's statutory rights, the customer may have to resort to law. This means seeking a judgement from a court in order to resolve the dispute.

Of course if a particular product or service offered by an organisation is not up to expectation, the consumer may choose to go elsewhere. This is possible in the UK, because for the most part the business environment is based on competition, giving us an element of choice. Thus market forces should have a greater influence on the quality of products than individual legal actions. Sometimes, as we have observed, this choice is restricted because an organisation has a monopoly in the market, as do the public utility corporations supplying gas, electricity and water. The user's voice on the quality of State monopoly services can be heard through the various consumer councils, or by complaining to a Member of Parliament who can raise the issue in Parliament (see Chapter 35). However, as organisations depend on scarce resources (see Parts D and E), goods and services must be produced by methods which make the most economical use of these resources – hence the wide adoption of mass production techniques which enable manufacturers to supply goods in such quantities and of an overall quality that satisfy consumer demand. In this process though, it is possible for goods to come on to the market with defects of which the manufacturer may not be aware.

Here, resort to the law can have a significant effect. Let us illustrate this by considering the circumstances surrounding the pregnancy drug 'Thalidomide' in the 1970s. When this drug became widely used it was noticed that children born to some women who had used it suffered from severe physical deformities. Although the drug was withdrawn immediately, what could those consumers do? The women affected in fact took the matter to law, and basing their action in the tort of negligence (drawn from the Donoghue 1932 case referred to in Chapter 2) sued the producer of the drug for damages, and succeeded.

On the other hand, organisations themselves may have to resort to the law if consumers fail to carry out their part of the bargain. Thus a person who fails to pay a telephone bill may, after appropriate warnings, be taken to court by British Telecom to seek a court order enforcing payment of the debt.

People in employment have a number of rights (discussed in Chapter 19) which protect them from unnecessary exploitation, because here again there may be conflicting interests between employees and employers. At its most basic, we as employees wish to get from our employment the best pay and conditions in exchange for our labour. Similarly an employing organisation seeks to obtain from our work the most economic and efficient return. Grievances that occur within the work environment can often be dealt with satisfactorily by the parties concerned. We may go to see the personnel officer or ask our trade union representative to act on our behalf. There may be times, though, where the internal procedures fail, in which case it may be necessary to go to law to get the matter settled.

Occasions may arise, then, where parties in dispute seek the assistance of lawyers and the courts in an attempt to settle their dispute.

Who should we see if we cannot resolve a dispute ourselves?

In the normal course of events people purchase items with which they are pleased, or work for organisations which treat them well, or live in a locality with no evidence of hostility. The world, though, is not free of problems nor is it populated by saints, and arguments will arise in any community. When an argument does arise each side will maintain its correctness and virtues. The law plays its part by setting down rules of behaviour and where these break down it provides procedures to settle arguments.

Solicitors

If we need advice or legal assistance we may need to employ the services of a **solicitor**, such as the partners Lore and Vice at 9 Sunhampton High Street. The main work of solicitors involves advising clients on the law and looking after their legal affairs. You and I in our private lives are bound to call upon the services of this legal expert at some time, possibly to carry out the legal work in connection with buying and selling our home, in preparing a will or in obtaining a divorce. We may also need help if we have been involved in a road accident or have been accused by the police of having committed a crime. Work with which solicitors may be involved in the business environment may be in giving advice to persons wishing to set up a trading organisation, or on the preparation of a formal contract, say between a pop group and their manager.

Solicitors too, have been seriously affected by certain changes, not least by the loss of their monopoly over conveyancing introduced by the Administration of Justice Act 1985. This Act amends the Solicitors Act 1974, by now allowing 'Licensed Conveyancers' (supervised by the Council for Licensed Conveyancers) to undertake conveyancing of land. You may recall that we have already made mention of the new powers of institutions such as the building societies to incorporate such a service. The 1985 Act further increases the power of the Council of the Law Society to impose sanctions on solicitors whose professional services fall below a quality that is reasonable in dealing with their clients' interests. Following a notorious instance in 1983 when a client was overcharged by £50 000 and his complaint against his solicitor was not investigated properly by the Law Society, an independent Solicitors Complaints Bureau was set up in September 1986. Although not divorced from the Law Society, the Bureau is intended to provide effective scrutiny over the handling of complaints about solicitors, as well as providing an adjudication panel to decide on disciplinary sanctions. The government announced in March 1987 its intention to remove the supervision of the Legal Aid system from the Law Society and to run it as a government-appointed Legal Aid Board.

Solicitors generally do most of their work outside the law courts, and in fact they should apply their expertise in civil disputes to trying to settle matters between their client and whoever is involved in the argument.

Crimes, however, are a different matter. Once a person has been arrested, questioned and charged with committing a crime, the matter must go before a criminal court. This is because a crime is a wrong committed against us all, represented by the State, and a person found guilty of a crime will be punished by the State, generally either by imprisonment or by a fine.

You will not see solicitors representing their clients in all the courts, because they have a restricted right of 'audience'. They may appear to argue a case only before a Magistrates' Court (mostly criminal cases), before a County Court (civil cases) and in certain cases before a Crown Court. In fact it is the Magistrates' Court in which solicitors most often appear arguing the case for their clients. Solicitors in 1985 pressed for an increased right of audience in formal matters before High Court judges, but not involving advocacy.

What happens if the solicitor cannot settle the dispute between the client and another? In such an event, if the matter has to go to a court in which the solicitor cannot appear, the professionals who can appear are contacted. These men and women are called **barristers**.

Barristers

Barristers are the lawyers whom you will see in a court of law, wigged and gowned, arguing their case on behalf of a client. They are so named because when they have completed their training they are 'called to the Bar' by one of the four Inns of Court to which they belong. The Inns are regulated by a body called the Senate of the Inns of Court and the Bar, which exercises disciplinary powers over practising barristers.

Barristers have the right to be heard in all courts of the land. They work from offices called 'chambers', both in London and in other parts of the country, in towns like Birmingham, Cardiff, Hull, Leeds, Liverpool, Nottingham and Swansea.

The important characteristic of the dual legal profession is that clients may only approach a solicitor for legal assistance and never a barrister. Only a solicitor acting on behalf of a client may contact a barrister. If a dispute has to go to court, the solicitor will present the details of the client's case in a document called a 'brief'. This brief will be sent to a set of Chambers and the clerk of the Chambers will pass the brief on to one of the barristers. This means that normally the first contact a client will have with a barrister is in the Court itself before the case commences. The barrister's fees are paid by the solicitor, who of course recovers the money from the client. The division is so strict that the professional rules of each type of lawyer require them not to carry out the functions of the other nor even to meet socially.

Crown Prosecutors

Headed by the Director of Public Prosecutions, a new Crown Prosecution Service took over, from 1 October 1986, the responsibility for the conduct of nearly all criminal proceedings instituted on behalf of the police. The police thereby ceased having responsibility for conducting prosecutions and after instituting proceedings must now submit a case to a Crown Prosecutor, who will have the final say on what cases are brought to trial. The decision on whether to prosecute in such cases as company fraud, terrorist outrages, official secrets cases and race relations cases will remain the preserve of the DPP.

To what extent is the dual legal profession a disadvantage in the modern business environment?

Suppose a client cannot afford lawyers' fees?

Stuck on the window of the offices of Lore & Vice & Co, we may see this logo which denotes that the partners are voluntary members of the **legal aid** scheme. This scheme is funded by the Home Office but is administered by the Law Society, and has a turnover about £4m a month. Under the Legal Aid Acts 1974 and 1979 financial aid is granted to persons on a low income (the ceiling of which is changed from time to time to keep pace with inflation). Solicitors who take part in this scheme (called the Green Form Scheme) may offer £40 worth of advice to such people on such matters as drafting a will, the grounds for divorce, or tenancy matters. The fee is refunded by the Law Society's Legal Aid Committee.

If a dispute involves going to a civil court a person who has a low income may apply for a **Legal Aid Certificate**, which may be granted if the case is reasonable. The Certificate entitles a person to representation before a court, but according to the applicant's income a contribution to the costs may be required.

In respect of criminal cases a **Legal Aid Order** may be applied for by the accused from the court. It will be granted to those with modest incomes, and in some cases such as murder it is granted automatically. Indeed a judge may refuse to try a case if the accused is not legally represented. Like the Legal Aid Certificate, the Order covers the solicitor's costs and those of the barrister. In 1987 the government introduced a Bill aimed to establish a Legal Aid Board (separate from the Law Society), and also to harmonise the civil and criminal procedure for the granting of Legal Aid.

Law centres

There are other agencies to which one can go with legal problems, such as the Citizens' Advice Bureaux and Neighbourhood Law Centres, both of which are funded by local government authorities. As these bodies charge no fees, people with low incomes are attracted to them.

To which court would you go if you were unfairly dismissed?

You would probably not go to a court at all. Going to law is an expensive matter, and most people probably earn too much to be entitled to receive legal aid from the Law Society. The total legal aid cost in England and Wales will be some £400m in 1986/7. We have already noted that the scheme might be run by a government-appointed Legal Aid Board.

A less expensive and quicker procedure has been devised to settle disputes – **tribunal hearings**. Tribunals are different from ordinary courts which deal with a whole gamut of types of cases, because they are established to deal with just one matter. The **Lands Tribunal** listens to complaints from home owners whose houses are intended to be compulsorily acquired by local authorities in carrying out their planning obligations (see Chapter 17, p. 148). Appeals from decisions of Social Security Officers who determine State benefits are heard by **Social Security Appeals Tribunals**. Complaints by employees that they have been unfairly dismissed by their employers are heard before **Industrial Tribunals**.

The second feature of tribunals apart from their specialist nature is that proceedings before them are informal, and instead of a judge there is a chairman who has some knowledge of the particular field in question. He or she is assisted, say in an Industrial Tribunal, by two ordinary individuals, one of whom will represent employees' interests on one side while the other may represent employers' interests. No one is robed, and deliber-

Fig. 14.1
The structure of the English courts, showing the lines of appeal

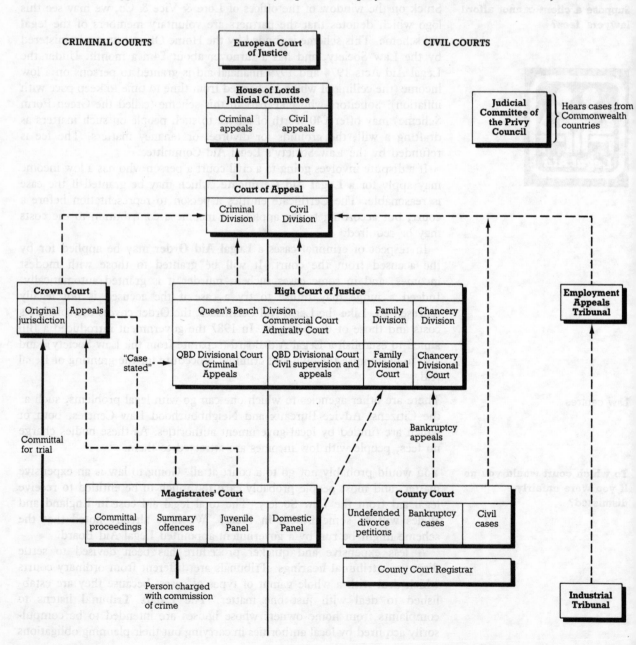

ations take place in an informal atmosphere with the minimum of legal formality. An employee who belongs to a trade union may be helped by a trade union representative. Appeals are possible on points of law from tribunals, which in the case of Industrial Tribunals are heard by the Employment Appeal Tribunal (see Fig. 14.1) and beyond that to the Court of Appeal. The working of tribunals is supervised by the Council of Tribunals set up by the Tribunals and Inquiries Act 1971.

Other bodies which deal with disputes

Inquiries

The Tribunals and Inquiries Act 1971 is also concerned with public inquiries which may have to be undertaken in order to give a chance for people to air their complaints. Public inquiries have to be held, under the Highways Act 1959, if the Minister of Transport proposes to put a motorway scheme into effect. The chairman of the inquiry has to arrange for an open session to receive evidence from local residents about a proposal. As these are not court hearings, a member of the public has no right of cross-examination. The evidence so collected is sent to the Minister, who must then come to a decision in the light of objections.

In 1980, the government decided to set up a public inquiry to assess the public's feelings about the proposed expansion of the nuclear plant at Windscale (now called Sellafield). The inquiry was not cheap; it took 100 days to collect evidence and cost some £2m.

More recently, the future of part of Britain's civil nuclear industry was decided, when in January 1987 Sir Frank Layfield reported the conclusions of a public inquiry on the development of the Sizewell plant. The inquiry had received many submissions from those opposed to nuclear energy. He recommended the go-ahead for the building of the first pressurised-water reactor by the Central Electricity Generating Board subject to the Board satisfying the government on a number of points concerning safety of the plant's operation.

Arbitration

Arbitration is another method employed to resolve disputes, and is governed by the Arbitration Act 1979. Widely used in commercial disputes, arbitration offers a quick, informal and cheap way to resolve differences. Many commercial contracts between organisations may have written into them that in the event of a dispute, the parties shall resort to arbitration. The parties agree on who shall act as arbitrator, and further agree to abide by the arbitrator's decision, called an 'award'. This award is usually as final as if it were a judge's decision.

ACAS

The Employment Protection Act 1975 created the Advisory, Conciliation and Arbitration Service (ACAS) which has the function of helping to improve industrial relations. Either employers or employees may call upon ACAS to intervene if a trade dispute is in the offing. If both parties agree ACAS may investigate the background of the dispute and issue an 'award'. The award may be published if all the parties consent. ACAS has reported that most issues over which it has been asked to make awards involve disputes arising over grading, holiday pay, bonus payments and other such matters. For example, in 1977 ACAS settled by arbitration a dispute between a trade union and British Nuclear Fuels for an increased allowance to compensate for the abnormal conditions which had arisen at the Windscale nuclear plant.

What sorts of matters are dealt with by the courts?

Going to the courts should be a last resort for parties involved in a civil dispute. Civil disputes may arise under contracts, where one person has promised to do something but has breached this promise. Other matters include matrimonial disputes; disputes where a landlord wishes to regain possession of rented premises; disputes over the payment of a debt; complaints by an occupier of premises that a neighbour is infringing his or her rights; claims in the tort of negligence; bankruptcy proceedings; arguments over the validity of wills; and claims that charitable trustees have misused trust funds. This is not a complete list, for the examples are very varied, but we can say that the characteristic of civil disputes is that they exist between private individuals or organisations and it is for those parties to use the courts to enforce their rights if they so choose.

In contrast, the criminal law is aimed at attempting to get people and organisations to conduct themselves in a certain manner, and nonobservance may lead to **prosecution**. This word denotes that a person (or organisation) charged with a crime will be brought for trial and if found guilty will be punished by the State, usually by fine and/or imprisonment. As a crime is regarded as a wrong against the State, most prosecutions are undertaken in the name of the Crown. Crimes include: theft, robbery, burglary, blackmail, criminal assault, grievous bodily harm, manslaughter, murder, rape, dangerous and reckless driving, selling alcohol from unlicensed premises and obstructing the highway. Persons charged with such crimes do not, as with civil disputes, have the choice about whether to go before a court, unless the accused is insane, when he or she will be committed to a mental institution rather than stand trial.

Figure 14.1 shows the relationship of the various courts within the English legal system. The criminal courts appear on one side of the dividing line, the civil courts and tribunals on the other.

To which court should you go in order to enforce a debt?

The answer to that question is firstly that as it involves a civil matter it should go to a civil court. In fact the great bulk of civil disputes are dealt with in the County Courts, of which there are about 400 in England and Wales. Actions can be heard by Circuit Judges who sit singly in a court without a jury (these being rarely called in civil actions), and hear the case put by each party to the action before giving judgement.

County Court jurisdiction

A County Court can only entertain an action relating to its own district, i.e. the district in which the defendant lives or carries on business or where the cause of the action took place. The essential feature of a County Court is that because it is an inferior court, it can only dispose of actions within certain defined limits, whereas the jurisdiction of the High Court is unlimited. So, actions founded on failure to comply with a contract, or the commission of a tort (i.e. a civil wrong, such as injury resulting from another's negligence) may be brought before a County Court, provided the plaintiff's claim does not exceed £5000.

Other matters within a County Court's jurisdiction include actions for the recovery of land, the management of certain estates of deceased persons, dissolution of partnerships, certain bankruptcies and actions involving undefended divorce petitions. Again, the County Court's jurisdiction is limited in certain of these matters by the value of property or the amount of money involved in the action. It is open to the parties in some cases in which the claim exceeds the limits to consent to the case being heard in a County Court instead of in the High Court.

Small claims

The permanent head of a County Court, the County Court Registrar (appointed from among solicitors with at least seven years' experience) will arbitrate in disputes where the claim does not exceed £500. This procedure was introduced in 1973 to provide a very quick system for dealing with small consumer claims. In the event of disagreement with the Registrar's decision, there is a right to appeal to the Circuit Judge of that Court.

Appeals from the decision of a Circuit Judge usually require his or her consent, and are made to the Court of Appeal Civil Division. Appeals in bankruptcy matters are heard by the Divisional Court of the Chancery Division.

In order to give you an idea of how a legal action in a County Court might proceed, look at our example here.

A County Court action commences with the party bringing the action, named the **plaintiff**, applying for a **summons** against the other party, the **defendant**. Look at Fig. 14.2 which shows a form of request for a default summons brought by Sunhampton's Housing Department against Mr S.L.P. Happi for arrears of rent of £329.63. The summons is to be delivered by County Court bailiffs on Mr Happi. If on receiving the summons he decides to pay up he will need to send the money to the Court, and that will be the end of the matter. However he may disagree with the facts stated by the Council in their particulars of the claim. For instance he may argue that he has withheld the rent because the Council refused to repair his leaking water tank. In any case, if he disputes the claim he must return the copy of the summons with his defence written on it.

When Sunhampton County Court officers receive Mr Happi's reply they will arrange for a preliminary hearing before the County Court Registrar, who may arbitrate in this dispute since the amount claimed does not exceed £500. If the Registrar cannot solve the dispute or if the parties disagree with the decision, a date for a hearing before a judge will be set.

If, after hearing the facts of the case, usually argued by barristers representing each side (although parties may represent themselves), the Court decides against Mr Happi it will order him to pay the claimed amount plus costs. Mr Happi may lodge an appeal, which will usually require the judge's consent, if he feels that justice has not been done.

The appeal is heard by the Court of Appeal, Civil Division. An appeal does not involve a rehearing of the facts already presented in the County Court. The Court of Appeal's three senior judges (Lord Justices of Appeal) merely hear the arguments put by barristers on behalf of each party only on that point on which the appeal is based. After having heard the argu-

IN THE **SUNHAMPTON**   COUNTY COURT

CASE No. *000001*

THIS SECTION TO BE COMPLETED BY THE COURT

Summons in form: N.1 Fixed Amount ☐   N.2 Unliquidated ☐

Service by: Bailiff ☐   Plaintiff('s solicitors) ☐   Post (Certificate) (overleaf) ☐   Post (At defendant) (company's R.O.) ☐   Date issued ☐

Statement of Parties   Please use block capitals

1. PLAINTIFF'S names in full, and residence or place of business.
2. If suing in a representative capacity, state in what capacity.
3. If a minor required to sue by a next friend, state that fact, and names in full, residence or place of business, and occupation of next friend.
4. If an assignee, state that fact, and name, address and occupation of assignor.
5. If co-partners suing in the name of their firm, add "(A Firm)".
6. If a company registered under the Companies Act, 1948, state the address of registered office and describe it as such.

SUNHAMPTON BOROUGH COUNCIL HOUSING DEPT. HIGH STREET SUNHAMPTON SUNHAMPSHIRE

Plaintiff's solicitors name and address for service

LORE & VICE & Co. 9 HIGH STREET SUNHAMPTON

Solicitor's reference

ALV/66/83

7. DEFENDANT'S surname, and (where known) his or her initials or fore-names in full; defendant's residence or place of business (if a proprietor of the business).
8. Whether male or female.
9. Whether a minor (where known).
10. Occupation (where known).
11. If sued in a representative capacity, state in what capacity.
12. If co-partners are sued in the name of their firm, add "(A Firm)" or if a person carrying on business in a name other than his own name is sued in such name, add "(A trading name)".
13. If a company registered under the Companies Act, 1948 is sued the address given must be the registered office of the company, and must be so described.

Mr S. L. P. HAPPI (Interior Decorator) 160° HALCYON COURT HAMPTON ESTATE AVENUE ROAD SUNHAMPTON SUNHAMPSHIRE

WHAT THE CLAIM IS FOR

AMOUNT CLAIMED	329	63
ISSUE FEE	32	00
Bailiff Service	4	00
SOLICITOR'S COSTS	22	00
TOTAL	**£387**	**63**

[Strike out if inappropriate:-

NOTES:

1. Two copies of the plaintiff's particulars of claim are required before a summons can be issued, and if there are two or more defendants to be served, an additional copy for each additional defendant.

2. Any claim for £500 or less which is defended will be referred to arbitration automatically, but the reference may be rescinded on application.

3. When a defended claim is arbitrated the right of appeal against the arbitrator's award is very limited.

4. If the defendant's address is outside the district of the court you must complete Section A overleaf.

5. The certificate in Section B overleaf should be completed and signed if service by post is required.

N.201 Request for default summons (single case) Order 3 Rule 3(1)

Fig. 14.2
Request for a default summons

ments raised by Mr Happi (the **appellant**) and the Council (the **respondent**) they may either accept or reject the point raised in appeal. If the appeal is accepted the judges may reverse the decision of the court below. Only in rare cases of miscarriage of justice will they use their power to order a wholly new trial. In some cases an important matter of public interest may be raised. Such questions may be raised on appeal to the Judicial Committee of the House of Lords, which consists of nine Lords of Appeal in Ordinary (who sit as members of the Lords), of whom usually 5 will consider an appeal from the Court of Appeal.

As the Lords of Appeal are superior judges they may overrule the Court of Appeal's decision.

Let us suppose that some while after the case has been heard and Mr Happi has complied with the court order, he becomes unable to meet his general debts and is petitioned in bankruptcy (see Chapter 20, p. 207). Except for London, where bankruptcy matters are dealt with by the Bankruptcy Court in the Chancery Division of the High Court, certain County Courts have jurisdiction to hear bankruptcy matters where the total debt does not exceed £5000. Our luckless Sunhampton resident again attends the County Court, where he is eventually declared bankrupt.

In the meantime, the Council wishes to regain possession of Mr Happi's council house. As we shall see in Chapter 17, a landlord may only regain possession by issuing a **fixed-dated order** before the County Court Judge (and only if the rateable value of the land is under £5000).

While this is happening his wife, who has been under considerable strain, petitions her husband for divorce on the grounds of her husband's association and adultery with Ms F. Luff. Mr Happi is anxious not to cause his wife any further misery and decides not to contest the petition. Undefended divorce petitions may be heard by a County Court Judge. As Mrs Happi's petition appears to be well-founded and Mr Happi does not defend the petition, the judge declares the marriage to be irretrievably broken down because of Mr Happi's adultery and issues a **decree nisi** (unless), which, if in 6 weeks the parties cannot reconcile their differences, will become a **decree absolute**.

What we have done is to give an outline of the sort of cases which may come before a County Court; the list is not exhaustive, but it does give you an idea of the nature of the Court's jurisdiction. If the action involves a greater sum than those mentioned above, it must be heard before the High Court.

What is the work of the High Court?

In the event of a claim by a plaintiff for a breach of contract, a demand for compensation for an injury resulting from another's negligence, or any matter beyond the jurisdiction of the County Court, the action must commence before the High Court. These actions commence with the presentation of a **writ**. Like a County Court summons, the writ contains a statement of the plaintiff's claim and the name of the defendant to the action. Usually it will be a solicitor, acting on behalf of the client, who will send the writ to the Central Office of the High Court (or the District Registry, outside London). On payment of a fee a copy of the writ will be sealed and returned to the solicitor, who can then serve it on the defendant. To avoid having judgement made against him or her the defendant must make a reply

Fig. 14.3
The Royal Courts of Justice, Strand,
London

within 14 days. When the case comes up for hearing it will be heard before
a single judge who will give a reasoned judgement after hearing the facts
of the case. Again, only in a few cases, such as a case of libel or slander
where a person's character is falsely damaged, will there be a jury.

The High Court was established by the Supreme Court of Judicature Acts
1873 and 1875 with the Court of Appeal, and is based in the Royal Courts
of Justice (the Law Courts building) in the Strand, London, which has over
50 separate court rooms. The High Court also makes an appearance in the

provinces, since by the Courts Act 1971 it may sit anywhere in England and Wales determined by the Lord Chancellor.

So as to achieve a degree of specialisation the High Court has been divided, since the passing of the Administration of Justice Act 1970, into three sections. These are the Queen's Bench Division, the Family Division and the Chancery Division. The Lord Chancellor appoints High Court judges, one to each Court making up the various divisions. There is what is called a Divisional Court attached to each division whose purpose is to handle appeals from the lower courts. These Divisional Courts carry out their appellate functions with usually three High Court judges.

In March 1987 the government published proposals with a view to amalgamating the County Court and High Court. This would end the limit to the jurisdiction of the County Court. Also proposed was the abolition of the court vacations and the extension of the working days of courts. Legislation is expected in the 1988/9 Parliamentary Session.

Let us now consider the types of civil disputes in which each of these divisions specialise, remembering that even though the Supreme Court, comprising the Court of Appeal, the Crown Court and the High Court, is centred in London, the High Court also sits in the provinces of England and Wales, and writs may be issued from what are called **district registries**.

The Queen's Bench Division

This is headed by the Lord Chief Justice of England, who is assisted by over 40 High Court Judges. Unlike the County Courts, the Division has no limit placed on its jurisdiction. In fact the Division will sit in judgement on disputes which the County Courts have no power to hear, principally in contract and tort actions where the amount claimed is over £5000. Whereas this Division deals with over 200 000 cases a year, the County Courts hear over 2 million disputes, reflecting the fact that most civil disputes between people do not involve great sums of money.

In addition to ordinary civil matters the Division has a special Commercial Court (though many commercial disputes are resolved by arbitration) and an Admiralty Court which hears matters such as those arising from collisions at sea.

The Queen's Bench Divisional Court hears appeals from certain tribunals, and also from the solicitors' Disciplinary Committee. The Court also considers complaints from people claiming to have suffered unfairly at the hands of lower courts and tribunals, public authorities (e.g. the police) or the government itself. We shall be examining these 'supervisory powers' of the Queen's Bench Division in Chapter 35. For the present we may instance orders issued demanding the release of anyone wrongfully imprisoned (the order is called **habeas corpus**), or orders transferring a trial of a matter from a lower court or tribunal to the High Court.

The Family Division

The work of this aptly named Division is mainly concerned with disputes relating to the validity of marriage, the wardship of children and defended divorce cases. The Division also handles the legal work connected with giving power to persons to distribute the property of persons who have died.

The Family Divisional Court hears appeals from Magistrates' Courts on

The Chancery Division

matrimonial matters such as orders for separation and payment of maintenance orders (see below, p. 117).

This Division hears disputes involving mortgages and trusts, partnership and company matters, arguments about the validity of wills or property left by someone who has died without making a will, and bankruptcy matters. A special Bankruptcy Court which comes under the Chancery jurisdiction handles all bankruptcy cases occurring in the London area. Outside London, you will recall, certain County Courts have bankruptcy jurisdiction.

Judges from the Chancery Division sit as the Patents Court under the Patents Act 1977 (discussed in Chapter 20, p. 212). The Chancery Divisional Court hears appeals on bankruptcy matters from County Courts outside London, and income tax appeals from the Commissioner of Inland Revenue.

The Restrictive Practices Court

In order to protect consumers from the effect of certain agreements say, between manufacturers and retailers by which the price for the supply of goods to consumers is fixed, the Restrictive Trade Practices Act 1956 established the Restrictive Practices Court with High Court status. The court consists of a High Court Judge assisted by two non-lawyers who have 'knowledge or experience in industry, commerce or public affairs'. The Act, amended by the Restrictive Trade Practices Act 1976 and the Fair Trading Act 1973, requires that certain classes of restrictive trading agreements must be registered with the Office of Fair Trading. Among the duties of the Director General of Fair Trading (apart from overall responsibility for fair trading, and control over monopolies and mergers) is the function of bringing before the Court any trading agreement considered to be 'contrary to the public interest'. If the Court agrees with this opinion, the agreement would be declared to be void and of no effect. This would be the case if a manufacturer of car tyres entered an agreement with a wholesaler seeking to enforce a minimum retail price on the sale of tyres, and the company failed to show that the practice was for the benefit of the public.

How do the Criminal Courts deal with cases?

Let us consider these circumstances. Mr B. Olshy is an employee of Insurall (Insurance Services) Ltd – a private company. His employers have done nothing to rectify a duplicating machine which is leaking harmful spirit fumes. The fumes adversely affect the health of Mr Olshy's colleague who works with him in a small confined office. Mr Olshy is aware that his employers are criminally liable under the Health and Safety at Work Act 1974 (see Chapter 19, p. 202) and may be fined by the Magistrates' Court. Indeed his friend is considering bringing an action before the High Court to claim £10 000 damages for deterioration in health.

Mr Olshy decides to take matters into his own hands and destroys the machine by dropping it out of the second-floor window. He also steals £1000 by appropriating the company's petty cash box. Unfortunately for him the sharp-eyed commissionaire spots him leaving the offices at 3 High Street, Sunhampton, in suspicious circumstances. This intelligence is reported to the company's manager, who demands to see Mr Olshy the next morning. On realising the 'game is up', Mr Olshy attacks the manager until restrained. The police are called; they arrest him and take him to the police station, where he is charged with an offence under the Criminal Damage Act 1971, with burglary contrary to the Theft Act 1968 and with criminal assault punishable under the Offences against the Person Act 1861. The Crown Prosecution Service will undertake the prosecution. However, Mr Olshy cannot be punished until the prosecution can prove beyond reasonable doubt that not only has he committed the acts in question, but that he also did so with a guilty mind.

Magistrates' Courts

The Magistrates' Court to which Mr Olshy will be brought consists of four parts. Firstly there is the **domestic panel** which has civil responsibilities such as making orders in connection with the failure to maintain the applicant or any child of the family, or to order custody of any child under 18 years of age, or to make an order prohibiting a spouse from molesting the applicant or a child of the family.

Secondly there is a **juvenile panel** before which children aged 10 to 17 years may be brought when they are charged with committing a crime. The magistrates (of whom one must be a woman) may order that the child be put in the care of the local authority, or in appropriate cases a child aged over 14 may be sentenced to an attendance centre or to a detention centre.

The third aspect of Magistrates' Court's work is the hearing and passing sentences on persons charged with **summary offences**. These are less serious crimes such as causing a breach of the peace, driving offences, cases of minor theft, less serious criminal assaults, and causing criminal damage to property where the damage caused does not exceed £200. The magistrates may impose a fine of up to £1000 and/or imprisonment of 6 months for an offence (but not more than 12 months where a person is charged with more than one offence). Some offences, such as theft, are 'triable either way' (i.e. before the magistrates or before the Crown Court), it being open to the accused to choose whether to be tried before the magistrates or not. If the magistrates find that because of previous convictions their powers of punishment are too limited they may require the Crown Court (see below) to pass sentence.

Fourthly, a person charged with a serious crime, called an **indictable offence**, which includes serious cases of theft, robbery, burglary, rape, murder and spying, must first come before the magistrates. These are called **committal proceedings**, and the function of the magistrates is to examine the evidence submitted by the prosecution, and if satisfied that there is a case to answer to commit the accused to the Crown Court for trial by jury.

Who are the magistrates?

The magistrates' bench will consist either of a single trained lawyer called a **stipendiary magistrate**, who receives a salary, or lay magistrates. Lay magistrates are appointed from local worthies such as people involved with one of the major political parties, trade unionists or voluntary workers. They are not lawyers and they are not paid more than their expenses. Their appearance in the court system is to ensure that ordinary people can be involved with the administration of justice. 'Justice must not only be done, it must be seen to be done.' The magistrates sit without a jury and may make use of the Clerk of the Court, who is a trained lawyer, if they need any advice on a legal matter. Another function they have is to issue licences to sell alcohol.

Appeals from the magistrates

There is a right of appeal from the magistrates claiming that they have made error in law or have exceeded their powers. The magistrates 'state the case' (the facts which they used to arrive at their decision) to the Divisional Court of the Queen's Bench. An appeal against conviction or sentence may be made to the Crown Court, which will consider the points raised on appeal before two to four magistrates and a judge. The result may be a confirmation or reversal of the decision of the Magistrates' Court, and the punishment may be reduced or increased.

Mr B. Olshy, it turns out, has caused severe harm to his manager, and the damage to property totals £4500. He is therefore brought before the Sunhampton magistrates, who after hearing the evidence against him commit him for trial before the Sunhampton Crown Court. His application for bail (under the Bail Act 1979) is not contested by the police and the magistrates set the sureties to the value of £5000. If he fails to turn up for trial the £5000 is forfeited and the police may ask a magistrate to issue a warrant for his arrest and detention.

Trial by jury

Twelve weeks later Mr B. Olshy, in the case of R. (for Regina, the Queen) *v.* Olshy 1987, is required to attend Sunhampton Crown Court, before Judge Fare. His solicitor, Mr N.O. Vice of Lore & Vice, sees him and introduces him to the barrister, Mr Justin, Q. C. (Queen's Counsel). The Crown Court consists of not only the judge but also a jury of 12 members of the public (see Fig. 14.4).

The function of the jury, appointed from among people over 18 years of age who are registered on the electoral roll and are not otherwise excluded, is to arrive at a verdict on the basis of the evidence produced by the prosecution or the defence. By the Juries Act 1974, a jury may arrive at a majority verdict (e.g. 11–1 or 10–2). The judge is bound by the jury's verdict and must then pass sentence or acquit as the case may be.

Mr Olshy for his part has pleaded 'not guilty' to the charges, claiming that he was right to be annoyed by management's inaction over safety matters and in any case he claimed that he was drunk, and furthermore was only acting in self-defence when 'attacked' by his manager. The case proceeds with barristers from either side calling witnesses, questioning them and allowing the other side to 'cross-examine'. After hearing the evidence the prosecution addresses the jury and submissions end with Mr Justin addressing the jury on the case for the defence. At this point Judge Fare sums up the case and directs the jury to consider their verdict. Two and a half hours later the jury returns with their verdict, which their foreman delivers as a unanimous verdict of 'guilty'. The judge then imposes a sentence of two years in jail for the unfortunate Mr B. Olshy who is taken from the court to serve his sentence in HM Prison, Sunhamptonshire. Of course he may lodge an appeal either against conviction or sentence.

The Crown Court

The Crown Court is concerned with trying indictable offences. The judges may be drawn from the Queen's Bench Division of the High Court but are more usually Circuit Judges. Since 1971, another type of judge may sit to

Fig. 14.4
A Crown Court

hear criminal cases in this court, namely the Recorder. A Recorder is a part-time judge who must be in practice as either a barrister or a solicitor. What is unusual in this is that it breaks with the tradition that judges were always appointed from among barristers.

What is the appeal system in Criminal Courts?

Court of Appeal, Criminal Division

This court is headed by the Lord Chief Justice of England, and three judges hear appeals from decisions made in the Crown Courts. The Criminal Appeal Act 1968 gives a convicted person the right to appeal against conviction based on a question of law. This may involve an employee questioning whether a conviction for attempting to steal from a colleague's handbag can be right because the handbag was empty at the time. Alternatively if the convicted person argues that the conviction is based on incorrect assessment of a fact raised in the Crown Court, he or she may appeal by either being permitted to do so by the trial judge or by getting leave from the Court of Appeal itself. In certain cases a person convicted on indictment may complain that the sentence is too severe and may so appeal with leave of the Court of Appeal.

The Court has power to annul a conviction, to substitute a conviction of an alternative offence, or to annul a sentence. If in the course of an appeal evidence not previously raised at the trial is disclosed, the Court may order a retrial.

Because the consequences of a criminal conviction are so much more serious than a finding of liability in civil actions, the rights of appeal in criminal cases are more extensive.

The Judicial Committee of the House of Lords

The Criminal Appeal Act 1968 enables either the accused or the prosecutor to appeal against the Court of Appeal's judgement, with the permission of either the Court of Appeal or the House of Lords. Leave will only be granted if the point of law which is questioned by the appellant is one of 'general public importance'. The reasons for allowing or dismissing the appeal are not normally delivered orally but are issued in writing.

The Judicial Committee of the Privy Council

The Judicial Committee listens to a limited variety of appeals. It is composed of the Lord Chancellor, Privy Councillors who have held high judicial office, Lords of Appeal in Ordinary and, among others, former superior court judges of certain Commonwealth countries, and there will be from three to five in attendance to hear an appeal. Appeals are heard from domestic tribunals such as those concerned with dentists, opticians, veterinary surgeons and medical practitioners. Most often we hear of this body's deliberations when deciding appeals from the few Commonwealth countries that still allow appeal to England, from Australian States and from the Channel Islands and the Isle of Man.

Law reports

In our previous discussion we have mentioned case decisions as being themselves a source of English Law. The reasoning that judges apply to a given set of facts will be based on legal principles, sometimes describing an area of liability (for example the case of Donoghue v. Stevenson 1932, discussed on p. 31), or by interpreting the meaning of an Act. In fact judges perform an important role in interpreting legislation, and occasionally parties may bring an action as a test case when the exact meaning of a new law is unclear. Invariably the cases we quote in this book, and those which lawyers employ as sources of law, are decisions of judges in the superior courts.

Any visit to a law court will enable you to see volumes on shelves or stacked on barristers' and judges' tables. These are reports of major decisions to which reference will be made by lawyers to support their argument. There is now a whole variety of reports of court and tribunal decisions. Decisions from many of the legal institutions we have described are recorded by organisations, some companies, others charities (e.g. the Incorporated Council of Law Reporting).

It is possible that a decision of long standing arrived at by a past Court of Appeal can be overturned today when the point of law is considered by the House of Lords. This is one of the reasons why the law is always in a state of flux and always changing. We should note that the only opportunity a court has to rethink a point of law is to wait for parties to come to court. Such a limitation does not apply to Parliament, which can make laws at will. In fact another reason for the continual change in law is that the government of the day, naturally, wishes to give effect to its policies.

Fig. 14.5
The EEC Court of Justice in session

The European Communities'
Court of Justice

Since 1 January 1973 when the European Communities Act 1972 came into effect, the UK has been a member of the EEC. We shall be discussing the nature of the EEC in Chapter 12, but for the purposes of this discussion we will examine the role of the Court of Justice.

Under the EEC Treaty certain obligations are placed upon signatory member countries, and these in turn create certain rights for inhabitants of those States. Moreover, the Community institutions make a variety of rules and regulations which have to be enforced in this country. In effect, all these rules emanating from the Community become part of our national law, and by virtue of the Treaty obligation are superior to any English law in cases of conflict.

One of these Treaty obligations states that, subject to some qualification, citizens of the EEC member states have freedom of movement throughout these countries. Community citizens must not generally be subjected to otherwise usual immigration controls. To put it simply, because Community law is superior to national law, any national law preventing free movement may be declared invalid. In the first instance it should be a national court that would listen to a complaint of expulsion or denial of entry into a country. If the court is in doubt on which law to apply, reference may be made to the Court of Justice in Luxembourg. This latter may then give a ruling on the interpretation of the Treaty, and direct how the matter should be dealt with, including a declaration that the national law is invalid.

Can you suggest some types of disputes that might arise between individuals within your organisation, and ways in which they might be resolved by the parties themselves?

Can you summarise the jurisdiction of the County Court?
Can you list the types of actions that may be heard by the various civil courts?
Can you draw up a plan of the English court system?

Summary, Part B

1 The bigger the organisation, the more likely it is to make use of specialisation and division of labour.

2 Organisations may use work study techniques to establish the best way of doing a job.

3 All substantial organisations have some hierarchical structure within which decisions are made by those in authority, who in turn may be accountable to others.

4 The bigger the organisation, the more likely it is to be subdivided into different departments.

5 Line departments have primary responsibility for achieving an organisation's objectives; staff departments support and advise line departments.

6 Sole traders, partnerships, and many clubs and societies exist as unincorporated associations.

7 Trade union organisations receive special protection under the law when acting in furtherance of their legitimate interests.

8 Individuals may seek the advantages of incorporation by registering an organisation under the Companies legislation.

9 Incorporated bodies must act within their powers, otherwise the act will be *ultra vires*.

10 The principal advantages of a company over the partnership and sole trader are limited liability for shareholders and a greater potential for raising funds for future expansion.

11 Many public corporations are created by Acts of Parliament to manage an industry which has been nationalised.

12 The major advantage of public corporations is that basic industries can be operated for the national as opposed to private interest. However, they are sometimes accused of being unwieldly and inefficient, because they are monopolies and face little or no competition.

13 The special feature of central and local government organisations is that Members of Parliament and Councillors who undertake administrative responsibilities are elected.

14 The policy of the European Community is considered and put into effect through its institutions. The major institutions are the Commission, the Council, the European Parliament and the European Court of Justice.

15 Building societies, hospitals and charities are organisations that are subject to special legislation.

16 Co-operative organisations exist as consumer co-operatives by which goods are purchased at bulk rates and sold cheaply to members, or producer co-operatives by which goods and services are produced by organisations in which the employees are the shareholders.

17 Most disputes occurring in the business environment will be resolved by agreement between the parties, without the need to consult a lawyer or go to court.

18 Administrative tribunals and domestic tribunals are established to settle

disputes of a specialist nature without the need to resort to the ordinary courts.

19 Public inquiries serve an important function in the business community by enabling protestors against government proposals to register their objections before a final decision is made.

20 Resort to a civil court by obtaining a summons or a writ may be employed as a means of providing an ultimatum which, if effective, hastens a settlement out of the court.

21 Lawyers are divided in the English legal system into solicitors and specialists, called barristers, who argue cases before judges.

22 The elaborate system of courts developed in the English legal environment permits dissatisfied litigants to appeal to superior courts, which may overturn the trial judgment.

23 Most civil actions are settled before County Courts and most criminal actions are settled before Magistrates' Courts. These are distributed throughout England and Wales and serve their own districts.

24 A person arrested for a serious crime, called an indictable offence, must first be brought before examining magistrates who may commit him or her for trial before a Crown Court on being satisfied that there is a case to answer. Prosecutions are now undertaken by Crown Prosecutors.

25 A consequence of the entry of the UK into the EEC is that European Community law supersedes our own laws where there is a conflict. References on the interpretation of community law may be made to the European Court of Justice.

26 As case decisions form a source of English law, there exists a sophisticated system of recording and reporting legal decisions made, mostly, in the higher courts.

27 Certain free advice from a solicitor is available to persons with low incomes, and representation in court may be paid for by the State by issuing a Civil Aid Certificate or a Legal Aid Order.

Assignments, Part B

1

Your organisation

a Describe the departmental or divisional structure of the organisation in which you work or study.
Illustrate by diagram the chain of authority responsibility and accountability of people employed in the section or department in which you work or study.
b By drawing information from documents and/or oral statements, set out the principal objectives of the organisation in which you work or study.

Skills
Identifying and tackling problems, information gathering, learning and studying, communicating.

2

The legal system

Find out what courts and tribunals are located in your area. Working in small groups, visit the different types of court to experience the contrast between civil actions and criminal cases.

Prepare individually an accurate summary of two cases you have observed. As a small group provide an oral account to the rest of your class of your visit(s).

Skills
Information gathering, learning and studying, communicating, working with others.

3

Business expansion

Brian Small runs a general store in Sunhampton High Street as a sole trader. The business has been very successful, especially as his son was helping him to manage affairs. His son, Lawerence, believes that the methods they employ and the extension of their product line to include home leisure equipment based on micro-computer technology means that the business could be expanded. Their main suppliers are Electrofactor (Products) plc, and Lawrence knows they are interested in increasing their own production.

Should Lawrence and Brian consider altering the form of their business?

If so, what would be the advantages in forming another organisation, perhaps to accommodate a second retail outlet? Prepare a detailed account for them, setting out all the matters they need to have in mind and the procedures they would need to follow to form an appropriate type of organisation.

Skills
Identifying and tackling problems, information gathering, learning and studying, communicating.

4

You the consumer

This assignment requires you to keep a record of your spending on goods and services over a period of two weeks. From this information you may analyse your pattern of expenditure according to the type of organisations whose goods or services you consumed.

a Keep a diary of every item of your expenditure on goods and services over a period of two weeks. Be sure to include use of public sector services for which you might not have paid a direct price.

You will need to consider how best to classify this information accurately and effectively, especially given the requirements of **b**.

b Analyse the information gathered so as to draw comparisons and contrasts between your spending on different types of products and organisations.
Classifications you might consider could include
- goods as opposed to services;
- categories of product (e.g. food, leisure and entertainment, clothing, rent, travel, etc.);
- public as opposed to private sector organisations;
- within the private sector, classifications according to type of business unit where the expenditure took place (e.g. plc, partnership, etc.);
- imported as opposed to home produced.
You might also consider other suitable classifications.

c Write a commentary on your pattern of expenditure, illuminating main features you discover. Calculate proportions of your spending on different categories such as those above to illustrate your commentary.

Skills
Learning and studying, information gathering, communicating, numeracy.

PART C
A BUSINESS ORGANISATION

When you have read this part you should be able to:
- Identify the external factors which led to each stage in the company's growth.
- Recognise the effects of growth on the organisation's internal environment.
- Understand the way in which the internal and external environments interact.
- Describe how increased size encourages an organisation to organise its internal structure on hierarchical lines.
- Recognise the importance of specialisation by department or function.
- Understand the role of acquisition and merger as a mechanism for growth.

15 Electrofactor (Products) plc

The history of Electrofactor (Products) plc began when James Dodd left the army at the end of World War 2; he was 24 years old, and determined that from now on he wasn't going to take orders from anyone. The Army had given him a skill and a small gratuity, and he decided to use them to set up his own electrical repair business called J. Dodd (Electrical Repairs).

He set up his workshop in his mother's garage, and equipped it by spending some of his gratuity. He spent more of the money on a regular advertisement in the *Sunhampton Echo* and on some printed business cards for display in newsagents' windows, etc. The rest of his gratuity he spent on two months' rent for his workshop.

His first customer was a friend of his mother, whose electric cooker needed a new hot-plate. James repaired it quickly and efficiently and his customer was pleased with the standard of the service and recommended James to other people. What with personal recommendations, and responses to his advertisements, James was kept very busy, though he began to find that spare parts were often difficult to obtain. It seemed no time at all before he was using his skill to produce his own spares, or to recondition those which experience showed were in shortest supply.

By 1948, this part of the business had become so important that James had to employ Harry to undertake some of the repairs while James spent more time in the workshop.

Until now, James had been in complete control of all aspects of his business, and had been in direct contact with suppliers and customers, with the bank (he now had a deposit account in which he was trying to build up some capital), and with his landlady; he still rented his mother's garage even though he was married with a house of his own (Fig. 15.1).

When Harry joined him, James's direct contacts with his customers became less frequent. When he took on Joe to help in the manufacture of the spare parts, his control over the quality of the goods was diminished, and this too, altered his relationship with his customers to some extent (Fig. 15.2).

Fig. 15.1

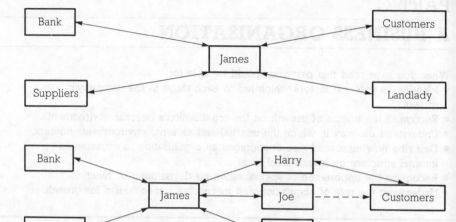

Fig. 15.2

By 1952, James and Joe had been joined in the workshop by Leslie, and they were producing parts for other electricians in Sunhampton. Meanwhile, James had also employed a young school leaver to work on repairs with Harry; John, at 15, was the youngest member of the team.

James's own work and responsibilities had also changed in the seven years since he first set up the business. He no longer saw his customers (they were dealt with by Harry and John), and the spares were now produced by Joe and Leslie. James's time was now spent in administration: he arranged the jobs for the day for the workers; he dealt with suppliers; he accepted and processed orders for spare parts; and he was spending more time dealing with the bank. He had, almost by accident, become a manager who was more concerned with planning, control, co-ordination, etc. than with operational issues such as producing a good (Fig. 15.3).

James's business had expanded quite considerably since 1945, both in terms of repairs and in manufacturing operations, and the old garage workshop was now too small. It was also rather inconveniently located if customers wanted to pop in with small goods for repair.

It was time, James felt, for a move to larger, more convenient premises in a more prominent position, preferably in Sunhampton High Street. This was one of the reasons why James had been seeing more of his bank manager; he had accumulated some capital and had decided to use it to move the business out of the garage. His capital alone was insufficient to

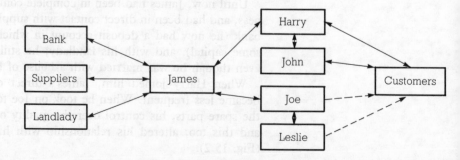

Fig. 15.3

cover the costs of a move, and he had been to ask his bank manager for advice about possible sources of finance.

James had two options open to him, and both required some capital:

1 He could look for an empty property to purchase, which would mean obtaining a bank loan which might cause a slight cash flow problem.

2 He could consider a partnership with Andrew Simpson, whose electrical retail and repair shop was located next door to Insurall in the High Street.

Andrew had bought spares from James's firm for some years and the two men had become friends. The subject of a partnership had already been discussed, initiated by Andrew, who, at 50 years old was keen to find someone to share the responsibility. James had been reluctant to commit himself at the time because he felt that he would find it hard to share in this way; he was his own boss, and he didn't want to lose the freedom which this gave him. On the other hand, there wouldn't be the problem of raising a bank loan, as Simpson's was in a good position in the High Street and there were workshops behind the shop. There was also some land on which James and Andrew had discussed the possibility of expanding the workshops.

Eventually, it seemed to James that a partnership might work well, since he and Andrew had different, complementary interests. Andrew could continue to run the shop and act as an agency for the repair of small appliances, while James could concentrate on manufacturing, meanwhile offering repairs and services on the goods sold by Andrew.

Each would bring some capital together with a considerable amount of goodwill into the partnership, and they would share the responsibility for managing the business, just as they would share the profits, liabilities, etc.

So, James and Andrew went to see Andrew's solicitors, Lore & Vice & Co who would draw up their deed of partnership. While they were talking to Mr Lore they sought his advice on how to obtain planning permission to build their extra workshops. Mr Lore was, at first, rather discouraging since he felt it was unlikely that planning permission would be granted. He suggested they should apply for a site on the industrial estate which had been established by Sunhampton Council in Dock Street, in an attempt to confine industrial development to clearly defined areas of the town.

In 1953, therefore, James found himself as one half of Simpson and Dodd Electricals, with a shop in the High Street and a manufacturing workshop (rented at a reasonable sum from the Council) on the Dock Street Industrial Estate, while his mother's garage, for so long the centre of his activities, had reverted to its original function and housed his mother's car.

Thus, a new era began for James: the changes in job content which he had experienced when his business began to grow were suddenly accelerated. The simple interaction between himself, the bank, suppliers, customers, etc. was no longer possible, any more than it was possible for him to spend much time on the factory floor. The combined workforce of Simpson and Dodd Electricals (which now included a number of new recruits who were needed if the manufacturing activities were to be expanded) meant that James could no longer personally supervise the whole workforce in Dock Street.

Fig. 15.4

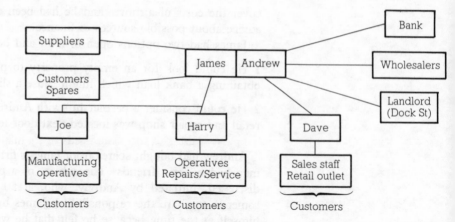

The merging of the two businesses has produced an organisation whose combined activities were more diverse, and James and Andrew had to decide how best to deal with this (Fig. 15.4). The obvious solution seemed to be through specialisation by each man, in those areas which interested him most. Andrew, thus, managed the retail outlet and also took responsibility for the firm's finances. He dealt with the accountant, with the bank, and he authorised payment of bills, including those incurred at the Dock Street site.

James on the other hand, was more involved in the activities at Dock Street. Although he was notionally in charge of repairs and servicing, James had long since delegated to Harry the authority for overseeing the operational or day-to-day aspects of this section. This allowed James to spend more time working closely with Joe on the manufacturing side. The firm was still mainly concerned with producing spare parts, though James had discovered that he had a talent for designing electrical appliances. Joe and his team had produced a prototype hairdrier from James's design, and Simpson and Dodd Electricals had now patented the design: they planned to retail the hairdrier initially through the firm's shop in time for Christmas 1954. If it was a success, they hoped to market it through other retail outlets as well.

Neither man regretted the decision to merge, since the partnership worked well, with each man retaining some autonomy while benefitting from the skill and expertise which the other had brought to the firm. Though James was at present the junior partner (Andrew had, after all, sunk more capital into their partnership), he was hoping, with the increasing importance of the manufacturing section, to increase his share of the profits.

Both found themselves less involved in the operational aspects of the firm, and more of their time was now spent in planning for the future. They were considering an expansion of their retail activities: the economic environment was more buoyant, and had brought greater spending power to working people who had more money to spend on luxuries. They were keen to improve their lifestyle and were buying electrical goods of all kinds – record players, radiograms, television sets and the new tape recorders which were being imported from Germany.

Simpson and Dodd Electricals had shared in this boom; the hairdrier had been a success and had been followed by a toaster, and there were other household goods in the development stage. Even the repairs and servicing section had increased to keep up with demand.

The partners were now confronted with strategic decisions affecting the long-term success of the firm. Clearly, the firm needed to expand: as its manufacturing base widened, the Dock Street site was becoming cramped. The firm was, in any case, no longer recognisable, as the number of employees grew to meet the needs of its manufacturing output. And as its output grew and the range of goods expanded, so a larger showroom was required to display what was available to the customers. It also seemed like a good idea to expand their retailing activities beyond Sunhampton, since there was a steady demand for their manufactured goods from shops all over the South-east.

It seemed then that the firm needed to increase its property holdings and its plant, and possibly to employ more staff, at least in retailing. However, any expansion seemed likely to precipitate other changes: an expanded manufacturing output needs an increase in marketing to improve the firm's market share; it may also need careful monitoring of the purchase of raw materials and of the levels at which spare parts, completed goods, etc. should be maintained. In short, there may be a need for expertise which is not available within the existing staff.

The partners agreed that the firm was doing well and that the time was indeed right to expand. However, with growth in turnover, etc. comes a parallel growth in liability and risk, so it also seemed a good time to change the status of the firm. By becoming a private limited liability company, they felt that they might be able to contain some of the risk. Consequently, in 1957, the newly named Electrofactor (Products) Ltd was formed, with Andrew and James as the major shareholders, taking equal shares. James's wife Mary, his children Ian and Ann, and Andrew's daughter Christine were the other shareholders.

James was to be the Managing Director and would continue to run the production and manufacturing section from Dock Street. This section as now known as Simdod Electrics, and the operation had taken over the factory space next door. Andrew would run the repairs and servicing function which would in future operate from the showrooms; he would continue to be responsible for the retail function, which had also been re-named as Simpson Dodd.

Two years later, the original showroom in Sunhampton High Street had become the administrative headquarters of Electrofactor (Products) Ltd, while a new larger showroom was opened at the other end of the High Street. There were also by now, three other showrooms: one on the outskirts of Sunhampton, another in Melbury, about 30 miles away, and the third in Netherton, which was about 40 miles away.

In theory, both partners were now based in Sunhampton High Street, together with most of the administrative staff. In practice, however, James still spent most of his time in Dock Street. The company had become so complex that James and Andrew relied more than ever on other people to ensure operational efficiency. Neither man had much direct contact with customers any more, and their contacts with suppliers were conducted more

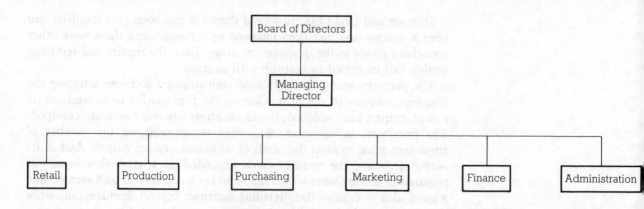

Fig. 15.5

frequently through intermediaries with delegated authority to act on behalf of the company.

By 1960, the company's organisation structure had been transformed. A perceptible hierarchy was now acknowledged to exist, headed by the Board of Directors; this itself had now been augmented by the various heads of the sections which had been formed in an attempt at rationalisation. The company was now organised on functional (or sectional) lines with each function headed by a director (Fig. 15.5).

There were 6 sections, each concerned with a specific function. However, two of the functions had additional areas of responsibility: the Production Section was responsible for co-ordinating research and development, while the Administration Section, in addition to providing secretarial and clerical services throughout the company, also dealt with personnel matters.

Over the next decade, Electrofactor (Products) Ltd continued to grow, helped in part by the continuing prosperity of the country, and the changing habits and lifestyles of the people. However, James's flair for design, and his ability to anticipate demand were also important factors; he identified early on the potential of the transistor, so that when the transistor radio became an important part of teenage life, Simdod Electrics had a range of models which Simpson Dodd were able to make available.

There was an increased demand for labour saving devices too, in the kitchen and in the home in general, as people continued to improve their lifestyles. As people bought more electrical goods, so Electrofactor (Products) Ltd acquired more showrooms; by 1965 Simpson Dodd was a prominent sight on many High Streets in the South-east of England, from Brighton to Reading.

The range of goods produced by Simdod Electrics had also expanded and the company had moved out of Dock Street and was now housed on the outskirts of Sunhampton, in a disused airfield which the company had acquired freehold in 1963. Production was currently being carried out in the converted hangars, though new buildings were being erected.

Electrofactor (Products) Ltd was also in the process of diversifying again, since the company hoped to increase its property holdings by developing the airfield as an industrial estate; they had sought, and been given, planning permission by Sunhampton Council, and on completion of their new factory buildings (which would cover about 60 per cent of the land) the hangars would be offered for rental as workshops.

In 1968 the company was once again in the throes of change. Its manufacturing base was in Sunhampton, while its products were sold throughout the United Kingdom. They had, until now, used the services of Unwin Karriers Ltd to deliver their goods, for which they were invoiced each quarter. By 1966, however, James and Andrew had already discussed the possibility of buying their own fleet of vans. At a subsequent board meeting, and on the advice of the Director of Finance, they had decided that it was too soon after the expenditure on the new factory; the idea was therefore shelved, though not entirely forgotten.

A year later, when James met Henry Unwin, the Managing Director of Unwin Karriers Ltd at a Rotary meeting, he was interested to learn that Henry was thinking of retiring. He was even more interested when he remembered that Henry and his wife had no immediate family to inherit the company.

The following day, James talked to Andrew (who was himself talking of retiring by now) and to the Director of Finance, and at the next board meeting it was agreed that James should approach Henry Unwin with a merger offer, in which Electrofactor (Products) Ltd shares would be offered in exchange for Unwin Karriers Ltd shares; Henry would join the board of the newly created company to ensure a smooth transfer of goodwill, etc. and some key personnel from Unwins would also join the new board.

The merger was agreed and in 1968 Unwin Karriers Ltd became the third division of Electrofactor (Products) Ltd, and since some of Unwin's assets consisted of property – mainly garages and warehouses, though there were some office premises too – it was felt that the time had come to create a property division to deal with the flats and offices which Electrofactor (Products) Ltd had acquired along with its retail outlets.

Electrofactor (Products) Ltd was now more and more a holding company, with the actual activity occurring at divisional level (Fig. 15.6).

Electrofactor (Products) Ltd entered the 1970s as a successful company, with a bright future. Indeed, James's only regret was at having had to accept Andrew's decision to retire from active business when he reached 65 in 1968. Though still healthy and fit, he wanted to withdraw from the centre of the action, while remaining on the board in a non-executive role. Once the merger with Unwin Karriers had been successfully completed, Andrew retired.

By 1970, Unwins had been successfully absorbed into Electrofactor (Products) Ltd and the company was doing well. It seemed to James to be a good time to review the company's position:

1 Electrofactor Properties now included van depots and warehousing in Sunhampton; several flats and offices above their shops; the Airfield Indus-

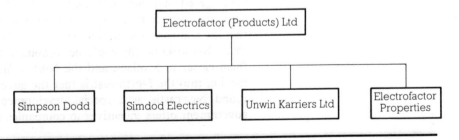

Fig. 15.6

trial Estate; and they had recently invested in a new shopping precinct currently being built in Sunhampton, thus ensuring a prime site for themselves together with several floors of office space to rent. The board had also been considering moving into the domestic housing market, and acquiring land to develop as housing units. Though James could see that there was indeed an increased demand for home ownership, privately he wasn't convinced that the company was ready for this.

2 Unwin Karriers Ltd was still carrying Simdod Electrics' goods to the nation's High Street stores. It was also taking advantage of the demand for road transport, and was providing a road haulage service for other companies. It had recently inaugurated an overnight delivery service for small parcels, and its future plans included offering a van and truck rental service. There had also been discussions about acquiring a small furniture removals firm, though as yet nothing concrete had emerged.

3 Simpson Dodd had been expanding slowly but steadily, so that there were showrooms all over the South-east; the acquisition of Dempsters of Merseyside had given them a substantial foothold in the North since their showrooms were to be found as far apart as Harrogate, Blackpool and Chester, with a toehold into North Wales in Wrexham.

Warehousing was still, by and large, in the South-east and the company was currently considering acquiring facilities a little nearer to the geographical centre of the country. Yorkshire had been suggested since this would give them better access to Scotland where, though they had no shops of their own, the company's products sold well.

4 Simdod Electrics was doing well and its products had obtained a reasonable slice of the home market. In addition, their export figures were also increasing in comparison with their competitors, to the delight of the board. They have high hopes of an expanding market with Britain's membership of the EEC. However, there are potential problems on the horizon, since membership of the EEC is a two-edged sword which cuts both ways; there has been an influx of electrical goods from the Continent, and the Italian company, Frigo, has begun to make inroads into the home market. The Japanese, too are beginning to be a threat and Simdod Electrics cannot afford to be too complacent.

James's solution to the increased competition is to introduce new products, and he is particularly keen to develop a home computer since his instinct tells him that this will be the next boom area; the board are not yet convinced that this is the right move.

Overall, then the Company's long-term prospects look reasonably healthy, and though they remain sceptical about home computers the board have agreed that there is a need to expand their research and development activities, and, hoping to kill two birds with one stone, they have decided that the company should find a site in the North-east of England. They feel that a R-and-D facility could be combined with warehousing, thus bringing them closer to Scotland and the North. Another convincing argument for moving into the North-east is that the government has designated the area round Newcastle as a special development area, which means that the government offers incentives to companies to move there.

James and some other members of the board have already been to Newcastle and have found somewhere which looked promising – a disused industrial estate with some usable factory units. Though some building would be necessary, the site was particularly attractive to James since there would be enough space for a small manufacturing plant as well as research and warehousing facilities. This was important to James since he was still hoping to talk the board round to his view on the matter of home computers. Over the years James had found himself in this kind of situation many times, and he had usually managed to get people to come round mainly by making sure that he was in total command of all the facts, being able to argue his case without losing his temper and by being able to counter other people's arguments without them losing face.

This particular talent had come to his aid in his many encounters with the trades unions which represented the workers at Electrofactor (Products) Ltd. James and Andrew had never been anti-union and the business had been unionised almost from the start. It wasn't a closed shop – and never would be while James had any say in the matter – but about 70 per cent of the workers were union members. James had sat down to negotiate with local union officials many times on a variety of issues; for example, quite early on, the firm had decided that it would pay its workers on a piece-rate system and this had led to a tough bargaining session with the local union officials. In the end, a compromise had been reached whereby the firm agreed to pay a basic rate (based on the figures agreed at national level during negotiations between the Federation of Engineering Employers and the Confederation of Engineering Unions) plus an additional bonus rate to be paid according to individual output.

There had also been some difficult discussions when the firm began recruiting women to work on the production line, especially when it became clear that many women preferred to work part-time. From the firm's point of view this made sense since:

a it gave them more flexibility in terms of hiring and firing,
b it cost them less in national insurance contributions etc.,
c they were able to keep up production levels by a more efficient use of machinery.

The unions saw it simply as a threat to the livelihood of the full-time workers, most (though not all) of whom were male.

This was now ancient history, and the company were employing more and more women. However, the work which the women did was, in general less skilled than that carried out by the men. An analysis of rates of pay might also show that the men tended to earn more than the women, even for comparable work. However, to some extent the employment legislation passed in the 1970s improved the situation and there has been no serious industrial disputes for some time, a fact for which James took some of the credit.

James knew that he was going to need all his negotiating skills if he were to persuade the board to agree to try and develop a home computer. Thus, while plans were going ahead to establish the new Research and Development Section in Newcastle, James got the Marketing Department to commission a survey on the potential market for home computers.

While waiting for the results of the survey James addressed himself to another problem. All through the 1970s competition from the Japanese and from the Continent had been increasing, and it had become clear that most of the competition had invested heavily in new methods of production, which were not as labour intensive as the traditional production line system which was, for the most part, still used by the company. Despite the cost of the initial investment in new production methods, in the long term, other companies were able to keep production costs low mainly through savings in the wage bills. Electrofactor (Products) Ltd was now encountering a price war, since its competitors were able to offer comparable goods at lower prices. This was James's most pressing problem, since he felt it was time to consider investing in new equipment; as this meant quite a large capital expense he was anticipating a tough time at the board meeting at which the matter was to be discussed.

James decided that his best tactic might be to try to present the need for a change to new technology and his plans to diversify into the home computer market as a package, on the assumption that if the company needed to raise capital, then it might as well raise enough to cover both. Armed with the sales figures and comparable data about their competitors, and a favourable report from the Marketing Department on the potential market for home computers, James went to the board meeting.

Some hours later, James emerged from the meeting with the board's agreement to pursue both policies. They had also agreed that the way to raise the capital required was for the company to seek to become a Public Limited Company, and they had authorised James to take the necessary steps.

Thus by 1979, the company had established its Research and Development Department in Newcastle, and plans to go public were well in hand; Electrofactor (Products) Ltd entered the new decade as Electrofactor (Products) plc. Unfortunately, however, for once, James's intuition let him down; the share issue was not as successful as he had hoped it would be; the world economy was fast sliding into a recession; while in the UK the inflation rate had reached double figures, which in turn had an adverse effect on production costs.

Imported goods became even more attractive to the home market and the export markets began to decline. Consequently the company found itself fighting for its market share, and for the first time in many years, 1982 saw a significant decrease in the company's profits. However, because they had anticipated this to some extent, the company had had its property holdings revalued, which did a little to increase its ostensible assets; it was also a preliminary to the business of offering some of them for sale, with a view to boosting the profits in the following year.

However such short-term and largely cosmetic activities did little but postpone the inevitable. James's plans had misfired: the investment in new production methods had been expensive and had come too late, while the boom in home computers had declined as fast as it had peaked leaving many casualties in its wake. The Electro, produced by Electrofactor (Products) plc in 1982 simply could not compete with the market leaders such as the Sinclair Spectrum with its wealth of software packages, games, etc.

In 1984, therefore, the Company bowed to the inevitable and agreed to a takeover by the Italian Frigo company. It was not the way in which James had hoped to enter the Continental market but he was now 63 and was beginning to think about retirement anyway. For this reason he took very little part in the negotiations, leaving them to younger people with more of a stake in the future.

Frigo was really only interested in the company's manufacturing capability and in its road haulage division; it was not keen to involve itself in the retail sector, and thus it announced its intention to sell off Simpson Dodd fairly early in the negotiations. Several senior executives of Electrofactor (Products) plc then decided to make a bid for what they considered to be a still potentially profitable part of the company; there had in fact been little loss of profit in this division and Simpson Dodd had built up a considerable reserve of goodwill over the years.

The executives managed to raise the capital, partly from sources in the City, but also by persuading many of the staff of Simpson Dodd to invest in the new venture; this was an attractive offer which many members of staff were happy to accept since it gave them a personal stake in a viable concern and would also allow them to share in the profits.

By 1985, therefore, Electrofactor (Products) plc had ceased to function as an independent organisation having been absorbed into the multinational activities of Frigo, while Simpson Dodd faced the future alone as a newly formed private limited company.

James, meanwhile, having taken very little part in the process emerged with some of the patents for his designs and tried to settle into retirement. It did not last long, however; he has recently been approached by a small firm who would like to manufacture some of his designs under licence. They have also told him that they would be interested in seeing any future designs which he may produce; James is now working from a workshop in his back garden and is currently interested in microwave technology!

Summary of the history of Electrofactor (Products) plc

1945	J. Dodd (Electrical Repairs) established.
1948	Business expands and James takes on more staff.
1952	Manufacturing activities expanded.
1953	Simpson and Dodd Electricals established.
	Factory rented in Dock Street.
1954	Simdod Hairdrier launched.
1957	Electrofactor (Products) Ltd established with two sections:
	Simpson Dodd
	Simdod Electrics.
1959	Shop moved to new High Street site; administrative headquarters established in old premises.
	Expansion of retail activities to Melbury and Netherton completed.
1960	Reorganisation of Electrofactor (Products) Ltd along functional lines completed.
1960–5	Continued expansion of retail outlets in South-east of England.
1963	Acquisition of airfield for development as new factory; planning permission granted for Airfield Industrial Estate.
1968	Merger with Unwin Karriers Ltd.
	Electrofactor (Products) Ltd reorganised along divisional lines:
	Simdod Electrics
	Simpson Dodd
	Unwin Karriers Ltd
	Electrofactor Properties.

1974	Acquisition of Dempsters of Merseyside.
1976	Plans to establish Research and Development Sections in Newcastle.
1978	Research and development and warehousing facilities established in Newcastle.
	Need to introduce new production methods recognised.
	Proposal to move into home computer production.
1979	Company plans to go public to finance new technology and development of home computer.
1980	Share issue announced on Stock Exchange.
	Electrofactor (Products) plc formed.
1982	Decrease in overall company profits.
	Revaluation of property holdings.
1983	Profits slightly boosted by sale of some property.
	Preliminary discussions with Frigo.
1984	Takeover of Electrofactor (Products) plc by Frigo agreed.
1985	Company absorbed by Frigo.
	Simpson Dodd Ltd established as an independent company.

PART D
THE ORGANISATION AND ITS NEEDS

When you have read this part you should be able to:
- Describe the various sources of finance for organisations.
- Understand the various legal constraints facing an organisation in its acquisition and use of resources.
- Understand the significance of information needs for an organisation.

16 Resources

At this stage we should ask just what are the various needs of our organisation if it is to produce its goods or services in an effective manner. What resources does an organisation require? How might it get them? Are there any physical limitations in the acquisition of resources, and what legal constraints are important when acquiring and using resources?

In order to meet its objectives it is crucial for an organisation to acquire the necessary quantity and quality of productive resources and use them efficiently. These ingredients for producing goods and services are sometimes called the **factors of production.**

Different organisations produce different goods and services in different ways. However, all organisations in the public and private sectors require finance in order to meet needs such as acquiring:

Land and **premises**
Capital goods like machinery, word-processors
Raw materials or component parts
Labour (which could be manual or non-manual)
Managerial expertise

In Part D we shall describe the nature, utilisation, means of acquisition and constraints on the use of these productive resources. We shall also consider the information needs of organisations, to aid effective planning and decision making.

The costs of production

The resources needed to produce goods and services seldom come free! Since goods and services can be produced in many different ways, a fundamental internal problem facing an organisation is to combine its inputs in such a way as to enable it to produce at the lowest possible cost. This combination is referred to as the **optimum** or **least cost** combination, and is achieved by using the cheapest factors of production in the most effective mix.

For example, the advent of cheaper computerisation has meant that many organisations have changed their methods of record-keeping, invoicing and wage payment. This use of silicon chip technology has reduced administration costs by providing speedier and cheaper systems.

$$\text{TOTAL COST} = \begin{cases} \text{FIXED COST} \\ \text{e.g. machines, premises} \\ \\ \text{VARIABLE COST} \\ \text{e.g. electricity charges,} \\ \text{weekly wage bill} \end{cases}$$

The total costs facing an organisation have two components – fixed and variable. **Fixed** costs are the costs of factors of production, which are fixed in quantity for the period under analysis. Therefore fixed costs do not change even when the organisation changes its level of output.

Variable costs are the costs incurred in the day-to-day running of the business. The quantity used of such factors of production varies with output. Thus, when the organisation expands output its variable costs increase.

Can you state the factors of production and their rewards?
What are the two functions performed by entrepreneurs?
Can you distinguish between fixed and variable cost?

17 Land and business premises

The law relating to land

Organisations of all types must occupy buildings and land which suit their particular activities. Land is a natural resource and as such may be occupied by an organisation in order to exploit the land itself. Such organisations may be concerned with farming, stone quarrying, coal mining, oil extraction or the collection of water in a reservoir. These organisations and others, such as those operating a railway network, require a substantial acreage of land. Urban areas, by contrast, have very large populations occupying a relatively small area. Here, organisations exploit the commercial expertise and enterprise available in the community.

The premises built on land are regarded as part of the capital stock used in the production of goods and services. Premises appropriate for industrial and commercial undertakings have been constructed over the centuries, and owing to the close co-operation between different organisations this has led to high density building. This is very true also for residential accommodation, where many of us live in flats and terraced housing. For us, as much as organisations, the occupation of land means the payment of rent to a landlord or repayment of a loan for the purchase of land.

What is the legal nature of land?

We have described the nature of land as a factor of production where, in the economic sense, land referred to a gift of nature.

To a lawyer, the word 'land' refers to more than just the soil. The term refers also to any structure built on the land, to fences and boundary walls, to things growing on the land, and to things below the land such as minerals. In fact the owner of land can be said to own the land itself, the airspace above it and the subsoil to the very centre of the Earth. The landowner may pass the legal title to his or her family on death, may allow someone to occupy it in exchange for the payment of rent, or may sell someone the right to be in possession for a term of years.

The origin of land ownership in this country dates back to 1066, when, after the conquest of England by the Normans, the Norman kings acquired

Fig. 17.1
Industrial premises in the North of
England

absolute ownership of the country. Recognition of loyal service to the king
was made by granting rights of occupation of parts of England to the
Norman knights. People who held land in this way were known as 'barons',
and the king demanded services from them such as the raising of armies
and the payment of taxes. The barons in turn demanded the services of the
English inhabitants, who then became tied to the land and to their respective baron. The system by which the king owned all the land and his
subjects occupied land subject to the performance of services is termed the
'feudal system'. Although these large baronial estates have been broken
down over many centuries into a vast number of small holdings, in theory
the Crown still *owns* the land comprising the United Kingdom.

**What are the types of
possession of land?**

Strictly, because the Crown is the true owner of land, every person claiming
to be a landowner is a tenant of the Crown. In practice though, a person

who has legal title to a piece of land is for all intents and purposes the only owner and may, subject to restrictions which we will examine, do with it what he or she wishes. However, that is not the end of the story, for the person holding the legal title to land may not be in possession of it. The possessor of the land may be an organisation or individual who pays a regular rent to the title holder, who may be another individual or another organisation like a local government authority. Alternatively the land may be occupied by someone who has purchased the right to possess the land for a period, say 99 years. At the end of this period the possession of the land returns to the owner. Our references to a landowner from now on apply as much to an organisation with legal personality as to an individual.

Freeholders

The owner of land is described as having what is called a 'legal estate' in the land, which is a right to be on the land. Under the Law of Property Act 1925 there are only two types of legal estates, what are commonly called **freeholds** and **leaseholds**. In law a freeholder is one who has, to use the legal terminology a 'fee simple absolute in possession'. These words denote the right of the owner to possession of the land for all time, passing the title to family or children for example, by making a will. The owner of the freehold may dispose of the interest by sale, or by granting a lease of part or all the land to someone else. Subject to the law, a freeholder is free to use the land in any chosen manner. Land, being a scarce resource, can only be obtained at a price, and the market price is such that it is beyond the finances of most people and organisations. Consequently, for many, the purchase of a freehold is only possible through the loan of the price of the land. Until the loan is repaid, after perhaps 25 years, the lender of the money has an interest in land.

How does an owner prove the title? Look at the facsimile of a Land Register in Fig. 17.2. Most of this country is composed of registered land, i.e. land which is recorded at HM Land Registry, which retains a central register of property. On the purchase of land from the owner, the purchaser's name will be entered on the register and is final proof that the person there recorded is the owner. In our illustration, the freehold land known as No. 11 Sunhampton High Street is at present owned by Arthur Things, the shopkeeper we introduced in Chapter 1. However, if we look at the third section of the register we can see that Arthur has had to borrow the purchase money from the Buyerpad Building Society, which has registered its interest in the land.

Leaseholders

The other type of legal estate is the leasehold or 'term of years absolute'. In contrast to a freehold title, the leaseholder has a limited right of possession of land, mainly to whatever term of years for which the lease has been created, such as 99 years, 200 years or 999 years. A leaseholder is so called because the formal document or deed is termed a 'lease', and contains the rights and obligations under which the person granted a lease holds the land. This deed will detail the various duties of treating the land properly, and observing restrictions on how the land may be used. The landlord (or landlady) for his (or her) part must ensure that the tenant has 'quite enjoyment' of the leased property. The Law of Property Act 1925 provides that a lease created for a term exceeding three years must be in

H.M. LAND REGISTRY

Edition 3 opened 1.3.1964   TITLE NUMBER 00002   *This register consists of* 2 *pages*

A. PROPERTY REGISTER
containing the description of the registered land and the estate comprised in the Title

COUNTY Sunhampshire   DISTRICT Sunhampton

The Freehold land shown and edged with red on the plan of the above Title filed at the Registry known as 11, High Street, Sunhampton.

registered on 12 October 1954

B. PROPRIETORSHIP REGISTER
stating nature of the Title, name, address and description of the proprietor of the land and any entries affecting the right of disposing thereof

TITLE ABSOLUTE

Entry number	Proprietor, etc.	Remarks
2.	Arthur Lawrence Things, Shopkeeper, of 11, High Street, Sunhampton, Sunhampshire, registered on 1 June 1970.	Price paid £15,000

Any entries struck through are no longer subsisting

TITLE NUMBER 00002   Page 2

C. CHARGES REGISTER
containing charges, incumbrances etc. adversely affecting the land and registered dealings therewith

Entry number	The date at the beginning of each entry is the date on which the entry was made on this edition of the register	Remarks
1.	1 March 1964-A Conveyance of the land in this title dated 30 September 1934 and made between (1) Jill Doe (Vendor) and (2) John Bull (Purchaser) contains the following covenant:- "The Purchaser hereby covenants with the Vendor for the benefit of the adjoining land known as 3, 5, 7 and 9 Station Road to observe and perform the stipulations and conditions contained in the Schedule hereto." THE SCHEDULE before referred to 1. No building to be erected on the land shall be used other than as a lock-up shop. 2. No building to be erected as aforesaid shall be converted into or used as flats, maisonettes or separate tenements or as a boarding house. 3. The garden ground of the premises shall at all times be kept in neat and proper order and condition and shall not be converted to any other use whatsoever.	
2.	1 March 1964-The part of the passageway at the side of the property included in the title is subject to rights of way.	
3.	1 March 1964-LEASE dated 25 July 1935 to Tim Ant for 99 years from 24 June 1935 at the rent of £45.	Lessee's title registered under 00003.
5.	1 June 1970-CHARGE dated 14 May 1970 to secure the moneys including the further advances therein mentioned.	
6.	PROPRIETOR-BUYERPAID BUILDING SOCIETY of 7, High Street, Sunhampton, Sunhampshire, registered on 1 June 1970.	

Any entries struck through are no longer subsisting

Fig. 17.2
A Land Registry entry

the form of a deed. Such leases are usually sold for the whole term of the deed, with only a small annual sum payable, called 'ground rent'. Look again at the title documents of Arthur Things, and you will see in the Charges Section that Entry 3 shows a lease taken by Tim Ant has been registered. Thus Arthur is the landlord of No. 11 Sunhampton High Street, part of whose premises are occupied by Tim for the remainder of the term of the lease. When Arthur bought the freehold in 1970, Tim's lease still had 64 years to run. Of course, Tim may at any time sell his lease to someone else for the remainder of the term.

Periodic tenancies

Not all leases have to be created by a deed, and as we have seen, leases with a term of less than three years need not be by deed. In fact these may be created by word of mouth, and a 'periodic tenancy' comes about with a tenant going into possession and the landlord receiving rent. A periodic tenancy may be created as a monthly or an annual one, although it may endure through continual renewal for many years.

Are there other interests in land?

A person or organisation holding either the freehold or leasehold may have with the basic title other interests and obligations. Examining Arthur's title documents again, in the Charges Section, we see that the first entry refers to an agreement (or 'covenant') dated 1 March 1964. The purpose of this agreement is to restrict the use and buildings of No. 11 Sunhampton High Street for the benefit of neighbours in the same block. If any building is used in a way prohibited by the covenant, the neighbours can ask a court to enforce the agreement. This type of agreement – a 'restrictive covenant' – was originally made between Jill Doe and John Bull, but it is not a *personal* agreement; it is intended to be part of the title and as such is a registered restriction. It therefore applies to Arthur and to anybody else who buys the freehold from Arthur. This agreement is one of the few which may be created by two parties to the original contract and yet bind a stranger to the agreement, like Arthur.

The second entry refers to a passageway at the side of the house, which is said to be subject to a 'right of way'. Obviously, the adjacent landowner has sought access to the back of the building along the passageway, and has at some stage in the past obtained a right of way. Again, these rights, known as 'easements' are usually registered as part of the title of the legal estate. Other easements are the 'right of support' and the 'right of light'. Thus, if Arthur's neighbour plans to demolish the building so as to withdraw support from Arthur's premises, or a neighbour builds an extension which blocks off the light to Arthur's conservatory or garden greenhouse, Arthur can complain. He may seek an injunction from a court ordering the neighbour not to infringe his easements.

Easements may be in a written form, granted formally by one landowner to a neighbouring landowner. Easements of this kind are called 'legal easements' owing to their being granted in a legal document, and will endure with the freehold or the leasehold estates of which they are a part. Thus a legal easement pertaining to a freehold will exist for ever, and because it has been created by formal document it will automatically pass with the title of the land. However, some easements may be taken to exist even though there has been no formal grant. For instance, adjoining landowners may enter into an agreement to create an easement of, say, a right of way. So long as there is some evidence that the parties wrote down the agreement, or alternatively that there is evidence the agreement was partly performed, as when someone has regularly used the right of way over a neighbour's land, an easement, will exist. Despite the fact that this particular right of way was not formally granted by the owner of land, it still has validity as what is termed an 'equitable easement'. The difference between a legal and an equitable easement is that the latter is valid only if the easement is registered. If it is not, and does not appear on the title deeds, the purchaser can ignore it.

Easements can also arise through long, continual use, so that if the person claiming a right over a neighbour's land can show it has been used for 20 years there is a right to it. Thus, when the owner of a freehold complained to a court that his neighbour's plan to build an extension to his house would block off the light to his greenhouse, the court granted the owner an injunction. He had built the greenhouse in 1957, and so had acquired the 'right to light' by long usage (Allen v. Greenwood 1978).

Charges

The way in which the lender of money for the purchase of land, such as a building society or a local authority, can seek protection for the loan is to have an interest registered against the title. This is registered as a 'charge'. We can see that the Buyerpad Building Society has registered a charge on Arthur's title documents, so that any prospective purchaser interested in buying the property is made aware of the society's hold over the property. In effect, the lender may be regarded as the real proprietor of the land, and remains so until the loan has been paid off. However, the lender has only an interest in the land, while the borrower owns the legal estate.

Mortgages

This form of financing for the purchase of land is known as a **mortgage** whereby the lender, or **mortgagee**, acquires a right over the borrower's, or **mortgagor's**, land by way of security. At any time before the final payment is due, the mortgagor may repay the outstanding amount. On the other hand, the mortgagee may apply to a court to end the mortgage if the mortgagor fails to make repayments. If the court approves this move, the whole of the legal estate comes into the ownership of the mortgagee.

As with easements, there may exist what are called 'equitable mortgages', the term used when the mortgage is not created by formal deed. These will be recognised if either the borrower or the lender have written evidence of the agreement or have shown by their conduct that there is an agreement. Such conduct might, for example, be that the borrower has deposited the title deeds with the lender. Again, as the interest is an equitable one, it must be registered as a charge against the particular land.

A mortgagor may sell the legal estate, but of course must repay the mortgagee any outstanding sum out of the proceeds of the sale. The mortgagor may also seek to raise a second mortgage on the land, a procedure often employed by persons who wish to raise capital to establish a business.

Holding land on trust

There is another type of ownership of freehold or leasehold land. It may be held under a **trust**. A trust is a device created by *equity* whereby any type of property, be it land, company shares or bone china figures, is held by persons called **trustees** on behalf of others known as **beneficiaries**. You will most commonly come across a trust when you are asked to make a donation to charity. These charitable trusts were described in Chapter 6.

Trusts are useful in that they make it possible for the legal title of property to be held by persons, not for their own benefit but on behalf of others. This may happen if a child under 18 years of age is made a gift of land the title of which he or she is too young to hold. Until the child reaches the age of 18, the legal title to the land is put in the name of adults, perhaps the child's parents. In the meantime the child does own something, mainly the right to have the land placed in his or her name in the future. This right is called an 'equitable interest'.

We also saw that an 'unincorporated association' like a local club or society lacks a legal personality and therefore cannot own land in its own name. A solution to this difficulty would be the creation of a private trust so that at least two of the association's members have the association's premises placed in their name, not, however, for their own personal benefit but on behalf of the association's members. If the trustees use the property for their own personal benefit in breach of the trust, the beneficiaries may complain to a court.

Are there any special tenancies?

So far we have discussed the two types of legal estates in land, freeholds and leasehold, and also certain other interests in land. Perhaps over 40 per cent of premises are occupied by persons or organisations who purchase neither the freehold nor the leasehold of premises. Rather, they pay a regular rent under various types of tenancy agreements. The landlord of such tenants may hold either the freehold or a leasehold of the land.

Private tenancies

Much of the law concerning tenants of private landlords is to be found in the Rent Act 1977 and also in the Housing Act 1980. Other tenancies arise where the landlord is a local authority, and in this respect the Housing Act 1980 gives tenants the right to purchase their home from the authority. Another form of tenancy arises where a group of persons interested in purchasing a home form a 'housing association' registered under the national Housing Corporation. In the latter two cases the lettings are referred to as 'secure tenancies'.

The most common form of private letting is called a 'regulated tenancy' (i.e. subject to the Rent Act 1977), whereby the whole or part of a house, flat, maisonette or bungalow is let for a rent. Generally the Rent Act applies to premises with a rateable value not exceeding £1500 in Greater London or not exceeding £750 elsewhere. The most important right of a regulated tenant is to be charged a 'fair rent'. This is a rent which is fixed by a Rent Officer and is recorded in the local Rent Register. Once it has been fixed, the landlord may not charge a rent above the one recorded. Either a landlord or a tenant can apply for an assessment of a fair rent, and if there is an objection to the rent fixed by the Rent Officer, a Rent Assessment Committee will decide what is a fair rent.

A new form of tenancy subject to the Rent Act 1977 was introduced by the Housing Act 1980 and is called a 'shorthold'. Here the private landlord lets the property for a fixed term, at a fair rent, of between one and five years. The tenancy ends when the term for which it is granted is up.

In the case of all these tenancies, the only way in which the landlord can regain possession of his property, is by seeking an order of possession from a County Court.

There is a form of tenancy which is not subject to the 'fair rent system' we have described. If the landlord and the tenant live in the same flat or house the tenancy is called a 'restricted contract' tenancy. However, it is possible for either the landlord or the tenant to apply to a Rent Tribunal for the fixing of a reasonable rent. As with the other tenancies, the landlord must seek the aid of a court if he or she wishes to eject the tenant.

At the conclusion of 1987 the government introduced a Housing Bill which on becoming law would substantially affect this area of discussion. The proposal would deregulate private rents by introducing a new concept of 'market rents' for new lettings. Tenants would be allowed to opt out of council control and seek a private landlord or form a tenants' co-operative. Housing associations would be extended. 'Assured tenancies' would allow landlords to increase rents, while shorthold tenancies would allow them to reclaim property after six months.

Agricultural tenancies

Because the encouragement of agriculture is regarded as important for the UK economy, the Agricultural Holdings Act 1948 sets our protection for tenant farmers. The protection afforded is to limit the free exercise by the landlord of giving a tenant farmer notice to quit. If the tenant farmer can therefore feel secure in the tenancy there is more likelihood of investing money in improving the quality of the land and buying stock. Notice to quit an agricultural holding must be at least one year.

Business tenancies

The same purpose is sought by the Landlord and Tenant Act 1954 Pt. II, which aims to protect business tenants who may be particularly vulnerable. After all, the tenant will have established an enterprise, perhaps requiring expensive alterations of the premises, and will have acquired the goodwill of clients. It would not be fair if all this was lost, because the landlord was able to rent the premises at a more favourable rent to someone else. Under the Act, therefore, the landlord can terminate the tenancy only upon giving proper notice to the tenant of at least six months. Moreover the tenant may counter this notice and apply to a court for a new tenancy. If the court considers that the tenant should be protected it may supervise the creation of a new tenancy.

Can the owner of land use it without restriction?

Have you already noticed that the mere fact that a person, like Arthur Things, is registered as the owner of land may make him subject to certain restrictions? For example, Buyerpad Building Society has a hold over the land which does not cease until the mortgage is repaid. A neighbour has a right of way over the passageway at the side of Arthur's house. Arthur became automatically restricted in what changes he might propose to make, when he bought No. 11 Sunhampton High Street, owing to the registered restrictive covenant.

Planning restrictions

Local authorities have various powers which restrict the owner of property in making structural alterations to the building. Thus the building of a garage, a loft extension or alterations to the front of a dwelling may only be undertaken with the authority's permission. If such alterations are made by the occupier without planning permission, the authority may order the occupier to return the premises to their original condition. Similarly, if the occupier wishes to alter the use of the property, say from a travel agency to a petrol station, such change of use may only be undertaken with local authority planning permission. Even a person's fence at the front of a house may not be built to a height of more than one metre.

The relevant law is the Town and Country Planning Act 1971, the Town and Country (Amendment) Act 1972 and the Town and Country Amenities Act 1974. These Acts make local authorities responsible for planning in their counties or districts under the auspices of the Department of the Environment. Each authority is required to prepare development plans for its area based on forecasts for the use of land for residential, commercial and industrial purposes. Included in this is improvement of the environment and traffic management. Proposals for development have to be submitted to the Secretary of State for the Environment and must be made known to the relevant community, with an opportunity for local people to object. If the proposals are controversial, a public inquiry may be held which can receive objections to the plan. If the plan is approved by the Secretary of State, the authority may seek the compulsory acquisition of the land affected, in effect, the authority enabling to purchase it from its owners. Any disputes that arise are resolved, not by the law courts but by the Lands Tribunal (see Chapter 14, p. 107). Planning legislation also seeks to protect the environment by preserving buildings of special interest and trees and by prohibiting the creation of unsightly buildings and advertising hoardings. Thus, local planning authorities may issue a 'tree preservation order' to preserve a forest – or even a single tree. The Secretary of State has also the duty of compiling a list of buildings of special architectural or historic interest, and once so listed a building may not be demolished by its owner.

Restrictions on the use of minerals

It has long been the rule at common law that the owner of land may not own things on or under the land if they constitute a 'treasure trove'. Any gold or silver which is found *hidden* in a house or in the earth, the owners of which are unknown, belongs to the Crown. The finders of treasure trove must hand over their find to the Crown, but they may be compensated. This is what happened when a couple came across two sixteenth-century gold coins in 1980. As there was evidence that the coins had been hidden by their original owner the coins belonged to the Crown. However the finders were paid £450 compensation by the Crown. If the gold or silver is taken to be *lost* by the owner, rather than hidden, the finder may keep the find because it would not be treasure trove.

The landowner is further restricted by statutes in the use of minerals on the land. By the Royal Mines Act 1688 all gold and silver in mines belongs to the Crown. The Crown owns any petroleum existing in its natural condition by the Petroleum (Production) Act 1934, while all coal found under land belongs to British Coal by virtue of the Coal Industry Nationalisation Act 1946. The Secretary of State for Energy has power to take over any uranium or plutonium found on land by a power granted under the

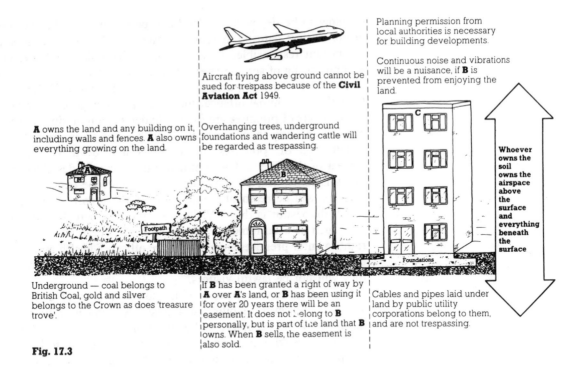

Planning permission from local authorities is necessary for building developments.

Continuous noise and vibrations will be a nuisance, if **B** is prevented from enjoying the land.

Aircraft flying above ground cannot be sued for trespass because of the **Civil Aviation Act** 1949.

A owns the land and any building on it, including walls and fences. **A** also owns everything growing on the land.

Overhanging trees, underground foundations and wandering cattle will be regarded as trespassing.

Whoever owns the soil owns the airspace above the surface and everything beneath the surface

Underground — coal belongs to British Coal, gold and silver belongs to the Crown as does 'treasure trove'.

If **B** has been granted a right of way by **A** over **A**'s land, or **B** has been using it for over 20 years there will be an easement. It does not belong to **B** personally, but is part of the land that **B** owns. When **B** sells, the easement is also sold.

Cables and pipes laid under land by public utility corporations belong to them, and are not trespassing.

Fig. 17.3

Atomic Energy Act 1946. Water in a pond or a lake belongs to the owner of land, but only the bed of a river may be owned, the flowing water being ownerless: although the landowner may extract water (and also fish) for his own purposes. However, the owner of land must generally have a licence to abstract water percolating beneath the land under the Water Resources Act 1963.

Public utility services supplying water, electricity, gas and telephone communications in pipes located under the land (and within dwellings) do not belong to the landowner, but are the property of the appropriate organisation (see Fig. 17.3).

What statutory duties are imposed on landowners?

First, a statutory duty is imposed on those who undertake work in connection with the provision of a dwelling by the Defective Premises Act 1972. The work must be done in a professional way and using proper materials, so that the dwelling will be fit for habitation. This duty is owed to any person who later acquires the dwelling. Moreover a landlord who owes a duty of maintenance to a tenant also owes a duty to any persons who might be reasonably expected to be affected by defects in the premises. If the local authority finds a dwelling to be unfit for human habitation, it has power under the Housing Act 1957 to make an order to close the house or to demolish it.

Under the Health and Safety at Work Act 1974 (see Employment section in Chapter 19) the owners of work premises may be criminally liable for failure to observe their duty to ensure, as far as is reasonably practicable, a safe place of work. They have this duty towards employees as well as those who might be affected by the activities at the work-place.

The Control of Pollution Act 1974 places a duty on persons not to deposit or allow to be deposited on land any poisonous or polluting waste. If any person suffers damage thereby, the Act gives a right of civil action against the person responsible. As regards excessive noise, as for example in the ground testing of aero engines, the local authority has powers to investigate and serve a notice requiring abatement of the noise. Failure to comply is treated as a criminal offence, for which the wrongdoer may be fined.

Occupiers of premises are further under a common duty of care to certain persons entering their premises. If such a person is injured as a result of a defect on the premises, the occupier may be liable for negligence in respect of the defect. The common duty of care is described by the Occupier's Liability Act 1957 as such care as could be expected to ensure that a visitor will be reasonably safe in using the premises for the purpose for which the visitor is there. Visitors are those persons lawfully on the premises, such as a customer in a shop, a house guest, or anyone with a legal right to enter premises such as a police officer, a health and safety inspector or an electricity or gas company official. If the last go beyond their duties they will not be lawful visitors.

Generally, the occupier owes no common duty of care to trespassers. There is, however, liability to a trespasser who is injured in a mantrap installed by the occupier, and apart from this, there is a 'humanity duty' to trespassers who the occupier either knows or ought to know might enter the premises, if there are dangers on those premises. This will be particularly so in respect of child trespassers who might be allured to the premises, say, because demolition workers on a site have built a fire. When a small child was injured on a railway line when taking a short cut home through a neglected and dilapidated fence, the occupiers were held liable. Although the child was a trespasser, the occupiers owed a duty to those children who might have been attracted to cross the railway line (British Railways Board v. Herrington 1972). This decision is incorporated now in the Occupiers Liability Act 1984, so that an occupier owes a duty of care to trespassers if he or she is aware (or ought to be) of dangers that might harm trespassers where protection against the danger might reasonably be undertaken.

Can a neighbour restrict an owner's use of land?

There are further reasons why owners of land cannot do what they wish on their own land. The judges, over the centuries, have developed common law rights for owners of land, to enable them to prevent interference with their enjoyment of the property. An adjoining landowner must not use the land so as to commit a 'tort' against another.

Private nuisance

For instance, someone who cannot enjoy their land owing to the unreasonable activities of an adjoining landowner may pursue a civil action in the **tort of nuisance**. The tort is committed by any person whose act unlawfully interferes with an owner or occupier's enjoyment of their own land. If the unlawful activity causes an owner of land some damage, the latter may pursue an action before the courts for either an injunction or compensation. In order to succeed the person complaining must prove that the nuisance was continuous. So, when one person complained that cricket balls from an adjoining club were a nuisance, the fact that this happened about 6 times in 30 years prevented the court regarding it as a nuisance (Bolton v. Stone 1951). However, when cocks crowed for a number of weeks in a residential area, the disturbance was held to be a nuisance (Leman v. Montague 1936).

The activity complained of must be unreasonable and substantial enough to merit a complaint. A company which operated a copper smelting plant in an industrial area was sued by an occupier of premises just over a mile away for nuisance from vapours which destroyed trees and shrubs on his land. Although the activity took place in an industrial area, the court decided that the emission was unreasonable and was an actionable tort (St Helen's Smelting Company v. Tipping 1865). Similarly, Mr Halsey succeeded in an action for nuisance when clothes hung out in his garden and the paintwork on his car were damaged by acid smuts emitted from a company's chimney, and also the pervasive pungent smell and the night-time noise of machinery caused substantial discomfort (Halsey v. Esso Petroleum Company 1961).

The fact that either a person or property are unusually sensitive may or may not be relevant to the reasonableness of the annoyance. When the owner of premises in which abnormally sensitive brown paper was stored brought an action against a neighbour who, as a result of heating his cellar, caused damage to the paper, the complainant failed to prove nuisance (Robinson v. Kilvert 1889). If on the other hand the annoyance is caused out of spite, then conduct may amount to nuisance. There was held to be a nuisance when a person clattered pots and pans whenever his neighbour gave music lessons (Christie v. Davey 1893). When, out of malice, Mr Emmett fired guns near a farm breeding foxes and so caused them to miscarry, the farm owner was granted damages and an injunction against the nuisance (Hollywood Silver Fox Farm Company v. Emmett 1936).

Even if the annoyance has resulted from natural causes, there may be liability for nuisance. This is what a court decided when land controlled by the National Trust caused damage to the property of neighbours. Earth, soil and tree stumps had fallen on neighbouring land when the bank of an ancient hill subsided owing to natural causes (Leakey v. National Trust 1978). Tree roots growing under neighbouring land were also held to constitute a nuisance (Butler v. Standard Telephones and Cable Company 1940).

Only a person with some title to the land may sue the creator of a nuisance, especially in view of the fact that the tort concerns an interference with the landowner's use or enjoyment of land. This means that the occupier's family, guests or lodgers may not sue in the tort of nuisance. We can see this in the case of Malone v. Laskey 1907 when the wife of an occupier was unsuccessful in her legal action against a neighbour. Machinery used by the latter caused vibrations, which resulted in a water tank supported on a bracket in a lavatory falling and injuring Mrs Malone.

Damaging escapes from land

Sometimes if a person keeps something on the land which would not naturally be there, such as electricity or gas, sewage, artificial lakes or chemicals, and these escape, that person will be liable for any damage so caused. Liability is based on the 'escape' of a thing which is likely to cause harm to another. For these purposes it does not usually matter that the keeper of the thing was not actually negligent or careless or had no wrongful intention. It is sufficient that something has escaped from land and caused damage to someone.

This principle of liability without fault was formulated in the case of Rylands v. Fletcher 1866. Rylands brought an action against Fletcher, who had employed independent contractors to construct a reservoir. Neither Fletcher nor his contractors could have known that water would escape into a disused mine shaft and then flood the mine shaft controlled by Rylands. The court decided that despite the absence of fault on the part of Fletcher, nonetheless there was an escape of something, water, which was not naturally on the land, resulting in damage to another person. Fletcher was found to be strictly liable for the escape, for it was something which if it did escape would result in damage.

The 'thing' which escapes may also be persons, so the controller of a caravan site was subjected to an injunction owing to the damage caused to a neighbour when caravan dwellers committed nuisances on the latter's land (Attorney General v. Corke 1933).

The rule in Rylands v. Fletcher will not be employed in cases where there has been no actual escape. When a person was injured by the explosion of a shell, while on the premises of a site controlled by the Ministry of Supply, there was held to be no escape (Read v. J. Lyons Company 1947). Here the injured person might have succeeded in a civil action in the tort of negligence based on the case of Donoghue v. Stevenson 1932 (see p. 31).

Trespass on land

A person who, without lawful authority, enters upon land or buildings in the possession of another commits the **tort of trespass** to land. Trespass to land takes place either when someone enters on land or leaves anything on the land without authority. The tort supports the general principle of the landowner's entitlement to exclude others from the land. Moreover, unlike other torts such as negligence, nuisance and the rule in Rylands v. Fletcher, the person bringing the complaint need not show any actual damage to the land.

Trespass is not only committed by personal entry on another's land without authority, as when a fox hunter trespassed on another's land in pursuance of a fox and was held responsible for the wrong (Paul v. Summerhayes 1878). Leaving rubbish on another's land also amounts to a trespass. This is what a court decided when hearing a complaint about a builder who left all the rubbish from demolishing part of the building on the premises (Konskier v. Goodman (B) Company 1928). Another builder, who worked from his own home, was held to have committed a trespass when he rested planks, building materials and ladders against his neighbour's wall (Westripp v. Baldock 1938).

You will remember that the owner of land also owns the airspace above it. In Fig. 17.3 you will see that B's tree overhangs into A's airspace; can A sue B in trespass? The answer to this may be found in the case of Lemmon v. Webb 1895, where Mr Lemmon was found to have a right to lop off overhanging branches because they constituted a trespass. While this was so, the branches still belonged to Mr Webb. In another case a large cigarette advertising sign which projected into a neighbour's airspace was held to be a trespass (Kelsen v. Imperial Tobacco Company 1957).

You might think that if there can be an interference with a landowner's airspace, aircraft must commit a trespass when flying through people's airspace. Although strictly aeroplanes do commit a trespass (and nuisance), in order to permit air flights the Civil Aviation Act 1949 denies persons legal actions. The Act prevents actions in the tort of trespass or nuisance in respect of flights by civil aircraft flying at a reasonable height. Flights by aircraft in the service of the Crown are also exempted from liability by the Crown Proceedings Act 1947.

If a person who is lawfully on premises does something which is contrary to the purposes permitted, that person may become a trespasser. Mr Harrison went on to a path, not for the purpose of using it as a highway but purely to frighten off grouse and so prevent the landowner from shooting them. As his purpose was unlawful, the court decided that he was a trespasser (Harrison v. Duke of Rutland 1893). It should be said that the public's rightful use of the Crown's highway is limited to passing and repassing. The use of the highway to dump rubbish or to obstruct it in any way will not be regarded as reasonable and may be a public nuisance.

Persons entering premises under a lawful authority will not be regarded as trespassers. So, two police officers were not trespassing when they entered premises to arrest a person for whom they had been issued an arrest warrant. They were trespassers, however, when they also seized documents because they had no lawful authority to do so (Elias v. Pasmore 1934).

A person who uses a right of way over neighbouring land in exchange for allowing the neighbour to trespass his or her land will not be a trespasser. This may be so even though the right of way has not been registered as an 'easement'. In E.R. Investment Company v. High (1967) the builders of a block of flats had built the foundations so that they encroached under Mr High's land. In exchange the company allowed him to use a short cut over their land, and even watched while he built a garage to take advantage of the right of way. When the flats were sold to E.R. Investments they tried to sue Mr High for trespass. They failed because even though the right of way had not been registered, the original owners had allowed Mr High to cross their land, owing to their own trespass (see Fig. 17.3, in which C's building trespasses under another's land), and he could not be sued.

Look further at Fig. 17.3. Suppose that farmer A's livestock were to roam on to B's property, would A be liable to B? The answer is provided by the Animals Act 1971, which states that owner of livestock is legally liable for any damage the animals do to another's property. This will be so even though the owner of the livestock was not at fault for their escape.

Criminal trespass

Is there any criminal liability for those persons who trespass on land? **Burglary** will be committed (under Theft Act 1968) by a person who enters a building as a trespasser with the intention to steal or damage property. There will be an **unlawful entry** if persons seek to gain entry to a building by the use of force or violence, and they may be punished under the criminal law (Criminal Law Act 1977).

The Public Order Act 1986 contains a section giving the police powers to direct trespassers to leave land unlawfully occupied, in certain circumstances. This goes beyond the usual right of landowners to seek eviction of trespassers by recourse to the civil courts.

Must land be sold in any particular way?

Land is not like other property, and so the law lays down strict rules concerning the sale and purchase of land. An organisation may wish to acquire either freehold or leasehold premises, and the purpose of the legal rules is to ensure that good title is obtained to the land. The method of transferring land is called a **conveyance**.

The most important stage is to obtain finance for the purchase of premises, either through a building society or local authority mortgage or through a bank loan. At the preliminary stage the prospective purchaser may wish to show an *interest to buy*, subject to certain negotiations. The parties will not at this point wish to be contractually bound. The purchaser will want to arrange a survey on the state of the property, so as to assess whether the asking price is fair. We have seen that local authorities may plan for commercial, residential or cultural developments, and so the purchaser will want to examine any proposals, in case the premises for sale are due to be redeveloped. There are certain questions the purchaser will want answered about the land, which only the vendor knows. If all this is satisfactory, and finance is also made available, the parties may be ready to be legally bound.

A legally binding agreement then follows, when the purchaser and the seller *exchange contracts*, that is, duplicate agreements setting down the details of the sale including the price. The transfer of title is not yet complete. Now, the purchaser will seek authority to search the seller's title, and will see a copy of the Land Registry entries, much as we observed when we discussed Arthur Thing's title. Not all land is yet registered, and where it is not the purchaser need only search the title for the past 15 years of ownership. Eventually all land in England and Wales will be registered at H.M. Land Registry. The purchaser may then ask further questions about the property; for example he will want assurance that the seller's mortgage in favour of, perhaps, a building society will be paid off when title is transferred. In the meantime the purchaser's building society will prepare a charge document (see above p. 145), which it will seek to have registered against the purchaser's title. Before completion, the purchaser will make a final Land Registry search to ensure that nothing has affected the seller's title in the meantime, and to ensure also that the purchaser can be registered as the new owner. Finally, at *completion*, the appropriate cheques are handed over, the mortgage documents are signed by the purchaser, and once the transfer document is signed the property is conveyed to the new owner.

It is wise for purchasers and sellers to be advised by solicitors in the conveyancing of land.

The location of industry

The choice of a suitable location is another crucial decision an organisation must make. An appropriate site and premises helps to reduce the total costs of the organisation and facilitate contact with customers.

A range of the influences affecting the choice will be considered below. Not all of the following points are relevant to every organisation. You might consider which factors are most relevant to the location of the organisation in which you work or study. Note that sites may be advantageous in some ways but undesirable in others. Thus, the decision on location involves weighing up the maximum net advantages of different sites.

Transport costs

Transportation cost of raw materials
(inputs)

FACTORY

Transportation cost to market outlets
(outputs)

As a locational influence transport has two distinct and significant dimensions: first, the transportation of raw materials to the factory and secondly, the conveyance of finished products to the market outlets.

The task facing the organisation is, therefore, to calculate whether it would be cheaper to set up production near a source of raw materials and power, for example near a port or a coalfield, or alternatively would it be cheaper to locate the organisation within or near the confines of a large market area such as London and South-east England? Obviously, this decision will be influenced by the relative weight and bulk of inputs and outputs, affecting transport costs.

The development and use of electricity as the prime source of power has made the location decision much more flexible for many organisations, which in years past were dependent on raw materials as a source of power. Furthermore, improvements in the motorway network have also helped to reduce transport costs and increase the speed of delivery.

Thus proximity and access to major urban markets has become more feasible in this century. Since the 1920s and 1930s, emerging consumer goods industries have often been located in the South-east or the Midlands, near the big urban conurbations.

Nevertheless, for some organisations using bulky materials, location near sources of the raw material is still important; e.g. oil refineries are coastal so that deliveries from oilfields do not have to be transported inland; wine is made very near vineyards.

Availability of labour

A supply of labour in an area could be important for an organisation, particularly if the labour possessed necessary skills. However, in many organisations operating division-of-labour techniques a large number of jobs can be unskilled or semi-skilled, thus allowing a more flexible choice of location.

Furthermore, some firms might hope to attract labour to an area chosen for its other advantages. For example, much of the housing in the Dagenham area was built as a result of Fords setting up their plant there in the 1930s. The prime advantages of the site were its coastal location proximity to the major market of London.

Accessibility and cost of a site

The centre of a city would be an ideal site in terms of proximity to the market for a firm selling consumer goods or services. However, the cost of premises would be very high. A more remote location would doubtless mean a cheaper site, but that would have to be offset against problems of accessibility and greater transport costs.

Localisation

Some organisations establish themselves in areas which have specialised in their particular activity. Ancillary services are likely to be located there, the labour force will have a tradition of working in that industry, and local banks and insurance companies will be associated with it. Northampton, for example, is noted for the production of shoes. Many organisations in the motor industry concentrated in the Midlands, an area that had a tradition in engineering.

Government influences – regional policy

Various governments have introduced policies to influence firms to settle in areas of high unemployment. Government aid to attract industry to such areas arose out of the national and international depression of the 1930s, when conditions in the regions were exacerbated by the decline of basic industries. The heritage of the regional problem is illustrated by Table 27.3 (Chapter 40), which quotes statistics on regional unemployment.

There are 4 major strands of regional policy.

1 The main initiative pertaining to regional policy in recent years involved the changes introduced in November 1984.

There are two categories of assisted areas – **development areas** and **intermediate areas** – as shown in Fig. 17.4.

Organisations setting up or expanding in development areas (though not intermediate areas) are eligible for **regional development grants** from the government, which contribute towards the cost of buildings, plant and machinery.

The grants are payable at a rate of 15 per cent of the capital cost of the project provided there is a suitable level of employment created. Alterna-

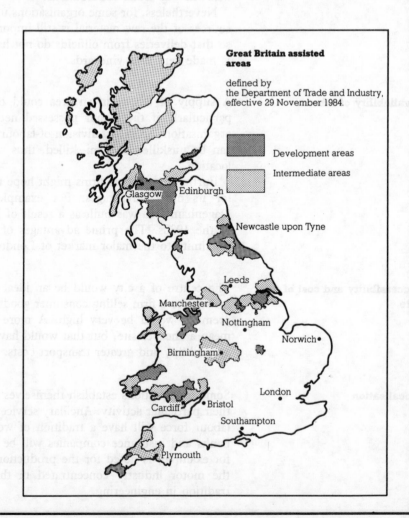

Great Britain assisted areas

defined by
the Department of Trade and Industry,
effective 29 November 1984

Development areas

Intermediate areas

Fig. 17.4
Source: *British Business* 30
November 1984

tively, there could be a grant of £3000 for each new job created by the project. The applicant organisation would receive whichever was the larger amount from the government.

As in intermediate areas, the government may offer selective assistance at negotiable rates in development areas for projects which bring regional and national benefit and create or safeguard employment. Grants are also available towards training costs of an approved project.

An example of such selective assistance occurred in the late 1970s when the government contributed £70 m of the cost of setting up and equipping the engine plant built by Ford at Bridgend in South Wales. Ford were considering other parts of Europe such as Spain, but the level of regional aid offered helped to swing the decision towards the UK.

Governments often make changes in the pattern of regional aid. The extent of assisted areas was sharply reduced by the Conservative Government in 1979 as part of a package of public expenditure cuts. By 1982 assisted areas were designed to cover only 25 per cent of the working population as opposed to 40 per cent previously. As problems become more acute in certain areas, extra regional provision may be made. For example, Corby was designated a development area after the closure of the British Steel plant in the town.

The regional policy revisions of November 1984 extended coverage to 35 per cent of the working population, given the notable inclusion of the West Midlands as an intermediate area. This move recognised the growing unemployment in the region reflecting the decline in manufacturing. The increase in coverage was coupled with a reduction in the extent of provision, saving £300 m a year by focusing on what the Government regarded as the most cost-effective measures.

2 To promote regional employment, governments have also taken the deliberate step of devolving some public sector activities to the regions. For example, the Royal Mint, Companies House and the Business Statistics Office have all been located in South Wales.

3 A new departure in 1980 was to introduce a number of enterprise zones (see Fig. 17.5). The aim was to attract new firms to the zones by charging no local authority rates for up to 10 years and minimising planning controls. However, rents increased inside the zones as demand for premises rose, and at the same time fell for premises outside. Thus the concession has to some extent been eroded by high rents.

4 As you will see in Chapter 44, some regional policy expenditure is financed from the EEC Regional Fund. Such money is proportional to that spent by the national government on regional aid.

Nissan – an illustration of location factors at work

In 1983 the Japanese motor manufacturer Nissan announced plans to set up a car-assembly plant in the UK, to open a bridgehead for further penetration into the EEC car market.

Nissan pondered between three British regions for a suitable site: Wales, Humberside and the North-east. In March 1984, the company announced its choice of Washington New Town, near Sunderland, in the North-east of England.

Fig. 17.5
Enterprise zones

The factors which drew Nissan to Washington were said to be:

a the geographical proximity to key Continental markets;
b the cheapness of the land and the ability to undertake further expansion on the site if the initial phase of development proved successful;
c the co-operation of the local authority in Sunderland.

Furthermore, given that Nissan were likely to set up the plant in an assisted area, the Trade and Industry Secretary stated that the government would provide selective financial assistance of up to £35 m towards the project.

The government has been subsequently keen to encourage Nissan to expand its plant further, and utilise a large proportion of British-made components rather than the imported Japanese kits which were initially used. If such further growth took place at the Washington site, in an area of high unemployment, the government agreed to offer regional development grants at a rate of 22 per cent rather than the usual rate of 15 per cent.

Keep abreast of news of any plans by Nissan to expand their operations in the UK. What would be the likely reaction of other motor manufacturers operating in Britain to such a move?

How do organisations acquire premises?

Small firms are likely to approach an estate agent which deals in commercial property, whereas big organisations seeking office blocks or factory sites would consult a major firm of chartered surveyors. Sites could of course be freehold or leasehold. Possibly a specific site is in mind. Alternatively the organisation might instruct the estate agent or chartered surveyor to find vacant premises of the desired type.

In some areas, bodies have been established to own and lease premises, e.g. the Welsh Development Agency. Some local councils operate similar schemes, such as Peterborough and a number of local authorities that contain designated enterprise zones. Interested organisations can contact such bodies to seek out potential sites.

18 Finance

Finance is crucial for an organisation to meet the costs of production. Inevitably, the raising of finance is essential to the development or even the very survival of an organisation. For example, if additional or replacement machinery cannot be introduced, the quantity or quality of output may stagnate or decline.

Finance for organisations

Different organisations utilise different sources of finance. We shall note differences particularly between private and public sector organisations in this respect.

For many trading organisations, their revenue from sales of goods or services is the most important source of funds, especially for the covering of variable costs of production. In this section we shall describe the various other sources open to organisations, both for current survival and future expansion.

Organisations require finance for both fixed and working capital.

Fixed capital

This involves raising funds for the acquisition of fixed factors of production, to cover fixed costs, e.g. new machines, an extension to a hospital, a new car park. Finance of this type is likely to be medium or long term.

Working capital

Circulating or working capital is needed for the financing of variable factors of production, to pay variable costs, e.g raw materials, weekly wage bills, electricity. Such finance is short term, covering the fundamental running costs of the firm.

There are no rigid demarcations over the periods for finance to be regarded as short, medium or long term. As a general guide, this classification can be followed:

- short term – less than 1 Year
- medium term – 1 year to 5 years
- long term – over 5 years

Where does such finance come from? We can first subdivide the sources into two types, internal and external, and then look at specific examples relating to private and public sector organisations.

Internal sources

This involves finance generated within the firm – retained profits or surpluses. In fact, as we shall see, such undistributed profits are the major source of finance in the private sector.

External sources

Firms are likely to find that internal sources are not always sufficient to cover the funds needed, and therefore they need to raise finance from other people or organisations, e.g. bank borrowing, new issues of shares.

Fig. 18.1
Major sources of finance for
different forms of organisation

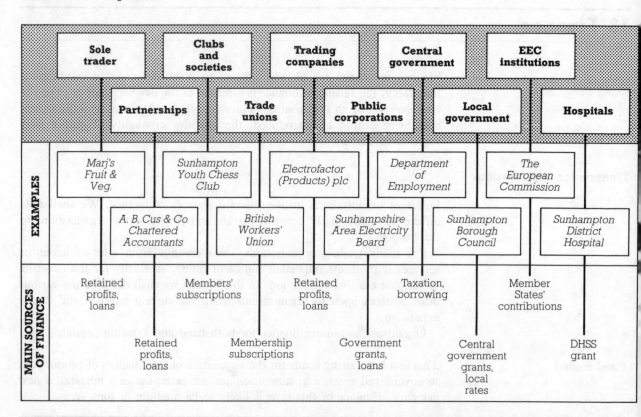

Information about finance

Before we explore possible sources of finance in more detail, how might organisations be aware of financial opportunities open to them?

Large organisations

Clearly, large, established organisations have much experience in the financial markets. The expertise of the Finance Director or senior employees like the Company Secretary or Chief Accountant will provide a valuable source of advice. Merchant banks, specialising in corporate finance, can also guide a client. Large organisations can afford to tap their services.

Small organisations

However, for small business organisations the level of 'in-house' expertise is unlikely to be as high. People newly in business are particularly likely to need advice about the financing of their project.

Certainly banks may assist. They provide personal advice and produce leaflets outlining the financial help they give. In addition, in recent years, government at both a central and a local level have extended the advisory services they offer to small businesses, in keeping with the government's aim to promote the growth of the small business sector.

The Department of Employment operates Small Firms Centres in major towns and cities to proffer advice and guidance. Increasingly, local councils have developed small business advisory services. Sometimes this has occurred through the Business in the Community scheme, whereby large companies second staff to assist new and existing small business people. For example, in the London Borough of Hammersmith and Fulham there is Hammersmith and Fulham Business Resources Ltd, while the Borough of Hounslow offers Hounslow Enterprise Ltd.

In some cases small amounts of financial support might be offered, or in other cases just guidance and advice. Check out what provision is made in the borough in which you live to assist small businesses.

Finance in the private sector

Short-term finance

Retained profits

By utilising profits from previous trading activity, all types of private sector organisations – sole trader, partnership, joint-stock company or co-operative – can generate finance. Obviously, the extent of such self-financing will depend on the prosperity of the organisation and its policy on distributing profits to the owners, be they shareholders, partners or the sole proprietor.

Bank lending

Short-term lending can be conducted either by means of a loan or, more commonly, an overdraft.

A loan involves the borrower receiving from the bank an agreed sum of money and repaying the loan at (usually) a fixed rate of interest within a stipulated time.

An overdraft enables the organisation to withdraw from its bank account more money than it has to its credit, up to a specified limit. Interest is paid at the prevailing rate on the amount overdrawn.

Small firms are likely to contact their clearing banks (the major High Street banks like Barclays, Lloyds, Midland and National Westminster) in order to borrow relatively small amounts for short- or medium-term periods.

Larger firms may well be clients of clearing banks or quite possibly of

Fig. 18.2
Major sources of finance for private sector organisations

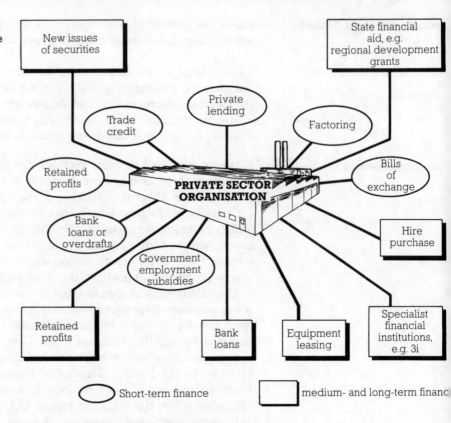

Short-term finance
medium- and long-term financ

a merchant bank – an institution specialising in corporate finance. A bank is likely to require security to back the advance it grants. For example, the loan or overdraft might be secured on the value of the firm's premises, so that the bank could recover its money if the funds were not repaid.

Private lending

Small firms, especially sole traders, may be able to arrange loans from friends or relatives. Larger firms inevitably need to contact an institution if they wish to borrow.

Bills of exchange

A large company can obtain credit, generally up to three months, if payment for a transaction takes place by means of a bill of exchange. This is a promissory note, a promise by one party to pay another party a sum of money by an agreed date. A specimen bill of exchange is shown in Fig. 18.3.

For example, firm B arranges to buy, say, rubber tubing from firm S worth £5m. If both parties agree, a bill of exchange could be drawn up stating that B consents to pay S £5m in 3 months' time. Firm S could hold the bill until it matures, when B would have to pay up. If S needs cash sooner, it might sell the bill, i.e. have it 'discounted' by a bank or a discount house. Discount houses are institutions in the London money market which specialise in the discounting of bills of exchange. Note that firm S would not be able to sell the bill for the full £5m. The bank or discount house wishes to make some profit on the deal, and so might discount the bill for, say, £4.9m. The amount of discount will reflect the

Fig. 18.3
A Bill of Exchange

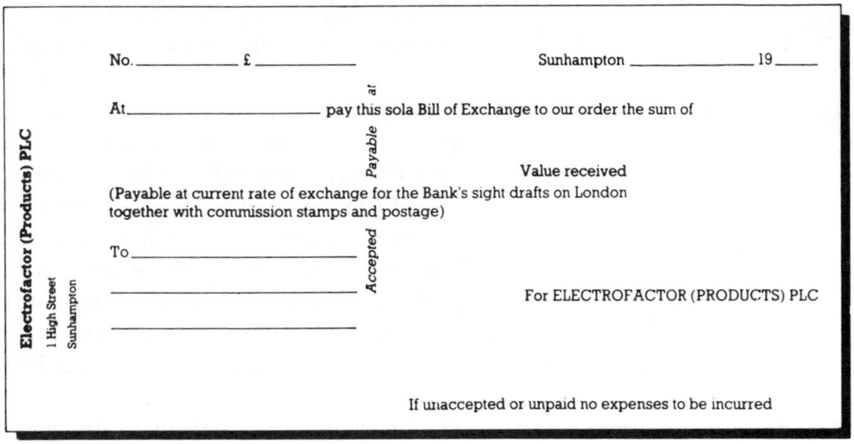

No. _____ £ _____   Sunhampton _____ 19____

At_____ pay this sola Bill of Exchange to our order the sum of

Value received
(Payable at current rate of exchange for the Bank's sight drafts on London together with commission stamps and postage)

To _____

_____

_____

For ELECTROFACTOR (PRODUCTS) PLC

If unaccepted or unpaid no expenses to be incurred

Electrofactor (Products) PLC
1 High Street
Sunhampton

Payable at

Accepted

prevailing rates of interest in the economy. The higher interest rates are, the lower will be the selling price of the bill and the larger the discount. Firm B must now pay £5m to the new owner of the bill on the date of maturity.

Trade credit

It is common for firms to give other organisations periods of grace, before payment for sale of goods or services is required. The buyer can benefit from interest-free credit for one month or more, just as the bill of exchange gives three months' credit. Trade credit is a very significant form of short-term finance. As an alternative, firms may grant a small discount off the purchase price if the buyer pays promptly.

Factoring

Factoring involves a firm of factors paying an organisation a sum of money in return for purchasing outstanding book debts due to that organisation from the sale of its products. Hence, the organisation obtains cash more quickly, but only about 80 to 90 per cent of the amount it would have received if it had waited for its debtors to pay up. The difference between the two sums reflects the return to the factoring institution. Factors are unlikely to take on the debts of small firms with low turnover or with many small customers because the administration costs become prohibitive. Like equipment leasing, factoring is an American practice, which developed in the UK from the 1960s.

Government employment subsidies

Governments in recent years have operated various policies designed to encourage or preserve employment. For example, the March 1986 Budget saw the introduction of the New Workers Scheme. Employers receive from the government a subsidy of £15 per week if they recruit young people aged 18 to 19 at below £55 per week, or workers aged 20 years at less than £65 per week.

Although such measures are primarily aimed at reducing youth unemployment, they do provide firms with additional funds.

Medium- and long-term finance

Retained profits

In most years the use of undistributed profits is the most important source of finance for the private sector, especially for small firms. After all, it is the cheapest method! By no means all profits are distributed to the owners, whether they are sole traders, partners or shareholders. Internal finance is important for future investment in capital goods.

Bank landing

Traditionally the clearing banks tended to concentrate their lending on the short and medium term. However, in recent years they have expanded the scale of their corporate lending, sometimes via subsidiaries, so that nowadays loans for over 10 years are not uncommon.

Large companies may well look to the merchant banking sector or overseas banks for large loans. Sometimes large loans are syndicated between banks, i.e the loan is split between several banks so that no single bank bears the risk of default in repayment. Also, large loans can be negotiated in overseas currencies and then switched into sterling.

Loan Guarantee Scheme

The Loan Guarantee Scheme is designed to encourage more venture capital to be lent to small businesses by banking institutions. It reduces the risk that the lender might face because the borrower in effect 'insures' the loan under the terms of the scheme. If the borrower cannot repay the bank, a claim can be made on the Loan Guarantee Scheme.

Specialist financial institutions

Investors in Industry

A number of financial institutions specialise in industrial lending. Prominent is Investors in Industry, which now covers the work of the Industrial and Commercial Financial Corporation and Finance Corporation for Industry.

Investors in Industry deals in loans to organisations, generally secured by a mortgage on the assets of the firm and can also purchase new issues of shares by companies as a means of injecting finance. It may provide funds from as little as £5000 up to £35m.

Hire purchase

Rather than pay at the outset the full amount for the purchase of an asset, the buying organisation might arrange finance on a hire purchase basis. This means that the firm has immediate use of an asset like a machine but staggers payments over a period of perhaps five years or more. The third party to such a transaction is likely to be a finance house, an institution specialising in HP. The seller of the good will receive payment from the finance house, while the buyer repays the finance house, with interest. The good remains the property of the finance house until full payment is made. Generally the buyer has to contribute a portion of the cost of the asset as an initial deposit.

HP finance is often used for capital goods like vehicles, agricultural machinery and machine tools. Also, of course, individuals sometimes use hire purchase to acquire durable consumer goods like TVs, freezers and cars.

Equipment leasing

Similar to hire purchase is the increasingly popular arrangement of leasing equipment. Again, this is a means of avoiding the large outlay necessary to purchase capital equipment. Generally, equipment leasing is available for more expensive assets than is usual under HP, e.g. a computer. Therefore, it is less likely to be a method used by small firms.

Leasing institutions include finance houses, subsidiaries of banks, specialist equipment leasing companies and the leasing departments or subsidiaries of equipment manufacturers. Fixed payments are made over the period of the leasing agreement. Such time spans are usually up to five years, when the agreement can be extended.

A prime difference between equipment leasing and hire purchase is that with the former, the lessee (the user) has no right to purchase the equipment on the expiry of the lease. With HP, the firm using the equipment can, for a small sum, claim ownership of the asset from the finance house.

By 1984, leasing accounted for 13 per cent of total investment in plant and equipment in the UK. It was thought, however, that the phasing out of relief from corporation tax for profits used for investment, as announced in the 1984 Budget, would thwart the sustained growth of the leasing industry.

State financial aid

There are a number of ways in which the State can provide long-term financial assistance for firms. The extent to which this is done has been reduced by the policies of the Conservative Governments since 1979, which prefer less government involvement in the economy. Nevertheless, let us consider some areas in which government aid can be given.

British Technology Group

The British Technology Group was formed in 1981 out of the merging of the National Enterprise Board and the National Research Development Corporation. It operates with a smaller budget than its predecessor organisations and aims to fund new ventures especially in the technological fields. For example, it injected funds into INMOS, the micro-chip manufacturer, which was subsequently acquired by Thorn-EMI.

Regional development grants

These grants are available to firms undertaking capital investment projects in assisted areas, as explained in Chapter 17.

Grants for micro-chip technology

Firms that both make and install information technology could qualify for State aid designed to stimulate this important sector of the economy. For example, in 1984 it was announced that small firms in the clothing, footwear and small-batch engineering industries would qualify for 20 per cent grants for investing in automation. Grants were also available to boost software innovation and to micro-chip producers themselves under the Micro-electronics Industry Support Programme, which aimed to encourage output of micro-chips.

New issues of securities

Joint stock companies can raise additional finance by the issue of new securities. The capital structure of companies can be composed of three main types of securities.

Debentures

These are loan stock, often secured to the assets of the company. The holder is entitled to a fixed rate of interest per annum through the lifespan of the stock. These interest payments are part of the costs of the firm, and thus are not paid direct from the profits of the company. Debenture holders are creditors, not owners, of the company.

Preference shares

If the Board of Directors decides to distribute any profit, preference shareholders are given priority in its allocation. A preference share entitles the holder to receive up to a maximum percentage dividend, but guarantees nothing. Some preference shares are cumulative, i.e. if last year preference shareholders were not paid up to their maximum, the shortfall can be added to their entitlement this year. Preference shares do not usually carry voting rights at a shareholders' meeting.

Ordinary shares

These shares normally carry voting rights, but are more risky since they give no guarantee to a dividend of any size, and are paid after preference shareholders have received their allocation of profit.

In a bad year, ordinary shareholders could receive little or no dividend, preference shareholders being ahead of them in the queue for whather level of profits were distributed. However, in a good year, the dividend to ordinary shareholders could well exceed the maximum payable to the preference shareholder.

The ordinary share is by far the most common type of security in the capital structure of UK companies.

Methods of new issue

The choice of method to raise finance by the issue of new securities largely depends on the sum involved and the prevailing economic climate as it affects the capital market. Are prospects for the economy and the particular industry of that individual firm buoyant enough to encourage buyers for the new issue? Are rates of return more attractive in other areas, e.g. government securities?

The new issues market

The public limited company involved in making the new issue is likely to call upon the services of Issuing House (usually a merchant bank) to advise on the amount, timing and composition of the issue, and to organise the new issue according to which of the methods below is selected. The Issuing House is likely to arrange for underwriters, often insurance companies or merchant banks, which will purchase any securities left unsold after the issue. The underwriters would only agree to buy left-over securities at a discount. If the underwriters are not called upon, they will still receive a fee for their services.

There are four common means for issuing new securities:

1 *Offer for sale.* This is an expensive method and could only be justified if the size of the new issue was itself very large. It involves the compilation of a prospectus about the company and its new issue, and advertisements in national newspapers proclaiming and informing about the new issue. Investors are invited to subscribe for the new issue by completing an application form.

This method has been used in the privatising of British Telecom (see Fig. 18.4) and British Gas. When Tottenham Hotspur football club became a plc in 1983, it raised £3m by an offer for sale.

2 *Offer for sale by tender.* Bids above a minimum price are invited from potential buyers, so that a price can be struck at which all securities can be sold, if there are sufficient bids. This method runs the risk of uncertainty of how much finance might be raised, but in a buoyant market companies with good prospects have successfully used this technique, such

Fig. 18.4
An offer of shares for sale

TELECOM

British Telecommunications plc
Offer for Sale

by **Kleinwort, Benson Limited**

on behalf of **The Secretary of State
for Trade and Industry**

of up to **3,012,000,000
Ordinary Shares of 25p
each at 130p per share**

50p is payable now
40p is payable on 24th June 1985
40p is payable on 9th April 1986

and underwritten by

Kleinwort, Benson Limited	S.G. Warburg & Co Ltd
Barclay Merchant Bank Limited	Baring Brothers & Co Limited
Charterhouse Japhet plc	County Bank Limited
Robert Fleming & Co Limited	Hambros Bank Limited
Hill Samuel & Co Limited	Lazard Brothes & Co Limited
Lloyds Bank International Limited	Samuel Montagu & Co Limited
Morgan Grenfell & Co Limited	N.M. Rothschild & Sons Limited
J. Henry Schroder Wagg & Co Limited	

as Virgin Group plc (see Fig. 18.5), Our Price, the records retailer, raise £3.5 m by this technique in 1984.

3 *Placing*. The Issuing House arranges for the purchase of the new securities by an institutional investor. This is a method often used by smaller companies. In 1984 Unibond (Holdings), the adhesives manufacturer, raised £2.5 m by this method.

4 *Rights issue*. This has been a prominent form of new issue in recent years. In 1985, for example, rights issues were the major mode of new issue. Existing shareholders are given the option to buy, at a reduced price, some new securities in proportion to their current holdings. For example, a 1 for 5 rights issue would give each existing shareholder the right to buy one new share for every five currently owned. The shareholder does not have to buy, and can sell the option if desired. This can be a cheaper method for the company since it avoids some of the external costs of new issue, e.g. advertising.

A number of the major banks have used funds from rights issue to improve their capital base and provide finance for further expansion. For example, Barclays raised £519 m in 1985, while National Westminster raised £714 m in 1986, at that time the largest ever rights issue. Tesco raised £151.6 m by this technique in 1985.

Fig. 18.5
An offer of shares by tender

Virgin Group plc

(Registered in England No. 1568894)

Offer of Ordinary Shares by Tender

by

Morgan Grenfell & Co. Limited

as agent for the Company and the vendors whose names are set out herein

of up to 50,000,000 Ordinary Shares of 10p each to raise £60,000,000

with a minimum tender price of 120p per share

the amount tendered being payable in full on application

The Business Expansion Scheme

A boost for new issues for small companies without a stock market quotation has been the Business Expansion Scheme. Introduced by the Government in 1981, it provides income tax relief to personal shareholders who subscribe to such new issues.

Comparison of sources of finance for companies

Generally, retained profits provide the major source of finance, as shown in Table 18.1. It is the cheapest method and is not subject to conditions imposed by outside bodies. Other sources vary in importance, reflecting such factors as the availability of bank leading, interest rates, prosperity or depression in the economy and the buoyancy of the stock market.

Bank borrowing and new issues tend to fluctuate from year to year in the face of such factors. Funds raised by new issues exceeded £5bn for the first time in 1983, of which £2bn came from rights issues. However, new issues are generally far less significant than bank borrowing in the share of total finance raised.

Table 18.1
Sources of funds for companies (£m)

	1980	1984
Funds from internal sources	18 613	31 138
Bank borrowing, other loans and mortgages	6 436	8 407
New issues	1 423	1 376
Overseas sources	1 910	356

Source: *Financial Statistics*, December 1985, Table 8.2.

The stock market

As was stated in Chapter 7, it should be made clear at the outset that the Stock Exchange is not a source of *new* funds for organisations in the UK. We have already described the new issues market and the possible methods by which new securities are sold. Stock Exchange dealings are not directly involved. Rather, the Stock Exchange is the market for second-hand securities. It aids the raising of finance by new issues by providing a forum where securities can later be bought and sold. Buyers of new securities feel more secure in the knowledge that they can dispose of their acquisitions in the future.

Government securities (gilt-edged) as well as securities of companies are traded on the stock market. The bulk of securities, about two-thirds,

Fig. 18.6
The Stock Exchange before 'Big-Bang'. Compare with Fig. 7.1.

are owned by institutional investors like pension funds, insurance companies, unit trusts and investment trusts. They utilise the aggregated savings of many individuals in order to increase the value of the money saved with them. Individual shareholders in contrast own a smaller proportion of securities.

Investors may buy securities to earn a return in the form of interest or dividends. Securities may be bought for speculative reasons, to be sold later at a profit, so that a capital gain can be made.

Traditionally, clients bought and sold shares by contacting a stockbroker who would strike a deal with a jobber operating on the floor of the Stock Exchange. Jobbers dealt on their own behalf, buying and selling the types of securities in which they specialise.

However, with the so-called Big Bang in October 1986, as part of the process of deregulation of the City of London, Stock Exchange rules were relaxed to permit the growth of financial conglomerates which could combine the broking and jobbing functions. This, along with the greater use of computer technology in securities transactions (as described in Chapters 3 and 7), is changing the face of the Stock Exchange.

Have you ever read the Stock Exchange listings in a newspaper? You will find a number of columns of information. For example, on 24 January 1987 *The Times* listed the following information about Rowntree Mackintosh, the chocolate and confectionery manufacturer, for the previous day:

| 1986 | | Price | | | | | |
High	Low	Bid	Offer	Change	Gross dividend (pence)	Yield %	P/E
540	365	463	467	+9	18.0	3.9	12.9

The high and low figures show the highest and lowest values, in pence, of the shares over the year. The bid and offer prices reflect buying and selling prices of the shares. The figure for change shows that the shares had risen by 9 p over the price the day before. The gross dividend represents the earnings paid to each share when profits were last distributed. In this case, each share earned 18 p. The yield, though, relates the earnings per share to the current market price (taken as the middle price between the bid and offer – 465 p in our case). Thus the percentage return can be gauged if shares were to be traded at the current price.

$$\text{Yield} = \frac{\text{Earnings per share}}{\text{Market price}} \times 100$$
$$= \frac{18}{465} \times 100$$
$$= 3.9\%$$

P/E stands for the price/earnings ratio. This is the ratio of the price of the share to the profits of the company (averaged per share) after corporation tax has been taken into account. Firms with a good record of profit growth tend to have a high P/E ratio. Their shares will be in demand and the price will rise. Investors compare P/E ratios between firms as a guide to relative profitability in relation to outlay on a share.

The Unlisted Securities Market

As described in Chapter 7 this market, originating in 1980, provides a forum for the sale and purchase of shares in smaller public limited companies, often in high risk industries like electronics.

Co-operatives

Co-operatives obtain finance in a similar manner to other private sector organisations. However, there are some qualifications to be made. The Co-operative Societies cannot make new issues of shares in the same way as a public limited company. Any new finance from shares is that which individuals subscribe on application. Worker co-operatives may seek assistance from specialist bodies like the London Co-operative Enterprise Board or Industrial Common Ownership Finance Ltd. As was mentioned in Chapter 6, the Co-operative Development Agency advises on establishing and expanding worker co-operatives.

Finance in the public sector

Government departments

Government finance is discussed more fully in Chapter 35. Here, it is sufficient to say that of all the organisations that this book is concerned with, the biggest spender is naturally the central government. The administration of the Houses of Parliament itself costs 8 p in every £100 of public expenditure. The Government as the body concerned with directing national policy has a myriad of responsibilities and these cost money. Every time someone says that 'something ought to be done about it', the fulfilment of this hope requires, perhaps, the setting up of another government office, the employment of more civil servants and the expenditure of government money. In general though, the government of the day is responsible for funding its services, including the maintenance of the health service, the social security system, the court system, transport policies, grants to private industries in the regions which need help and the national defence. Central government departments like the Ministry of Defence, the Department of the Environment and the Department of Health and Social Security are not permitted to raise finance in their own name. They are allocated funds out of central government revenues.

Much of the government's income is raised by the Exchequer by various forms of personal taxes, taxes on goods and services and levies imposed on corporations. The government also borrows money by issuing bonds, certificates and stocks (see Fig. 18.7), known as 'gilt-edged' securities or 'gilts'. One purpose of the Chancellor of the Exchequer's annual budget statement, to which we all look eagerly or with grave anticipation, is to adjust the income to meet the projected expenditure needs of government.

What, then, are the controls on public expenditure? Certainly every five years or so (see Chapter 35) the electorate may have a say by voting into government a party which may to a lesser or greater extent meet the majority of the population's view as to what priorities to adopt. However, such control, although ultimately important, cannot effect how a party elected to government actually behaves. After all, the bulk of the expendi-

Fig. 18.7
Notice of issue of Treasury Loan

THIS FORM MAY BE USED
TENDER FORM

This form must be lodged at the Bank of England, New Issues (J), Watling Street, London, EC4M 9AA not later than 10.00 A.M. ON WEDNESDAY, 16TH JULY 1986, or at any of the Branches of the Bank of England or at the Glasgow Agency of the Bank of England not later than 3.30 P.M. ON TUESDAY, 15TH JULY 1986.

ISSUE OF £900,000,000

$8\frac{1}{2}$ per cent TREASURY LOAN, 2007

MINIMUM TENDER PRICE £94.50 PER CENT

TO THE GOVERNOR AND COMPANY OF THE BANK OF ENGLAND

I/We tender in accordance with the terms of the prospectus dated 11th July 1986 as follows:—

Amount of the above-mentioned Loan tendered for, being a minimum of £100 and in a multiple as follows:—

Amount of the Loan tendered for	Multiple
£100—£1,000	£100
£1,000—£3,000	£500
£3,000—£10,000	£1,000
£10,000—£50,000	£5,000
£50,000 or greater	£25,000

1. NOMINAL AMOUNT OF THE LOAN

£

2. AMOUNT OF DEPOSIT (a)

Amount of deposit enclosed, being £25.00 for every £100 of the NOMINAL amount of the Loan tendered for (shown in Box 1 above):—

£

3. TENDER PRICE (b)

The price tendered per £100 of the Loan, being a multiple of 25p and not less than the minimum tender price of £94.50:—

£   :   p

I/We hereby engage to pay the balance of the purchase money when it becomes due on any allotment that may be made in respect of this tender, as provided by the said prospectus.

I/We request that any letter of allotment in respect of the amount of the Loan allotted to me/us be sent by post at my/our risk to me/us at the address shown below.

———————— July 1986

SIGNATURE...
of, or on behalf of, tenderer

PLEASE USE BLOCK LETTERS

MR/MRS MISS	FORENAME(S) IN FULL	SURNAME

FULL POSTAL ADDRESS:—

POST-TOWN	COUNTY	POSTCODE
G		

a A separate cheque must accompany each tender. Cheques should be made payable to "Bank of England" and crossed "New Issues". Cheques must be drawn on a bank in, and be payable in, the United Kingdom, the Channel Islands or the Isle of Man.

b The price tendered must be a multiple of 25p and not less than the minimum tender price. If no price is stated, this tender will be deemed to have been made at the minimum tender price. Each tender must be for one amount and at one price.

ture is unavoidable in that it is necessary to preserve the basic structure of government spending.

The major examination of government expenditure is exercised by Parliament itself. This may be through the ordinary activity of Members of Parliament asking questions of ministers trying to raise support in public for criticisms of government expenditure.

Examination of public expenditure is undertaken by the Comptroller and Auditor General, who is independent of the government, receiving a salary, as also do judges, from the Consolidated Fund, a major Exchequer account. This officer's function is to carry out an annual audit of the accounts of each government department and to issue a report to Parliament. In Parliament there exists a group of 15 MPs formed as the Select Committee on Public Accounts, whose job it is to investigate how government money has actually been spent. The Public Accounts Committee then issues a report which is published in Parliament and in which it may level charges of serious government overspending and wasting of public services. While it does no more than report, its findings are made public and do give the public the opportunity to hear about any excessive government expenditure.

Local authorities

Local authorities have more latitude in raising finance than individual central government departments. A large proportion of their funds (46 per cent in 1984/5) comes directly from the central government in the form of the Rate Support Grant, but they also have the power to levy rates on residential property and business premises in their area in order to provide additional finance to meet local needs. About one-quarter to one-third of their revenue comes from rates.

However, the 1987 Local Government Finance Bill would, when enacted, replace the rates system with a community charge. This would be a flat rate charge affecting every adult in England and Wales.

Further, local authorities borrow money. This may be done on a short-term basis by the sale of local authority bills of exchange, or by short-term loans (known as temporary deposit receipts) from banks and the money market. In the medium term, they sell bonds offering a fixed rate of interest which are attractive to many savers prepared to commit their funds for a few years. However, the extent of all this borrowing is ultimately controlled by the Bank of England and the Treasury.

Additionally, local authorities receive revenue from services they offer, e.g. rents from council housing and admission charges to municipal swimming pools, golf courses, etc. Funds may also be raised by the sale of council houses to tenants.

Control over a local authority's use of capital

The Rate Support Grant and the local rates provide most of a local authority's capital requirements. What control, though, do the providers of these monies have over the way the local authority spends its income?

Ratepayers are under a legal duty to pay local levies, which are assessed on the grounds of what an imaginary tenant would pay were the premises to be rented. A sum of say £300 per annum might be decided upon as the rateable value of the premises. The actual amount paid by the ratepayer depends on the level at which the rate is set, e.g. 65 p in every £1, at which rate the amount payable on property with a rateable value of £300 would be £195.00 a year. This gives us an idea of what might affect a local resident's view on how the elected local councillors are conducting themselves. As the local authority is elected, the final control is in the hands of residents to vote out of office councillors who they believe not to be spending the authority's income for their benefit. They may wish for more rather than fewer services to be available, in which case again, their voice may be heard at election time. Beyond this, residents may canvass their local councillor to get their point of view over at council meetings.

A more powerful control over the spending of capital is exercised by the Secretary of State for the Environment. It is more powerful because central government is the major source of a local authority's money. The central government's interest in controlling local authority expenditure is that uncontrolled public expenditure may be seen as having the effect of increasing the nation's rate of inflation. At any rate, under the Local Government Planning and Land Act 1981 the Secretary of State for the Environment is empowered to penalise so-called 'overspending' local authorities. Under the Act, the Minister can order that particular capital projects be halted and can reduce the Rate Support Grant to an offending authority. In effect these powers give the Minister some ability to direct local authorities on how they may spend their income.

As discussed before (see Part B), local councillors who refuse to raise a rate can be fined and removed from office (as happened to Lambeth councillors who were taken to court by district auditors in 1986). The obligation to fix a rate by 1 April is laid down in the Local Government Act 1986. In essence the financial controls on local councils amount to: the setting of the level of central funding through the Rate Support Grant, earmarked for given purposes; limiting through rate capping the sum which may be collected; determining the amount of money which a council may levy; and by penalising overspending local councillors.

The government has also introduced another means of supervision – the Audit Commission. Established in the 1982 Local Government Finance Act, the Commission works with local authorities to help them ensure that their services are provided economically, efficiently and effectively. It is responsible for the District Audit Service, and appoints external auditors for local authorities, who give their opinions on the accounts and report on any findings of public interest. To give you an idea of the content of the Commission's reports, in 1986 it recommended a possible saving of about £100m in housing administration, a reduction of council rent arrears of £100m and the possibility of bringing 25 000 dwellings for letting.

Do you remember that the general governing legislation for local authorities is the Local Government Act 1972? Apart from any additional powers that it may have obtained through the passage of a private bill through Parliament (see Chapter 2), a local authority has limited powers. What this means is that expenditure of matters outside these legislative provisions, will amount to an *ultra vires* act. An authority which spends money *ultra vires* may be taken to court (see Chapter 11).

Sources of finance for other organisations

The EEC

The prime source of finance for the EEC to carry out its operations comes from contributions by member States. Generally, the larger, richer countries make the biggest contributions.

Specifically, the EEC obtains finance from three sources:

1 Levies on agricultural imports from non-member States under the Common Agricultural Policy.

2 From customs duties on imports of other goods from non-member States.

3 From tax revenue from each member State of an amount equivalent to that collected from a Value Added Tax (VAT) rate of up to 1.4 per cent.

Hospitals

The vast bulk of finance for an individual hospital comes from the Department of Health and Social Security. A smaller fraction comes from sources such as charges to private patients and for prescriptions.

In 1985/6 the total expenditure of the Hounslow and Spelthorne Health Authority in West London was £52 158 321; all bar £577 576 came from the DHSS.

Public corporations

Once again, public corporations, e.g. British Steel and British Coal, receive much of their new finance from central government by way of loans and grants. Any profits (or surpluses as they are called) of public corporations officially accrue to the Treasury. However, such funds are often used by the corporations for investment purposes or the repayment of previous borrowing.

With Treasury permission, public corporations can issue stock to raise finance and can also borrow from banks, sometimes from overseas banks on international financial markets.

Such finance is of course aside from revenues obtained in the provision of the goods or services of the public corporation.

Trade unions

Trade unions' revenue derives primarily from subscriptions paid by members. Unions invest funds surplus to immediate needs and derive income from the proceeds. Such investments are mainly in public sector securities or in property.

The largest trade union in the UK is the Transport and General Workers' Union with a membership at the end of 1985 of 1 434 005. Its income comes mainly from members' subscriptions. In 1985 £44 570 222 came from that source, whereas £3 900 100 was investment income.

Charities

Charities raise funds needed to aid their cause mainly from donations from individuals and also from organisations. Some large firms allocate money to certain charities. Charities may operate fund-raising events, from the local jumble sale to sporting events like the Football Association Charity Shield match. Note that people and organisations may obtain tax relief on donations to charities, a significant fund-raising advantage for charitable organisations.

The acquisition of capital goods

Given that an organisation is able to raise the necessary finance, how does it set about acquiring capital goods? In Chapter 17 we described the acquisition of premises. How does an organisation obtain machinery and raw materials?

Machinery

Machinery will obviously be sold by specialist suppliers. By studying catalogues and viewing demonstrations of the relevant machines an organisation can attempt to gauge their suitability for its needs. For example, to acquire office machinery or computers, a major business-machines firm would be a likely supplier. For lorries, leading commercial-vehicle dealers or manufacturers are the prime source. Specialist industrial machinery can be sought from specific engineering firms.

Organisations may well visit a Trade Fair to compare the performance and price of machines produced by competing organisations. Remember also, the growing popularity of equipment leasing as opposed to outright purchase.

Raw materials

Very large orders of raw materials can be acquired on the commodity markets, for example the London Metal Exchange. There, large scale deals are struck for the immediate or future purchase of commodities.

Smaller transactions are conducted with supplier organisations which themselves are likely to have bought on the commodity markets.

19 Labour and employment laws

The labour requirements of organisations change if markets are expanding or contracting, or if changes are made in methods of production.

Apart from land and capital, a third 'factor of production' is labour, or human resources. Organisations need labour of varied types, be they skilled or unskilled, manual or clerical, qualified or unqualified people. Consider for a moment the range of jobs in your work-place or college. How many different types of employees are there? Particularly in large organisations, there will be an array of qualifications and experience necessary for people to fill the various posts adequately. These organisations very often have personnel departments who have the task of filling vacant posts with the people the organisation needs to carry on its business.

An organisation must enter the labour market through one of its many avenues in its search for suitable employees. Such avenues may be through:

- placing advertisements in newspapers, or specialist journals, or radio and sometimes on television;
- approaching either a private employment agency or the government-sponsored Job Centres and Careers Services;
- or accepting the direct approaches of people seeking employment.

While obtaining a job is uppermost in the minds of people once their education is completed, the availability of jobs is dependent on the general economic state of the country. Thus, in times of recession in the economy, organisations in the business environment may close down or at least reduce their operations and so shed all or some of their labour force.

Organisations as employers have to be aware of the various legal restraints that exist when hiring labour. What might appear to be a straightforward proposition of an organisation wishing to employ the services of a person it desires is in fact fraught with legal regulations. These have become necessary to set down the rights and duties of employers and employees and to afford protection to employees. Thus the basic right of an organisation to 'hire' whom it wants and to 'fire' a person when it wishes is in practice hedged by many restrictions. Let us now examine the various facets of these constraints in order to understand their importance to organisations' policies on employment.

Regulations affecting selection of candidates for a post

Parliament has introduced laws to protect people from discrimination based on sex (the Sex Discrimination Act 1975) and race (the Race Relations Act 1976). Under these laws, which you will be able to examine later, it is generally unlawful for an organisation to discriminate against a candidate for a job because of his or her sex or race. Sometimes applicants with criminal convictions of long standing are entitled not to be discriminated against only for that reason (the Rehabilitation of Offenders Act 1974.) Organisations employing more than 20 persons must ensure that at least 3 per cent of their work force consists of disabled persons (the Disabled Persons Employment Acts 1944 and 1958). In contrast, an employee who deceives a prospective employer into wrongly believing that he or she has obtained qualifications necessary for a post may be guilty of a crime (Theft Act 1968).

Can a previous employer restrict an employee's future employment?

The general rule is that there is no restriction on persons to seek employment for which they are properly or adequately qualified. However, it is recognised that employers may wish to protect their industrial and trade secrets or clients from being lost to a competitor. The law, therefore, permits restrictions placed on an employee, which may have been written into the contract of employment, but only if the restriction is reasonable and not against the public interest.

Mr Skilton entered an agreement when he was employed as a milk roundsman, part of which stated that for a year after terminating his employment he must not deliver milk to the dairy company's customers. In fact, on leaving he did work for another dairy and served his previous employer's customers. The court decided in favour of the employer, holding that Mr Skilton was bound by the restraint because it was reasonable, and that he should cease contravening it (Home Counties Dairies *v.* Skilton 1970).

However, the court will not uphold restraints which are against the public interest. When Tony Greig and other world-class cricketers joined World Series Cricket, an Australian company which was seen as a threat to the established International Cricket Conference, those cricketers were banned from playing in games organised by the ICC. The Test and County Cricket Board also barred them from playing cricket in the UK. The court judged that both these bodies had acted in an inappropriate manner and so were not pursuing their legitimate interests as promoters of cricket. The ban was therefore an unlawful restraint on the cricketers' employment opportunities (Greig *v.* Insole 1977). On the other hand a covenant between doctors practising in the NHS which restricted an outgoing partner from practising within a two-mile radius of the partnership premises for two years was held valid and not against the public interest (Kerr *v.* Morris 1986).

Employing organisations and trade unions

An important influence on employing organisations' acquisition and treatment of workers is played by trade unions. Are you a member of a trade union?

We have already discussed the nature of trade union organisations in Section B and you may remember that we set out their special legal status. There has been a steady decline in trade union membership since 1979 when TUC-affiliated unions had 12 171 508 members, compared with 9 580 502 at the end of 1986. In Chapter 1 we referred to factors which might be regarded as having influenced this decline. Can you recall these?

The largest unions are: the Transport and General Workers Union, the Amalgamated Engineering Union, the General and Municipal Workers Union, and the National Association of Local Government Officers (see Table 19.1). However, there are 400 trade unions registered with the Certification Officer for Trade Unions (see Section B) and of these 88 are affiliated to the TUC. Examples of some of the smaller unions include the Association of Somerset Inseminators and the Society of Cricket Ball Makers.

Table 19.1
The largest trade unions (1986)

Trade union	Membership (thousands)		Assets (£m)	
	1979	1985	1979	1985
T & GWU	2090	1430	39.6	66.5
AEU	1510	970	24.9	21.6
G & MWU	970	830	20.9	33.6
NALGO (local government)	750	750	12.6	36.6
NUPE (public employees)	690	660	13.3	20.4
USDAW (shop workers)	470	390	5.8	10.4
ASTMS (scientific/managerial)	490	390	4.2	8.1
EEPTU (plumbers/electricians)	440	380	8.3	14.4
NUT (teachers)	290	260	7.2	14.1

What are the roles of trade unions?

We may regard trade unions as performing three main roles.

Improving members' conditions of work

This is likely to come about by the process of 'collective bargaining' which trade unions undertake with employing organisations. In such negotiations the union is the bargaining agent acting on behalf of its members. Bargaining strength is increased if there exists what is known as a 'closed shop', indicating that all employees working for a particular organisation must belong to a relevant trade union.

Improvements in work conditions would be sought on a number of fronts, predominantly:

wage rates
hours of work
holidays
the work environment, e.g. canteen facilities
pension rights
resisting redundancy
disciplinary procedures

Employers and unions must seek compromises for agreements to be reached. Sometimes the trial of strength may result in some sort of industrial action such as a strike (or even a lock-out of workers by employers) before agreement is reached. Here, as we saw in Chapter 14, the role of the Advisory Conciliation and Arbitration Service (ACAS) is important in attempting to resolve industrial disputes before the parties take any action.

Taking part in national politics

Many unions are affiliated to the Labour Party. Unless members choose otherwise, they will pay as part of their union subscription a 'political levy' to the Labour Party. This recognises that the Party and trade unions are part of a labour movement, particularly in the historical context. The Party actually evolved in the early part of this century as the political arm of the trade union movement. Thus the unions have an important role in the formation of Labour policy.

Acting as pressure groups

The Trade Union Congress (TUC), which represents most unions, often acts as the vehicle for promoting unions' views, particularly on economic issues, to the government of the day.

In a similar way the Confederation of British Industry (CBI) speaks on behalf of employers in private industry.

What is the structure of trade unions?

Trade unions are fundamentally democratic organisations. The views of members at local branch level can be transmitted to regional or national executives. Union policy is decided at a national conference. In manual trades, a shop steward is likely to be elected to act as the workers' immediate representative of the trade union.

In fact, the majority of people at work either have weak trade union representation or none at all. In many cases these workers are amongst the lowest paid, with the poorest working conditions also. In order to give some protection to these low-paid workers the government has set up Wages Councils which set minimum levels of pay for certain jobs. We shall discuss these bodies later. It should be said at this stage that these councils have been criticised for having restricted the development of collective agreements, so hindering the setting of wages above the minimum levels.

Employment law

Must the employment agreement be a signed document?

All agreements to work establish a legal relationship between the employee and the employer. However, there is generally no legal necessity for the agreement to be in writing, and in fact most employment agreements (or contracts) are made by word of mouth. Therefore, the contract of employment may be oral or in writing. A contract imposes both rights and duties

* For details the law of contract, see Chapter 30.

on the parties, and failure to observe the terms of a contract may entitle the injured party to seek redress at law.* Unlike other contracts though, an employment contract requires a good deal of flexibility in view of the fact that it may survive over a person's whole working life. In some cases the employment contract is unsuitable for legal formalities to be insisted upon, so that it is rarely worth an employer's while to sue an employee who leaves a job without giving proper notice, if that post is easily filled.

On the other hand, certain employees may be required to sign formal legal documents, as will screen actors, music performers and tennis players. Sometimes the nature of the work is subject to strict terms, so that many civil servants have to sign a statement under the Official Secrets Acts 1911 and 1920: once they have signed, such workers are prohibited from divulging information which might be prejudicial to the interests of the State.

Are employment contracts individually negotiated?

Some employment contracts may be the result of negotiations about the terms and conditions between an individual employee and employer. It is far more common for an employee to be offered a contract in a standard form, having terms and conditions which are common to all employees. Indeed, most workers are employed subject to 'collective agreements'. These agreements are made between trade union representatives, on behalf of all their members, and employers' representatives. The terms and conditions may be agreed on a national scale for particular industries or organisations, very often allowing for local differences. In such circumstances an applicant for a post is referred to a collective agreement to discover full details of individual contracts of employment. There has been an increasing tendency to agree at a national level but to allow local differentiation.

However where central government in effect controls the amount of money available for services, whether by direct financing or the imposition of cash controls, organisations can be prevented from agreeing to too high wage settlements. Indeed the government has most control over local councils (see Chapter 11) and has been willing to intervene in their pay negotiations. For instance, after two years of being unable to agree new terms of pay and condition with all the various teacher unions, the government introduced legislation actually imposing the terms set out by the Secretary of State in the Teachers Pay and Conditions Act 1987. Further, the government indicated in February 1987 that it was in favour of an ending to national bargaining, and therefore preferred local pay and conditions bargaining.

What is the definition of an employee?

In our references to the 'employer' we include an individual, such as a sole trader, as much as an organisation like the Pearl Assurance Company or British Rail. As regards workers, the law recognises two categories: 'employees' and 'self-employed persons', the latter also called 'independent contractors'.

Employees are engaged under a contract *of service*, and as such are entitled to wide statutory protection and benefits such as unemployment pay, industrial injury benefit and in certain circumstances the right to sue for unfair dismissal (see below). Such rights are not available to self-employed workers who work under a contract *for services*. Although the latter enjoy fewer statutory benefits, they are equally entitled to a safe place of work and to protection from discrimination in pay and conditions on grounds of sex.

What is the importance of distinction between employees and self-employed persons?

1 At common law employers owe a special duty to provide their employees with a reasonably safe system of work. In addition, the Health and Safety at Work Act 1974 places duties on employers towards employees which are more extensive than those owed to independent contractors.

2 The common law provides that an employer may be made to answer for an employee's careless conduct (this liability is known as 'vicarious'). Only in exceptional cases will an employer be vicariously liable for the acts of an independent contractor. (For example, a local authority may be held liable for any injuries resulting from work carried out on the highway by independent contractors.)

3 Under the Employment Protection (Consolidation) Act 1978 self-employed workers do not share with employees the right to sue for unfair dismissal, to claim a redundancy payment or to receive paid maternity leave.

4 The payment of National Insurance contributions is fixed at levels dependent on the category of worker. The contribution levied from employees, with a contribution from the employer, under the Social Security Act 1975 is higher than that applicable to self-employed persons.

5 Income Tax paid by employees is by way of the PAYE (Pay As You Earn) system, under which the appropriate liability is deducted – by the employer – from wages or salary. Self-employed persons are responsible for making an annual declaration of their income against which they may set certain expenses. The Inland Revenue then assess the tax liability.

The advantages of being classified as a self-employed worker are to be found in the short-term benefit of paying a lower social security contribution. Additionally there is the ability to limit the burden of taxation by claiming business expenses, such as transport and the cost of work materials, and there is a considerable saving in administrative costs as compared with an organisation with employees. A self-employed person receives payment from which there have been no deductions – tax and social security contributions are paid separately, usually at the end of the person's tax year.

A legal test is needed to determine whether or not a worker is an employee, but a satisfactory one has not been easy to devise. The question, said a court (Market Investigations *v.* Ministry of Social Security 1969), was whether the worker – in this case a canvasser – was working as a person 'in business on his own account'. A sub-postmaster who, although under substantial control of the Post Office, also ran a general store on his premises was held to be carrying on the business on his own account. As such, he was not an employee, and so could not claim that the Post Office had unfairly dismissed him (Hitchcock *v.* Post Office 1979).

In a dispute over whether part-time orchestra players were employees, the Employment Appeals Tribunal decided they were essentially *freelance* musicians and were therefore self-employed persons. The tribunal arrived at its decision (Addision *v.* London Philharmonic Orchestra 1980) after considering such questions as:

a the degree of control exercised by the employer;
b the workers' prospect of profit or risk of loss in a venture;
c whether the workers were part and parcel of the business;
d the responsibility for payment of tax and insurance contributions;
e whether the workers were carrying on business on their own account;
f the parties' own view of the relationship.

How are workers protected by the law?

The employment relationship is one in which the employer has the basic right to 'hire and fire' a worker and so is placed in the stronger bargaining position. As a way of redressing the balance Parliament has intervened to grant employees a variety of forms of protection, which are to be found principally in the Employment Protection (Consolidation) Act 1978 and the Employment Acts of 1980 and 1982. Let us see the extent of some of these provisions relating to such matters as the right to receive written details of employment terms, equal pay, maternity rights and time off from work.

Right to receive written details of the contract

As most workers do not sign a written contract they may not know about all the terms applicable to their employment. In many cases these will be set out in an accessible copy of a collective agreement. Failing such conditions, i.e. where there is no *written* contract and no terms set out in a collective agreement, most 'full-time' workers, i.e. those engaged for at least 16 hours per week, are entitled to receive from their employers, within 13 weeks of commencing employment, a written statement detailing the contract terms. (Some full-time employees such as Crown servants and registered dock workers are excluded.)

Apart from identifying the parties, the written statement, according to the Employment Protection (Consolidation) Act 1978, must state the title of the job, the mode of payment, the periods of notice, conditions relating to holidays, sickness and injury, pension rights, and procedures for dealing with grievances.

Pay protection

In contrast to some countries, the UK has no statutory minimum wage, but there do exist some measures to protect low paid workers. Wages Councils have power to make wages orders fixing wages for workers in particular industries, such as agriculture, catering, footwear and clothing. Employers and appropriate trade unions are represented on each council. The councils were reformed by the Wages Act 1986, which also restricted their influence to workers over the age of 21.

The Act also modernised the law on deductions from pay, so that employers making deductions for other than tax, national insurance or agreed deductions would be acting unlawfully.

As payment in cash now no longer suits modern conditions, the Payment of Wages Act 1960 permits the payment of wages or salary by money, postal order or cheque, or by directly crediting the employee's bank account, provided the employee agrees.

All employees governed by the Employment Protection (Consolidation)

Act 1978 must receive an itemised statement of their pay describing both gross and net amounts and the amount and purpose of deductions.

Guaranteed payments

The same 1978 Act (as amended by Employment Act 1980) provides that all full-time employees and some part-time employees are entitled to receive a payment even if their employer provides no work at all. This helps those in industries where production is not constant and so workers are from time to time laid off or put on short-time working. For those not subject to a collective agreement providing for a guaranteed wage for a workless day the Act allows them a statutory payment.

Equal Pay

As long ago as 1888 the Trade Union Congress called for equal pay for men and women, and such a principle was included in the 1951 convention of the International Labour Organisation. Now, since 1975, the Equal Pay Act 1970 entitles both employees and self-employed workers to equal terms and conditions of employment as persons of the opposite sex engaged in similar work (see also the section on Equal value, p. 186).

Treatment of pregnant workers

The law entitles a woman not to be dismissed for reason of her pregnancy. An exception might arise where the nature of her employment is such, as working in a nuclear plant, that damage might be caused to her unborn child. If a pregnant worker cannot carry out her normal duties, she should be offered a suitable alternative job. Again under the Employment Protection (Consolidation) Act 1978 (as amended by the Employment Act 1980), a woman continuously employed for two years by the same employer, is entitled to return to her original job up to 29 weeks from giving birth, so long as she has given her employer sufficient notice of this intention. If such reinstatement would not be reasonably practicable and the woman refuses a suitable alternative job, her employer will be released from the duty to re-employ her. Businesses with five or fewer employees may disregard the obligation to reinstate a woman if it would not be reasonably practicable to do so.

Following the Social Security Act 1986, changes were made to the law on maternity pay. As from April 1987, Statutory Maternity Pay was introduced, payable by employers rather than by the DHSS. The basic rate (equal to that of Statutory Sick Pay) will be paid for 18 weeks to a woman who has worked for her present employer for at least 6 months. Women having worked with the same employer for two years are entitled to an increased Statutory Maternity Pay of nine-tenths normal wages, for the first 6 weeks of absence on maternity leave.

Women in receipt of Income Support or Family Credit (both introduced by the Social Security Act 1986) may qualify for £75 grant, payable from the Social Fund managed by the DHSS.

How far is the present law adequate in protecting the position of a woman worker who becomes pregnant?

Time off from work

Both the Employment Protection (Consolidation) Act 1978 and the Employment Act 1980 entitle certain workers to time off from their normal employment duties:

a for ante-natal care for a pregnant employee;
b to carry out public duties such as a justice of the peace, or membership of water or health authorities;
c to undertake duties as an official of an independent trade union;
d to take part in trade union activities at an appropriate time;
e to look for another job if made redundant (see below).

Trade union membership

Many of us who work in jobs are members of trade unions, and in some occupations a trade union and an employer may have agreed that all employees must belong to a particular union. Under the Employment Act 1980, employees have a right not to be unreasonably excluded or expelled from a trade union. This is particularly important to those who would lose their jobs as a consequence of being refused membership of a union or being expelled from it.

Hours of work

There are few statutory restrictions on the hours worked by adult male workers. Those whose hours of work are limited by statutory restrictions include sheet glass workers and bakery night workers, and those employed in underground work. Public service, locomotive and heavy goods vehicle drivers may not drive for more than $5\frac{1}{2}$ hours at a stretch and 10 hours a day (Transport Act 1968). Women, on the other hand, are governed by the Factories Act 1961 and are subject to general restrictions such as not working for more than 9 hours a day. Moreover, nightwork is generally forbidden for persons under 18 years of age and for women. Children who are two years below school-leaving age may work for two hours on a school day (but not before 6.00 a.m. nor after 8.00 p.m.). Local authorities have general powers under the Education Act 1944 to regulate the employment of children.

Sickness or injury at work

We have seen that an employer must bring to the notice of employees any provisions under the contract of employment relating to sickness or injury. Often an employee will continue to be paid if absent from work owing to sickness. Only if the sickness involves prolonged absence from work may an employer be entitled to regard the contract at an end. The contract can be terminated then, by what is called 'frustration', because it cannot be carried out.

From April 1982 employers became responsible for payment of sick pay for the first 8 weeks of sickness of their employees. Thereafer, under the Social Security Act, employees who have made sufficient contributions are entitled to State benefits. If the illness is chronic and lasts more than 168 days, an employee may claim State Invalidity Benefit. Illness brought on by alcoholic excess will disqualify an employee from receiving benefit. See below for accidents at work.

What are the duties under an employment contract?

Some terms and conditions will be fixed by the parties, or set out in collective agreements. In the absence of such terms, an industrial tribunal or court called upon to determine the existence of terms will *imply* those which, although not mentioned, seem to be obvious.

A term will be implied if it is well established through custom and practice. So, when a weaver objected to a deduction for bad workmanship from his wages because there was no such express term in his contract, the court upheld the deduction because it reflected a long-standing custom at that time among Lancashire weavers (Sagar *v.* Ridehalgh 1931).

Employers' implied duties

Even if nothing is said about certain matters, the common law *implies* certain duties.

Duty to pay for work

At common law the principal implied duty of an employer is to pay employees wages, salary or other payment. Normally, payment is dependent on the employee being available for work.

Duty to provide work

There is, in general, no implied duty at common law on an employer to provide an employee with work. As a judge said: 'Provided I pay my cook her wages she cannot complain if I choose to take any or all of my meals out.' This principle was brought home to Mr Langston, whose car-worker colleagues refused to work with him and who was paid but not put to work by his employers. The court decided that there was no *right* to work 'for any particular employer or in any particular place' (Langston *v.* Chrysler/AUEW 1974).

Duty of respect

As employer is under an implied duty to treat employees with respect and courtesy.

Duty to provide a safe place of work

This important implied duty to ensure the reasonable safety of employees will be fully discussed below.

Note The Companies Act 1980 provides that directors of a trading company should have regard for the interests of the company's employees as well as the interests of shareholders.

Employees' implied duties

Duty of faithful service

When it is remembered that an employment contract involves the giving of *personal* service, it will be appreciated that loyalty and good faith are demanded of employees. Conduct by an employee which destroys this implied 'duty of fidelity' causes a breach of the contract. Fidelity will be spoilt by stealing from the employer or disclosing the employer's trade secrets, or perhaps by taking part in a strike.

Although a strike legally breaks the contract between an employee and employer, the usual attitude is that the contract is merely *suspended* for the duration of the industrial action. In a previous chapter we noted that the Trade Union and Labour Relations Act 1974 (as amended by the Employment Act 1980) grants immunity from legal action to trade unions so long as the action is taken 'in contemplation or furtherance of a trade dispute'.

Although an invention made by an employee and arrived at in the course of carrying out normal duties belongs to the employer, the Patents Act 1977 does entitle the employee to receive some compensation. As regards copyright (Copyright Act 1956) any original literary or musical work belongs to the employee unless the work is created as part of the worker's employment duties.

Duty to obey orders

Implied in the duty of faithful service is the obligation on an employee to obey all reasonable and lawful orders. However, an order which is lawful and reasonable may be disobeyed if it would mean the employee acting outside contractual duties. For actions to be taken against the employee, the disobedience must generally amount to more than an isolated act. For instance, when a gardener became abusive when told by his employer to pot some plants, the employer was held to be entitled to dismiss him because there had been a history of disobedience (Pepper v. Webb 1969).

Duty to be of good conduct

An employee is under an implied duty not to commit any misconduct. So, when an employee took £15 from the till of a betting shop which he managed, leaving an IOU in its place, he was held to have been rightly dismissed for behaving in manner inconsistent with his employment (Sinclair v. Neighbour 1967).

Misconduct outside employment will not generally be relevant, unless it reflects on the job that the employee does. For example, an accountant convicted for theft may not be trusted with the employer's money.

How are workers protected from discrimination?

We noted earlier that people seeking work are protected from discrimination based on sex, race and sometimes criminal convictions. We must now examine these laws in more detail.

Sex discrimination

The Equal Pay Act 1970 (substantially amended by the Sex Discrimination Act 1975) was aimed at tackling the problem of unequal employment terms based purely on grounds of sex. Though equally applicable to discrimination against men, the main effect of the Acts is necessarily in respect of female workers.

Under the Acts all workers' contracts of employment are taken to include an 'equality clause'. This states that a worker is entitled to receive no less favourable terms than a fellow worker of the opposite sex who is employed on *like work* or on work rated as equivalent (i.e. through a job evaluation exercise).

The question to be decided is whether, if any practical differences exist, they are of a type which could be expected to be reflected in different terms and conditions in a contract. Thus Mrs Lawton, who was employed to cook and serve meals to a company's directors, complained that she received a lower level of pay than her male counterparts who served the company's general staff. Her claim was upheld as there was no practical difference in their work, and so she was entitled to the same rate of pay for a basic working week (Capper Pass Company v. Lawton 1977).

The equality clause will not operate if the employer can prove that the variation in pay and terms is due to 'genuine material differences' other than differences of sex. Differences may therefore be a reflection of the level of qualifications possessed by the employee or the degree of responsibility borne by the employee.

Equal value

The British Government was obliged to introduce in 1984, an amendment to the Equal Pay Act following an adverse ruling on the Act by the European Court. The Equal Pay (Amendment) Regulations 1983 was enacted in order that English law conformed with the EEC Treaty. A woman can now take advantage of an equality clause where she is employed on work of equal value to that of a man in the same employment. Comparison can be made with workers of the opposite sex who do *different* but comparably skilled and responsible jobs. This means that, say, a woman cook could claim equal pay with higher paid males doing different but comparable work in a shipyard (Hayward *v.* Cammell Laird 1986. In this particular case she is to appeal against a decision that she gets better sick pay as well as a free daily meal.). This and a number of cases to be decided in 1987 will determine the extent to which English courts will recognise the notion of 'equal value' in equal pay claims. However the influence of Community Law in the English courts can be substantial. In 1987, the Court of Appeal applied the equal value provision in the EEC Article 119 in a case decided in favour of Mrs Pickstone in her claim for equal pay for work of equal value against her employer (Pickstone *v.* Freemans (Mail Order) plc 1987). This ruling gave Mrs Pickstone a remedy which she would not have had under the Equal Pay Act 1970.

Are you able to chart the progress of the Hayward case, and the cases of Leverton *v.* Clwyd County Council, Pickstone *v.* Freemans, and Enderby *v.* DHSS?

The Equal Opportunities Commission

Set up by the Sex Discrimination Act 1975, the Commission has the task of promoting equal opportunities for men and women and to review the working of the 1970 and 1975 Acts. It may conduct formal investigations, and may issue a 'discrimination notice' to an employer. This notice sets out steps to be pursued to end the discrimination complained of. Subject to a right of appeal against a notice either to the Commission or to an industrial tribunal, the employer has 5 years within which to comply with the notice.

Despite over 10 years of laws aimed at equal pay, the Commission reported in 1986 that women still earned less than 75 per cent of the average hourly pay for men. This is set against the background of the fact that women comprise 51.3 per cent of the population and 41.4 per cent of the workforce. By 1985 men earned an average £190.40 as against £125.50 for women.

The Sex Discrimination Act 1975

This Act makes unlawful certain forms of discrimination based on grounds of sex or marital status. Subject to qualifications, there must be no discrimination in education, the provision of goods and services or advertising, as well as in employment. Private households and organisations with less than 6 employees are excluded from the provisions of the Act. Discrimination based on sex is allowed with regard to employment in the police or the prison service, the Church and mines. The Crown, too, is excluded from provision of the Act, so it is the eldest son who must still succeed the throne. Moreover, some jobs may be reserved for workers of a particular sex to preserve decency or privacy.

Discrimination may be *direct*, as where a woman is treated less favourably than a man, or *indirect*, as where an employer sets down conditions which men rather than women can meet. A person who has either brought or taken part in proceedings, or has alleged discrimination, has a right not to be victimised. Complaints in the field of employment may be brought before an industrial tribunal.

The EEC's view

Since the UK joined the European Economic Community through the European Communities Act 1972, some of the articles of the Treaty of Rome are binding law. For example Article 119 states that each member State must apply 'the principle that men and women should receive equal pay for equal work'. This has the consequence of giving rights to individuals so that English Courts may have to refer a question involving the interpretation of a Treaty Provision to the European Court of Justice.

In 1980 a female part-time clothing workers, Mrs Jenkins, had her case for the same basic rate as a full-time male worker referred to the Court of Justice. A favourable decision to her could have led to some 4 million claims by female part-time workers for equal rates of pay. In fact, in the case of Jenkins v. Kingsgate Productions (1981) the Court of Justice decided that part-time work was a material difference which entitled the employer to pay women less.

The European Court decided in a case brought by Miss Marshall against her employers in 1986, that the dismissal of a woman from her job merely because she had reached the qualifying age for a state pension, and where that age was different for women and men, amounted to sex discrimination. This infringed the principle of equality of treatment laid down by a European Council Directive (No. 76/207). This led to the passing of the Sex Discrimination Act 1986 which, among other things, makes it unlawful to discriminate against women in respect of retirement from employment. This has the effect of enabling both sexes to share a common retirement age.

Racial discrimination

The existence of racial discrimination in society is reflected in the unfair treatment of certain racial groups. In many areas with a high black population in this country, unemployment is above average. It has been suggested by some commentators that the city riots in Bristol, Liverpool, Manchester and London between 1980 and 1985 were due to the exceptionally high unemployment rate amongst black people. Parliament has attempted to tackle the problem of racial discrimination through the Race Relations Act 1976, which was itself influenced by the laws relating to sex discrimination. Thus the Act created the Commission for Racial Equality, whose functions include investigating and reporting instances of racial discrimination. It may draw up Codes of Behaviour in consulation with employers and trade unions. In cases of organisations thought to be committing an unlawful discrimination, the Commission may issue a Discrimination Notice. If after 5 years the discrimination does not cease, the Commission may obtain an order from a County Court requesting the ending of the practice described in the Notice.

The Act makes it unlawful to discriminate against a person on the grounds of race, i.e. colour, race, religion, nationality, or ethnic or national origins. An employee must not be directly discriminated against by being treated less favourably because of race. Neither must there be conditions which cannot be met, which would leave the effect of indirectly discriminating against employee by reason of race. It is unlawful to practise discrimination in the selection of employees or in the employment terms including promotion, training, benefits and other facilities and services. In the first case of victimisation under the Act a woman personnel officer claimed she had been unfairly dismissed after she had reported her employers to the Commission over their treatment of her West Indian colleague, who was moved out of the reception area 'because of her colour and negroid appearance'. An industrial tribunal awarded the personnel officer £562 for victimisation and £300 to the West Indian woman (Wild & Joseph *v*. D. Clulow of Earls Court 1980).

However, if membership of a particular racial group is a genuine occupational qualification the Act does not apply. This might occur in entertainment, in artistic or photographic modelling, in a restaurant, or where a person is required to provide personal services promoting the welfare of racial groups.

A restriction on the employment of persons wearing beards was held 'justifiable' because it was imposed in the interests of hygiene, even though it affected the employment prospects of an orthodox Sikh (Panesar *v*. Nestlé Company 1979).

Convicted persons

After a 'rehabilitation period' a person convicted of committing a criminal offence involving no more than imprisonment for 30 months may in particular circumstances be regarded as a rehabilitated person by the Rehabilitation of Offenders Act 1974. Such a person is regarded as having a 'spent conviction' after a period of 10 or 7 years, depending on the term of imprisonment imposed, with a shorter period applicable for offenders under 17 years of age. There is, however, a wide range of excluded employments, including the Crown and the Post Office; the police; prison officers and probation officers; judges and magistrates ; doctors, lawyers, accountants, teachers and midwives.

How can employment be terminated

Notice

Most people terminate their employment by giving notice of their intention to their employer. The Employment Protection (Consolidation) Act 1978 requires employees to give at least one week's notice. Employers must, according to the same Act, give their full-time employees (i.e. those working over 16 hours a week) at least one week's notice after four weeks' service and up to one year's service. Further, an employee must receive at least two weeks' notice for two years' service, and an additional week's notice for each year of service up to a maximum of 12 weeks' notice for a period of 12 years' service. Payment of wages in lieu of notice is permitted.

Redundancy

Every organisation exists within an economic environment and so must be adaptable as economic conditions change. For example, an organisation may decide to adopt new, less labour intensive methods and techniques or to move to a less expensive location. In extreme cases, the organisation may have to cease business altogether.

Employees who lose their jobs as a consequence of such events may be regarded as being **redundant**. The need to compensate workers who through long service had acquired a sense of ownership of their jobs was recognised by the Redundancy Payments Act 1965. Now, this Act has been substantially replaced by provisions of the Employment Protection (Consolidation) Act 1978.

Who qualifies?

Employees who are more than 18 years old and are below retirement age (see Sex Discrimination Act 1986, page 188) may qualify for a redundancy payment, but must have been continuously employed with the same employer for two years. Some workers are not able to qualify, such as those who ordinarily work outside the UK, those employed by their spouses, and Crown servants.

Employees must have been dismissed through the termination of their contract by the employer, either with or without notice. If different, unfavourable terms such as a lower rate of pay and reduced status are imposed on an employee, the contract of employment may be regarded as repudiated and the employee therefore as dismissed. An employee who is given advance warning of redundancy but finds another job before actually receiving notice, is not regarded as dismissed and so will not qualify for redundancy pay.

Compensation will be lost if the employee, before the end of the existing contract, is offered re-employment under different terms and conditions and unreasonably turns down the offer. However, the offer of alternative work must be suitable for that employee in relation to pay, status and prospects. The question of the reasonableness of the refusal will be judged by taking into account personal factors such as hours of work or the need to travel. An employee who accepts an offer of alternative employment is entitled to a 4-week trial period, during which the offer may be rejected without losing redundancy rights.

How is the compensation assessed?

The State, through the Department of Employment, helps to finance a Redundancy Fund which is otherwise funded from the employers' social security contributions. It is the employer who pays the redundancy money to the employees, after which there is entitlement to a rebate (about 40 per cent of the total payment) from the Fund. The compensation is assessed by reference to the employee's age at dismissal, and the period of continuous service. A redundant employee aged over 41 is entitled to 1½ weeks' pay for each year of service. Employees aged between 22 and 41 receive one week's pay for each year of service, and those aged between 18 and 22 half a week's pay. In any case, a claim for payment is restricted to a maximum of 20 years' service.

Complaints about redundancy are heard by industrial tribunals. In assessing continuity of employment, up to 26 weeks of absence from work because of pregnancy, sickness, injury or a temporary cessation of work will count towards the qualifying period. Any period during which the employee was either on strike or locked out by the employer cannot be counted towards the qualifying two years, but at the same time it does not break the continuity of service.

In calculating redundancy pay, the maximum allowable weekly limit is £158.00 (since 1 April 1987). However the 35 per cent government rebate is now only payable to employers employing 9 or fewer (employees) workers up to a limit of £30 000. No rebate is payable in respect of workplaces with 10 or more employees.

Must employers consult over redundancy proposals?

The Employment Protection Act 1975 requires an employer intending to make employees redundant to consult with representatives of a recognised independent trade union. Consultations must take place at least 90 days before any proposed dismissals of more than 100 workers are put into effect. If an employer proposes to make redundant 10 or more workers consultations must begin at least 60 days before those dismissals are to take place.

Unfair dismissal

An employee who is dismissed after being continuously employed for a period of at least 26 weeks has a right under the Employment Protection (Consolidation) Act 1978 to ask the employer to provide a written statement setting out the reasons for dismissal. If the employer fails to do this, the employee may complain to an industrial tribunal, which may order the employer to compensate the employee by paying two weeks' pay.

The same Act provides that a full-time employee, that is, someone working under a contract of at least 16 hours a week (or someone who has worked 8 hours a week for 5 years), has a right 'not to be unfairly dismissed'. To qualify for this protection, the employee must have been in continuous employment for the same employer for 52 weeks and must be below retirement age.

Different conditions apply to workers employed by an organisation having fewer than 20 employees. In such a case, the right to sue for unfair dismissal arises only after two years' service (Employment Act 1980).

Moreover, some employees have no right to sue for unfair dismissal. Amongst those excluded are those employed by their spouses, members of the police force, registered dock workers and those who ordinarily work outside the UK.

An employee will be regarded as dismissed if the contract of employment is terminated by the employer with or without notice.

Is an employee forced to resign regarded as dismissed?

If an employer commits an act which is an important breach 'going to the root' of the employment contract, it may be fair for the employee to consider it a reason for release from performing his or her side of the contract. An employee resigning a post because of such repudiation, may be regarded as being 'constructively' dismissed. Such a dismissal may be claimed to be unfair.

This is what Mrs Austin claimed when she complained that she was not provided with eye protectors which could fit over her spectacles. Hearing nothing further about the provision of suitable goggles, she resigned after 6 months. The Employment Appeal Tribunal found in her favour, holding that her employers had failed to investigate her complaints in respect of safety matters and so had committed a fundamental breach going to the root of her contract. She was considered as unfairly dismissed (British Aircraft Corporation v. Austin 1978).

On the other hand Mrs Walker who, on being given 7 weeks' notice of dismissal, did not return to work, had terminated her own employment, and therefore had not been dismissed (Walker v. Cotswold Chine Home School 1977).

When will a dismissal be fair?

It is for the employee to show that he or she has been dismissed. The employer has to satisfy an industrial tribunal that the reason for the dismissal was proper. In assessing the fairness of the dismissal the tribunal must (Employment Act 1980) take account of the merits of the case, including the size and administrative resources of the employer's undertaking.

Under the Employment Protection (Consolidation) Act 1978 the employer must show that the reason for the dismissal was proper and that it falls within one of the following categories:

a **Incapability** of a worker to carry out duties by reference to such matters as the degree of skill possessed and state of health or disability brought about by injury. The dismissal may also be fair if the worker's qualifications are found to be wanting.

b **Misconduct** on the part of the employee may be a fair reason for dismissal, but it must be of a nature to warrant dismissal. In any case, the employer will be expected to have complied with fair disciplinary procedures (of which the Advisory Conciliation and Arbitration Service has produced a code of conduct). The employee should have been given adequate warnings and an opportunity to state his or her case. Misconduct outside working hours may only be regarded as grounds for dismissal if it is grave or capable of hurting the employer's business.

c **Redundancy** of an employee may be regarded as a fair reason for dismissal. However, if the reason for the redundancy is connected with the employee's trade union membership or is in contravention of agreed procedures the employee may be regarded as unfairly dismissed.

d **Statutory restrictions** may give rise to a fair reason for dismissal. This may occur where a person who is employed to drive commits an offence under the Road Traffic Act whereby the person's driving licence is revoked.

e **Other substantial reasons** may be pleaded by an employer as providing for a fair dismissal. For example, an employee may unreasonably refuse to accept changes in terms and conditions of employment in an organisation which wishes to adapt to changing circumstances.

When will a dismissal be regarded as unfair?

Any reason falling outside those already discussed may be unfair. Beyond that, statute law specifies particular reasons for dismissal being unfair. Thus the Employment Protection (Consolidation) Act 1978 states that a female employee who is dismissed only because she has become pregnant may be regarded as unfairly dismissed. Only if it can be shown that her employment was contrary to the law, e.g. the Ionising Radiation Regulations 1968–9, will the dismissal of a pregnant worker be regarded as fair, because the radiation would be harmful to the unborn child.

In connection with dismissals relating to trade union membership, the 1978 Act provisions have been redrawn by the Employment Act 1982. Regardless of an employee's length of service, a dismissal will be regarded as unfair if the employee:

● was or proposed to become a member of an independent trade union;
● had or proposed to take part in the activities of such a union at an appropriate time;

- was not a member of any trade union, or of a particular trade union, or had refused or proposed to refuse to become or remain a member.

In addition, an employee has a right under the 1978 Act (as amended by the Employment Act 1980) not to be unfairly dismissed for refusing to join a trade union where there exists a Union Membership Agreement (UMA – whereby workers agree to a 'closed shop' under which trade union membership is compulsory). The objection to joining needs to be based on genuine grounds of conscience or other deeply held personal conviction concerning trade union membership. Indeed, unless a *new* UMA has been supported by a ballot off 80 per cent of those employed by an organisation, the dismissal of an employee for refusing to join a trade union will be unfair. Related to this is the right of employees not to have action short of dismissal taken against them to compel them to join a trade union if they object on genuine grounds. Employees so victimised may complain to an industrial tribunal, which may make an award. The Employment Act 1982 added the requirement for a five-yearly review of a closed-shop agreement in a secret ballot.

An employee dismissed for taking part in a strike or other industrial action will be regarded as unfairly dismissed if victimisation can be shown.

How can an industrial tribunal help a dismissed worker?

If, after hearing each side in an industrial dispute, the tribunal decides that the employee was dismissed unfairly, it may make an award. The complainant may be awarded reinstatement and the employer ordered to give the old job back. Alternatively re-engagement with the same employer may be offered, but not necessarily in the previous post. Whether these are possible depends on the circumstances of the case and the amount of acrimony felt on each side.

Failing these remedies, the tribunal may award the complainant compensation for loss of employment. This is made up of a **basic award** based upon the employee's age and years of service (see redundancy provisions), up to a maximum of £4050 for an employee aged 41 or over with 20 years' service. Any amount already received for redundancy is set against the basic award. Additionally an employee's loss of income, pension rights and loss of future employment prospects may be met by the order of a **compensation award** up to a maximum of £7000. For dismissals regarded as unfair because related to trade union membership (see above) there is a special award, subject to a maximum of £20 000.

Wrongful dismissal under the common law

You will recall that the employment relationship is based on a legally enforceable agreement, and so a serious breach of such of a contract entitles either party to pursue a legal action. An employee, therefore, who commits an act 'going to the root' of the contract may be dismissed summarily, i.e. without notice. Unlike the other forms of termination we have looked at, wrongful dismissal is based not on statute but on common law. An employee who claims wrongful dismissal because of the employer's breach of contract brings the action before the law courts and not an industrial tribunal. Whether or not the dismissal was wrongful is then determined by the court according to the facts of each particular case, and by quoting previous court decisions.

Therefore, on the point of whether disobedience entitles an employer to dismiss a worker summarily, we have seen (Pepper *v.* Webb 1969) that the disobedience must be the 'last straw' in a history of complaints, and not a sole incident. Only an act of a grave and serious character which has the effect of repudiating the contract or one of its essential conditions will entitle the employer at common law to dismiss a worker summarily. Theft of the employer's property and making a secret profit from the employer's undertaking may be such acts.

How can a court help a wrongfully dismissed worker?

The employee who becomes the plaintiff in a court action must show the court that the employer, the defendant, committed a breach of contract by not giving proper notice as required by the contract. The most appropriate help that the court can offer a wronged employee is to order the employer to pay a compensatory amount as damages. The amount awarded might be that sum which the employee would have received as wages had the full notice period been served out. The award might take into account the loss of future prospects, as where an apprenticeship was wrongfully curtailed, thus depriving the employee of the acquisition of skills (as in Dunk *v.* Waller and Son Company 1970).

What if the employee who has been wrongfully dismissed does nothing to help the situation? At common law any person who has suffered a legal wrong is expected to lessen or 'mitigate' the loss. Thus the County Court of the High Court before which the employee pursues the legal action for breach of contract will want to see evidence that the dismissed employee has tried to find alternative employment. If the employee has made no attempt to mitigate the loss the court may reduce the amount of damages. In assessing damages the court will make a deduction in respect of any payments of income tax, unemployment benefit and redundancy pay.

Another type of award is an **injunction**, which is granted only at the discretion of the court. The effect of this is that the court orders the employer not to dismiss the employee wrongfully, on pain of punishment. In practice an injunction will only be awarded in highly exceptional cases. There is another discretionary equitable remedy, **specific performance**, by which a court may order a person to carry out that which he or she specifically promised to do. However, as a rule, a court will not order specific performance of a contract of personal service. Thus a court was prepared only to issue an injunction to restrain the actress Bette Davis from doing something she had contracted not to do, namely, to work for another film producer without her employer's consent (Warner Bros. Pictures Inc. *v.* Nelson 1937). Indeed, the Trade Union and Labour Relations Act 1974 states that no court can, either by an order of specific performance or by injunction restraining a breach of contract, compel an employee to do any work or attend at any place for the doing of any work.

The expense of pursuing a legal action before the law courts, despite legal aid (see Chapter 14, p. 107), and the time taken to resolve a dispute make this sort of action unpopular. Most dismissed employees allege statutory unfair dismissal before an industrial tribunal, which is informal and less expensive.

How does the law ensure that organisations provide a safe place to work?

What are the rights of a worker who is injured through coming into contact with an exposed electric cable, loses a finger on an unguarded saw, or suffers concussion when driven in a firm's van by a colleague who engaged in horseplay? The answers to these questions will be found in rules laid down by the common law as well as statutory provisions. However, there can be no doubt that none of us (except perhaps members of the armed forces or the police) undertakes to be injured or killed as a result of doing our work.

At common law there is a defence to an action alleging negligence, whereby the person injured is claimed to have voluntarily undertaken the risk of injury. However, this is a harsh principle to apply to the working environment. The fact that a worker knows that the workplace is dangerous does not thereby mean that he or she consents to being injured. As far back as 1891 a Mr Smith was taken not to have consented to being injured by falling stones carried by a crane in the quarry in which he worked. His employers could not escape their liability (Smith v. Baker and Sons 1891).

Not every job carries such hazards, so for example a bank clerk, a shop assistant, and a civil service clerical officer are exposed to less danger than a manual worker using factory machinery or a merchant seaman. An implied duty is placed on employers to ensure that their employees are not exposed to avoidable dangers at work. The clearest statement of this common law duty was that expressed by the judge in the case of Wilsons and Clyde Coal Company v. English (1938). Mr English had suffered an injury owing to the very dangerous conditions of the mine in which he worked. After hearing both sides to the dispute the judge decided that the employer could not escape his duty to care for the safety of his employees by placing the blame on the coalmine manager. Employers are under a fundamental duty to take reasonable steps to protect their employees from dangers at work. This duty covered 'the provision of a competent staff, adequate material and a proper system, and effective supervision'. We shall consider these points below.

Let us be clear first about the exact nature of an employer's duty. The duty not to allow employees to suffer unnecessary risks, if broken by an employer, gives an employee who has been injured the right to sue in the courts under the tort of negligence. You will recall that in Chapter 2 we explained that this tort arose from the legal principles laid down by the judges in the House of Lords in the case of Donoghue v. Stevenson (1932) (see p. 31).

Accidents in the work place normally occur because someone has been careless, so, before an injured employee can sue the employer in the tort of negligence, the latter must be shown to be at fault. The employee must give the court evidence that:

a the employer owed the employee a duty of care;
b there was a failure to observe this duty; and
c as a consequence the worker suffered an injury.

As we shall see, employees unable to work because of an accident at work may be entitled to certain State welfare benefits. However, the tort of negligence allows employees to seek compensation from those at fault for injuries. In order that employers can meet such claims for compensation

Parliament requires employers to purchase a policy of insurance against liability to employees for injury or disease arising 'out of or in the course of their employment'. This law is the Employers' Liability (Compulsory Insurance) Act 1969.

What is the standard of care expected of an employer?

The standard of care owed by employers to their employees will vary according to the individual worker's age, experience or physical wellbeing. Normally, an employer cannot escape liability by raising the individual's susceptibility to injury as a defence. The employer must take the employee 'as he finds him', so a higher standard of care would be expected in respect of, for example, a one-eyed worker. Such was the disability of Mr Paris, who was not supplied with goggles in work in which flying splinters were a hazard. He therefore succeeded in showing that his employer breached his duty of care when a splinter blinded his remaining eye (Paris v. Stepney Borough Council 1951).

On the other hand, an employer cannot be held responsible for outlandish behaviour, as when Mr Lazarus was injured in the rush to be first in the tea queue (Lazarus v. Firestone Tyre and Rubber Company 1963).

Similarly, an employer is entitled to expect that employees will use their skill and experience in carrying out their duties. A court decided that a skilled steel worker should have been familiar with an obvious risk, like the spilling of molten metal on himself. When this happened to him, his employers were found not to be liable, particularly as Mr Haynes had not worn the protective spats which his employers had made available to the moulders (Qualcast Company v. Haynes 1959). Of course, an employer would be expected to take reasonable steps to ensure that protective items, such as goggles, masks and spats, are actually used by employees.

Must the injury be one which is foreseeable?

A court will hold an employer liable for negligence only for those risks which a reasonable employer would have foreseen. Regarding the tort of negligence, the test of what can be foreseen is that of what 'the reasonable man' would have anticipated. This non-existent figure, described by a judge as 'the man on the Clapham omnibus', affords a court the opportunity of considering a case from the standpoint of an ordinary person, ignoring personal idiosyncracies.

It will depend very much on the circumstances as to what a reasonable employer might foresee. If a hazard would not be reasonably foreseeable, because medical awareness of a particular danger is not far advanced, the employer may not be liable. Thus, only recently have the dangers of asbestos to a person's lungs and lead poisoning in the air been fully appreciated. If the knowledge of a risk is known, the failure to take steps to avoid it will result in liability. Thus Mr Stokes's company was ordered to pay him compensation when he contracted scrotal cancer through wearing oil-soaked overalls in his work. The company doctor was negligent in failing to keep abreast of medical developments (Stokes v. GKN Company 1968).

Obvious negligence

On some occasions it may be very difficult for a person suffering an injury to be able to put a finger on just who was to blame. What is certain is that an injury did in fact occur and that it happened in or around premises controlled by another. Indeed, 'the facts speak for themselves' (this principle is called by lawyers *res ipsa loquitur*), so that a person suing in negligence pleads that although the fault cannot be proved to be that of another, there is no other reasonable explanation. For instance, Mr Scott was injured when bags of sugar fell on him as he passed through a doorway of a company's warehouse. In the case which he brought against the company, the court allowed him to plead *res ipsa loquitut*, because the accident was one which could have been avoided by the management exercising proper care. He was entitled to assume that the company was at fault (Scott *v.* London and St Katherine Docks Company 1865).

Is the employer liable for remote hazards?

Set against the fact that an employer may be liable for foreseeable risks, is that an employer may not be expected to take steps to avoid the risk of harm which is too remote. The balance of the risk and the economic cost of avoiding it was considered in the case of Mr Latimer who injured himself when he slipped on a factory floor. A freak rain storm had flooded the factory floor, causing it to be very slippery. The employers had put as much sawdust as was available on the floor in order to restart work. The court agreed with their contention that it would have been unreasonable to close the factory in the circumstances (Latimer *v.* A.E.C. Company 1952).

In another case, the risk of an asbestos lid covering a cauldron of molten metal slipping and splashing someone was foreseeable. In the event, when the lid slipped into the cauldron it actually exploded, injuring Mr Doughty. This explosion was held to be too remote for a reasonable employer to have been expected to guard against (Doughty *v.* Turner Manufacturing Company 1964).

The Wilsons case

Let us now consider the points raised in the Wilsons case referred to on p. 195.

Reliable colleagues

We are all entitled to expect that our employers will appoint sufficiently experienced and qualified colleagues. For this reason a company was made responsible for an injury suffered by Mr Hudson when he was tripped by a colleague who was well known as a practical joker (Hudson *v.* Ridge Manufacturing Company 1957).

Safe premises and equipment

Employees should expect that their work premises and equipment are safe. The duty on an employer to ensure such safety applies even where the work is to be carried out on someone else's premises. An experienced window cleaner was awarded compensation for injuries he suffered while attempting to clean windows on a customer's premises (General Cleaning Contractors *v.* Christmas 1953).

By driving a firm's van which had no heating Mr Bradford suffered frostbite, and he successfully sued his employers for failing in their duty to provide safe equipment (Bradford *v.* Robinson Rentals 1967).

Of particular assistance to employees who may find it difficult to prove that the employer was aware of defects in equipment, is the Employers' Liability (Defective Equipment) Act 1969. The Act provides that if an employee suffers an injury in the course of employment through using defective equipment the employer can be sued. This is so even if the reason for the defect is attributable to the maker of the equipment.

Safe system

The method for carrying out work must be safe, and protective equipment, training and supervision must be adequate. The Stone Manganese Company discovered that it was not sufficient merely to provide protective ear-muffs; they had to ensure that their employees used them so as to avoid the risk of injury (Berry v. Stone Manganese Company 1971).

As a result of the Unfair Contract Terms Act 1977 an employer may not exclude his liability in negligence by inserting a term in employment contracts to this effect, or even by posting a disclaimer of liability notice.

Is an employer liable for the wrongful acts of employees?

So far we have looked at the personal duty owed by an employer to all of the employees individually. You may have noticed that in some of the cases we have seen the company itself is sued for accidents that may well have been due to the careless acts to its employees. Under the common law an employer may have to answer for the wrongful acts of employees. This type of liability is called **vicarious** liability. This principle arises from the practical point that an employer rather than an employee can meet a claim for damages.

A person injured at the hands of a negligent or careless worker may succeed in recovering compensation from the worker's employer if it is proved that:

a the wrongdoer was an employee;
b the employee's conduct was wrongful, for example, a negligent act; and
c the conduct occurred at a time when the employee was 'in the course of his or her employment.'

An employee may be regarded as acting within the course of his or her employment, and so doing the job, even if he or she is the chief beneficiary of the wrongful act. The managing clerk of a firm of solicitors deceived a client in the sale of her land to his own advantage. Mrs Lloyd won her action against the clerk's employers, on the grounds that they were vicariously liable for their employee's misconduct (Lloyd v. Grace, Smith and Company 1912).

However, if the employee's act is outside the scope of the job, the employer will not be vicariously liable. In the case of Hilton v. Thomas Burton Company (1961) a widow failed to show that the company was vicariously liable when her husband was killed in a van driven by a colleague on an unauthorised trip to a local café. The judge described the workers as being 'on a frolic of their own', and so could not be acting in the course of their employment.

Even if a worker is carrying out work in a manner forbidden by the employer, so long as it is still work for which he or she is paid, the employer may be vicariously liable for wrongful acts. Thus, when a driver of a horse-drawn bus raced a driver of another bus company to pick up passengers despite being instructed not to do so, and caused an accident, the employer was liable (Limpus v. London General Omnibus Company 1862). However a bus conductor who drove a bus and caused an accident was held not to be acting within the course of his employment, because he was not employed as a driver. The company could not be held answerable for their employee's conduct (Beard *v.* London General Omnibus Company 1900).

Do employers answer for the acts of independent contractors?

We have met this type of worker at the beginning of this chapter, and we have stated that the term independent contractor refers to a person who is not actually an employee. Because the relationship between an employer and employees is different, the general rule is that an employer of an independent contractor is not vicariously liable for the latter's misconduct.

An exception to this rule occurs in cases where the employer chooses an incompetent contractor, in which case there will be liability for any injuries caused to others exposed to the contractor's misconduct. Also, where legislation, such as the Factories Act 1961, imposes strict obligations to ensure safety, a failure on the part of a contractor to observe such duties will cause the employer to be vicariously liable.

An employer of a contractor engaged on particularly hazardous work will again not be able to escape liability. A company was therefore held liable for a fire which broke out in their client's cinema when a photographer they had hired ignited a magnesium powder to obtain a flash-light (Honeywill and Stein Company *v.* Larkin Bros 1934).

A further exception arises where contractors are employed to carry out work on a public highway and cause an injury to someone. Mr Holliday succeeded in his action against the employers of a contractor who had dug a hole in a road and whose lamp had exploded, causing Mr Holliday an injury (Holliday *v.* National Telephone Company 1899).

Finally, an employer who specifically instructs a contractor to do an act and knows it to be wrong will be vicariously liable for any resulting injuries. This is what happened when a contractor was ordered to dig up a street in the absence of any permission from the local authority. It was the employer who was liable (Ellis *v.* Sheffield Gas Consumers Company 1853).

Is an organisation liable for its employees' crimes?

We noted in Chapter 5 that corporations are *artificial* persons, being only legal creations, and so are different from human persons. It so happens that liability for criminal acts is normally based not only on the doing of a criminal act but also on *intending* to do the act in question. So, a person who leaves a supermarket without having paid for an item is not guilty of theft unless it can also be proved that the person intended permanently to deprive the supermarket of its property.

Clearly, a corporation does not have a mind as possessed by one of us, so on that ground it could never be convicted before a criminal court for committing a crime. Yet it would not be right for corporations to escape the consequences of criminal activity. In order to get round this problem, the judges have decided that a corporation can be responsible for criminal acts because it can be said to have a 'mind'. This 'mind' is that of the corporation's executives who decide what the organisation does. In effect, what the executive decides is what the corporation decides. If that involves committing a crime, then the corporation is taken to commit the crime.

However, no criminal liability attaches to a corporation if the decision to commit a criminal act is taken by one of the corporation's employees.

A company was decided not to be vicariously liable for a crime committed contrary to the Table Descriptions Act 1968 because the act was carried out by a branch manager. This employee did not occupy such a senior position in the company's management to be described as part of the 'mind' of the corporation (Tesco Stores Company v. Nattras 1972).

Can workers rely on breach of statute when suing employers?

Parliament has long intervened in conditions at work, particular with work in factories and mines, for here the accelerated production brought about by the Industrial Revolution in the nineteenth century produced terrible casualties amongst the workers. Many of the principles contained in various statutes are now to be found in the Health and Safety at Work Act 1974 (to be discussed below).

Often, an employee claiming to have been injured at work will base a civil action on the ground that the employer has failed to observe a statutory duty. For example, the Factories Act 1961 (which is being progressively replaced by the above 1974 Act) places duties on employers with a view to preventing work accidents. The statutory duties affect those working in a 'factory', namely a place involved in the making, altering, repairing, cleaning, destruction or adapting for sale of any article. A very important duty under the Act is that a factory owner shall securely fence 'every part of the transmission machinery' (Section 13), and 'every dangerous part of any machinery' (Section 14).

An injured worker may thus claim that the injury was the result of a failure of the employer to comply with this statutory duty. A dangerous part of machinery has been taken to include 'swarf' or shavings driven out of a piece of metal being drilled by Mr Millard, which entangled his hand and pulled it into the drill. The court decided that the machine should have been fenced to hold in any swarf, and this the employer had failed to do, so Mr Millard was entitled to be compensated (Millard v. Serk Tubes Ltd 1969).

What happens if the worker was partly responsible for the injury?

We should not be surprised, in view of the nature of accidents at work, that an employer sued for negligence may wish to complain that the employee was also at fault. Recognition in law that the injured person may share responsibility is to be found in the Law Reform (Contributory Negligence) Act 1945. Under this law the judge may reduce the amount of damages he might otherwise have awarded, according to the injured person's contribution to his own injury.

In Stapley v. Gypsum Mines Company (1953), the widow of a miner killed in a roof collapse received only 20 per cent of the damages awarded, on the grounds that her husband had been 80 per cent responsible for the accident. It was found that the deceased and a colleague had failed to carry out orders to make the roof safe.

If an employee is killed at work, can the relatives sue?

We have seen in the last case that the widow of a man who had been killed at work sued the man's employer. The Fatal Accidents Act 1976 enables certain dependents of the deceased to pursue a legal action against a person or organisation alleged to be responsible for the death. Normally the action must be brought within 3 years of the death, but a court has power to extend this period. The court will assess damages on the basis of the loss of the prospective earning power of the deceased. Any money payable to the deceased's dependents under an insurance policy or pension scheme is ignored by the court in assessing damages.

Is there a time limit on bringing court actions?

The Limitation Act 1980 provides that in respect of personal injuries, or death, an action for negligence or breach of statutory duty must be brought within 3 years of the incident. Sometimes this period commences from the time when the injury or disease became apparent. A cancer, for example, takes a long time to develop and so a right of action will date from the time of its discovery. Of course, the injury must be shown to be partly or entirely attributable to the behaviour of the wrongdoer.

What is the State's responsibility for industrial injuries?

You will realise that much of what we have discussed in relation to injuries at work depends on the injured worker taking someone to court. As the court has to discover fault, it may very well turn out that this is not proved and so the employee will not receive damages. At other times even if the employee does succeed the award may be reduced to reflect the employee's own contribution to the accident. In any case though, the litigation process is very slow and so it may be some while before a court is ready to issue its decision. The delay may amount to 2 or more years. How is the employee cared for in this time?

The State, through an insurance scheme (set up originally in 1948) provides contributors, both employed and self-employed persons, with certain welfare benefits. The national insurance scheme, now to be found in the Social Security Act 1986 provides for the deduction of regular contributions from working people's earnings. In exchange for these contributions allowances may be paid if a worker is unable to work owing to illness or injury, and, for those who have lost their jobs, unemployment benefit may be paid. Working women who become pregnant are entitled, as we have seen above, to allowances under Statutory Maternity Pay according to their circumstances.

Workers who suffer from injuries received from accidents at work or industrial diseases are entitled to various benefits according to whether the accident has caused an injury or disablement. Assessment of the extent of a worker's disability is carried out by doctors who are members of a Medical Board. Claimants are entitled to appeal against the ruling of the Social Services. Unlike the tort of negligence, fault is not so much the issue, as whether or not the accident occurred in the course of employment. Even if the employee was disobeying an employer's orders when the injury occurred, he or she will be entitled to a State benefit as long as what was being done was in connection with his or her work.

Because these benefits are available as a right, there is no reason why an injured worker should not also pursue damages by way of civil litigation. However, the Law Reform (Personal Injuries) Act 1948 requires a court to take into account half of any State benefits received by the worker in a period of 5 years from the date of the accident. This will be deducted from the award of damages made by a civil court.

The Health and Safety at Work Act 1974

In many areas of employment there is an obligation to report industrial accidents, and from the accidents reported to the Health and Safety Execu-

In 1985, 2427 injuries were reported to the Executive of which 414 were fatal.

tive we can get an idea of the severity of the problem. The figures are drawn from the records of the Inspectorates of Factories, Explosives, Mines and Quarries, Agriculture, Railways, Nuclear Installations, Alkali and Clean Air provisions.

The alarming level of industrial accidents and the unsatisfactory implementation of safety procedures caused the Robens Committee to be established, and its recommendations formed a foundation for legislation. That was the Health and Safety at Work Act 1974. As we have already observed, this Act is intended progressively to replace legislation such as the Factories Act 1961 and the Offices, Shops and Railway Premises Act 1963. Unlike previous legislation, the Act refers not to types of premises but to all employed persons (save for domestic employees).

A highly distinctive feature of the 1974 Act is that a breach of certain duties results not only in a right to sue in civil law, but in a criminal prosecution. Any person or corporate body can be charged with committing a crime under the Act. Treated as a summary offence before a Magistrates' Court, fines of up to £1000 may be imposed. In more serious cases offenders may be tried on indictment before a Crown Court, which has power to impose unlimited fines and in certain cases up to two years' imprisonment on officers of the organisation concerned. In 1985 there were 1534 prosecutions initiated under health and safety legislation.

The Health and Safety Executive, which was created by the 1974 Act, has as its main responsibility the enforcement of the legislation, and has the duty to appoint inspectors. The inspectors have power to enter work premises, taking with them a police officer if necessary, and there to make such examinations and investigations as are required. They may put any question to persons on the premises and may require the production of any relevant books or documents.

If the investigation reveals a failure to observe safe procedure for employees, an inspector may issue an Improvement Notice, which calls upon the ceasing of a breach within a specified period of not less than 21 days. In graver cases, where an inspector suspects a risk of serious personal injury, the issue of a Prohibition Notice may be made. The behaviour complained of is thereby forbidden. There is a right of appeal before an industrial tribunal against the issue of these notices (so that a Prohibition Notice becomes deferred). A total of 4655 enforcement notices were made in 1985.

Criminal liability

Employers may face prosecution for failing to observe certain general duties imposed by the 1974 Act. Section 2 calls upon employers *as far as is reasonably practicable* to ensure the health, safety and welfare of employees, mainly:

a to provide and maintain safe premises, equipment and systems for carrying out work;

b to ensure the safety and absence of risks to health in connection with the use, handling, storage and movement of articles and substances;

c to maintain any place of work over which the employer has control so as to ensure that it is safe and without risks to health;

d to ensure the provision and maintenance of a working environment

Fig. 19.1
Protecting equipment: metal worker,
chemical worker and firemen.

without risks to health and adequate for employees' welfare, i.e. toilet facilities, control of noise and fume levels and so on;

e to provide such information, training and supervision as is necessary to ensure the health and safety and welfare of employees.

Safety representatives

Safety representatives chosen from among employees must be appointed, the Act states, and, if it should be requested, there must also be established a safety committee. Employers are under a duty to consult such representatives on matters concerned with safety at work. Investigation of any potential hazards may be undertaken by safety representatives, who may also deal with any complaints made by employees. Representatives are entitled to be present and to represent the interests of employees in consultation with the Health and Safety inspectors. They have a further right to carry out an inspection of the work place every 3 months.

Section 6 of the Act imposes a duty to ensure the health and safety of users of any articles in the work-place. This duty is placed on any person who imports or supplies or designs such articles. Designers and manufacturers must also undertake any research necessary with a view to eliminate any risks to health and safety of articles. Any person who manufactures, imports or supplies any substance for use at work is also placed under this statutory duty.

Not only employers and suppliers have duties placed upon them, for by Section 7 all employees are also under a duty while at work to take reasonable care of their own and their fellow workers' safety.

The Health and Safety Commission is charged with the responsibility for the issue of codes of 'good industrial safety practice' which provide guidance on such matters as noise levels, toilet facilities, handling noxious substances and so on. Failure to observe these codes, which are always being added to, may lead to prosecution under the Act itself.

In 1986 the government proposed changes to some aspects of the law outlined in this chapter:

Proposals for changes in employed matters

1 Charge a conditional returnable fee to deter ill-founded unfair dismissal cases;
2 Extend to two years the period before an employer is required to give a detailed statement of reasons for dismissal;
3 Exempt firms with less than 10 employees from obligation to take back a woman after she has given birth;
4 Restrict the range of duties for which time off from work is allowed;
5 Introduction of a model employment form.
6 The 1987 Employment Bill proposed to outlaw in effect all closed shops, and to bar trade unions from disciplining members who defy strike calls. Rules on strike ballots will also be tightened and the Secretary of State will be empowered to issue codes of conduct.

20 Enterprise

You should recall that enterprise as a factor of production involves the performance by entrepreneurs of two functions:

- risk taking
- organisational decision making

Enterprise in the public sector is confined to the second of those tasks, since risk taking by investors does not take place.

In the private sector, those who are entrepreneurs vary according to the type of organisation. Consider Table 20.1.

In small-scale organisations like a sole proprietorship, a small co-operative, a partnership or a private company, ownership and control are likely to be vested in the hands of the same individual(s). However, in large private or public companies, there is likely to be a divorce between ownership and control.

Table 20.1
Enterprise in the private sector

Organisation	Risk taking	Major decision making
Sole proprietor	Owner	Owner
Partnership	General and limited partner(s)	General partner(s)
Company	Shareholders	Board of Directors, Senior management
Co-operative	Shareholders	Board of Directors, Senior management

Recall our description in Chapter 15 of a large organisation like Electro-factor (Products) plc of Sunhampton. It is common in such organisations that major shareholders are big institutional investors. Their interest in the organisation is financial. They are unlikely to be directly involved in the running of the organisation. While the shareholders are the risk takers, directors and senior management are the main decision makers.

We shall consider next the legal duties and protection relating to risk-taking entrepreneurs.

The legal consequences arising out of the supply of capital to companies

You will recall that when we discussed the nature of organisations registered as companies we saw that they are not free to trade in any way they wish. They are limited to those activities for which the company was created. These are set out in the organisation's 'objects clause' (see Chapter 5, p. 73). If the company's directors decide to engage in activities outside these objects, the company will be acting *ultra vires*. In order to get around this limitation, companies in practice draft very wide objects clauses to allow them to engage in a whole host of activities. Nevertheless, in principle the *ultra vires* doctrine has the aim of restricting a company's activities. Of course, if a company wishes to alter its objects, it may do so under the terms of the Companies Act 1985, by getting the authority of its shareholders. However, one of the consequences arising out of the purchase of shares is that a shareholder is entitled to see that directors of a company act for the benefit of the company. This general duty on directors is owed not to individual shareholders but to the shareholders as a whole.

The duties of directors may therefore be summarised as follows:

1 To act, when carrying out their functions, for the benefit of all share-holders. When, therefore, the directors of a firm, hoping to hold off a take-over bid from another organisation, issued unauthorised shares to its employees, a shareholder took the matter to court. It decided that the directors' act was a wrongful exercise of their powers (Hogg v. Cramphorn 1966). After all, the shareholders might have been financially benefited by the takeover.

2 Directors must act with such care in exercise of their powers as can reasonably be expected of a person having their particular knowledge and experience. Most important is that they act honestly, and so long as they do so they may be excused by the law for stupid acts.

3 Directors are expected to be reasonably diligent in carrying out their functions. If shareholders feel that a director is not carrying out his or her job properly, they may vote at a company meeting for the director's removal.

These duties to some extent place the directors in the position of *trustees* that is, they are holding and dealing with the property of others, and in this sense they owe a duty of care and skill to the shareholders, who may be regarded as beneficiaries. Therefore, a director will be in breach of trust if acting contrary to shareholders' interests. When a company director placed orders for supplies with certain companies as part of his duties, he received a commission which he kept for himself. In considering whether his dismissal was justified, the court held that he had breached his duty to act in good faith and so was rightly dismissed (Boston Deep Sea Fishing and Ice Company v. Ansell 1888). A director then, must now allow a conflict of interests to arise, and if he or she does, any secret profit made will have to be paid over.

In fact the Companies Acts place an obligation on directors to disclose any interests they may have in a contract in which their company is involved. Indeed, any loans made by a company to its directors must also be declared to the shareholders, and the Companies Acts oblige directors to declare their interests, or those of their spouse or children, in the company's shares or debentures.

To protect further the interests of a company, the Companies Act 1985 sets out certain rules in the event of takeover moves by another organisation. The relevant part of the Act prohibits 'insider dealings', e.g. the secret selling or buying of shares by directors and other persons closely connected with the company.

You will remember from Chapter 13, that the Company Securities (Insider Dealing) Act 1985 makes it an offence for persons to engage in 'insides dealings', e.g. the secret buying or selling of shares in a company subject to a takeover or merger bid not yet publicly announced. Persons taking advantage of their insider knowledge in this way commit a criminal offence carrying a maximum sentence of two years. Others who must not take advantage of a confidential relationship with a company are company officers and professional advisers, including accountants and solicitors.

Any theft of company property can be dealt with as a criminal offence under the Theft Act 1968.

Every company must produce annual accounts, and in the case of public companies these accounts must be distributed amongst shareholders; you will often see a major company's accounts printed in the business section of your newspaper. This is an important indication of how the company is spending its money, and it allows the members of the company (the shareholders) to raise questions about its management.

Can providers of capital protect their investment in the event of failure of a business?

We live in a society of credit, with most of us being unable to afford many big purchases like a home, a car or even consumer products such as refrigerators and washing machines, without borrowing money. This is no less true for business organisations, which have to own premises, buy plant and machinery, pay for raw materials and meet the cost of employees. Apart from government institutions and public corporations, businesses in the private sector of the economy have to be prepared to undertake a risk. There are many adverse factors, discussed in this book, which may make it difficult to succeed in business. It may be that the demand for an organisation's product falls or that profit margins are so small that the business is not worth pursuing. For public limited companies whose shares are quoted on the Stock Exchange, investors may lose confidence owing to circumstances occurring in the national or even international economy. For example, civil disruption in another country may permanently affect the supply of raw materials to a UK company. In short, in extreme cases, the investors may wish to withdraw their support by selling shares, and in some cases may actually call for the company to be wound up.

Insolvency

If a business like a trading company, a partnership or even a sole trader cannot meet its debts, the business can conclude matters by pursuing bankruptcy proceedings, before the courts. The proceedings for personal bankruptcy, as with a sole trader, or company bankruptcy have the same purpose. That purpose is the calling in of available assets and so far as possible distributing them amongst the creditors and, in the case of public companies, the shareholders.

Either the individual or the company, or alternatively the creditors or shareholders may present a petition in bankruptcy. The main protection available to shareholders of a public company if it is wound up, is that their personal financial liability is limited to the amount they have contributed for the purchase of shares. Beyond this, if there are funds after the payment to major creditors (see below), shareholders are entitled to a share of the surplus.

If it is a company which is to be wound up, whether it be by the shareholders, the creditors, in some cases a court, or the company itself, a liquidator must be appointed. The liquidator, usually an accountant from a firm of accountants, takes over running the affairs of the company. From that time on, the powers of the directors cease. The liquidator has the job of winding up the company's business, collecting in any assets and paying off employees (see redundancy rights, Chapter 19).

Some of the company's creditors will have protected or **secured** their loan by what is called 'charging' the company's property. Do you remember in the section dealing with law relating to land that a building society protects its loan by entering a 'charge' against the title of the landowner? This not only protects the society's interest, but also ensures that if the land is sold the prospective purchaser will become aware that the seller owes money to another. In respect of companies similarly, a lender, such as a bank will insist that the money is secured so that, in the event of the business failing, its loan will be paid out of the sale of the company's property. The property to which the charge might apply could be the company's premises.

One of the major aims of bankruptcy proceedings after a petition has been accepted by a court, is to ensure that there is a distribution of company assets amongst creditors. Certain debts are regarded as 'preferred debts'. Such debts as income tax and inland revenue debts; VAT; Social Security contributions; pension scheme contributions; and employees' wages must be paid in priority to other debts. Of course, it is possible that there will be insufficient funds to meet all these debts, or if there are that there will not be enough left to pay other debts. Where this occurs, debts have to be scaled down.

Just how this is done is now set out principally in the Insolvency Act 1986. This law describes the insolvency procedures as applying to companies, whether wound-up by the company itself, or by the company's creditors through a court of law. The Act, also, explains the process to be followed should an individual be petitioned as being unable to meet financial liabilities. Both in the case of a company or an individual, if the total indebtedness is £750 linked with an apparent inability to repay debts, there may be a commencement of a process either to wind-up a company, or to bankrupt a person.

As regards companies in severe financial difficulties, the Insolvency Act 1986 enables a court to appoint a Company Administrator to take over the company where there are reasonable prospects of a return to profitability. If the Administrator's proposals are accepted by creditors and shareholders, the court may approve them and they can be put into effect. This avoids the bankruptcy procedure, activated by the company nominating a Liquidator in a 'voluntary winding-up' by the company, or with the appointment of an Official Receiver where the company is compulsorily wound-up by a court. The aim of bankruptcy procedure is to end the company's affairs and to distribute the assets to pay off debts as far as is possible and, if sufficient, to distribute any remaining assets to shareholders.

Individual bankruptcy

What is the position of an individual, say a sole trader, who is unable to satisfy the claims of creditors owed in excess of £750? Either the creditors can petition or the debtor can. The process involves the appointment of an Official Receiver, who will receive from the debtor a statement of financial affairs, and will call a creditors' meeting at which the debtor may offer a partial settlement of debts. If this is not accepted there may be a public court hearing, followed by a handing over of the bankrupt's estate to a Trustee in Bankruptcy whose job it is to distribute amongst creditors. Some property is protected such as tools of the bankrupt's trade or vocation, and clothing and domestic items essential for the bankrupt and the bankrupt's family. Discharge from bankruptcy will usually be automatic after 3 years. Second or subsequent bankruptcies will not be automatically discharged, but after 5 years the bankrupt may apply to a court for discharge. Once

Fig. 20.1
(a) Company and personal bankruptcies
(b) Bankruptcies according to industries

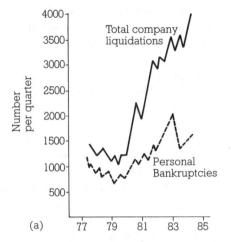

Activity	% of total 1984
Builders	11.6
Shops	10.5
Hotels & catering	7.7
Restaurant, cafes	6.4
Transport	6.1
Manufacturing	5.0
Business services	2.9
Motor traders, petrol stations	2.5
Wholesaling	2.3
Farming & gardening	2.0

(b)

(a)

declared bankrupt, a person loses certain rights; for instance, there is a denial of membership for Parliament.

Partnership bankruptcy

If the organisation is a partnership, and one of the partners is declared bankrupt, this has the effect of bringing about the end of the partnership. Otherwise partners may seek the court's assistance to dissolve the partnership. On bankruptcy of the partnership, the partnership's assets must be used to pay off the partners' joint debts, and if need be also the partners' personal assets must be applied for this purpose.

The law relating to creative enterprise

Good ideas are the foundations for enterprise, whether they are a unique invention, a new design, a catchy product name or a different marketing approach. Great fortunes are possible for the owner of such ideas, and so the law seeks to protect ownership from unlawful exploitation by others. Enforcement, though, is difficult as many breaches (called 'copyright piracy') take place in other countries, many of them newly industrialised nations. In 1986 the government received reports that the annual cost in lost sales was £1 bn. British recording and publishing companies assessed their loss at £158 m in just 8 countries, including Singapore, Nigeria, Korea and Indonesia. In Korea for example 90 per cent of recorded cassettes sold are pirated, thus depriving the composers and artists of their royalties, and the recording companies of potential sales. The governments of these countries generally are slow in taking any effective action.

Innovation is such that account now has to be taken of new technology involving computers and satellites, and so protections need to be updated continually.

Goodwill

Some organisations are based on various types of creative enterprise. Think of the shop you most often use to buy clothes, records or food. There is usually more than one to choose from, so what makes people buy in one shop and not another? The custom that an organisation attracts either through the quality of its goods, its prices or its service must be regarded as something of value. Do you remember when we talked of the case of Salomon *v.* Salomon and Company 1897 in Chapter 5 (see pp. 69–70)? Mr Salomon formed a company registered under the then Companies Acts and so created a different legal person – Salomon and Company. Not only did he sell the company his premises, his stock in trade and his tools; he also sold it the business's *goodwill*. Goodwill refers to the customer loyalty which has grown up over time, and when a business is sold it will be included in the deal.

Legally, goodwill must be recognised as something that can be owned, even though, unlike other property, it has no legal existence. Let us look at a common example. A debt as such is not a physical thing at all. What it really amounts to is a *right to be paid*. This right is something of value to a creditor, because in the event of not being paid, the creditor may pursue a legal action before a court (see Chapter 14). Lawyers have a name for this type of property; they call it a 'chose in action', which means a thing which, despite not being physical, can be enforced by a legal action. Other examples of 'choses in action' are trade marks, registered designs, copyrights and patents. Organisations and individuals owning these things need protection of the law against those who might deny them the opportunity to exploit their enterprise.

The Copyright, Designs and Patents Bill was finally introduced at the end of October 1987. The Bill will redraw the laws (see below) covering copyright, trademarks, computing programmes and patents.

Trade marks

Fig. 20.2
Some registered trade marks

It would surely be accepted that it would be unfair competition if a new manufacturer chose to call its product by the same trade name as the producer of the goods which have established themselves in the marketplace. After all, consumers identify the name of certain products so closely with the type of goods that they may be synonymous. You must have heard your family talking about 'hoovering' the carpet. What can a manufacturer do to protect its trade marks?

You will often see examples of trade marks such as those illustrated here, with either the ® symbol or the words 'Registered Trade Mark'. This denotes that the owner of a trade mark has had it registered in accordance with the provisions of the Trade Marks Act 1938. The registration of any organisation as proprietor of a trade mark in respect of any product grants the owner the exclusive right to use that mark in relation to the product. An infringement will occur if another uses the trade mark itself or any other mark so nearly resembling it as to be likely to be misleading.

The owners of the trade mark 'Daks' for clothes failed to show that the mark 'Kidax' might be confused with theirs, as did the manufacturers of 'Goya' cosmetics; who tried to prevent another company calling their products 'Gala' cosmetics. On the other hand Pan Books succeeded in preventing a company registering the name 'Pem Books'. Names that sound too much like a general description will not be registered, as for example, 'Electrix' and 'Shredded Wheat'. Nor will initials alone normally be registered, although 'BP', 'BL' and 'EMI' were accepted.

The Patents, Designs and Marks Act 1986 allowed service businesses in the same way as product manufacturers, to register their trade marks. The Prudential has registered its woman in the flowing headband, Lloyds Bank its black horse and Abbey National Building Society its thumbs up symbol.

Passing off

Apart from the 1938 Act, there exists the common law tort of 'passing off'. This civil wrong is committed by anyone who so conducts business as to lead customers to mistake their goods or business as the goods or business of another. 'Passing off' cases involve not the infringement of a trade mark so much as the deception of a customer into believing that the goods are those of a well-known manufacturer. Thus the appearance of a package of razor blades which has an uncanny resemblance to that of Wilkinson blades, or the manufacture of a soft-drink bottle which has the exact shape of that of Coca Cola may be regarded as 'passing off'. The description 'champagne' denotes the wine-producing area in France, and so an organisation calling its product 'Spanish champagne' was held to have no justification. Again, there is no law preventing a person using their own name for a business, but if unfair advantage of that name is taken, they may be stopped by a court from using it. This might happen if a Mr or Ms Parker decided to attach that name to ballpoint pens and fountain pens which an organisation manufactured.

Industrial designs

An organisation wishing to be protected on industrial design must comply with the requirements of the Design Copyright Act 1968. Once the design is registered, its owner may bring a legal action against anyone who copies it. Either the original model of the designed article or the artistic work, perhaps a set of drawings, must be registered. Registration gives the owner protection from copying of the design for a period of 15 years from the date when articles bearing the design were first marketed. In order to be valid, the design must consist of some novel factor which differentiates it from any existing articles. It is for the court to decide to what extent an alleged copy resembles the article whose design is registered, in an action brought by the owner of the design.

Copyright

You will have often seen the symbol © followed by the name of an organisation or a person, in the first few pages of a book, at the end of a television programme on the credits, or in the titles of a film. The symbol denotes that a **copyright** exists in that particular work, entitling the owner of the copyright to sue a person who infringes the copyright. The governing law is the Copyright Act 1956. The works that may be copyrighted include novels and literary works, including tables and compilations; lectures and sermons; and dramatic works such as plays, scripts for films, and ballets. Artistic works are also covered, such as paintings, drawings, photographs and architectural designs, and also music, gramophone records and tapes. In general, an original work is protected under the Act without regard to its objective merits. Protection for literary, artistic, dramatic and musical works extends over the period of the creator's life and for 50 years after the creator's death. If an original work is not used during its creator's lifetime, the 50-year protection will run from the time that it is first used.

Unlike some of the other forms of creative enterprise we have been discussing, a copyright need not be registered. It is normally acquired at the moment of creation. No other formality is required than merely indicating that the work is copyrighted by simple insertion of the © symbol.

Any person who reproduces the original work, in whole or in part, without permission may be restrained by a court injunction from repeating the breach. The court may also order the wrongdoer to pay damages or account for any profits obtained through breaching another's copyright. The issue before the court is whether the subject matter contains sufficient work, skill or taste to enable it to be regarded as an original work. The court, however, may find all this present, but if the work is immoral or illegal it cannot receive the protection of the law.

As copyright gives the creator the exclusive right to exploit to work, generally speaking no part of the work may be reproduced without permission. The Act, however, does allow copying for private study and research and the quoting of passages for review and report, which are regarded as 'fair dealing'.

It would appear that educational establishments are major culprits in the infringement of copyright. An organisation representing the interests of music publishers, the Music Publishers' Association, estimated that some 8 million copies of copyright music and written material have been unlawfully copied in British schools. In 1981 one of Britain's oldest public schools, Oakham, was found to have unlawfully copied sheet music for years and was ordered to pay £4250 damages to the music publishers Novello and Co.

In an attempt to meet the problems faced by those whose creative talents involved computers, Parliament passed the Copyright (Computer Software) Amendment Act 1985 to extend protection to computer programs.

Inventions

Most inventions are made by persons employed by organisations to carry out particular research. We have talked of this matter in the section relating to employees (see p. 185). If the invention is made in the employer's name, the employer will own the invention; otherwise the invention will belong to the inventor. An invention may be protected by registration as a **patent** under the Patents Act 1977. In essence an idea is patentable if it is 'new' and involves an 'inventive step', i.e. a step not obvious to a person skilled in the particular field to which the invention relates. It has also to be capable of industrial or agricultural exploitation. While drugs may be patented, medical treatments may not.

Applications must be made to the Comptroller General of Patents, who then can make a decision about the granting of a patent. Disputes arising therefrom may be settled by the Patents Appeal Tribunal. The Comptroller will not register patents for scientific theories, mathematical methods or computer programmes (which may receive protection under copyright law). After examination and search of other patents, a patent will be granted on payment of a fee. A patent is protected for a period of 20 years, an annual fee, adjusted to keep pace with inflation, being due. If someone can prove that a patent should not have been granted, it may be revoked by the Patents Court. However, once it has been granted, the inventor may protect his monopoly on the idea by suing those who infringe the protected idea in the High Court. An inventor granted a patent by the London Patents Office may sue for infringements in the courts in England, Scotland and Northern Ireland. If the inventor wishes to extend the ambit of protection he or she may apply for a European Community Patent from the Munich office of the European Patent Office, and designate in which of the member States the patent is to apply.

The Copyright, Designs and Patents Bill 1987 will replace the Copyright Act 1956, and will attempt to give protection far more widely to products of the human imagination (such as computer programmes and satellite output).

Do you think that the providers of capital have sufficient control over how it is used?

Can you give some examples of everyday articles with a registered trade mark or design?

What inventions in your home, on the road and in college or your office do you consider to be the most novel?

21 Information in organisations

You will find many references in this Chapter about the need to gather and assess information. All organisations, regardless of size or type, need information to enable them to function effectively. Information which is accurate and relevant and obtained at the right time is important if managers are to plan properly in an increasingly complex environment.

Importance of information

The business world is becoming more complex, and organisations are having to come to terms with a more challenging environment:

a Organisations must grow, either internally or through merger or acquisition, if profit maximisation is to be maintained.

b Many organisations may feel the need to diversify their operations.

c Overseas competition is becoming an important factor for more and more organisations.

d Major technological changes are taking place in production methods.

e Legislation, government policy, economic factors, etc. can change rapidly.

In order to anticipate (or even to react to) these issues, organisations need information.

At the same time, organisations generate a great deal of information as a result of their daily activities: e.g. production levels, staffing levels, income and expenditure accounts, etc., and this information must also be taken into account by managers.

Clearly, then, organisations must recognise the importance of information which comes from both the internal and external environments, and apply it in all aspects of planning. An example of a typical problem faced by Electrofactor (Products) plc may serve to illustrate this.

The company needs to re-assess its production levels, and therefore must consider (among other things) the following factors:

a its production capacity – i.e. potential output in relation to actual output per worker and production machinery;

b the market – actual and potential;

c costs of production – i.e. maintenance of machinery, wages and bonuses, etc.

Once they have done this, they can determine:

a where there is a market for more goods;

b whether the company has spare capacity;

c how much the increased output is likely to cost.

Most of this information is readily available. Much of it will come from internal sources (i.e. information on costs, production levels, wages, etc.) Some of it will be more difficult to acquire, since it concerns matters from the external environment, and therefore will come from external sources. In this example, the marketing information may have to be obtained by means of a survey, specially commissioned by the company; in other situations, however, even external sources of information may be easy to tap: information on the economy (e.g. interest rates, balance of trade, etc.) and on actual and proposed legislation is freely available through the media, libraries, etc.

While service industries and public sector organisations may not be concerned with producing a good, nevertheless they too need information about potential and actual markets and on the likely cost (at least in human resources) of any plans to expand or change the service. They too will need to consult both their own records and outside sources.

Internal sources of information

As we have already suggested, organisations generate an enormous amount of information relating to their day-to-day activities. Each department is responsible for collecting data about its own activities, for storing it and for making it available (often on a 'need to know' basis) to other members of the organisation.

For example, the Marketing Department will keep records concerning such things as the type of product(s) manufactured or sold; type of market – home, overseas, wholesale, retail, etc.; percentage of market share held, etc. Other departments will cover their own relevant areas, and will collect information relating to such diverse topics as liquidity, sales turnover, stock policy, investment levels in research and development, and so on.

This information will then be processed and distributed in memoranda, reports, etc. for discussion at meetings. In an attempt to improve the efficiency of information storage, etc. many organisations have begun to make use of computers since, arguably, they can:

a store information more effectively and efficiently, in larger quantities in a central data base;

b be updated more quickly;

c organise, process and re-present information in a variety of formats;

d be accessed easily by means of desk-top terminals in managers' offices.

However, use of computerised data base may well mean that an organisation needs to be aware of the main provisions of the Data Protection Act 1984.

Data Protection Act 1984

This Act, which came into force in 1985, places certain statutory obligations on the use of data concerning individuals. Broadly speaking, its intent is to protect information about individuals and to establish a mechanism whereby people may have access to the information which is held about them. From 11 November 1985, data users (i.e. organisations and computer bureaux who compile computer files) must register with a Registrar whose function is to oversee the functioning of the Act.

Despite these new formalities, computerisation of internal records still remains one of the most effective ways of dealing with information, particularly since it then becomes easier to disseminate information to managers as and when they may need it to carry out their functions effectively. A computerised system can help organisations set up an integrated Management Information System (MIS)

MIS

This is an attempt to ensure that managers can obtain accurate, relevant information at the right times, to improve their decision making. It should provide information on the past (historic information about production levels, etc.), the present (i.e. current production figures, markets, etc.) and the future (i.e. projected or forecast profits, etc.); it should include information from both the internal and external environments.

An efficient MIS can be useful for:

a planning future strategies;

b logistic purposes – i.e. linking the activities of the various divisions of the organisation. For example, payroll administration can be improved with better access to productivity figures since any bonus rates can be calculated more quickly.

c control purpose – i.e. monitoring, correcting, improving operations, etc. can be carried out more quickly and easily.

Many large organisations establish their own library and information service whose function is to acquire information, mainly from external sources, on behalf of the organisation; it also often acts as the repository for internal information, and reports on company research projects, etc. will be stored in the library. Its other function is to disseminate information to key personnel within the organisation, and if there is a fully integrated, functional MIS operating, then the library can often use this as a communication channel.

In an organisation known to you (e.g. your workplace, College, etc.) consider:
(i) How is information disseminated to members? and (ii) If there is a Library Service, what role does it play in the organisation's activities?

We have discussed the importance of information in organisations and have recognised that internal and external information sources need to be taken into account. However, it may be useful to consider how organisations acquire information about the external environment.

External sources of information

There is a wide range of information sources available to organisations, from obvious ones like newspapers, periodicals, radio, television and the teletext services (e.g. Prestel, Ceefax, Oracle) to the less obvious such as local authority departments, government agencies, etc. and it may be helpful to consider some of these.

Local authority sources

Many local authorities have established advisory services which can provide help to people who want to set up small businesses; even in the absence of such a service, however, most organisations will need to consult some of the departments which are responsible for providing local services.

For example, any organisation which wishes to extend its premises must consult the local *Planning Office* before building; when Electrofactor (Products) plc wanted to build a workshop behind the shop in Sunhampton High

Street, the planning laws would not allow it; later, when the shop became their administrative headquarters they found that they needed to check with the Planning Department because they were changing the use made of the building. Later still, as their property division grew to include flats they found that they needed permission to convert flats into office space.

They also needed to be aware of the existence of the *Department of Environmental Health*, since this department is concerned with a range of issues such as noise levels, waste disposal, etc.

The *Public Library* is also a useful source of information, containing, as it does, a wide selection of business and commercial directories, etc. Sunhampton Libraries (having seen the success of the London Borough of Bexley's Bextel service) have introduced a local Prestel service; Suntel is a subscription service which can be accessed on-line from Electrofactor (Products) plc's headquarters in the High Street at any time, night or day; it contains local information and a comprehensive business and commercial information service. Local organisations can obtain information on, for example, local planning, the Stock Market, the latest exchange rates, etc. simply by pressing a few keys on a desk-top terminal.

Government sources

All government departments have a library and information service, most of which are happy to answer enquiries from organisations and members of the public.

For example, organisations can contact any of the following for advice:

- The *Department of the Environment* for information on planning, environmental health, pollution, etc.
- The *Department of Trade* will provide advice on overseas trade policy; on the administration of statutes governing company affairs; patent, trade marks and copyright matters, etc.
- The *Department of Employment*, in addition to providing information on employment matters, supports 3 agencies which are, themselves, very important sources of information:

  a Advisory, Conciliation and Arbitration Service,
  b Manpower Services Commission,
  c Health and Safety Executive.

Other sources

Chambers of Commerce, which are local associations of business and commercial organisations, can often be approached for advice.

Research Associations (RAs) exist in most of the major manufacturing sectors to carry out research on behalf of the industry as a whole. For example, Electrofactor (Products) plc is a member of the Production Engineering Research Association which is located in Melton Mowbray.

RAs are funded partly by the government and partly by members' subscriptions; in return for their subscriptions members may receive copies of reports describing the results of research, or they may ask for advice.

Development Associations such as the Copper Development Association (CDA) are groupings of manufacturers in the same field, and are established to promote members' products; for example, the CDA will promote the use of copper goods for the whole industry. Development Associations provide an advisory service to members, supported by a library and information unit.

Trade Associations are set up by organisations in a particular industry to assist members in all aspects of the industry's legal and trading interests. They are particularly useful to small businesses, and often cover very specific industries: for example, the Small Potteries Trade Associations of Haverfordwest, South Wales, helps to set standards in a manufacturing sector which is generally characterised by one- or two-person businesses. Trade Associations can be approached by members for help and advice.

This is a small selection of agencies, etc. which exist to advise and inform organisations; they are sufficient, however, to underline the importance of establishing links to ensure a steady flow of useful information from the external environment.

Summary, Part D

1 In order to produce, an organisation needs to acquire the use of land, labour, capital and enterprise which collectively are referred to as the factors of production.

2 The factors must be combined in such a way as to enable the organisation to produce at the lowest possible cost per unit. The combination is known as the 'optimum combination'.

3 There are two so-called legal estates in land: a freehold estate and a lease-hold estate.

4 The law on landlord and tenant has a wide scope in protecting tenants in private dwellings, business premises tenancies and agricultural tenancies.

5 Statute law has placed a number of restrictions on what the occupier of premises may do to alter the character of their land.

6 Among the common law duties imposed on landowners are that they must not cause a nuisance, or allow dangerous things to escape or interfere with another's land.

7 Organisations require finance for working or fixed capital.

8 Funds may be generated internally or externally.

9 Short-term finance for private-sector organisations may come from retained profits, bank lending, private loans, bills of exchange, trade credit, factoring and employment subsidies.

10 In the medium and long term, private sector organisations can raise finance from retained profits, banks and other financial institutions, regional aid, the issue of new securities, hire purchase and equipment leasing.

11 The Stock Exchange is not directly a means of raising new finance. It is the market for secondhand securities.

12 Government departments are funded primarily from tax revenue and government borrowing.

13 Public corporations may receive grants from central government and, with government permission, can issue stock or borrow from banks.

14 Finance for local authorities comes mainly from the Rate Support Grant, borrowing and rates.

15 Trade unions primarily gather funds from members' subscriptions, and charities receive donations.

16 Local authority expenditure may be controlled by the Secretary of State

for Environment under powers in the Local Government Planning and Land Act 1981.

17 Central government expenditure may be examined by Parliament itself either through the normal Parliamentary procedure or by the Public Accounts Committee.

18 Trade unions act on behalf of their members to improve wage rates and conditions of work.

19 The legal relationship between employing organisations and their employees is based on contract.

20 A variety of statutory rights such as a pregnant worker's right to return to work and the right not to be unfairly dismissed are set out in the Employment Protection (Consolidation) Act 1978.

21 An attempt to lessen discrimination against employees based on sex or race has been made by the Sex Discrimination Act 1975 and the Race Relations Act 1976.

22 A dismissed employee may claim either wrongful dismissal, unfair dismissal or redundancy.

23 An employee injured through an accident at work may sue the employer in the tort of negligence or for breach of a statutory duty. In any case the employee is entitled to industrial injury benefits administered by the State.

24 The Health and Safety at Work Act 1974 has as its purpose the establishment of the adoption of safe systems of work by employers.

25 Investors in a company may protect their capital by ensuring that company directors carry out their duties.

26 The bankruptcy procedure enables creditors to receive as much as is available when assets are distributed.

27 Creative enterprise is protected by the law by protecting the right of the owner or creator of an invention, a design or an artistic work to exploit their enterprise to the exclusion of others.

28 Information is important to organisations if they are to function effectively in the complex business world.

29 The departments of an organisation must collect and make available information derived from its activities.

30 Computerising information storage and other data may increase efficiency, but may bring an organisation within the scope of the Data Protection Act 1984.

31 Introducing a MIS may facilitate the dissemination of information, thus improving management performance.

32 Information obtained from sources outside the organisation must also be taken into account.

Assignment, Part D

Jabula Ltd

Jabula Ltd is a small company which makes and sells candles. Trade is seasonal, most candles being sold in the winter months. They need short-term financial aid to cover the costs of raw materials and labour while they make and store candles in readiness for periods of high demand.

You are employed as an assistant to the Managing Director, Mr Patel. He requests advice from you on suitable financial options open to Jabula Ltd to raise the necessary finance. Write a memorandum to Mr Patel giving the necessary information and outlining the main advantages and disadvantages of the use of each mode of finance you suggest.

Seven years have elapsed and Jabula Ltd's sales have expanded 5-fold. The current premises are proving inadequate both for production capacity and administrative space. You are now part of a management team of 4 people, given the growth in the company.

The Managing Director has eyes on larger premises. He estimates that 20 new employees (15 in production and 5 in administration) would be needed. Three new machines are also likely to be required if sales grow to the amounts predicted.

The Managing Director requests the management team to draw up a checklist of needs and requirements to be met if the proposed expansion is to take place. A plan of action can thus be formulated.

Working in a group with 3 fellow students, you are to form the management team to devise the checklist of needs and requirements.

Consider how the organisation might acquire the necessary resources to engage in this expansion. Describe procedures involved and state any legal requirements to be met.

Particularly you should consider:

- information needs;
- premises;
- labour;
- possibilities for raising finance.

Skills
Working with others, communicating, information gathering, identifying and tacking problems.

PART E

THE EFFECTIVE USE OF RESOURCES BY ORGANISATIONS

When you have read this part you should be able to:
- Understand how an organisation makes decisions in order to operate at an appropriate scale and to produce efficiently.
- Recognise the need to plan for effective staffing levels, both in terms of numbers and skills, in a changing environment.

22 The efficient use of resources

All organisations, large or small, in the public or private sector, need to mix productive resources to produce their goods or services. Clearly, the resource recipe will differ from organisation to organisation, just as we use different ingredients to make omelette as opposed to a pizza.

Some organisations are **labour-intensive**, which means they use a relatively large amount of labour compared to other productive resources. This would be especially true of organisations supplying personal services, where customer contact is important, for example in many areas of retailing like clothes shops.

Also, some organisations are **land-intensive**, so that by the very nature of the operation, a relatively large amount of land is required relative to other productive resources. This is obviously so in agriculture and also for large productive concerns whose premises cover a great amount of space. For example, the Ford Motor Company plant at Dagenham stretches for approximately 4 miles.

Other organisations are more **capital-intensive** where mechanisation rather than labour is the predominant element in production. Heavy industry like iron and steel and chemicals have long been of this type. However, increasingly in recent years, the onset of micro-chip technology has caused change towards more capital-intensive methods of operation. The greater use of, for example robotics, computers and word-processors, has meant the shedding of labour and the substitution of machines. It was estimated that by 1990, 17 per cent of typing and other secretarial jobs would be displaced by the word processor.*

* E. Bird, Info Tech in the Office, *Commission Report* 1980/81.

What about the organisation in which you work or study? Would you say it tended to be capital-intensive or labour-intensive? Is it land-intensive?

Efficiency

Irrespective of whether an organisation is labour-, land- or capital-intensive, it must consider using resources efficiently. At the start of this chapter we noted that organisations need to combine resources to produce output at the least cost, as efficiently as possible.

What exactly does efficient production of goods or service mean to an organisation? Consider, by example, Electrofactor (Products) plc of

Sunhampton. The Production Director is considering replacing the machines which press out the casings for hairdriers which the company produces. He has studied the catalogues of two manufacturers which produce the appropriate type of machine. From the information he notes that both machines have an expected life of 5 years, but the Borton 'Hi-Speed' can produce 60 casings per hour whereas the Milburn 'Reliable' produces only 30 per hour. Which would you choose if you were the Production Director?

Clearly the 'Hi-Speed' is superior in output terms. It is thus *technically more efficient* than the 'Reliable'.

However, technical efficiency is not the sole criterion to be considered. The catalogues also show that the 'Hi-Speed' costs £4m whereas the 'Reliable' is priced at £500 000. Although the 'Hi-Speed' produces twice as much output per hour as the 'Reliable' it is 8 times more expensive.

The Production Director will have to consider which machine is the more cost efficient, not merely which is technically superior. Assuming that space is available, two 'Reliables' could be purchased for £1m to get the same output as one 'Hi-Speed'. Given that costs of power, materials and labour do not increase considerably, then the 'Reliable' is the machine with greater *economic efficiency*: it enables production to take place at a lower cost.

We noted in Chapter 2 that resources are scarce. It is thus all the more important that organisations use them with strong regard to cost efficiency. Inefficient use of resources means higher costs, less ability to compete, lower profits and possibly higher prices to the consumer.

This issue is just as important in the public sector as the private sector, even if profit is a less prominent yardstick for gauging performance. However, we shall see in Chapter 34 that particularly in the public sector there are broader issues of social costs (costs felt by others as a result of the activities of an organisation – see p. 324) which are sometimes considered in a broader, more society-wide view of efficiency.

For the present, in the other chapters in Part E we shall analyse the use of resources more from the angle of particular organisations. What are the factors which affect an organisation's mix of resources and influence the level and scale of its production?

Before you read on, consider how efficiently the organisation in which you work or study is operated. Could you recommend changes to improve efficiency?

23 Planning human resources

One of the most important and most expensive factors in any organisation is the workforce; in an increasingly complex external environment it is important to ensure that an organisation's personnel is adequate to its needs. This requires that staffing levels are appropriate while ensuring that the correct mix of skills is available. This is the function of human resources planning. A further important aspect of efficient human resources management (which also helps in manpower planning) is good training and education.

Human resources planning

This is a fairly new phenomenon, the view that organisations should adopt what the Institute of Personnel Management calls 'a strategy for the acquisition, improvement and preservation of an enterprise's human resources'. In other words, organisations must plan their human resource needs, taking a long-term view, in relation to the changing external environment.

So far, few organisations have felt the need to do this in a systematic way and it is hardly surprising, given the relative ease with which they have been able to hire people at need, only to lay them off in times of depressed demand with minimal cost to the organisation. It is no longer quite so easy to operate in this somewhat haphazard fashion, since the rules of the game have changed substantially.

In effect, we have here a very good example of the way in which the external environment has affected the internal environment of organisations. We have already noted that the business world is becoming more complex, and organisations have had to adapt and to respond to change more rapidly in the past 20 years or so than at any time since the Industrial Revolution. Nowhere has this been more evident than in its effect on an organisation's workforce.

Consider, for example, the following factors:

a the technological revolution which has radically changed production methods, etc. and has affected staffing levels;
b the effect of UK membership of the EEC in terms of competition, and the increasing importance of overseas markets in general; these have emphasised the need to control production and other costs;
c the state of the world economy and its effect on, for example, exchange rates and interest rates;
d the general affluence in the UK; the increased demand for consumer durables; and the rapid change in public taste, e.g. the boom followed by a decline in demand for home computers.

These factors, among others, have prompted many changes in the ways in which organisations function: they demand a more flexible approach to staffing needs to enable an organisation to respond quickly and efficiently to stimuli from the external environment.

Organisations of all kinds must utilise the workforce efficiently, economically and effectively, and the rapid changes in the external environment mean that human resources planning may be the best way of ensuring the proper utilisation of personnel.

Human resources planning is, specifically, a technique whereby an organisation can plan the size and the composition (i.e. according to skills required) of its workforce, and in principle, the mechanics are simple enough.

Phase 1 Analysis and prediction

This needs to take into account such factors as:

Assessment of existing workforce

a the number of people currently employed;
b the range of skills/activities in which they are involved;

c their ages – to establish how many are near retirement, or who might qualify for early retirement;

d their length of service – to help calculate potential cost in redundancy payment;

e the possibility of redeployment and retraining.

Forecasting employment needs for the future

This must be done as specifically and as precisely as possible, and a date should be set by which the target should be achieved, e.g. 'On 1 April 19— we will require . . .'. The forecast will cover:

a the number of people required;

b the various job categories, and the number of people needed to fill each category;

c the number of skills required to enable the organisation to continue to function effectively;

When this is done, the organisation will have a clear idea of its future employment needs.

Estimating employment supply

It is as well to consider this at the same time as forecasting needs, since availability of the workforce will affect an organisation's ability to recruit. It may be necessary to move the organisation (or part of it) to where the labour can be found. Indeed, the information sources (e.g. *Social Trends*, *Monthly Digest of Statistics*, etc.), which will provide information on labour supply, may also suggest where the labour is located.

Another possibility is to consider whether any of the existing workforce can be redeployed from their existing occupation and retrained for something else.

This brings Phase 1 to a close, and it should now be possible to identify areas of overstaffing (i.e. where there is a surplus of labour), and of potential labour or skills shortage. It is time now to move on to Phase 2.

Phase 2 Evaluation of information

Inevitably, some evaluation has already taken place during Phase 1, and what we are concerned with here is an attempt to identify:

a alternative courses of action which the organisation could adopt;

b any cost factors which are likely to occur as a consequence in each case.

For example, when Electrofactor (Products) Ltd found itself in competition for a limited market with other companies which were using high technology production methods and therefore needed a smaller more highly skilled workforce, Electrofactor found that its production costs and therefore its pricing policy were higher than its competitors.

A human resources plan for Electrofactor would need to respond to the technological change and the threat from competitors by:

a introducing new technology;

b shedding/redeploying staff.

Alternatively, it can simply go on as before.

Whichever alternative is adopted, it will cost Electrofactor either in lost profits if the status quo is maintained, or in redundancy and/or retraining costs and the cost of new plant if they introduce new technology.

The long-term view would suggest that change is necessary, since the short-term expenditure on redundancy and equipment costs can be seen as an investment which will prove beneficial in the long term.

Phase 3 Planning and implementation

Once the alternatives have been assessed and a choice made, then the organisation can produce its human resources plan. This will:

a outline the organisation's future staffing needs;
b indicate how these are to be achieved;
c outline the expenditure which may be necessary in the short or medium term.

This process can be seen in a simplified form in Fig. 23.1

What we have here, in effect, is a decision-making model (as will be explained in Chapter 24) being used in a problem solving situation; it is therefore desirable to add a further stage or phase.

Fig. 23.1
Model of human resources planning

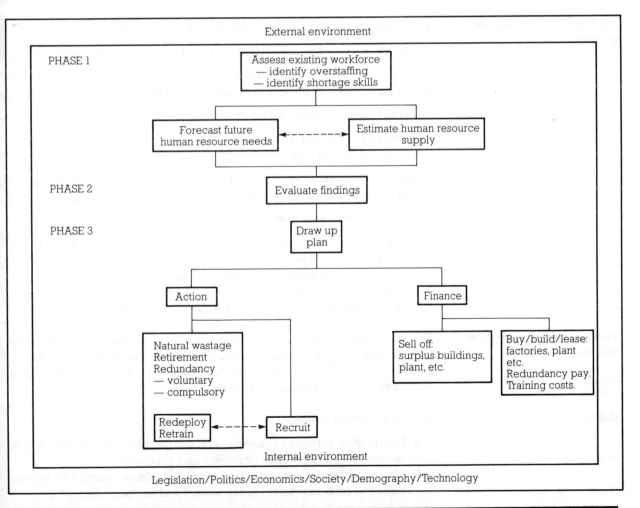

Phase 4 Monitor and control

Once the plan has been drawn up and implemented, it then becomes necessary to check that the forecasts which we made in Phases 1–3 were accurate.

We shall need to check whether our original objective – i.e. to arrive at a workforce which reflects our needs in terms of numbers, skills, etc. – has been met by:

a checking performance;
b noting any variations from the targets which were set;
c acting to correct the deviation.

We must not, at this stage, lose sight of the importance of the external environment, since changes in social taste, technology, economics, etc. can occur quickly and can affect our human resources plan.

For example, if the bottom falls out of the market, it doesn't matter how good the original human resources plan, it no longer reflects the current needs of the organisation (see Electrofactor's experience in Chapter 15).

Human resource planning needs therefore, to be ongoing, taking both internal and external factors into account in an attempt to ensure that the workforce reflects the organisation's needs in a changing world.

Benefits of human resource planning

1 It is possible to identify overstaffing, inefficiencies, shortage of skills, etc.

2 Recruitment in shortage areas can be carried out in good time.

3 It may be possible to minimise redundancies by redeployment and retraining, and through relying on natural wastage.

4 Training programmes can be considered at the same time, thus:

a training needs can be assessed;
b new training programmes can be devised in plenty of time.

5 Working conditions can be assessed to see whether they will be affected by the plan; for example, will existing canteen facilities be adequate?

6 It should result in a more flexible workforce:

a staff can be trained in a number of skills, thus making redeployment from job to job easier within the organisation;
b staff can be increased quickly at need, though the relationship between employer and employee may change, with staff being employed on a short-term contract – i.e. for as long as the organisation needs them.

Problems of human resource planning

Forecasting the future

Human resource planning is concerned with the future, and is therefore high in risk and uncertainty; forecasting the future of the market, the economy, etc. is far from easy and the manpower plan is only as good as the predictions upon which it is based.

Costs

It is an expensive process:

a Information gathering, analysis, etc. on the kind of scale which this exercise requires is time consuming and expensive.
b The resulting human resources plan will almost inevitably require extensive (and expensive) redundancies and/or retraining.

Change

The whole point of a human resource plan is to change the organisation's workforce, and most people's response to change is to resist it. This means that it may be necessary to pave the way for the change through extensive consultation with staff, thus giving them an opportunity to participate in the planning stage. Staff are more likely to respond positively to a negotiated change than to a change programme imposed from above.

Ideally, all staff should be consulted individually: however, given the logistical problems (particularly in a large organisation) it may be necessary to fall back on the framework of collective bargaining and negotiate with the trade(s) union(s).

In conclusion, then a human resource plan can help an organisation establish staffing levels, identify redundant/shortage skill areas and enable the organisation to adopt a more flexible workforce in response to changing needs; in particular it can help reduce staffing costs significantly since, in the long term, pay negotiations may take place at plant level rather than at national level through the collective bargaining machinery with its emphasis on across-the-board pay increases. Organisations may, in the future, find it easier to discuss relativities and differentials in pay at local level without much account of what is happening nationally.

So far we have considered human resource planning as a voluntary response to external pressures in an effort to maintain maximisation of profit, and to a large extent this is probably the driving force for most organisations. However, there are other factors which have also caused organisations to reassess their personnel policies; these are, by and large, the many Acts (mostly dating from the 1970s, and often based on the premise that an organisation has a responsibility to society as a whole) which cover employment and labour relations.

Social responsibility

The body of employment law passed in the 1970s (see Chapter 19) has inevitably affected the recruitment and treatment of an organisation's workforce. The origin of much of the legislation arose from a view that all members of society deserve an equal opportunity in the job market, and that once in a job, they deserved protection against unfair dismissal, redundancy, etc.

All this must be seen against background which included:

a the women's movement with its view that marriage and motherhood should not put an end to a woman's career aspirations and that, furthermore, a woman doing the same job as a man was entitled to the same rate of pay;

b the number of children, born in Britain of ethnic minority parents, coming onto the job market often with higher expectations than their parents, only to experience discrimination;

c the refusal by many disabled people to accept the fact that their disability made it impossible for them to lead a useful, economically active life.

It is now illegal to discriminate on grounds of race, gender, disability, etc. and, whatever happens covertly, organisations must now take this legislation into account in its human resources planning; few jobs now can be seen as being exclusively 'men's' jobs or 'women's' jobs, while organisations are obliged to reserve a certain percentage of jobs for the disabled.

While it would be naive to think that the legislation actually gets rid of discrimination, there is now a legislative framework which organisations must at least acknowledge.

If retraining and redeployment and a flexible workforce are to become the norm, then a system of *staff performance appraisal* may provide a framework through which staff skills, aptitudes, etc. can be assessed.

Staff performance appraisal

In essence, staff appraisal is an ongoing process whereby an organisation attempts to monitor or review the progress, performance, output, etc. of an employee, with a view to promotion, improvement, etc. It may take place once a year (as in the Civil Service) or on a more regular, structured basis at 3- or 6-monthly intervals. It is generally carried out from the top down (i.e. supervisors appraise workers; supervisors will, in turn, be appraised by their superiors), though it should be essentially a participative process in which the appraiser and appraisee discuss the latter's performance against a set of previously agreed yardsticks.

Appraisal depends heavily on the existence of such things as clear job descriptions, explicit output targets or performance criteria to be successful, since it is important that each worker knows what is required of him or her; it is unfair to assess a worker's performance if there is a lack of clarity as to the yardstick against which he or she is to be measured.

It is often easier to appraise staff involved in the production function where there is a specific outcome (i.e. a completed good) and where the task has been carefully designed (see Work Study p. 56). However, an *Organisation and Methods* (O and M) survey, a refinement of work study, can be used to measure clerical and administrative activities, since it is possible to estimate the percentage of time spent on each task by:

a observing a clerk at work for a given period of time, e.g. a day/week/month;

b during that period, watching the clerk several times each day, at random;

c recording what the clerk is doing (e.g. answering the phone, reading letters, filing, etc.) during each visit.

For example, by recording how many times during the observation time the clerk is seen answering the phone, we can calculate that perhaps 15 per cent of the clerk's time is spent in this way as opposed to 10 per cent spent reading letters and 25 per cent spent filing. Subsequent analysis of the data may suggest how, for the same expenditure of energy, performance can be improved; the data can also be used to produce a set of criteria for staff appraisal.

Purpose of staff appraisal

In brief, a staff appraisal system may be seen as a control mechanism to ensure that all parts of the organisation are performing well; however, it can also be useful in more specific circumstances:

a It can be used as the basis for rewarding staff, either through increased salary, or by payment of a bonus, or through promotion;

b It can motivate or encourage employees to improve their performance;

c It can help identify potential strengths, talents, etc. among employees which are not currently being utilised;

d It can help identify whether or not an employee is in the wrong job, i.e. it may show the employee's talents could be better used elsewhere;

e It can often highlight flaws in the current training programme, or identify new training needs.

In particular, (c), (d) and (e) become increasingly important in the context of human resources planning, since an organisation which has an established staff appraisal system already has some of the information required to hand; if regular staff appraisal is carried out, then the company has a profile of its existing staff's actual and potential skills, which may make it easier to identify candidates for redeployment and retraining.

Appraisal methods

There are a number of appraisal methods in current use, ranging from getting the superior to write a report on an individual; or using some kind of ranking or grading system where employees are ranked on a scale from 1 to 5 or Good/Satisfactory/Poor; or by appraisal interview based on completion (by the employee) of an appraisal review form.

Inevitably, each method has its strengths and weaknesses: for example the appraisal report and the grading system are both susceptible to the subjective views of the reviewer; the interview and appraisal review form are an attempt to overcome this problem by allowing the employee/appraisee to list his or her own strengths and weaknesses, his or her own perception of the performance under review, etc. The appraiser is then given an opportunity to read through the form in preparation for the interview, at which time a frank exchange of views should be possible. This method does ensure that both parties can prepare for the appraisal, and the subsequent dialogue should be mutually beneficial, and the end result should be perceived as fair by both appraiser and appraisee.

An appraisal is often perceived as threatening to many workers, but it is important to note that even where there is no formal system in operation, staff appraisal is nevertheless going on all the time; a staff appraisal system provides a framework within which the appraiser and the appraisee can be aware of the ground rules.

One important prerequisite for a successful appraisal system is the existence of an effective in-service training programme:

a so that appraisees whose performance is deemed inadequate can be helped to improve;

b so that staff who are identified for redeployment or retraining can be dealt with effectively.

Consider whether you are subject to an appraisal system either at work or at college: What form does it take?

Training and education

A good training programme is essential if staff are to perform well, and it is often beneficial to both the organisation and to the employees if there is someone who has responsibility for co-ordinating training across all departments. This should ensure that training standards are the same across the board.

A typical training programme should include the following:

1 Induction training, given to all new employees to introduce them to the organisation's objectives, structure, etc.

2 Training which will equip staff to carry out their duties:

   a On-the-job training which is usually done at the place of work by getting trainees to 'sit-by Nellie'; i.e. being shown how to do the job by someone experienced;
   b Off-the-job training which takes place away from the normal work-place in specially designed workshops, practice offices, etc.;
   c Other methods include use of training films, programmed learning packages, staff instruction manuals, etc.

3 Topping-up training in specific aspects of the job. These, more often than not, take place away from the work-place: a group of employees will be brought together for a short course on a single aspect of work: e.g. letter writing, interviewing skills, employees' duties under the Health and Safety at Work Act 1974, etc.

Overall, though, organisations in the UK have a poor record where training is concerned, partly because training is an expensive business when it is done properly; organisations which do take training seriously have often complained in the past that other organisations are not above poaching their trained staff. Furthermore, until recently, few organisations have taken their responsibilities for training women at all seriously, and few women were offered more than the basic training designed to produce functional efficiency. Until the arrival of the equal opportunities legislation on the statute books women were seen as being short-term employees who would leave to start families, and though things are changing there is still a long way to go.

Successive governments have attempted to improve training standards by introducing a number of training initiatives. For example, the Industrial Training Act 1964 enabled the establishment of a number of Industrial Training Boards (ITB) which together covered the major industrial and commercial sectors. Their responsibility was to encourage effective training of people employed in their respective sectors by offering courses, setting training standards, etc. However, over the years, it became apparent that there was a lack of consistency in the ways in which different boards operated, and since 1981 most of the ITBs have been abolished.

Since then, most government initiatives have come through the Manpower Services Commission (MSC) the most notable of which are the Youth Training Scheme (YTS), recently extended to two years, the Job Training Scheme (JTS) and Restart.

However, the fact is that the responsibility for training lies mainly with employers, who have little legal obligation to undertake training except in such areas as health and safety at work (mandatory under the terms of the Health and Safety at Work Act 1974), so there is little that can be done, at present, to change things.

An effective training programme nevertheless remains an essential factor in the efficient use of human resources, and it may well be important to incorporate the means whereby staff can attend educational courses at local colleges.

Consider a skill which you have learned either at work (e.g. filing, etc.) or at home (e.g. cooking, driving, etc.). How were you trained for the task?

Education

In a changing external environment, it may well be that the most efficient means of equipping staff with the necessary skill is to send them on the courses which are offered at local colleges of further education.

There is a wide range of courses catering for staff of all abilities, levels, etc. from the various BTEC courses – BTEC First; BTEC National Certificate in Business and Finance, or in Computer Studies or in Public Administration, etc.; BTEC Higher National Certificate – to courses validated by the London Chamber of Commerce and the City and Guilds of London Institute, to Diplomas in Management Studies and first degrees.

Many of these provide a grounding in basic business skills which will be useful in the working environment. Other, more specialised courses are available for workers in the engineering, building and craft industries in general. They are taught by staff who usually have experience of the individual industry concerned and are designed to take account of the latest developments in the real world.

All of these courses are available to people who are in full-time employment, and a good employer will be sufficiently aware of the organisation's needs and of the staff's needs to encourage them to attend college on an appropriate course either on a day-release (i.e. one day each week) basis or in the evenings.

Unfortunately, however, unlike most of the rest of Europe, the UK has no legislation which makes this obligatory; staff who wish to follow a course of study must, therefore, rely on the goodwill and the foresight of employers, some of whom are happy to support staff by granting day release, paying fees, etc.

There is little doubt that, in the long term, human resources planning is simplified somewhat when an employer adopts an enlightened attitude to training and education. However, in the absence of any legislation which would make this mandatory, improving and preserving the organisation's human resources is dependent on management's willingness to recognise its importance voluntarily.

24 Decision making

Business planning and decision making

People in organisations are faced with problem-solving situations as part of the process of effective management of resources. Problems are solved through good decision making, a skill which requires a logical, systematic and objective approach. While some decisions are made by individuals, many more are made by groups of people, working together. Group decision making often generates conflict within the group, and decisions may be bargained compromises, reached through negotiation.

The resources of an organisation need to be managed, and one of the key functions of management in this respect is business planning. The mechanisms through which this is carried out are the skills of decision making and problem solving. They are fundamental skills which we all exercise in our private lives, and the processes through which we solve problems and make decisions are the same, whether we are trying to decide between different micro-wave ovens for use in the home, between different candidates for the same job, or even to decide whether or not to merge with another company. The scale of activity may be different, but in each case we want to find the best solution, and in arriving at our choice we will, either consciously or unconsciously follow the same process. Indeed it is the extent to which we apply the process that should distinguish our business decision making from our personal decision making, since the latter tends to be more intuitive and less formalised.

In principle, decision making is an essentially *objective* activity, where the decision maker finds a solution to a problem by assessing information, identifying alternative courses of action and making a choice based on the facts. Again, in principle, feelings and emotions should play no part in the process.

Decision making inevitably takes place within the constraints imposed on all organisations by the external environment in which they operate, and by the limitations set by their internal environment.

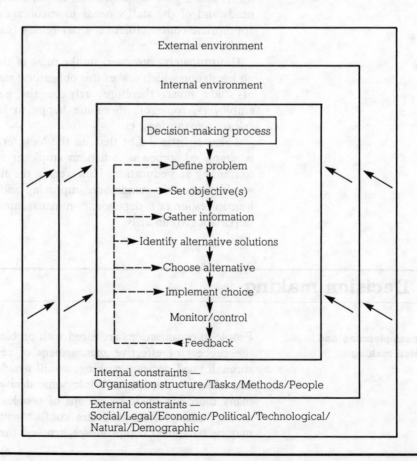

Fig. 24.1
A basic decision-making model

If we apply this model or procedure to the problems of the micro-wave oven and the new recruit posed earlier, we can see that the process is basically the same.

1 Define problem

Need new micro-wave oven   Need replacement Accounts Clerk.

2 Set objectives

To purchase best available model   To advertise/recruit for suitable replacement

3 Gather information

Probable uses   Job – duties prospects, etc.
  Useful features
  Space available in kitchen   Person – qualifications, personal
  Available models, etc.   qualities, etc.

4 Identify alternatives

Match models to requirements   Advertise job
                                          Preliminary selection for interview

5 Choose alternatives

Identify best model – match to   Interview/select – match to re-
requirements   quirements.

6 Implement choice

Purchase   Appoint

7 Monitor/control

Test it/use it   Induction/training/supervision/assess
  Does it do what you want?   Probationary period?

8 Feedback

In both cases, if the choice has been successful – and this should become clear during the monitor/control stage – then the decision-making process may be considered complete.

If, however, the choice has been unsuccessful, then the process (or at least part of it) will begin again. For example, it may be that we made the wrong choice of alternatives, in which case the feedback loop will return to Stage 5 and we will select another alternative. However if we feel that we made a wrong choice because of inadequate information, then the feedback loop will go back to Stage 3.

If we follow this model when trying to solve problems and make decisions, then the quality of our solutions should improve.

Analyse a problem which you have encountered at work, at college or in your private life using the decision-making model in Fig. 24.1

Operational decision making

There will be times, however, when some of these stages can be by-passed, since all decision making does not require such a complex approach.

For example, workers on a production line faced with a faulty machine do not need to gather information, or identify alternative courses of action, etc. They will be guided by the rules and procedures laid down by the organisation: they will know that they need to report the fault to their supervisor who will, in turn, follow his or her rules and procedures and contact the person in charge of maintenance. There is a decision-making process going on here, but the problem to be solved is one which occurs often enough to allow organisations to provide instructions for dealing with it.

Similarly, an accounts clerk who receives an invoice for payment from for example the Purchasing Department, can in most cases pass it on for payment according to the standard instructions laid down by the organisation. Though the arrival of the invoice is not a problem in the same sense as the faulty machine, nevertheless a decision must be made about how to deal with it, and normally, if the invoice is correct, the clerk can follow procedure. Even when there is a problem – where the quantity or the price is wrong – it is likely that this again happens often enough to justify a standard procedure.

This day-to-day (or operational) decision making is variously called *routine* or *programmable* decision making: the real decision has already been made by management, and it is the result of that decision-making process which forms the basis for the programme of instructions, or the routine which the worker must follow.

This is another aspect of the notion that managers manage (i.e. plan, coordinate, lead, etc.) while workers, for the most part, follow instructions. Our decision-making model is therefore more applicable to the work of the manager since he or she tends to be confronted more often by non-routine or non-programmable problem-solving situations.

Tactical and strategic decision making

Managers are concerned with problems which are out of the ordinary perhaps even unique, and which tend to have tactical (i.e. medium-term) or strategic (i.e. long-term) implications for the organisation.

For example, you may recall from Chapter 15 James Dodd's dilemma in 1952, when he needed to move from his garage workshop. This was a strategic problem since his decision would affect the long-term success of his business; should he buy or lease premises of his own? or should he merge with Andrew Simpson? This is not the sort of problem which face an organisation very often, and it is therefore impossible to lay down a standard procedure.

Put yourself in James's shoes and use the decision-making model in Fig. 24.1 to solve the problem. Do you think James made the right decision?

Problems which are likely to have long-term repercussions in the future must be approached logically and systematically, since there are high levels of risk and uncertainty involved. A decision-making model can be helpful here to ensure:

a that none of the stages are overlooked;

b that the major risks and uncertainties can be considered – e.g. changes in taste, change in interest and exchange rates, etc.

If managers follow this model, and approach decision making in an objective fashion, can we assume that decision making is a simple process? Unfortunately, there are too many variables involved in decision making for it to be that simple.

All business planning, and therefore all decision making, takes place within the environment in which the organisation functions, and the environmental factors often place *constraints* on decision making.

Constraints on decision making

External environmental constraints

No organisation can make plans without taking the social, legal, economic, technical, political, natural and demographic factors into account, since these all limit the activities of organisations.

For example, the planning laws forced James Dodd and Andrew Simpson to abandon their ideas for building a workshop behind the shop in Sunhampton High Street. Political and economic factors influenced their move to Newcastle, while social and demographic factors affected product development, and to some extent, the nature of the workforce with the demand from women for part-time work.

Similarly, employers must take note of the provision of other legislation such as the Health and Safety at Work Act 1974 and the various employment and industrial relations Acts.

These constraints are very important since they come from outside the organisation and are, therefore, largely outside its control. There are, however, other constraints which come from within the organisation's internal environment and some of these may be the source of even greater problems.

Internal environmental constraints

We have already noted that an organisation's internal environment consists of people, tasks, methods and structure, and all of these can, and do, affect decision making.

For example, a move away from the traditional production line approach to a more team-production approach (as in Volvo p. 57) will require a change in the structure of the organisation.

A production line can operate effectively with quite a wide span of control: in other words, a supervisor can be responsible for overseeing up to 40 staff. A team-production approach where workers pace themselves, organise the work themselves and control the quality of their own work may need a different form of supervision, where one supervisor controls perhaps, 20 staff.

Any decision, therefore, to change production methods is likely to affect the organisation's structure, and this must be taken into account. In fact, a decision to change any of the 4 variables will inevitably have a knock-on effect, and all 4 will be affected.

However, there is an even greater constraint which arises from one of the variables (people), because decisions are made by people, and they tend to bring to the decision-making process a whole range of *behavioural constraints*.

Behavioural constraints

People vary enormously in their abilities, expertise, etc., and they are also prone to behave irrationally and emotionally and all of this will obviously affect the quality of decision making. We are all products of the society in which we live and therefore we are all equipped with certain views and values which vary from person to person and from culture to culture.

The cultural influences and the emotions which we bring with us to the decision-making process can be a real problem, since it is considered to be a rational and objective process; this is aggravated by the fact that most

Rational decision making

people would argue that their problem solving *is* the result of *rational decision making*.

To claim that our decision making is rational is to make a brave (if not rash) claim, since rational decision making, in its pure sense, attempts to turn decision making into a 'scientific' activity, and it requires certain adjustments to our original decision-making model, since there are significant differences to those stages concerned with information gathering and with identifying and selecting alternatives.

A purely rational decision-making model is a far more comprehensive process than that implied in our original model, and it is an attempt to ensure that all our decisions are good, successful decisions based on an assessment of all relevant information, etc. It is argued that a decision made without all the facts is less likely to be successful.

In this way, decision making becomes more scientific, and risk and uncertainty are decreased, and clearly, if this scientific approach were possible, then good decision making would be within everyone's reach. Unfortunately, the purely rational decision making model contains within it its own problems.

It assumes a number of factors:

a all the information is readily available/obtainable/identifiable;

b the decision maker can assimilate/analyse/process, etc. this wealth of information, alternatives, etc.;

c that information gathering costs are negligible;

d there is enough time available to make comprehensive information gathering possible;

e the decision maker can always be relied on to behave totally rationally and so will always choose the solution which offers maximum benefit to the organisation.

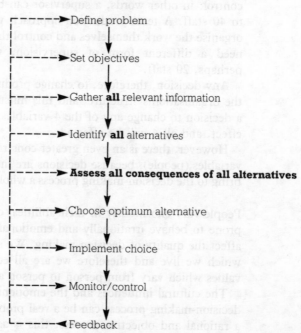

Fig. 24.2
A purely rational decision-making model with additional elements in **bold**

In practice, however, this is far more difficult than it might appear since, in the first place, information gathering on this scale presents enormous difficulties:

a it is extremely time-consuming and is, therefore, very expensive;
b if there is a deadline (and there always is) then it may not be possible to collect all the information in the time allowed;
c even if we perform the impossible and succeed in collecting perfect information within the deadline, decision day will find more information cropping up too late for inclusion;
d it is impossible to tell whether we have gathered all the information or not.

In any case, even if we can overcome these problems, we are then confronted with the greatest constraint of all, which is human nature itself, since, in the first place, few, if any, of us could cope with the amount of information an exercise like this would produce. Even more significant is the fact that people, by and large, are rarely capable of behaving in a totally objective, rational fashion: this is what makes us human, and we bring to the decision-making process all our values, beliefs, prejudices and all the other things which make us individual beings.

Like organisations, we too function within an environment which includes the family, our friends, the education system, the socio-politico-legal system, etc., and all of this affects the way we think and behave.

This means that even if we were able to cope with all the information – assuming we could collect it all and be sure that we had missed nothing – it is quite likely that we would still ignore or suppress that information which did not conform with our beliefs, and our decisions would be tempered by such factors as our opinions, experience, skill based on our work and so on.

In short, humans intend to be rational and objective in decision making; we try to suppress emotion, etc. and argue that most of our decisions are reached objectively. In practice, however, we cannot always suppress the human, subjective factor and this must be recognised and acknowledged if decision making is to be effective. There are many instances where managers (who might well sneer at the idea of a woman's intuition) have themselves 'played a hunch' in the teeth of the evidence, and have been proved right.

So, if human beings are rarely purely rational in their decision making, is the concept or rational decision making a realistic one? The answer is, of course, yes, providing that we recognise that:

a there is an element of subjectivity involved;
b it is impossible to collect and assess all the information.

These limitations can affect the quality of the decision. It may not, for example, be possible to be sure that the decision reached is the best or the optimum solution. In fact, most managers will reach what is known as a 'satisficing' decision which satisfies minimum criteria: in other words, many of our decisions will be compromises, or the best solution/decision given the prevailing circumstances/conditions/constraints.

Most of us, if we are honest, will acknowledge that the quality and the quantity of the information upon which we base our decisions are impaired in some way, and we make up this shortfall by using the skills which we have acquired at work; for example we may rely on opinion based on past experience, or we may respond to our intuition and play our hunches. Decisions made in this way may work just as well as those which have been attempted through a purely rational process.

To sum up so far, then, we can say that decision making and problem solving are part of the process of business planning, and therefore take place in situations of high risk and uncertainty.

Decision making is a predominantly rational process which is constrained by factors from the environment – internal and external – of the organisation, in particular by the behavioural factors such as the decision maker's abilities, attitudes, etc.

While the intention is to find the optimum solution, most people make satisficing decisions because of the inherent constraints of:

a the cost of information gathering;
b the need to meet deadlines;
c the behavioural aspects of information collection, assessment, etc.

Consider a recent problem in your own life – at work, at college, at home. Was the decision which you reached a maximising or satisficing decision? Try and identify the factors, constraints, etc. which influenced your decision.

Group decision making

So far, we have considered decision making by the individual manager and have identified some of the difficulties which we encounter in this important process. Decision making is, however – perhaps unfortunately – not always a solitary occupation. Few of us work in isolation since we tend to be members of departments, project teams, etc., and it is usually within these groups that decision making takes place. The great advantage of this is that two heads, as the saying goes, are better than one and the combined abilities and expertise of group members often lead to better decision making. On the other hand, all the behavioural constraints which we considered earlier are multiplied by the number of people in the group, since each member brings his or her values, beliefs, etc. to the decision-making process.

For example, when the board of Electrofactors decided not to buy its own fleet of delivery vans, some members of the board might have felt quite strongly that the decision was wrong. After all, the company was expanding, its products were being marketed all over the UK, and the cost of transporting the goods was largely outside their control since they were using an outside contractor. It is also possible that someone on the board could see the possibility for some personal empire building if the company acquired its own transport fleet, since personal ambition can also play a part in decision making.

On the other hand, as the Director of Finance pointed out, the company had recently been involved in an expensive programme of expansion when they purchased the airfield, and therefore this was not a good time to spend more money, however desirable, in the long term, acquiring their own transport facilities might be.

In a situation like this one, the group leader will be seeking a positive outcome, preferably a unanimous decision. However, given the fact that all groups consist of individuals, and that no two individuals are likely to see eye to eye on every issue, often the best we can hope for is a decision which reflects a consensus view, representative of the views of most group members, while trying at the same time to minimise *conflict*.

Conflict

Conflict, however, is an inevitable part of a group decision making. Indeed, it is to some extent an inevitable part of the internal environment of all organisations, and, contrary to popular belief, it is not always a negative force. Its existence, though, needs to be acknowledged, and managers need to develop strategies for dealing with it, since unresolved conflict can have a negative effect; it can lead to a lack of motivation, low morale, and to poor worker performance.

The keys to managing conflict are to be found through consultation and participation: managers must ensure that staff are consulted and given an opportunity to express their views; they should also be encouraged to participate in a formal, structured and controlled exchange of views. The role of group leader is crucial here, and if successfully carried out, consultation and participation can result in effective decision making without group members feeling resentful; they may not all be totally happy with the decision, but nor will they feel that they have been railroaded into accepting a decision in which their views, feelings, etc. have been ignored.

Groups are a very important aspect of any organisation, since the individual is likely to feel a greater sense of identity and loyalty to the group within which he or she operates than with the organisation as a whole. This means that members of the Finance Department will see the needs of the department as being more important than the wellbeing of the organisation. In the Research and Development Department, members of Project Team A and Project Team B will feel a greater sense of responsibility, loyalty, etc. to their respective team members than to the department or to the organisation.

This factor can often affect decision making within departments, teams, etc., since decisions may be reached because they are acceptable to the views, values and feelings of group members rather than because they are good for the organisation.

Either at college or at work, consider to whom you feel most loyalty – to the group/class/team/department? When you have done this, make a list of the reasons why.

The ultimate form of group decision making is to be found in *negotiation*, when two groups get together to try to reach a decision which is agreeable to both sides.

Negotiation

This kind of decision making can happen between two individuals, where each has a viewpoint or a proposal, and each wants to persuade the other to that point of view. At its simplest, it can be seen in the discussion between a parent and a child who wants an increase in pocket-money, while at its most complex, perhaps, we have the arms discussions between the USA and the USSR.

In both cases, there are common features:

a both sides want a satisfactory resolution as the outcome of discussion;
b both sides have a series of proposals to put to the other;
c both sides have a number of counter proposals;
d both sides have prepared for the encounter to try and anticipate demands so that counter proposals can be formulated;
e both sides have decided on a base line, or limit, beyond which they are unwilling to compromise.

Negotiations tend to follow a similar pattern: one side suggests a proposition, which is followed by acceptance, or discussion, or rejection, whereupon the other side offers a counter proposal and so on, until either a bargained compromise is reached, or until the negotiations break down.

Given the potential for conflict discussed earlier when considering group decision making, then it seems clear that there is an even greater potential for conflict in negotiation. For this reason it is helpful if the groups can appeal to a less partial third party, or arbitrator, if negotiations do break down.

In a business organisation, the third party may be the Head of Department, or the Managing Director or even the board, depending on the issues and the level of staff doing the negotiating. In this case, the decision of the arbitrator, or referee, is likely to be binding on the groups. However, some arbitrators lack the power to enforce their recommendations, and must rely on the commonsense of the participants. For example, the Arbitration, Conciliation and Advisory Service (ACAS) has no legal powers to force acceptance of their advice or recommendations on employers and trade unions who have reached stalemate.

The role of arbitrator is not an easy one, since it, too, requires an objective, rational decision based on an assessment of information. It is often the fate of the arbitrator to be reviled; notably by the losing party, but sometimes by both parties. It is not unknown for both groups to join forces to attack the arbitrator if neither is happy with his/her decision.

25 Mixing resources

You may recall from Chapter 16 the distinction between fixed and variable factors of production. The quantity of fixed factors of production does not change as output changes, whereas the quantity of variable factors does change.

An organisation may operate for some time without altering the quantity of its fixed factors of production (e.g. using the same amount of factory space and the same number of machines). This period is known as the 'short run'. In its longer-term planning the organisation may decide to build another factory or acquire more machines (i.e. to increase some of its fixed factors of production). The period when these new factors are in use is called the 'long run'.

We shall first analyse production behaviour in the short run, so demonstrating the Law of Diminishing Returns.

The law of diminishing returns

At the Electrofactors (Products) plc plant near Sunhampton, one of their small workshops contains a fixed number of work-benches for preparing materials, and specialised machines which produce components for their video games. In addition to these fixed factors of production the company needs to utilise the variable factors of labour and materials to produce components.

Consider the pattern of output per day in Table 25.1 as additional workers are employed.

Table 25.1

Number of workers	Total product	Average product	Marginal product
1	30	30	30
2	70	35	40
3	120	40	50
4	180	45	60
5	200	40	20
6	210	35	10

The terms at the heads of the columns merit explanation.
Total product (TP) is the total output produced.

Average product (AP) is the total product divided by the number of variable factors (in this case labour).

e.g. AP of 2 workers = TP ÷ 2
= 70 ÷ 2 = 35 units.

Marginal product (MP) is the increase in the total product as an additional unit of the variable factor is employed.

e.g. MP of the 2nd worker = TP (after 2 workers are employed)
− TP (after 1 worker is employed)
= 70 − 30 = 40 units.

You will note that as extra workers are employed, the average and marginal product at first rise, but then fall. Total product increases only slowly by the time the fifth and sixth workers are employed.

Why should this be so? By employing only one worker, Electrofactors are not fully utilising the fixed factors of production. As the second, third and fourth workers are employed there is an increasingly efficient use of the fixed and variable factors. However, when the fifth and sixth workers are employed there are evidently insufficient fixed factors for the services of the extra employees to be fully utilised. The organisation will not now be operated as efficiently as it was when 4 workers were employed.

The pattern illustrated above is not peculiar to Electrofactors. It would be apparent in any organisation facing the barrier of a set amount of fixed factors of production. Thus we can develop a general rule, known as the Law of Diminishing Returns or the Law of Variable Proportions. It states:

Fig. 25.1
Average and marginal product

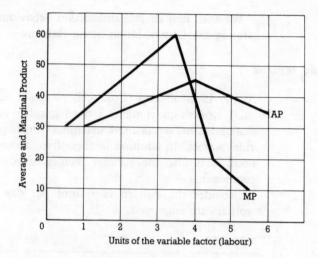

If one or more factors of production are fixed in supply and additional units of a variable factor are added, the marginal product will eventually diminish.

The Law of Diminishing Returns can be illustrated by means of a graph (see Fig. 25.1). Note that the marginal product is plotted above the values $\frac{1}{2}$, $1\frac{1}{2}$, $2\frac{1}{2}$, etc. on the horizontal axis. This is because MP relates to the *change* in total output as an *extra* factor is employed.

The shapes of the curves confirm the deductions made from the table. The rising AP and MP curves indicate improved technical efficiency since progressively fuller use is made of the fixed factors of production. However, following the employment of the fourth worker the curves enter the downswing. Diminishing returns have set in. It now becomes more difficult to produce extra output because of the constraint of the fixed number of work-benches and machines. Extra output and average output per worker declines.

At which point is the firm operating most efficiently? Consider this before you read on.

The most efficient point, given the present level of fixed factors, is where AP is greatest. That occurs where the fourth worker is employed. AP is at its highest value, 45 units.

Costs of production in the short run

As well as the relationship of inputs and outputs just described, an organisation must also consider the costs of producing goods and services. An analysis of costs is crucial to determine the cheapest levels of output, and as we shall see in Chapter 27, is an important influence in the setting of the price of the goods or services produced.

Again we shall initially consider a short run situation.

In Chapter 16 we introduced the two components of total cost. Do you recall what they were?

Total cost is made up of:

Total fixed cost The total cost of fixed factors of production, e.g. rent for premises, interest on money borrowed. Fixed costs do not change as output alters.

Total variable cost The total cost of variable factors of production, e.g. weekly wage payments, costs of materials and power. Variable costs change as output alters.

We shall illustrate the cost structure of a firm by reference to a further feature of Electrofactors. The data in Table 25.2 show the costs of the weekly production of batches of video games.

Table 25.2
Costs in the short run (£)

Batches of output of video games	Total cost	Total fixed cost	Total variable cost	Average total cost	Average fixed cost	Average variable cost	Marginal cost
0	500	500	—	—	—	—	—
1	900	500	400	900	500	400	400
2	1200	500	700	600	250	350	300
3	1410	500	910	470	167	303	210
4	1560	500	1060	390	125	265	150
5	1900	500	1400	380	100	280	340
6	2400	500	1900	400	83	317	500
7	3500	500	3000	500	71	429	1100

$$\text{Average total cost (ATC)} = \frac{\text{total cost}}{\text{units of output}}$$

$$\text{Therefore ATC at output 2} = \frac{£1200}{2} = £600$$

$$\text{Average fixed cost (AFC)} = \frac{\text{total fixed cost}}{\text{units of output}}$$

$$\text{Hence AFC at output 2} = \frac{£500}{2} = £250$$

$$\text{Average variable cost (AVC)} = \frac{\text{total variable cost}}{\text{units of output}}$$

$$\text{Thus the AVC at output 2} = \frac{£700}{2} = £350.$$

Marginal cost (MC) means the change in total cost as an extra unit of output is produced. Therefore the MC of output 2 = total cost at output 2 minus total cost at output 1 = £1200 − £900 = £300.

What do you notice from the pattern of data in the table as output grows?

Inevitably total cost increases as output rises. To produce more costs more! However, the fixed cost, by definition, is constant, whereas the total variable cost increases as output grows.

Note that average fixed cost continuously decreases as output gets larger. Why is that? Consider an answer before you read on.

The fall in AFC occurs because the constant amount of total fixed cost is being spread over a higher and higher level of output.

Average total cost, average variable cost and marginal cost all decline at first, but then increase as output rises further. How do you explain this initial fall and later rise? Again, consider this question before you read on.

The reason is closely related to the behaviour described earlier of increasing returns (rising average and marginal product) followed by diminishing returns (falling AP and MP). Falling ATC, AVC and MC reflect the more efficient use of extra variable factors in unison with the fixed factors of production. Output becomes cheaper to produce. However, eventually, by adding more variable factors to the set amount of fixed factors, extra output becomes more difficult to achieve, i.e. it begins to cost progressively more to produce extra goods because of the constraint of limited fixed factors.

This behaviour can be demonstrated by a graph of cost curves. In Fig. 25.2 note that MC (like MP in Fig. 25.1) is plotted at the mid-point values, of each unit of output in this case. MC, like ATC and AVC, first declines, then rises as output grows, for the reasons explained above. AFC continuously falls as output expands, as fixed costs are spread over a larger output.

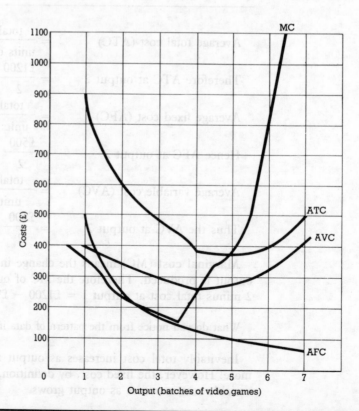

Fig. 25.2
Short run cost curves

At which level of output will the firm be operating most efficiently? This will be the level at which average total cost is at its lowest (output 5 in this case). This point, where output is on average cheapest to produce, is known as the **optimum output**.

As well as considering the Law of Diminishing Returns and costs of production, an organisation must also analyse its sales revenue possibilities (including the setting of a price) before deciding exactly at which output to produce.

Costs of production in the long run

If an organisation faces an expanding market it may find that its current stock of fixed factors of production prohibits the desired expansion of output. The answer would be for the organisation to alter the scale of its production, e.g. acquire more machines or bigger premises and offices, given that it can raise the necessary finance.

If this is done the organisation is now operating in the 'long run' production period. That is the time in which the firm can change its quantity of fixed factors of production.

Whilst increasing and diminishing returns are key influences on cost curves in the short run, economies and diseconomies of scale are similarly influential in the long run.

Economies of scale

Economies of scale cause the average costs of production to decrease as the scale of output increases. Internal economies of scale occur through expansion within the firm itself, whereas a firm benefits from external economies of scale by taking advantage of forces outside its immediate control.

Internal economies

These include **technical economies**. Large organisations are more likely to be able to adopt techniques like the division of labour and to acquire specialised machinery. Also, bigger firms can afford to utilise large-scale methods of transportation, e.g. supertankers for the movement of oil. Such technical economies mean that bigger volumes of output can be produced more cheaply.

Marketing and distribution economies Larger firms can afford to advertise in the mass media, so stimulating sales further. In addition, discounts can be negotiated for bulk buying, enabling goods to be bought more cheaply.

Financial economies Larger organisations stand a much better chance of raising large sums for capital investment, be it from retained profits or bank borrowing.

Managerial economies Larger organisations should be able to attract better quality managers and to adopt managerial specialisation, giving senior management sizeable responsibilities.

External economies

An expanding organisation can take advantage of opportunities potentially open to any firm in the industry, e.g. obtaining finance from government grants or benefiting from the advantages of localisation (which were described earlier as an influence on the location of industry – see Chapter 17 page 155).

Diseconomies of scale

In spite of the economies of scale, which push down average costs as output expands, organisations can run up against barriers which force up average costs in the long run. Such diseconomies of scale can be both internal and external to the firm.

Internal diseconomies

Large organisations can suffer the disadvantages of division of labour (as described in Chapter 4 – see page 57), such as industrial strife, absenteeism and defective work. Also, there can be managerial and administrative diseconomies in large organisations, caused by problems in co-ordination and communication within the firm.

External diseconomies

The effects of competition between expanding firms in an industry can cause shortages of factors of production. This can drive up average costs of production.

In addition, some diseconomies of large-scale production may be suffered by those outside the organisation too. Pollution of rivers and the air or excessive noise due to the production processes of large organisations cause disadvantage and discomfort to local residents.

The long run average cost curve

How do economies and diseconomies of scale influence the long run average cost curve? Three possibilities for the shape of the curve (denoted as LRAC) are shown in Fig. 25.3. Economies of scale outweigh diseconomies in Fig. 25.3(a), so that average cost falls as output grows. Figure 25.3(b) indicates that economies of scale are eventually offset by diseconomies. Average cost becomes constant as output grows. Figure 15.3(c) indicates the power of diseconomies over economies of scale, such that eventually average cost is forced up. An organisation in this situation should investigate its production and administrative structures to reduce such diseconomies.

Can you pick out any economies or diseconomies of scale in the organisation in which you work or study? Do you think the economies of scale outweigh the diseconomies, or vice versa?

These cost considerations will recur when we later discuss how an organisation goes about setting a price for its output.

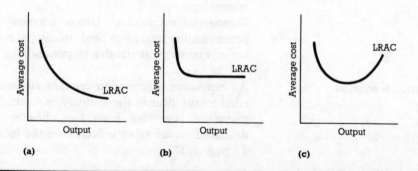

Fig. 25.3
Long run average cost curves   (a)   (b)   (c)

Takeovers and mergers

In Chapter 4 we stressed the significance in the economy of large organisations in both the public and private sectors. Organisations can grow in size through internal expansion, by exploiting economies of scale. However, many firms have grown by taking over or merging with other organisations. A takeover occurs when an organisation buys a controlling interest in the shares of another. A merger involves the exchange of shares in the original companies for shares in the newly formed organisation.

Such integration in the private sector will primarily occur to increase profitability. In the public sector nationalisation is the key form of integration, the reasons for which were explained in Chapter 8 (see page 85).

There are three types of integration by firms – horizontal, vertical and conglomerate. We shall describe the features of each.

Horizontal integration

This involves integration by firms at the *same stage* of production of the *same product*. For example, in the late 1960s the Westminster Bank and the National Provincial Bank linked to become the National Westminster. International Computers and Tabulators, English Electric, and Plessey united to form International Computers (ICL). In 1984 Woolworth took over Comet, the electrical goods retailer, while in the summer of 1985 the two strongest companies in the UK textile industry, Vanton Viyella and Nottingham Manufacturing linked. The main reason advanced was to combat foreign competition more effectively.

The nationalisation of an industry is a further example of horizontal integration.

The advantages of horizontal integration include:

a more control of the market by reducing the extent of competition;
b greater ability to compete with larger competitors, especially in overseas markets;
c greater opportunity to exploit economies of scale.

Vertical integration

Integration by firms at *different stages* of production of the *same product* is known as vertical integration. For example, large oil companies have bought the rights to explore oil fields, then refining the product and selling it at petrol stations. Also, major breweries own public houses (tied houses), ensuring a retail outlet for their beer. Banks and building societies have acquired estate agents.

The prime benefits from vertical integration are:

a more security over the supply of an input;
b cheaper inputs, since profit made by previously independent suppliers is removed;
c the security of a retail or wholesale outlet;
d economies of scale.

Conglomerate integration

This occurs through the integration of firms producing *different products*, e.g. Cadbury-Schweppes. Unilever is another large organisation which has

Fig. 25.4

developed by conglomerate integration. A selection of Unilever products is shown in Fig. 25.4.

Conglomerate integration occurs for the following reasons:

a risk diversifying – spreading the range of output so that if demand for one product line declines there are others with potential for development;

b if little growth is forecast in the original market (i.e. there is market saturation; this was a prime motive behind the expansion of the tobacco giants Imperial Tobacco and British American Tobacco, which have each become large conglomerates);

c economies of scale.

Whilst economies of scale could be amongst the motives when firms integrate it should not be forgotten that the larger organisations run the risk of experiencing diseconomies of scale, especially of the administrative type. Further, as organisations draw up plans to control a larger market share they may find potential mergers or takeovers referred to the Monopolies and Mergers Commission. If the Commission recommends that the proposed 'marriage' could prove counter to the public interest (e.g. by giving a firm too much market control), the Secretary of State can veto the merger or takeover.

Summary, Part E

1 Economic efficiency involves producing at the lowest cost.
2 Human resources or manpower planning is concerned with taking a long-term view of an organisation's staffing needs.
3 Human resources planning attempts to identify:
  a appropriate staffing levels;

b relevant job categories;

c essential skills.

4 Organisations must recognise that they have social responsibilities, notably in respect of equal opportunities, etc., which may well be mandatory under the law.

5 These social responsibilities must be taken into account in human resources planning.

6 Staff performance appraisal can help gather information which will be helpful in human resources planning and in identifying training needs.

7 Staff training and retraining will help ensure an efficiently functioning and flexible workforce.

8 Further education courses can help staff acquire new skills to improve efficiency and adaptability.

9 Decision making occurs at operational, tactical and strategic levels in all organisations.

10 Decision making is, in principle, an objective, rational activity.

11 Rational decision making is constrained by the difficulty involved in gathering *all* relevant information, and by the values, abilities, expertise, etc. of the decision maker.

12 Many decisions are taken by groups of people, and this may lead to conflict, which must be managed effectively.

13 Negotiation, whereby individuals or groups are allowed to bargain, can often result in a compromise decision where neither party feels resentment.

14 Where negotiation breaks down, the intervention of an independent arbitrator can often help resolve the difficulty.

15 Costs and output in the short run are influenced by increasing and diminishing returns.

16 In the long run costs are influenced by economies and diseconomies of scale.

17 The expansion of an organisation can also occur by means of mergers or takeovers.

Part E, Assignment

1

Change

This assignment involves you investigating a major change that has occurred in the organisation in which you work or study. (Or possibly you might choose to investigate another organisation in which change has occurred.)

For example, there may be a government policy change which has had an impact on an organisation. Maybe there has been the launch of a new product, or the closure of a branch. Perhaps new technology has been introduced. Possibly the structure of the department in which you work has been revised.

You need to:

a describe the change which has occurred;

b give reasons for the change;

c describe how the decision to change was made and by whom (consider if possible influences on the decision);

d consider the financial implication of the change;

e consider the effects of the change on, e.g. profitability, employment levels and training, efficiency (or other effects relevant to the specific change under analysis).

Skills
Learning and studying, numeracy, information gathering, identifying and tackling problems

2

Motorspares Ltd

Motorspares Ltd is an old established company which manufactures spare parts for the motor industry. For many years the company has been highly profitable, with a large share of the market both at home and overseas. For the past 5 years, however, they have experienced a decline in demand and a consequent loss in profit. They have recently appointed a new Managing Director who has a great deal of experience in this field, and whose first task is to investigate why the company is losing ground to its competitors.

It soon becomes clear that Motorspares' major competitors are all offering goods which are comparable in quality to Motorspares' goods, but at a much lower price. The Managing Director feels that they are able to do this because they have all invested in new technology and new production methods, whereas Motorspares is still using machinery which was installed in the 1950s. There has been little investment in new machinery since then, and maintenance and repair costs are increasing each year; the machinery is also labour intensive to operate.

The answer, then, seems to be an investment programme over the next few years to introduce new production methods to Motorspares. However, the Board will take some convincing, and the Managing Director asks for your help in preparing evidence.

You are required to:

a produce a checklist of factors which will strengthen the case;
b draw up an outline human resources plan indicating the main issues which need to be taken into account.

Skills
Identifying and tackling problems, communicating

HE MARKET

y the time you have read this part you should be able to:
Understand the nature of markets.
Describe how organisations set prices.
Appreciate the importance of marketing and describe the major elements
involved in it.
Understand what makes an agreement a legally binding contract.
Understand the effect of untrue sales talk on such a contract.
Understand the effects of and remedies for breach of contract.
Understand the effect of frustration on a contract.
Understand the nature of exemption clauses.
Understand the nature of contracts for the sale of goods and contracts of
hire purchase.
Understand the nature of Negligence and Product Liability.

6 The nature and form of the market

hat is the market?

The term 'market' can be used in three contexts: as the interaction of
buyers and sellers, as the demand for goods or services and as the mechanism helping to determine prices.

nteraction of buyers and ellers

This involves the fundamental market activity in which potential and actual
buyers and sellers are in contact and deals are transacted. When you
purchased this book you were participating in a market. Everything you
purchase involves you as a buyer interacting with a seller.

This interaction can depend on personal contact between buyer and
seller, as with stalls in a street market like Portobello Road in London, livestock markets, fruit and vegetable markets like New Covent Garden or
the counters at Marks and Spencer's. In London there are commodity
exchanges, buildings where prospective buyers and sellers of primary products like copper, tin, sugar and coffee interact. In all such cases, buyers
and sellers meet and transactions are agreed.

However, in some markets such immediate personal contact is not
necessary. Deals may be conducted by telephone or telex, with payments
made by cheques passing through the banking network. For example, the
foreign exchange departments of banks transact the sale and purchase of
currencies by telephone. No immediate personal contact occurs. In fact the
contact between the actual buyers and sellers is seen to be even more remote
when one considers that the banks are merely acting as agents for their
customers who need the currency. Their clients are the true buyers and
sellers. It is between them that any contract is made. The bank is simply

an agent whose job it is to make the contract. Once the contract has been made the banker agent drops out of the deal.

A recent variation on the market theme has been the growth of mail order business. Again there is no personal contact between purchaser and vendor. Buyers order by letter and the goods are similarly received through the postal system. As we shall see later on in this part, the law has a considerable part to play here. Mail order catalogues, advertisements, order forms etc. all have legal implications.

The market as demand

As well as considering the market as interaction between buyers and sellers, organisations refer to the market for their goods or services as the number of purchasers, or the number of units of the commodity bought by these consumers.

For example, if a manufacturer claims that his market expanded by 10 per cent last year, he means that his firm sold 10 per cent more goods. Therefore 'market' is used to mean actual demand, the quantities consumers bought.

An organisation may also refer to its market share. This means the percentage of sales of the whole industry which were made by that firm. For example, if total sales in an industry were 1 million units, and firm 2 sold 300 000 of those, its market share would be 30 per cent. In the new car market in the UK, the market share of British manufacturers, especially British Leyland (BL), declined from the late 1970s. Foreign-made cars took an increasing market share.

The market mechanism

In Chapter 2 the distinction between types of economic system was made. At the extremes were free market and command economies, with the mixed economy filling the middle ground. You should recall that in a pure market economy the market mechanism, or price mechanism as it is also known, is the determinant of price and allocator of resources. In a mixed economy

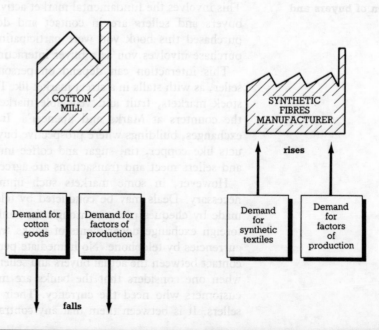

Fig. 26.1
The effects of the market mechanism

varying degrees of State involvement temper some of the apparent disadvantages of the market mechanism. In a command economy, the market mechanism has a far smaller role to play, with State direction of resources far more prominent.

The market mechanism involves the interplay of the forces of demand (on the consumers' side) and supply (the sellers') in order to determine prices of commodities and quantities bought and sold. Hence, varying quantities of factors of production will be utilised in particular industries, so reflecting conditions in the market for the goods they produce. However, as changes in demand or supply occur the market mechanism works to reallocate resources. For example, demand for cotton and woollen clothing has fallen in recent decades because of the development of synthetic fibres like rayon, nylon, terylene, etc. As illustrated in Fig. 26.1 the market mechanism has operated to reduce the demand for factors of production in the natural textile industry where some mills have closed down. On the other hand there has been growth in the chemical industry and in the manufacturing of synthetic fibres. Additional factors of production have been attracted into those industries.

Forms of market

Considering markets in the first of the senses we have mentioned, as inter-action of buyers and sellers, we can distinguish two fundamental types of market, perfect and imperfect.

The perfect market

A perfect market is one which portrays the following characteristics:

1 There must be a homogenous product. This means that there is no difference in the nature and quality of the supply of each seller. There is no branding or advertising to differentiate the product of one supplier from another.

2 There must be many buyers and sellers with free entry to the market. This implies the absence of monopoly elements, which would make the operation of free competition less likely.

3 Buyers and sellers must be fully aware of market conditions. Prices charged by various suppliers will be known to other participants in the market.

4 There must be no consumer loyalty. Consumers will buy where goods are cheapest, not always from the same supplier through tradition and habit.

It is difficult to think of an actual market which accords with all these features. Can you think of one?

Some markets bear many of the characteristics, e.g. the stock market, the foreign exchange market, or a string of street market stalls selling, say, fruit and vegetables. Perhaps they do not fit the role precisely. Where do you think these examples fail the test of being perfect markets?

If perfect markets rarely exist, why bother to discuss them?

The perfect market is the backcloth for perfect competition, where ther
is competition between many small firms, each trying to maximise i
profits. The lack of monopoly elements and the keenness of competitio
eliminate excess profits, and ultimately firms produce at the output wit
the lowest average cost. This leads to the optimum or best allocation c
resources in the economy, via the market mechanism. However, perfe
markets are rare. Our economy involves a collection of imperfect market
Let us analyse their characteristics.

The imperfect market

Quite simply, an imperfect market exists where one or more of the chara
teristics of a perfect market fail to hold. For example:

Products in most markets are not homogeneous.

This can be caused by brand names and advertising. To illustrate, ther
is no simple output of a common product 'washing powder'. We hav
Persil, Daz, Tide, Omo, etc., each trying to create a brand image an
individuality in the mind of the consumer.

The existence of non-price competition.

Competition between suppliers is not only on the battlefield of price. Fre
gifts may be given, e.g. plastic beakers with a packet of washing powde
trading stamps, etc. One example of the importance of non-price comp
tition and the success of firms in individualising their brands relates to Su:
washing powder. The manufacturers, Lever Brothers, decided to offer mor
powder per packet than rival brands at a similar price ('Square Deal Surf'
If consumers were purely price conscious, logically they would be expecte
to switch in large numbers to Surf.

However, the rise in demand was not especially large. It would appea
that if consumers identify with a brand and are content with it, a small pric
variation or a larger quantity in a substitute product is unlikely to b
sufficient to induce a change.

Research into consumer behaviour suggests that many consumers wer
attracted to the offer of a free gift with their washing powder.

Large firms in a market.

It is rare for markets to be composed of many sellers. Often selling :
concentrated into the hands of a few large firms. This type of a market for
is known as an 'oligopoly'. For example High Street banking is dominate
by the four major clearing banks. The market for washing powder :
concentrated between two large suppliers, Lever Brothers and Procter an
Gamble, who make most of the well-known brands.

A monopoly literally means just one seller of the product in a marke
The occurrence of a private monopoly is rare, though State monopolies ar
more common. In the UK some public corporations, and as in the ele
tricity industries, are sole suppliers.

The term 'monopoly' is sometimes used to indicate a dominant influenc
by a firm in an industry, rather than its literal interpretation of so
supplier. By the 1973 Fair Trading Act, if a firm controls at least 25 p
cent of the market, the Secretary of State for Trade and Industry or th
Director General of Fair Trading can order an investigation by th
Monopolies and Mergers Commission to consider whether the firm
abusing its monopoly power by acting against the public interest. This Ac

regards control of 25 per cent of the market as potential monopoly, an example of a situation where the law is intervening in the economy.

A market in which there is a sole buyer is known as 'monopsony', e.g. a nationalised industry could be the sole demander of labour, as is the Post Office for postal workers.

Lack of knowledge of market conditions.

There is no guarantee that buyers or sellers are fully aware of market conditions in the industry. For example, there is likely to be a time lag before all buyers and sellers become aware of a price change by a particular seller, especially if the market covers a large geographical area and sellers are many.

Consumer loyalty.

As was illustrated in the washing powder example of Surf above, consumers can become attached to a brand image and might not switch to a substitute, even if it were relatively cheaper. The friendliness apparent in one shop might overcome the cheaper prices but curt service of a competitor.

The geographical spread of the market

In considering the market according to demand, it can be analysed in relation to its geographical size.

The local market

Some organisations supply goods or services purely at a local level, e.g. newsagents, fish-and-chip shops. Their customers are residents of a locality. They are usually small firms, lacking the funds to expand, or, in some cases, lacking the desire to do so. The objective could simply be to run a relatively uncomplicated small business. There are exceptions to the small size, of course. London Regional Transport, a very large organisation, caters for a local market – the London area.

The national market

Many well-known firms supply their commodities on a nationwide scale. Public corporations like the Electricity industries and the Post Office operate to supply the whole country. Some of the supermarket chains, e.g. Tesco and International Stores, are likely to have branches in most major towns and cities.

The international market

Some big organisations may serve export markets in addition to their home sales, e.g. UK manufacturers like BL, Ford and Vauxhall sell vehicles to

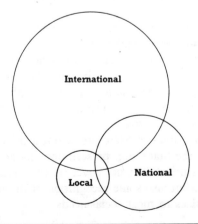

Fig. 26.2
The overlapping geographical spread of markets

a number of foreign countries. The major banks have overseas divisions, e.g. Barclays International, with banks in many countries.

Note that some firms operate on 2 or even all 3 levels, as illustrated in Fig. 26.2. The national newspapers supply the whole country, but most papers cater for regional markets by varying their sports coverage to include local news and reports. The major banks operate at all 3 levels. With branches overseas and in most cities, towns and even some villages, they operate in international and national markets. However, at the local level the individual bank manager should be flexible enough to cater for the needs of people in that area. He should be aware of the problems of local industries or agriculture, and able to gear banking services accordingly.

Does the organisation in which you might work serve local, national or international markets?

The spot and futures market

In many commodity markets and in the foreign exchange market, it is possible to negotiate a deal at today's price, or alternatively to contract future delivery at an agreed price. This is the distinction between operating in the spot market and in the forward or futures market.

On the commodity exchanges, copper, rubber, tin, silver, sugar, etc. prices are quoted by sellers for immediate sale (the spot price) or for purchase some months later (the forward price). For example, on 22 January 1987 the spot price for zinc on the London exchange was £490 per tonne, whereas the 3-month forward price was £486. The forward price will reflect likely future demand and supply conditions. Futures markets are important when buyers do not have immediate use for a commodity. An agreed price provides certainty, since if the commodity were bought at the spot price in 3 months' time, the price then would reflect the prevailing market conditions. It could be higher, or lower, than the current futures price.

Similarly, foreign exchange rates can be quoted at spot (today's rate) or at forward rates.

Markets for priced and non-priced goods and services

The vast bulk of goods and services we buy have a price which reflects the forces of demand and supply. However, there are a number of goods and services provided by the State which are priced below their cost or are not priced at all.

We do not pay a direct price for services like the armed forces, the police and the judiciary. Major parts of the National Health Service, e.g. visiting your GP, are not priced. State schooling is available without fees. Such services are known as public goods – services of inherent quality that require public production. Every member of society has access to these services irrespective of income and wealth, though they are financed by State revenue raising.

In some areas of State provision, a price is charged, but is partly subsidised by the State, e.g. prescription charges. The price for the average item on prescription does not cover its cost. Here there is an element of cost to the user, but also some recognition of the need for State provision of goods and services to meet social needs.

The marketing mix

If organisations are to tap market potential to the full and meet customer needs, then effective marketing of their goods or services is crucial.

You may recall in Chapter 15 we described the departmental structure of Electrofactor (Products) plc of Sunhampton. The Marketing Department there, as in other large organisations, is responsible for establishing and meeting customer needs and anticipating changes in them. In so doing, the marketing function involves pricing, advertising and sales promotion, and distributing the goods or services to buyers by appropriate means. In this chapter we shall introduce some basic principles of marketing and develop a fuller analysis in Chapter 4 along with a description of marketing research methods.

Essentially the Marketing Department of an organisation should establish the appropriate **marketing mix** so that sales are suitably stimulated.

The marketing mix relates to the following key issues:

a Is the range and quality of the product suitable?
b Is the product readily available to customers by likely channels of distribution?
c Is the price appropriate (involving, too, discounts to suppliers and possible credit terms)?
d Are methods of advertising and sales promotion suitable?

These factors are sometimes known as the 4 Ps:

- Product
- Place
- Price
- Promotion

It is important that the 4 factors are integrated and complement each other if the product is to reach its target market to the optimum.

Take the case of Buyerpad Building Society. When it opened its Sunhampton branch 5 years ago its Marketing Department (based at its headquarters in Manchester) certainly considered the marketing mix both at the local level at Sunhampton, but also by using their established national image as a major building society.

Product

Buyerpad offers a range of saving facilities for the personal investor. They range from small accounts for children to high interest bearing accounts for those prepared to commit leaving their money in the building society for lengthy periods.

A few months ago an automatic cash dispenser machine was installed outside the branch for ease of use of customers with the Buyerpad dispenser card.

Of course, importantly, Buyerpad prides itself on its prompt service to prospective home buyers who apply for a mortgage. In 1986 Buyerpad was busily making plans to engage in lending for customer goods, as permitted in the Building Societies Act 1986.

The Marketing Department regard it as crucial to offer a wide variety of accounts and borrowing facilities in order to attract a range of clients, and to be able to compete on product range with major competitors like Nationwide and Halifax, as well as the High Street banks.

Place

Buyerpad is pleased with the location of its Sunhampton branch. A prime site was acquired when a restaurant closed. The position is convenient for shoppers and office workers. The branch is of course fitted out with the familiar Buyerpad sign, logo and counter design common to their branches throughout the country.

Price

Prices to a building society are the interest rates it charges and offers. These must be competitive with other societies or banks which provide similar services. The interest rates Buyerpad offer to savers and the rate it charges to borrowers must thus be closely aligned to those of competitors. Otherwise, Buyerpad will find it difficult to attract sufficient funds, or borrowers might seek loans elsewhere.

Promotion

Buyerpad advertises nationally on television and in the major newspapers, since it aims at a national market of all ages and incomes. When the Sunhampton branch was due to open, the manager invited the local press along. As a result local papers then included feature articles on the opening. A crowd of people also attended, no doubt attracted by the presence of a famous television personality who had been hired as part of this sales promotion.

So far in this section we have illustrated the marketing mix by reference to large organisations. It is just as important for small organisations to consider the mix too. Although they will not necessarily have specialised marketing departments, it is still important that the owners or managers pay attention to those basic principles of marketing. They may do so in a less systematic way, but to ignore the significance of marketing imperils the future of any business organisation.

27 Demand and supply

One important element in the marketing mix is price. In this chapter we shall focus directly on the factors that affect the determining of a price for goods or services.

The price you pay for goods and services reflects the interaction of the forces of demand and supply.

Demand is the amount of a commodity that consumers are willing and able to buy at particular prices over a period of time.

Suppy is defined as the amount of a commodity organisations are prepared to put on the market at particular prices over a period of time.

We shall explore the influences on demand and supply before bringing the forces together to demonstrate the determination of price.

Demand

To illustrate consumer behaviour, assume that people would buy the following quantities of bacon each month in the market as a whole. This is expressed in a demand schedule, stating amounts people would be willing and able to buy at different prices.

Table 27.1
Demand schedule for bacon

Price per lb (pence)	Quantity demanded per month (lb)
120	550 000
160	400 000
200	300 000
240	250 000
280	200 000

You will notice that at higher prices people buy less bacon than at low prices. Such behaviour is usual for the vast bulk of goods and services. It is due to two fundamental reasons. As prices rise, they make bigger inroads into people's limited incomes. Hence it is likely that demand will fall as prices rise. This is known as the *income effect*. Furthermore, as a commodity becomes dearer, consumers are likely to turn towards relatively cheaper substitutes, and cut their consumption of the product in question. This is the *price* or *substitution effect*. A fall in price will induce greater demand, so that the income and substitution effects will be working in the opposite direction to that first described.

Although it is generally true that demand falls as price rises, there are rare exceptions. Some people might wish to buy a good *because* it is highly priced and therefore more exclusive, e.g. expensive perfumes or *haute couture* clothes. This is known as the 'snob' effect, in that such people would not buy the commodities if they were lower priced.

Another example occurs when people buy more of a commodity when the price has risen because they anticipate even bigger price rises in the near future. Such actions sometimes happen on the Stock Exchange when speculators buy shares with the intention of selling them later at a still higher price. These speculators are known as 'bulls'. Conversely, some speculators sell shares in anticipation of a price fall in order to buy them back more cheaply; they are known as 'bears'. Consumers have rapidly bought up supplies of sugar and coffee in recent years when there were fears of imminent shortage and rising prices. However, in the vast majority of cases one can state with confidence that at higher prices people buy less than at lower prices.

A demand schedule can be expressed in graphic form as a **demand curve**. The demand schedule for bacon is displayed in this way in Fig. 27.1.

The demand curve slopes downward from left to right. Why? It is because at high prices people buy less than at low prices. As we move down the demand curve, the quantity demanded gets bigger. Such a movement *along* the demand curve is an **extension** of demand. Moving *up* the demand curve is a **contraction** of demand, since the quantity declines.

Fig. 27.1
Demand curve for bacon

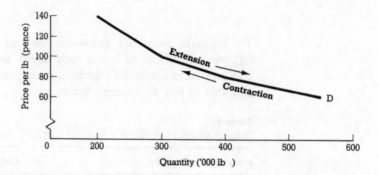

Fig. 27.2
A demand curve

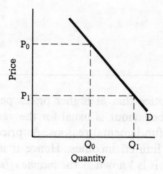

Rather than use specific figures, we can illustrate the concept of demand by using a graph as in Fig. 27.2. The demand curve relates price and quantity. At price P_0, consumers would buy Q_0. At a lower price of Q_1, demand extends to Q_1.

Factors influencing demand

Why should people be willing and able to buy exactly those particular amounts of bacon in the example above? Why not more, or less? Why does a demand curve for a product occupy the specific position it does?

There are a number of factors which explain consumer behaviour concerning goods and services in general. Some of these will be familiar to you from our earlier description of the marketing mix. The factors can be a split into two categories – the price and the conditions of demand. The reasons for this separation will be explained later.

The price

As we have already seen, at lower prices people are likely to buy more than at higher prices.

The conditions of demand

Income

The size of income levels in the population is an important influence on demand. As an economy expands and income levels grow, the demand for many commodities is likely to increase, whilst the demand for others will decrease.

The effect of the rise in real incomes in recent decades showed that quantities consumed of, say, alcoholic drink, clothing and durable consumer goods rose, whereas demand for products like coal and bus travel fell. In the latter cases there was substitution for improved or more convenient commodities.

Conversely, if real incomes were to fall, one would expect demand for many commodities to decrease to varying extents.

As well as changes in income from employment, a consumer's income could be affected by changes in income tax or National Insurance contributions announced in a Budget. The consumer's disposable income (his or her 'take-home pay') would alter. Similarly, the demand of dependent members of the population who receive welfare benefits from the State, e.g. retirement pensioners or the unemployed, would be affected in the light of changes in these benefits.

Population size

As was discussed in Chapter 2, changes in population size, allied with income levels, can cause increases or decreases in demand for goods and services. A significantly larger population would lead to increases in demand for many products, given that income levels would have grown in at least a similar proportion.

Availability of credit facilities

Many people do not spend simply from their current income or savings. There has been much growth in borrowing to supplement funds for expenditure, hence increasing demand. Increased lending has not only emanated from the High Street banks, but also from finance houses (for hire purchase) and the use of credit cards.

Prices of other goods

Changes in the price of substitute or complementary goods could exert an effect on the demand for a product.

Firstly, let us consider substitutes. If two brands, X and Y, of the same product are regarded as close substitutes by consumers, then a rise in the price of X alone will lead to a fall in its demand and an increase in demand for Y. A rise in the price of BP petrol could cause more demand for Texaco, Esso, etc.

Complementary goods are related products, e.g. cars and petrol, fountain pens and ink. One is of no use without the other. Hence a rise in the price of fountain pens would cause a fall in their demand, and consequently a decrease in demand for ink as well. Goods which portray such a relationship are said to be in *joint demand.*

Tastes

Individual likes and dislikes will influence the demand for a product. This reflects the degree of utility or satisfaction derived from consuming the product. There are doubtless some products that you dislike, and you consume little or none of them. Others that you are keen on you will buy in greater quantities.

The amounts demanded of some fundamentally necessary products are likely to be substantial and stable, e.g. milk, salt, bread, etc. There is a basic degree of necessity for many people to consume these products, and the demand is likely to change only little, even if income levels grow.

Fashion can often dictate taste. Why might you buy denim jeans? Changes in demand for colours or styles of clothing or hairstyles are often at the whim of new fashion. It is a moot point whether sellers can create a fashion through advertising, or whether it is that growing demand for a product makes it fashionable.

Whichever is more generally true, there is no doubt that advertising can exert significant influence on consumer tastes. Widespread use of eye-catching and ear-catching advertisements on television, in newspapers and magazines, and on roadside hoardings can reinforce demand.

Advertising can be informative or persuasive, though the distinction is not always clear. Informative advertising should merely present salient features about a good or service, e.g. 'Milk is good for you' as used by the Milk Marketing Board. Persuasive advertising tries to convince the prospective buyer that the product certainly is worth acquiring, e.g. 'Persil washes whiter, and it shows.' The milk advertisement may be more factual and less gimmicky, but there is still the element of hidden persuasion inducing us to buy more milk.

As we shall see later in this part, advertisers must keep within the law. If an advertisement makes a false statement the advertiser can be prosecuted under the Trade Descriptions Acts 1968 and 1973. Some manufacturers have been prosecuted for making false claims about products – for example cosmetics. It is very rare, however, for advertisements to make false statements. Often they make no statements at all but seek to create an impression – for example of glamour – by a photograph and words like 'magic', 'exotic' or 'tingling fresh'. Look at some cosmetic advertisements and draw your own conclusions. J.K. Galbraith in his book *The Affluent Society* claims that advertisers can *create* a demand for their products and 'convince' us that we need to buy their wares, even if basically we do not need them.

What do you think? How far are you influenced by advertising?

Packaging and display

As well as advertising, packaging and display are important. Product research has shown that consumers are more attracted to products with alluring, colourful wrappers rather than plain ones.

There are legal rules about the labelling of contents and weight which must be followed. Recently a cosmetics manufacturer was successfully prosecuted, even though the correct amount of face cream in the package was given, because the container, which had a smaller inner container, gave the impression that you were getting more face cream for your money than was actually the case. There is a great deal of EEC law on labelling and packaging which has become part of our law.

Further, consumers can be induced to buy a product if effective after-sales service is available, or if special offers or trading stamps are given.

Seasonal factors

A final influence on demand for some products is seasonal factors. There are some commodities which we are unlikely to want to buy continually through the year, but only at certain times. For example, the demand for Christmas cards is not going to be great in June, nor the demand for fireworks in April.

In analysing the factors which influence demand we distinguished between 'price' and the 'conditions of demand'. The reason for this distinction should now be made clear.

When a demand schedule is constructed and a demand curve drawn from the data, the conditions of demand are regarded as constant. If any one of them changes, there is likely to be an effect on the quantities demanded. Hence the demand schedule will alter and so will the position of the demand curve. While a particular demand curve and demand schedule hold, the only influence on demand that can vary is the price. Remember, the demand schedule and curve relate quantities that people are willing and able to buy at different prices. If a condition of demand changes, it is likely to lead to a shift in the demand curve. Consumers will now be prepared to buy different quantities at the range of prices.

For example, if income levels rise, the demand for beef will increase (except among vegetarians!). The demand curve will shift to the right from D to D_1, as shown in Fig. 27.3(a). At the original income level people would buy Q_0 of beef at price P_0. However, when income levels rise, demand increases such that consumers are now prepared to buy Q_1 units of beef at the same price.

If, say, the price of a substitute like lamb became much cheaper, then consumers would increase their consumption of lamb, to the disadvantage of sellers of beef. This can be demonstrated in Fig. 27.3(b). Originally consumers buy Q_0 beef at price P_0. Owing to the fall in the price of lamb, a condition of demand has changed. This causes the demand to decrease and the demand curve to shift to the left. Now, only Q_1 will be demanded at price P_0.

Can you think of any other reasons which could cause the shift in the curves illustrated in Fig. 27.3.

To summarise, a change in a condition of demand causes an **increase** or **decrease** in demand, and will bring about a change in data in the demand schedule, and thus in the position of the demand curve (as shown in Fig. 27.3).

A change in the price of the product alone will not shift the demand curve, but merely causes a movement along the demand curve. This is known as an **extension** or **contraction** of demand (as shown in Fig. 27.1).

Supply

Can you remember how supply is defined? Check back to page 258 if not.

Note that the quantity supplied is not necessarily the amount produced, but rather the amount put on the market. Sellers often hold stocks of prod-

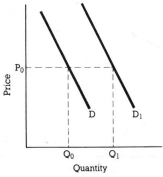

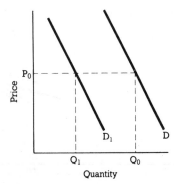

Fig. 27.3
The effect of changes in conditions of demand

(a) Demand increases

(b) Demand decreases

ucts so that all that is produced is not automatically offered for sale straight away.

Just as with the demand schedule, a supply schedule can be constructed to illustrate the likely pattern of supply. Assume that the following data relate to suppliers of bacon.

You will notice that at lower prices, firms would prefer to put less on the market, at higher prices more. The reason for this is twofold. Firstly, higher prices are likely to bring in more revenue and more profit, and therefore may encourage greater quantities to be put on the market. More firms may be encouraged to enter an industry if the rewards are greater. Hence supply will be bigger.

Secondly, to put more on the market could incur rising costs of production. You should recall from Chapter 25 how marginal costs eventually rise as output grows. Correspondingly, if firms incurred higher marginal costs to produce more output and put it on the market, they might need to charge higher prices in order to cover the greater costs.

The supply schedule for bacon can be expressed as a supply curve, illustrating the quantities that would be supplied at various prices (Fig. 27.4). You will notice that the supply curve slopes upwards from the left to the right. The reason is that more will be put on the market at high prices than low prices. As the price falls supply **contracts**. As price rises supply **extends**. Both involve movements along the supply curve.

As with the demand curve, we can generalise on the relationship between quantity and price, avoiding the use of figures from a supply schedule. In general terms, as in Fig. 27.5, a supply curve slopes upwards from left to right. At price P_0, Q_0 is supplied. If the price rises to P_1, supply extends to Q_1.

Table 27.2
Supply schedule for bacon

Price per lb (pence)	Quantity supplied per month (lb)
120	—
160	150 000
200	250 000
240	300 000
280	350 000

Factors influencing supply

What are the factors which influence precisely how much of a good or service an organisation will put on the market at particular prices? We shall distinguish between the role played by price as opposed to other factors collectively called the conditions of supply.

Price

As already explained, at high prices firms put more on the market than at low prices.

Fig. 27.4
Supply curve for bacon

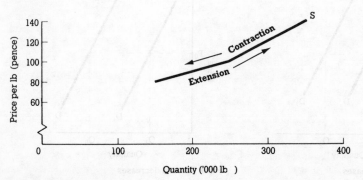

Fig. 27.5
A supply curve

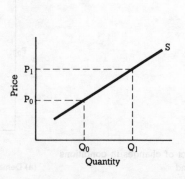

Conditions of supply

Costs of production

The costs of factors of production exert an important influence on the quantity supplied at particular prices. Rises in wage costs or costs of raw materials, for example, are likely to mean that a firm will only continue to supply a certain amount if it can now do so at a higher price. Lower costs of production or improved productivity (higher output per worker) would have the opposite effect. Firms would be prepared to sell more at lower prices.

Availability of factors of production

As well as their costs, the very availability of factors of production affects supply. A lengthy strike, for example, can restrict output and thus put pressure on the supply of commodities. Some firms have still found it difficult to recruit labour in spite of high unemployment, e.g. London Regional Transport, whose ability to provide full services on all bus routes has consequently been impeded.

Restrictions on supply of a raw material, as with oil in the mid-1970s, could also lead to cutbacks in production and ultimately reductions in the amount supplied.

Often, shortages of a factor of production lead to higher costs of production, since firms need to pay more for the tighter supply.

Technological change

The introduction of new machinery can lead to more efficient, cheaper, methods of production. Once again, greater quantities can be made available on the market at prevailing prices. Micro-chip technology, for example, will mean lower administrative costs through cheaper and more adaptable computers.

Objectives of organisations

The goal an organisation seeks to achieve can strongly influence its supply strategy. The quantity supplied over a range of prices is likely to vary depending on whether the organisation is a profit maximiser, is intent on increasing sales revenue or is a public sector organisation in which covering costs rather than maximising profit is a prime concern. More is likely to be supplied at the going price in the sales revenue maximising and public sector cases than in the profit maximising firm. The sales revenue maximiser or public corporation will not make so much profit but they are likely to offer a bigger supply. For the sales revenue maximiser growth of sales and control of the market is the prime target. Firms sometimes pitch their prices as a percentage mark-up over costs. The size of this mark-up will influence profitability, and may well vary according to the objectives of firms.

Price changes by competitors

Such a move could provoke a similar response from an organisation. If one firm lowers its price others may follow suit, so that there is a change in the pattern of supply. Such price-cutting competition has occurred in the market for holidays in recent years as tour companies light on bookings tried to increase sales. Both price cutting and price rises have occurred in the market for petrol, reflecting excess supply in relation to demand or movements in exchange rates. It has often been the pattern that as one major petrol company has adjusted its prices, so others quickly follow suit.

Government activity in a market

If the government imposes taxes on a product or grants subsidies to suppliers, this will affect the amount firms will be prepared to supply at particular prices. If a higher tax is imposed, a firm would hope to pass the tax burden on to the consumer by offering goods for sale at a higher price. This often occurs in a Budget when Excise Duty is increased on items like cigarettes, alcoholic drink and petrol.

Conversely, if the government grants a subsidy to an organisation, as has occurred in agriculture for example, the opposite effect transpires. Goods can then be supplied at lower prices. Such subsidies to farmers were common in the UK prior to our joining the EEC and participating in its Common Agricultural Policy.

Weather

Natural factors can affect supply, as explained in Chapter 2. Good or bad weather can particularly affect agriculture. A bumper crop will increase supply whereas bad weather will cause the reverse. Similarly, bad weather can disrupt the transportation of goods and hence restrict supply.

Seasonal factors

Many crops grow only at certain times of the year, not all year round. Hence their supply is governed by seasonal climatic factors, e.g. fresh strawberries will be supplied in summer, not winter, and the supplies of products like ice cream will be greater in the summer months.

As when analysing factors influencing demand, the same distinction between price and conditions is made when focusing on supply determinants.

While conditions of supply remain constant, a particular supply curve is a valid indicator of the pattern of supply. The only influence that can vary is the price of the product. As the price changes, there will be a contraction or extension of supply and a movement along the supply curve. However, if a condition of supply changes, then data in the supply schedule will alter and so will the position of the resultant supply curve.

For example, in Fig. 27.6(a), if costs of production for the product rise, the supply will decrease from Q_0 to Q_1 at price P_0. Alternatively if firms were to continue supplying quantity Q_0, they would charge a price of P_1 so covering the extra cost burden.

In Fig. 27.6(b), if the government were to grant a subsidy to the industry, this could enable firms to increase supply. This could mean that at the original price P_0, supply could increase from Q_0 to Q_1. Another

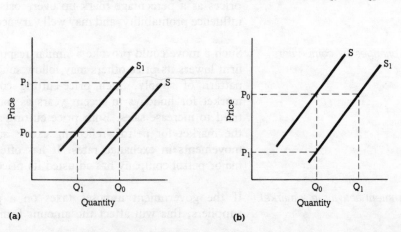

Fig. 27.6
The effect of changes in conditions of supply

interpretation could be that the firm could offer Q_0 for sale but at the lower price of P_1.

To summarise this section on supply, conditions of supply are constant while a particular supply curve holds. As price changes, there will be an **extension** or **contraction** of supply – a movement along the curve.

If a condition of supply changes, this causes a shift of the supply curve. Such a movement is called an **increase** or **decrease** of supply, depending on the direction of the change.

Determining a price

Price is determined by the interaction of demand and supply. Where there is compatibility between the intentions of consumers and suppliers, a price will be determined at which there will be neither surplus nor shortage.

The demand and supply curves for bacon from Figs. 27.1 and 27.4 are restated in Fig. 27.7 on the same diagram. We can see that the curves cross at a point corresponding to a price of 220p and quantity 275 000 lb. At this point demand and supply are equal. An **equilibrium price** has been determined, a price where demand equals supply.

At any price above 220p, the supply is greater than demand, so there is excess supply. For example, at 240p supply is 300 000 lb whereas demand is 250 000 lb: there is excess supply of 50 000 lb, meaning that at the end of the month suppliers would have 50 000 lb of bacon left unsold. Suppliers should reduce their price and contract supply.

At a price below 220p, demand exceeds supply – a situation of excess demand. When the price is 160p for instance, demand is 400 000 lb, whilst supply is only 150 000 lb. Bacon would be sold out well before the end of the month. Suppliers should raise the price and extend supply.

In order to pitch their price, organisations are likely to consider the average cost of making and selling a product or service, and add on an amount ('mark-up') reflecting the level of profit or surplus they feel they could make in relation to market conditions. This technique is known as 'cost plus' pricing. Having set this price, the organisation must await customer reaction. If the goods sell out more quickly than expected, or there is a rush for the services, then the firm would be likely to raise its price to increase profit.

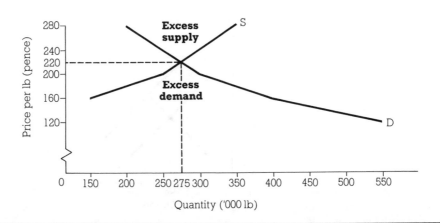

Fig. 27.7
Determination of price

Conversely, if there was excess supply, the organisation would evidently have set too high a mark-up and would have to lower the price to expand sales.

The effects of changes in demand or supply

An equilibrium price can be disturbed by a change in a condition of demand and/or a condition of supply. Some examples can illustrate the effects.

Originally in Fig. 27.8, P_0 and Q_0 are the equilibrium price and quantity. If the firm launches a successful advertising campaign, there will be an increase in demand since consumer taste has changed. This will cause the demand curve to shift to the right from D to D_1. People are now willing and able to buy more of the commodity. As a result, there will be excess demand at the old price. The firm will extend supply and raise the price so that the new equilibrium price will be P_1 and quantity Q_1. Within that industry there will be a need for additional production, or at the very least the releasing of stocks of the product for rapid sale.

Figure 27.9 illustrates the effect of the large rise in oil prices in the mid-1970s on the market for petrol. Countries which were members of the Organisation of Petroleum Exporting Countries (OPEC) agreed to raise the price of crude oil and restrict supply to the oil companies like BP, Texaco, etc. OPEC is a **cartel**, a group of suppliers acting together rather than competing on price or quantities sold. A major intention was to pressurise the Western oil importing countries into supporting the Arab rather than Israeli cause in the Middle East conflict. They also recognised that by adopting this policy they would increase their revenues and lengthen the period of years over which they could sell their oil, a non-renewable fossil fuel.

The effect on the market for petrol was to shift the supply curve to the left, a decrease in supply. If we simplify to suggest there is just one price for petrol (as opposed to different prices for 2, 3 or 4 star petrol), then the original price P_0 will be displaced. Suppliers face higher costs of crude oil and a restricted availability – conditions of supply have changed. The supply curve hence shifted from S to S_1. Petrol is a vital commodity for an industrialised society, so that demand is unlikely to contract very much. The new equilibrium price is P_1, with a small change in quantity bought and sold, which has dropped from Q_0 to Q_1.

Fig. 27.8
The effect of a shift in the demand curve

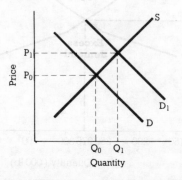

Fig. 27.9
The effect of a shift in the supply curve

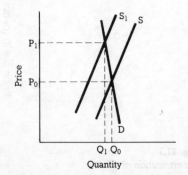

Fig. 27.10
The effects of shifts in the demand and supply curves

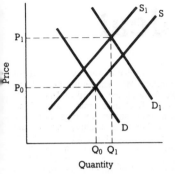

Note that there is no cause for the demand curve to shift – there has been no change in any condition of demand. What has happened is that the supply curve has moved up the demand curve. Supply has decreased and demand has contracted.

A third example relates to the market for wine. Originally, the price of wine was P_0 and quantity Q_0, as shown in Fig. 27.10. Over the years, people's income levels have grown, but also successive governments have raised the tax on wine.

The growth in income means a change in a conditon of demand, causing an increase in demand and a shift in the demand curve to the right.

The increase in tax on wine affects a condition of supply, so moving the supply curve to the left. Firms wish to recover as much of the tax as possible by passing it on to the consumer in the form of higher prices.

Thus there are two forces, increasing demand and decreasing supply, pushing the price up. However, some of the additional demand for wine due to the growth in income will be reined back by the higher tax. The new equilibrium price is P_1, with a larger quantity Q_1 bought and sold.

Try to analyse changes in other market conditions by the use of demand and supply analysis. If you work for an organisation selling priced goods or services, consider recent changes in price or quantity sold. Why have the changes occurred? Try to apply demand and supply techniques to the situation.

28 Merger Mania

There was a spate of very large takeovers and mergers in 1985/6 particularly in the retail field, to exploit superstore potential on the fringes of towns and cities or to develop larger, more varied High Street stores.

In 1985 in April Asda and MFI merged (see Fig. 28.1); in August the Burtons Group won control of Debenhams; November saw the merger of Habitat Mothercare with British Home Stores.

You might monitor what changes occur in the operations of these well-known names. Visit such stores and check what differences occur in layout, display and product range as a consequence of the integration.

In 1987 Asda announced plans to sell off MFI. Investigate why the merger had not worked out.

Away from the stores sector, in December 1985 there was the largest takeover yet recorded in the UK when Argyll Holdings bid £1.87bn to gain a controlling interest in Distillers, the alcoholic drinks manufacturer. Argyll believed they could increase the profitability of Distillers whose whisky brands had been losing market share to rivals.

The record takeover was surpassed in 1986 when the conglomerate Hanson Trust bid £2.5bn to acquire the Imperial Group.

Read press articles on further takeovers and mergers as they occur. Why do they take place? Does the general public benefit from such integration?

Fig. 28.1
Source: *The Guardian* 16 April 1985

Asda and MFI chains merge in £2bn deal

By Andrew Cornelius

Associated Dairies, the Asda and Allied Carpets stores group, is taking over MFI Furniture group in a £2 billion deal creating the fourth largest retail group behind Marks and Spencer, J Sainsbury and Great Universal Stores.

After three months' discussions the companies agreed terms late last week.

Asda and its advisers have bought a 17.5 per cent share take in MFI and yesterday announced details of a near £600 million takeover.

Mr Noel Stockdale, Asda's chairman, will become chairman of the new group. Mr Derek Hunt, MFI's chairman will become joint managing director.

"This is a unique opportunity," said Mr Stockdale, a deal taking both companies into the 1990s, and creating an "enormous platform for growth."

Asda, Allied and MFI will continue to trade under their existing names, and shoppers and staff will not immediately notice any difference.

Asda is offering 15 of its own shares for every eight of MFI, valuing MFI at 311p per share. There is a cash alternative worth 270p per share to MFI shareholders.

The offer terms were warmly received on the stock market. MFI shares jumped 52p to 305p, while Asda closed up 6p at 164p.

The Stock Exchange may launch an investigation into share dealings late last Friday when there was a sharp rise in the MFI price, in advance of any announcement.

The new group will have a dominant position in the grocery, carpet and furniture trades. Asda has 100 superstores and plans to open another six within a year.

Its empire includes Allied Carpets, which has 67 stores with 9 per cent of the UK carpet market. MFI is the biggest UK furniture retailer with 11 per cent of the market.

The new group would have annual sales of more than £2 billion and pretax profits of £144 million.

Mr Hunt said: "There is a lot of similarity in the development of the businesses over the past 10 years. Both are out-of-town retailers and both have ambitious young management."

The merger will immediately help the companies to combine their resources to find new out-of-town shopping sites.

MFI will also benefit Allied's buying power in the carpet business.

Monopolies and mergers

One aspect of interference with the market mechanism is statutory intervention to prevent unfair trading practices. As you may recall from Chapter 13 one example of this kind of intervention is the Monopolies and Mergers Commission which exists to investigate monopolies or possible monopolies referred to it by the Director General of Fair Trading and mergers referred to it by the Secretary of State for Trade and Industry on the advice of the Director General of Fair Trading. The Commission has to decide whether such monopolies or mergers are against the public interest by, for example, restricting consumer choice or preventing fair competition.

An example of a monopoly investigated by the Commission was the purchase of part of European Ferries by P and O. The Commission's report said that the merger would not operate against the public interest as there would still be freedom of entry into the markets.

As we have seen monopoly situations produce no-choice situations which put the consumer at a disadvantage. This is one of the criticisms levelled against nationalised industries. Contractual terms – the price and the nature of the service – are dictated to the consumer who cannot protest by taking custom elsewhere because there are no rival companies or corporations. The consumer is in a very unequal bargaining position as against a large public corporation or a conglomerate of companies. Mergers creating possible monopoly situations have been very much the trend in the 1980s.

Fig. 28.2
Asda Superstore in High Wycombe

Another example of the way in which legislation intervenes to prevent unfair trading practices is the Resale Prices Act 1976 which makes illegal the enforcement of minimum selling prices by manufacturers or distributors of goods unless this is held to be in the public interest by the Restrictive Trade Practices Court. At the time of writing only producers of books and medicines have the Court's permission to operate this kind of agreement.

There is a problem with making resale price maintenance generally unlawful. On the one hand it allows free competition, but on the other small businesses may be forced out of business by large multiple retailers and thus the consumer will have less choice. We then have, in effect, another kind of monopoly situation.

EEC Rules on Competition

Article 85 of the Treaty of Rome prohibits all agreements between business organisations which may have the effect of restricting competition within the Common Market. Article 86 provides that the abuse of a dominant position in the market structure is not compatible with the Treaty of Rome. Practices infringing these Articles may be referred to the European Commission by the Director General of Fair Trading. Cases of alleged infringement can be decided by domestic courts as well as by the Commission and the European Court of Justice.

In a recent case, Lucas Asjes and Others (1986), the European Court of Justice took a major step in clarifying the application of the competition provisions of the Treaty of Rome to air transport. The airline industry has often maintained high prices on certain routes by agreements to peg prices or restrict flights. The Court has now said unequivocally that Articles 85 and 86 do apply to air transport and the Commission has now written to a number of European airlines requesting that they change their practices in the light of evidence of abuses of competition provisions, e.g. fixing our fares.

29 Influencing and meeting customer needs

Setting a price

We saw in Chapter 27 that the price of a good or service is affected by demand and supply factors. The equilibrium price lies where demand and supply are equal.

An organisation might then have to adjust its price if it has not anticipated consumer response accurately. But how does a seller go about setting a price?

Fundamentally a calculation of the cost of producing a range of output is made. Depending on the principles employed this cost figure may or may not include an allocation for overheads. The cost is apportioned per unit of output on an average or marginal cost basis (see Chapter 25). Students who study marketing may come to know these methods as full, direct and marginal costing.

Having established a cost base, a mark-up is added to allow for the profit element and possibly overheads if they have not already been included.

A crucial decision is how large this mark-up should be. This is where a close understanding of the market, the degree of competition and anticipation of consumer behaviour is important. What price does the organisation reckon consumers would be prepared to pay?

A more detailed study of marketing would reveal a number of approaches to this problem. Prominent influences could be:

Pricing at the going rate This means setting your prices comparable with the going rate for the industry. This would be especially important in a highly competitive industry. It is true for example of the market for petrol. If, say, Shell continuously charged higher prices then Esso or Texaco they would surely lose sales and market share.

Penetration pricing The logic of this approach is initially to price below competitive levels in order to penetrate a market, increase market share and in so doing benefit from economies of scale, leading to reduced average costs and higher profitability. This is a principle employed successfully by many manufacturers with spare capacity to increase output significantly and speedily as demand picks up.

Market skimming

A high price would be charged for a new product which would attract at first a relatively small market of 'price-insensitive' consumers, probably of relatively high incomes.

Over time, a wider span of consumers begin to view the product more favourably so that lower prices might later be charged as a consequence of economies of scale and as a means of attracting more 'price-sensitive' customers. This has been the pattern in markets like calculators, video recorders and home computers.

Clearly the influences on pricing will vary according to the type of product and the nature of the market.

Consider the organisation in which you may work or consider products you buy. Do you think they are priced appropriately from the standpoint of the seller? What would be the effects if prices were raised or lowered?

The wisdom of changing a price is discussed in the next section by describing and analysing a concept known as elasticity of demand.

Price elasticity of demand

We have established the usual relationship that as the price rises people buy less of a good. But how much less? As the price falls demand will extend. But by how much?

Organisations must consider the likely reaction of demand if they alter the prices they charge for their products. If the price were raised but demand fell to a large extent, then a bad policy decision would have been made.

The responsiveness of demand to changes in price is known as the **price elasticity of demand**. The concept measures the extent that demand 'stretches' as a result of a price change.

A numerical measure of price elasticity can be obtained by this formula:

$$\text{Elasticity of demand} = \frac{\text{\% change in demand}}{\text{\% change in price}}$$

Some examples can explain its use. In this extract from a demand schedule, the price rises from 10p to 12p:

Price	Demand for A per week
10p	500
12p	480

$$\% \text{ change in demand} = \frac{20}{500} \times 100 = 4\%$$

$$\text{\% change in price} = \frac{2}{10} \times 100 = 20\%$$

$$\text{Elasticity of demand} = \frac{4\%}{20\%} = \frac{1}{5} = 0.2$$

Here the demand has evidently fallen by a smaller percentage than the price has risen. In fact, the proportionate change in demand has been only one-fifth of the proportionate change in price.

Where elasticity of demand has a value less than 1, demand is **inelastic**. The percentage change in demand is smaller than the percentage change in price.

Consider also the following example, where the price rises from £1 to £1.10.

Price	Demand for B per week
£1.00	1000
£1.10	700

$$\text{\% change in demand} = \frac{300}{1000} \times 100 = 30\%$$

$$\text{\% change in price} = \frac{10}{100} \times 100 = 10\%$$

$$\text{Elasticity of demand} = \frac{30\%}{10\%} = 3$$

Here the demand has fallen 3 times the proportionate rise in price.

Where elasticity of demand has a value greater than 1, demand is **elastic**, meaning that the percentage change in demand is greater than the percentage change in price.

By reference to demand curves, some judgement can be made about their respective elasticities.

Assuming that the curves are measured with the same numerical values on the axes in Fig. 29.1, the same price change from P_0 to P_1 in each case provokes a markedly different response of demand.

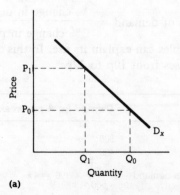
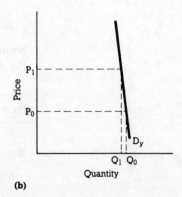

Fig. 29.1
Demand curves and their elasticity   (a)   (b)

Which demand curve do you think is the more elastic and which the more inelastic? Why?

The demand in Fig. 29.1(a) contracts by a far greater extent than in Fig. 29.1(b) for the same price change. This must suggest D_x is the more elastic and D_y the more inelastic demand curve.

We have established that if the elasticity of demand value is less than 1, demand is inelastic. If demand did not change at all when the price changed, demand would be **perfectly inelastic**. This could happen, for example, if the price of a very necessary item like bread or milk rose (or even fell) by a small amount. People might well continue to buy exactly the same amount of the commodity as before.

The numerical value of perfect elasticity of demand would be zero. To demonstrate, if the price of a good rose by 5 per cent but the demand was unchanged then:

$$\text{Elasticity of demand} = \frac{0\%}{5\%} = 0$$

A demand curve, or at least a section of a demand curve, over which demand is perfectly inelastic would be vertical as shown in Fig. 29.2.

At the other extreme demand is **perfectly elastic**, the numerical value of which would be infinity. In this case the minutest price change would provoke an infinitely large change in demand. It would imply that consumers would buy at one price but would not buy at any other. The demand curve would be as in Fig. 29.3. This is an unusual situation in reality.

Unit elasticity, where elasticity of demand equals 1, would occur where the percentage change in demand exactly matched the percentage change in price. For example, if a 10 per cent fall in price leads to a 10 per cent extension of demand, then the value of price elasticity of demand = 1.

Diagrammatically, a demand curve portraying this feature over its whole length would look as shown in Fig. 29.4. For the mathematically minded, this curve is a rectangular hyperbola. (Non-mathematicians, do not worry about the term: it does not affect your understanding of the concept.)

Remember that a demand curve need not be continuously elastic or

Fig. 29.2
Perfectly inelastic demand

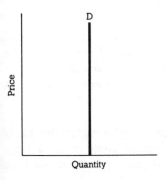

Fig. 29.3
Perfectly elastic demand

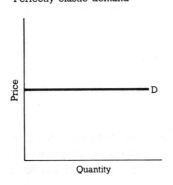

Fig. 29.4
Demand curve with unit elasticity

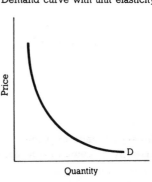

continuously inelastic over its whole length. The degree of elasticity could vary at different points on the curve, reflecting the responsiveness of demand to price changes at those various points.

Factors influencing elasticity of demand

Why may the demand for some goods be more inelastic than for others?

The following factors will explain.

Necessity

Some commodities are fundamental to our lives, and demand is unlikely to alter much even if the price rises. Basic commodities such as bread, milk and petrol fall into this category. Their demand is likely to be highly inelastic. They are fundamental products with few alternatives.

Habit

For some people certain products like cigarettes, alcoholic drink or other drugs are habit forming. A price change is unlikely to induce much variation in consumption. Demand is likely to be highly inelastic.

Level of income

The higher the income level of consumers, the more inelastic their demand for commodities in general is likely to be. Price rises make less of a dent into high incomes and hence demand need change less. For low-income families, every penny of a limited income counts. Such consumers are more likely to be price sensitive and to rearrange their pattern of demand in response to price changes.

The proportion of income spent on the product

The demand for low-priced goods is likely to be more inelastic than the demand for high-priced commodities. The former make less of an inroad into limited incomes. If, for example, the price of a box of matches rose by 50 per cent, the change in demand would be small. However, if the price of beef rose 50 per cent, the change in demand would be far more significant.

Substitutes

The degree of substitution is an important influence on elasticity of demand. If there are close substitutes for a product, a change in its price would lead to significant extensions of demand. However, for a product with no immediate substitutes one will find little change in demand in the event of a price movement. For example, if there is much interchange of demand between substitute brands of a product, their demand will be highly elastic. Note that although the demand for bread, a basic foodstuff, is highly inelastic, the demand for different brands of bread will be far more elastic as consumers switch between them when prices change.

The size of the price change

A very small price change will not provoke such elastic demand as would a large change in price. If the price of petrol changes by 1p per gallon, the impact on demand will be minor. A price change of £1 per gallon, a much larger percentage change, will cause a far greater proportionate response in demand.

The significance of price elasticity of demand – to firms

When firms contemplate changing their prices, they consider the likely response of demand. If price is raised and demand contracts to a large extent, a poor policy decision has been made. If price is lowered but little

To raise or lower price?

extra custom is gained, once again an inappropriate policy will have been adopted.

The revenue that organisations receive is an important indicator of the impact of price changes. Their revenue is what consumers spend: the price of a commodity × the quantity bought. Price elasticity is significant here. For example, if a firm raises its price from £1 to £1.10 per article sold, consider the possible reactions of demand in each situation A and B below:

Price	Quantity demanded A	Quantity demanded B	Revenue A	Revenue B
£1.00	10 000	10 000	£10 000	£10 000
£1.10	8 000	9 500	£8 800	£10 450

You should be able to ascertain that demand in case A was elastic (a 20 per cent contraction in demand due to a 10 per cent price rise), whereas demand was inelastic in case B (a 5 per cent contraction in demand due to a 10 per cent price rise).

In situation A, the revenue received by the organisation fell from £10 000 to £8800. To consider the effect on the firm's profitability one would need to know about costs of production and distribution. They would also be lower since the firm is now selling 2000 units less than originally.

Nevertheless, situation B is certainly healthier from the firm's point of view (though not necessarily from the consumers'!). The price increase has led to greater revenue. Remembering also that costs of producing and selling are lower (sales down from 10 000 to 9500), then inevitably profitability will have improved.

In general, then, if price is raised and demand is elastic, the total revenue of the firm will fall. If price rises and demand is inelastic, then total revenue will increase.

Can you reason out the impact on total revenue if price is lowered and demand is (a) elastic or (b) inelastic?

There has been debate in recent years about the pricing policy of British Rail as a means of reducing losses. The approach that British Rail has taken is to raise fares when costs increases have been faced. Their belief is that demand for rail travel in general is inelastic, so that demand will fall only slightly in the event of fare increases.

Pressure groups representing some commuter passengers into Central London have argued that British Rail will reduce loss if it *lowers* its fares. They claim this might attract more people to travel on the railways and would help to reverse the trend of people moving out of Greater London by reducing the cost of their journey to work. Hence these pressure groups are in effect assuming that demand for rail travel must be elastic if their policy is to improve the finances of British Rail.

Have British Rail or the commuter groups analysed the market more correctly? What do you think? Which factors influencing elasticity are especially important in this case?

Price discrimination

You are doubtless aware that some organisations, especially those which have full or near monopoly control in their industry, offer varied prices for their product. British Rail, for example, offers cheaper fares for off-peak as opposed to rush-hour travel. It is cheaper to telephone between 6 p.m. and 8 a.m. than during normal working hours. This is known as **price discrimination**, charging different prices to different sections of a market for the same good or service.

Why do you think this is done?

One important reason is that the rush-hour travellers or peak-time telephone users place greater demands on the respective systems. The large volume of railway rolling stock and the huge telephone network are fundamentally necessary to cater for peak usage. Therefore rail fares and telephone call charges must reflect the costs of these systems.

But why not charge the same prices to off-peak users as well? Elasticity of demand is an important consideration. By offering cheaper off-peak prices there is more likelihood of enticing the casual travellers or phone users. Their demand will be more elastic than that of the rail commuter or the businessperson for whom the phone is indispensable during office hours. Demand in the latter cases will be far more inelastic. Additionally, by offering lower off-peak prices, there is the bait for less urgent telephone calls or rail journeys to be made at times other than when the networks are already heavily burdened.

Hence, price discrimination can be effective where the elasticities of demand differ between categories of consumer, and where the commodity cannot be resold at the dearer rate. With a service there is no chance of resale, but a physical good might possibly be resold at the higher price.

Pricing strategy

Think back to the beginning of this chapter where we described penetration pricing and market skimming.

For these approaches to work, do they require elastic or inelastic demand? Think about this before you read on.

You may recall that penetration pricing involves pricing below competitors' levels in order to make inroads into the market. The success of this technique depends on demand being elastic, so that there is a more than proportional growth in sales given the cheaper price.

However, the market skimming method at first involves a relatively high price for a new product. This relies on a solid level of demand to establish the product. Thus the demand should be inelastic.

The significance of price elasticity of demand – to the government

Those of you who smoke, enjoy alcoholic drink or drive are probably aware that a large part of the price you pay for these pleasures is a tax imposed by the government. For example, in 1984 54 per cent of the price of a gallon of petrol was the tax element.

The reason is not that the government wishes to be particularly vindictive to smokers, drinkers or drivers. Rather, it is that the demand for commodities like cigarettes, tobacco, beer, wine, spirits and petrol is highly inelastic.

The taxes on these commodities are very good revenue raisers for the government.

Because these commodities are habit forming or virtual necessities and are relatively cheap and accessible, their demand is very inelastic. Thus when in a Budget taxes are increased on these products and firms pass the tax on to the consumer through higher prices, the fall in demand is relatively small. The government is therefore sure of getting revenue. There is generally little impact on quantities demanded, so that in most cases companies selling the products do not suffer much fall in sales revenue.

The participants in a market

We have described a market as the interaction of buyers and sellers. However, there are a number of ways in which goods and services are made available to the customer. The traditional means of distributing consumer goods to customers involves the chain shown in Fig. 29.5. In some markets, however, the wholesaler is by-passed. In others, the manufacturer sells direct to the customer. Recent trends in selling include mail order and hypermarkets, both of which will be discussed later. Customers, logically, are going to buy from retailers in their area who provide the range of products they desire.

Fig. 29.5
The traditional distribution network

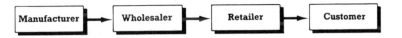

One effect of this kind of traditional distribution network is that the customer has no contact with the manufacturer and thus will not be able to sue the manufacturer for breach of contract. Any action taken against the manufacturer for damage caused by defective goods will either be a tort action, probably for negligence, or under the new consumer protection legislation referred to in Chapter 31. The EEC Directive on Liability for Defective Goods was adopted in July 1985 and new legislation will impose strict liability on manufacturers. In the absence of 'privity' of contract between the manufacturer and the retailer (i.e. they are not linked by a contract), the manufacturer cannot impose obligations on the retailer, e.g. as to the price at which goods should be sold. In any event under the Resale Prices Act 1976 this is unlawful. This Act was passed for economic reasons to stop price fixing, which interfered with free competition. The retailer has a price 'recommended' by the manufacturer but is not bound by that price. There are some exceptional cases where price fixing is allowed by law, e.g. the sale of books. The Resale Prices Act had profound economic consequences because it allowed supermarkets to undercut small grocery shops, thus putting many out of business.

The wholesaler

Let us consider the role of the wholesaler and discuss the advantages and disadvantages of having this link in the distribution chain.

Wholesalers act as intermediaries in a number of markets. They buy from manufacturers and then sell to retailers who, in turn, deal with consumers.

The advantages listed below relate to wholesalers in general. By no means all wholesalers perform every function discussed.

Advantages

1 From the manufacturer's point of view, wholesalers allow certain economies of scale to be achieved. Wholesalers buy in bulk from manufacturers. Thus manufacturers can:

a Save on administration costs, with fewer orders to process than if many small retailers were their customers.

b Operate bigger production runs than is possible for many small, less co-ordinated orders.

c Employ a smaller sales force than if a large number of retailers had to be approached.

d Cut delivery costs by transporting in bulk to relatively few destinations.

e Keep smaller levels of stock. The wholesaler can store large quantities of the product, especially if demand is seasonal.

2 From the angle of the retail organisation:

a It need deal with one or perhaps a few wholesalers as opposed to a larger number of manufacturers. This saves on time and administration costs.

b It can obtain supplies in small batches if necessary, a boon to small retailers with little storage space.

c It can obtain advice and information from some wholesalers on new products and retail display.

d It can receive trade credit from wholesalers, a valuable form of short term finance.

3 Some specialist wholesalers perform certain functions beyond the ability of small manufacturers, like blending (e.g. tea) or packaging.

4 Fruit and vegetable wholesalers perform an important role in speeding up the distribution of these perishable products in an industry in which small suppliers and small retailers proliferate.

Disadvantages

There is one fundamental disadvantage in the presence of the wholesaler. The wholesaler's profit margin can well increase prices beyond those that might apply if the retailer dealt directly with the manufacturer.

How valid is this criticism? Surely for the many small firms, the operation of the wholesaler helps to keep prices down. Consider the cost savings listed under advantages of the wholesaler.

However, for large retailers the disadvantage is more apparent. There has been a trend in recent years for a number of large multiple stores (those with 10 or more branches) and supermarkets to by-pass the wholesaler and buy direct from the manufacturer. Supermarkets like Tesco, Fine Fare, Waitrose, Sainsbury, and other multiple stores like Boots, W.H. Smith, Currys and Dixons have negotiated discounts from manufacturers and passed them on to the consumer. This development has accentuated the decline in importance of the small shop and the greater market share of the large retailer.

Compare prices in a supermarket with those in a small independent grocer. The effect of direct buying from manufacturers as opposed to the need to use a wholesaler is apparent in price differentials on many products. Some large retailers market goods under their own brand name, again the result of deals for bulk orders with established manufacturers.

Furthermore, major supermarket chains, for instance, have their own large delivery vans. Retailing over 10 000 products, supermarkets often need daily rather than weekly deliveries, especially where they sell fresh foodstuffs. By avoiding the wholesaler, the supermarkets can organise their own deliveries for easier integration into their distribution systems.

The big supermarkets and large multiple stores like Marks and Spencer have area support or consolidation depots. In these warehouses, they store items from manufacturers so as to provide deliveries in their own vans of ranges of products to local branches. Such deliveries can even be made several times a day if necessary.

Thus, for the many small retailers, supplying a shrinking share of the market, the wholesaler still plays an important role. However, for the growing large supermarkets and multiple stores, the functions of the wholesaler have been virtually eliminated.

Wholesalers are also less apparent in industries where goods are bulky and expensive, and turnover is not rapid. For example, car showrooms buy direct from manufacturers. Figure 29.6 shows the more varied patterns of distribution evident in recent years.

Supermarkets

As well as the features already noted about supermarkets, some other changes in the operations of these self-service retailers have occurred in recent times.

In order to increase profitability in a highly competitive industry, some supermarkets have extended their range of products beyond the original pre-packed and canned food and household goods. Larger supermarkets offer fresh foodstuffs. e.g. cooked meats, cheese and vegetables, and have a butcher's counter. Some supermarkets have expanded into selling clothes

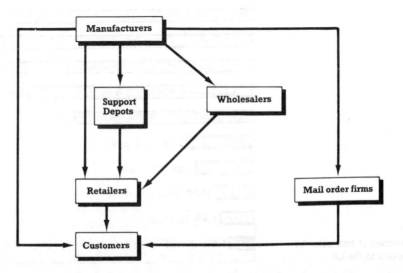

Fig. 29.6
The main channels of distribution

and durable household goods like crockery and even furniture. These products have bigger profit margins than foodstuffs.

A newer trend has been the growth of superstores, larger-scale supermarkets with a selling area of at least 25 000 square feet and attached car parking facilities. Firms like Tesco and Asda see the key to a greater market share in these larger stores.

Figure 29.7 illustrates the market share of Britain's major supermarket chains consequent upon the takeover of Safeway by the Argyll Group, which owns Presto supermarkets.

Hypermarkets

Hypermarkets are still larger in size than superstores and supermarkets, normally covering over 50 000 square feet, and offer a wider range of products. The originator of the Hypermarket was Carrefour in France. They are not to be found in expensive High Street locations, but are generally sited on the fringe of towns, where leases are cheaper. Sites can be purpose built, aiding warehousing and delivery facilities and offering large car parks for customers. Their growing importance reflects greater mobility of the population. As more families own cars, shopping in hypermarkets on the cash-and-carry principle becomes feasible. This extended mobility also enables the hypermarket to cover a larger catchment area of customers.

As a consequence of the growth in ownership of freezers, a freezer centre is another likely feature. Frozen foods can be bought in bulk relatively cheaply and stored at home until needed.

Hypermarkets generally operate a scrambled merchandising policy, i.e. they sell a wide variety of goods but with a limited assortment of brands. They get discounts from suppliers for stocking their brands. Many hypermarket precincts nowadays offer a very wide range of services as well as

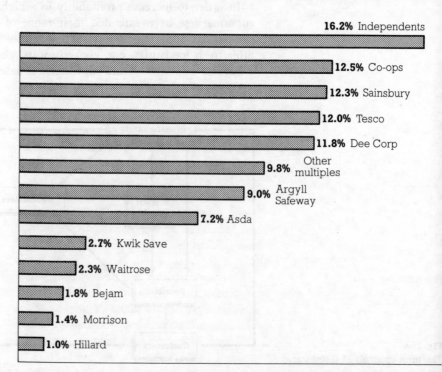

16.2% Independents
12.5% Co-ops
12.3% Sainsbury
12.0% Tesco
11.8% Dee Corp
9.8% Other multiples
9.0% Argyll Safeway
7.2% Asda
2.7% Kwik Save
2.3% Waitrose
1.8% Bejam
1.4% Morrison
1.0% Hillard

Fig. 29.7
The proportion of total sales by supermarkets in the UK

goods, including opticians, car repair and servicing, garden centres, DIY. Some hypermarkets also cater for families without cars by operating a private bus service.

Direct selling

This is a more traditional form of distribution, though it is not widespread. Examples include milk deliveries from dairies to your door, or the purchase of large machines by firms. In both cases, the potential size of the market is limited. In the former instance, it is essentially localised. In the latter, there are unlikely to be many purchasers of specialised machinery. The need for intermediaries is reduced.

Mail order

Of American origin, mail order business has grown in recent years and by the mid-1980s contributed approximately 5 per cent of total sales in the UK. It involves the ordering and sending of goods through the postal system. Some firms, e.g. Littlewood's, publish catalogues and operate through agents who take orders and collect payments. Credit facilities are available so that payment may be staggered over a period of time.

Smaller firms advertise their wares in newspapers and magazines, and so contact is more direct between buyer and seller. The choice of newspaper or magazine is deliberate, reflecting the income levels of the readership, so as to reach potential buyers. Specialised magazines are selected if the product is of particular and not of general interest.

With both large and small mail order firms, costs are saved by avoiding the need for retail premises, sales staff (other than agents) and transportation. Although costs are incurred with postal charges and packaging, there is the possibility of cheaper goods for the customer; but there is a time lag before the goods are actually delivered, and the goods cannot be inspected before purchase.

This is of course a problem which can have legal consequences. The advertisement to which the customer responds is the basis of the contract between the mail order firm and the customer. If the firm promises a refund should goods be returned after an inspection period, that is a legally binding promise. In addition, the law has intervened to give further protection to the mail order customer. The Director General of Fair Trading, under powers given by the Fair Trading Act 1973, has made some delegated legislation, in the form of a statutory instrument called the Mail Order (Transactions) Information Order 1976/1812 which lays down that mail order advertisements, circulars and catalogues must contain the name of the person carrying on the business and the address where it is managed. As far as a company is concerned it is enough to give the address of its registered office. The Office of Fair Trading has negotiated a code of practice for 'guidance in safeguarding and promoting the interests of consumers in the UK' in mail order trading.

Franchising

This is an emerging form of retailing whereby a large organisation contracts to a franchisee the right to sell that firm's goods or service in a local area. Selling a particular make of new car by a dealer has been a longstanding example of franchising, but more recently names like Kentucky Fried Chicken, Burger King, Wimpy, Prontaprint and Dyno-Rod illustrate the growth in this field.

Fig. 29.8

What are the advantages of franchising? To the major organisation (the franchisor) it means that capital investment does not have to be risked in premises in many areas. Such funds must be raised by the franchisees, those buying the franchise.

To the franchisee it means that a small business person has the advantage of selling a brand name which is well-known nationwide, having purchased stocks of the product and main fixtures and fittings from the franchisor. Furthermore, training would be given by that organisation to assist the franchisee to operate the business effectively.

Marketing boards

For some agricultural products, selling is conducted through marketing boards. This involves the many farmers selling produce like milk, potatoes and hops to the relevant marketing board at a fixed price. The board then acts as a centralised selling agency, saving on time, selling and transportation costs for small farmers. The farmers themselves contribute to the cost of running the marketing boards.

30 Contracts and consumer protection

As we have seen, the buying and selling of goods and services at a market price largely reflects economic forces. However, there are certain legal influences present in market activities as well. This chapter describes and analyses the market from the angles of the law of contract and consumer protection generally.

Consumer protection has been very much in the news in recent years and a tremendous amount of legislation has been passed to protect the consumer (defined by the Fair Trading Act 1973 as a person to whom goods or services are supplied in the course of a business carried on by a supplier, the consumer not being a business person but an ordinary one). We shall be looking at some examples of that legislation and at two branches of the common law which are particularly relevant – the law of contract and the law relating to the tort of negligence. We shall see that business people, manufacturers and government departments must be aware of these branches of the law because they frequently limit or inhibit their activities. We must remember that what may be desirable from an economic point of view may not be legally permissible. For example it may be a good idea to cut manufacturing costs by using a cheap synthetic, but if that synthetic is potentially harmful or if the manufacturer does not take sufficient care in the manufacturing process and people suffer injury as a result, then the manufacturer may well incur both civil and criminal liability. This must be taken into account. The manufacturer must also be aware that in advertising the product it is against the law to make misleading statements. In addition, there are legal consequences if there has been an agreement to supply machinery by a certain date and the date is broken. These are the kinds of problems and constraints that we shall be looking at in this chapter and Chapter 31. We shall be examining them both from the point of view of the business organisation and from the point of view of the individual consumer.

Finally there are two important points to note. One is that the law may look very good when we read about it but it has to be enforced. If businesspeople ignore the law and get away with it, the law is no use. It is mere words. The activities of pressure groups like the Consumer Association, of private individuals who bother to complain when things go wrong, and of the press and the media generally (can you think of any well-known TV programmes about consumer problems?) can bring unwelcome publicity to organisations that conveniently forget about the law.

The second thing to bear in mind is that consumer protection was not invented in the 1960s. In 1266 the Assize of Bread and Ale laid down rules to punish people who gave false measure. In 1321 it was recorded that the London Justices approved regulations made by hatters to enforce the labelling of caps of inferior quality.

In this chapter we shall begin by looking at the law of contract, which lays down the basic rules governing agreements of all kinds. You may get a few surprises when you realise just how many contracts you have been making unawares.

Then we shall look at two special kinds of contracts – contracts for the sale of goods and contracts of hire-purchase – where legislation has been passed to protect the consumer.

In Chapter 31 we shall look at the tort of negligence and manufacturers' liability to the consumer of their products, and again we shall see how Parliament has intervened to pass legislation to protect the consumer.

Throughout we shall be concerned with the practical side of things, and so references to case-law and detailed legislative provisions will be kept to the minimum.

The law of contract

You have seen in the previous chapters in this part how firms are influenced by market factors and how they research the market to see what the consumer wants, or arguably what the consumer can be persuaded to buy. In this section we shall be looking at the market from the point of view of the legal framework in which the organisation operates.

The basic common law which underlies agreements made by business organisations, manufacturers, government departments and private individuals is the law of contract. This is largely common law (see Chapter 2) but where this case-law system has proved inadequate, particularly in the field of consumer protection, legislation has been passed to add to or change the common law.

The common law of contract as it developed in the eighteenth and nineteenth centuries echoed economic ideas of *laissez-faire*. People were free to make what bargains they liked. If they made a poor bargain that was their fault. The law assumed that people knew what they were doing and that both parties to a contract were equally powerful. This was and is often manifestly not the case. The law has changed as the economy has changed. Just as there has been increasing State intervention in the economy, so there has been increasing statutory intervention in the common law of contract to protect the consumer who is in an unequal bargaining situation as compared with big companies or nationalised industries. We can say that the law has intervened to correct the balance.

What is a contract?

A contract can be simply defined as *an agreement that is legally enforceable*. Both parts of this definition have to be looked at closely.

1 In some contracts – for example the agreement you have with your local Electricity Board – the element of real subjective agreement is very small. Unless you prefer candlelight to electricity you have to take your electricity on the terms dictated to you by the Electricity Board. You are in a 'can't win' situation.

2 An agreement is legally enforceable in the sense that, if it is broken and the injured party brings an action to court, then the court will recognise the validity of that agreement, usually by granting money compensation (called **damages**) to the injured party, but only occasionally by actually compelling performance of the agreement. 'Enforceable' therefore does not mean quite what it seems.

Do contracts have to be in writing?

A contract does not, generally speaking, have to take the form of an impressive written document. Some contracts, like hire-purchase contracts and contracts for the sale of land and houses, do have to be in writing, but most of the contracts we make do not have to be written to be legally enforceable. An oral contract is just as legally binding as a written one, though it is obviously a good idea to confirm agreements made face to face or on the telephone in a letter and to keep copies of all correspondence on file so that, if there is any dispute later on, you can prove your case.

If a contract is in writing and you sign it, as a general rule you are bound by all its terms even if you have not read them. Remember that next time you sign a holiday booking form for example. Read the small print! You may find that you are agreeing to some terms of which you were not aware and which you do not like.

Implied contracts

Some contracts are neither written nor oral. They are implied by the law from what we do. When we drive into a car park and get our ticket, when we pick up a newspaper at a stall, when we buy a packet of cigarettes, when we travel on a bus, we are making contracts. If anything goes wrong and a case comes before the courts it is the rules of the law of contract which will apply. Remember that the law is not just a set of rules brought out for special occasions. It is, or should be, a safety-net underlying all sorts of transactions.

Intention to create legal relations

Not all agreements that you make are legally binding contracts. An agreement to share a holiday with someone or to play tennis with them is not a contract, and there can be no action for breach of contract if the agreement is broken. That should reassure you if you have made a date with someone who looked lovely in the dim light of the discotheque but turns up at the rendezvous point with bright orange hair and a safety pin through his or her nose. You can slink away without fear of being sued for breach of contract. The agreement you made to meet was not a binding contract. These and other 'social' agreements are not legally binding.

The same is true, generally speaking, of agreements between husband and wife, and certainly of agreements containing the phrase 'binding in honour' only. An example of the latter, by the way, is a football pools coupon. If a football pools company failed to pay out on a winning coupon they could not be sued. The reason for making this kind of agreement 'binding in honour' is to protect the football pools company from false claims. A lot of people might claim that they had won and allege that the company had lost their winning coupon. In theory, therefore, pools companies need never pay out at all; but of course if they failed to do so people would stop doing the pools.

Who can make a contract?

Nearly everybody, including 'people' like companies and other kinds of corporation, can make a contract. There are a few exceptions. People under the age of eighteen years, 'minors', can as a general rule only make two kinds of contract. These are:

- contracts for **necessaries** – goods or services which they need, e.g. food, dental care, or books if they are students; and
- **beneficial contracts of service** – agreements to serve an apprenticeship or to take on some form of training. If, however, such a contract exploits the minor he or she can ignore the contract. It is not binding.

Contracts made by a minor for goods or services which are not necessary and contracts of loan are void, i.e. the minor is not bound by them.

When is a contract made?

A contract is made when a firm offer has been unconditionally accepted. An offer, made by the offeror, might be, 'I will sell you my motor-bike for £300.' If the offeree, i.e. the person to whom the offer is made, accepts the offer by saying, 'OK. Done.', then a contract has come into being. It does not matter that the £300 has not yet been paid. Once an offer has been accepted there is a contract. If one of the parties then breaks the promise he or she risks an action for breach of contract.

An exception to this rule is where a contract is made for the sale of a house. Here the offer is made and accepted 'subject to contract'. The effect of these words is surprising to the ordinary person. They mean that the deal is not legally binding until a written contract has been signed. You may have had your offer of £40 000 accepted by the vendor, but, in English law,

Fig. 30.1
The Carbolic Smoke Company's
offer
Source: *Illustrated London News*

the vendor is perfectly entitled to break the promise to you and accept a higher offer. This is called by the slang name of 'gazumping'.

Offers to the general public

An offer does not have to be made to a specific person. It can be made to the general public and accepted by anyone.

Let us look at an example. In the famous case of Carlill *v.* Carbolic Smoke Ball Co 1892 the manufacturers of a smoke ball said to have wonderful medicinal properties showed their confidence in their product by saying in an advertisement that if anyone used the smoke ball and nonetheless became ill they would pay that person £100. Mrs Carlill read the advertisement, used the smoke ball and nonetheless became ill. She claimed her £100. The Carbolic Smoke Ball Co, perhaps fearing thousands of such claims, refused to pay up. Mrs Carlill sued for breach of contract and won. The court held that the advertisement was a firm, precise offer which Mrs Carlill had accepted by her conduct in reading the advertisement, buying and using the smoke ball, and then becoming ill. An offer of a reward would also be an offer made to the general public which could be accepted by anybody.

Offer/invitation to treat

Supposing you have a situation where a householder says, 'Would you be able to paint the outside of my house this summer? About how much would it cost?' and a decorator replies, 'I should be able to do it by the end of August and it might cost in the region of £800–1000, but I can't give a definite estimate until I've looked over the property.' Is there a firm contract there which binds both parties? The answer is No. The decorator is not making a firm offer in response to the householder's enquiry, but is opening negotiations about a possible contract. This is called an **invitation to treat** ('treat' being used in an old sense still used by lawyers, meaning to 'bargain, discuss'), i.e. a situation where someone is inviting offers but not making a firm offer to be bound. Many situations are deemed to be invitations to treat rather than firms offers, e.g. an auctioneer asking for bids is making an invitation to treat, inviting offers (bids).

Shop displays

It is perhaps surprising that goods on display in a shop window or a supermarket are not firm offers in law but invitations to treat. The practical effect of this is that if goods on display in a shop window are wrongly priced by mistake the shopkeeper does not have to sell at that price. The customer is making the offer to buy at the price given in the window display. The shopkeeper need not accept the offer. (Of course if the shopkeeper consistently misprices or misdescribes goods he or she may incur criminal liability under the Trade Descriptions Act 1968 and be prosecuted in a Magistrates' Court.)

Similarly if you select goods from the supermarket shelf you are making an offer which may be accepted or rejected by the cashier at the check-out point. Thus, if the supermarket is rationing customers to 2 bags of sugar each because of shortages, the cashier is perfectly entitled to refuse to allow a customer to have 10 bags of sugar.

Supermarkets

In the case of the Pharmaceutical Society of Great Britain v. Boots 1951, the courts were faced with the problem of whether or not a supermarket shelf display in the first Boots self-service chemist's shop constituted an offer or an invitation to treat. It was decided that the display was an invitation to treat and that therefore Boots was not contravening the Pharmacy and Poisons Acts which stated that certain 'dangerous' drugs (e.g. patent medicines like aspirin) must be sold under the supervision of a qualified pharmacist. This case was really concerned with the exact moment of sale. If the goods on the supermarket shelf were an offer and the customer accepted the offer when putting the medicines into the wire basket, then the sale was unsupervised, but if, as the court decided, the goods were an invitation to treat, then the customer made the offer when selecting the medicines. The sale was therefore supervised, since the check-out point was next to the dispensing section of the shop, where a qualified pharmacist was in attendance.

Buying by post

Many other kinds of situation are considered by law to be invitations to treat, e.g. mail order catalogues. When you order goods by mail and send off your money, your offer can be rejected by the seller (if the price of the materials has risen for example), but in that event your money must, of course, be returned. If the seller accepts the money the goods must be sent off reasonably quickly.

Advertisements

These may be deemed by law to be firm offers or they may only be considered to be invitations to treat, depending on the words used in the advertisement. In the Carlill case, you remember, the court held that the Carbolic Smoke Ball Co had made a firm offer. Thus when an advertisement promises a refund if the customer is not satisfied that is a firm offer. However, many advertisements are deliberately worded in a vague way so that they do not constitute offers, and also so that the advertiser cannot be prosecuted under the Trade Descriptions Act 1968 for making false claims for the product. Many advertisements try to give an impression of a product without being specific. They say that a face-cream will make your skin feel smoother, not that you will definitely look younger when you have used it. If they do say, as happened in one case, that a bath preparation is lanolin rich when it in fact contains only a minute amount of lanolin, they can be prosecuted under the Act. If an advertisement constitutes a firm offer, they can also be sued for breach of contract or, as we shall see later on in this chapter, for misrepresentation. There is an EEC Directive on Misleading Advertising which will further strengthen the law.

Revocation of an offer

An offer can be revoked or withdrawn at any time before it has been accepted. It is only when the offer has been accepted that there is a binding contract. An offer by itself does not bind anybody; but if you decide to withdraw your offer you should let the other person, the offeree, know that you are doing so.

Counter-offer

An offer must be accepted unconditionally. If the offeree varies the terms of the offer in some way then there is no contract. For example, if I offer to sell you my car for £1000 and you say, 'It's not worth that; I'll take it for £800', you are making a new offer on your own account and incidentally rejecting my offer to sell.

Acceptance of the offer

Acceptance of an offer must generally be communicated. It is not enough to accept an offer in your mind; you must let the other person, the offeror, know that you have accepted it. There are two exceptions to this rule:

1 As in the case of Carlill *v.* Carbolic Smoke Ball Co, acceptance can be by conduct when an offer is made to the general public.

2 When the contractual negotiations are carried on by letter, acceptance of the offer (and therefore the coming into existence of the contract) takes effect when the letter of acceptance is *posted*. It is therefore always a good idea to send important letters of acceptance by Recorded Delivery so that you have proof both that the letter was sent and of the time of its dispatch. Remember – even if a letter of acceptance never arrives there is still a contract. Your only problem is proving that the letter was sent.

Unsolicited goods

Supposing you have been sent goods which you did not order, do you have to pay for them or send them back? The answer is No. You can:

- either write to the sender explaining the position and asking for the goods to be collected. If they are not collected within 30 days the goods are yours: or
- do nothing at all except keep the goods safe for 6 months. If the sender has not collected them by the end of 6 months, they belong to you.

The above points are provisions of the Unsolicited Goods and Services Act 1971, which was passed to protect the consumer against 'inertia' selling – the practice of sending goods unasked for through the post and then demanding payment. The common law would say that you do not have to pay for goods you have not asked for because you have not communicated your acceptance of them. They have in a sense been 'dumped' on you. The Act makes the position clearer and also provides that if the seller writes threatening letters demanding payment this may be committing a criminal offence and can be referred to the local Trading Standards department or the police.

The price of the contract – consideration

Every simple contract (i.e. a contract not made by deed, which is a special formal document which must be drawn up by a solicitor) requires **consideration**. This is the lawyers' way of saying that in every contract there must be an element of bargain, a price for which the promise of the other party is given. English Law will not tolerate a something-for-nothing situation. If I promise to clean your windows in return for your promise to pay me, we have a contract. But if I simply promise to clean your windows and you promise nothing in return, we have no contract and I can break my promise.

Adequacy of consideration

There must be some price to make a contract, though not necessarily money. It could be another promise to do something or to refrain from doing something. What is clear is that, strangely enough, the law does not require that the consideration be adequate in any commercial sense. In the case of Chappell v. Nestlé it was held that silver paper wrappers from bars of chocolate were good enough consideration for a promise to dispatch the record 'Rockin' Shoes'. Nestlé had a campaign to sell more chocolate. Any customer sending in a certain number of silver paper wrappers from their chocolate bars would receive the record, over which Chappell had the copyright. Chappell argued that the record was a free gift. The court held, however, that there was a contract of sale between Nestlé and the customer who 'bought' the record for bits of silver paper (an unusual price but nevertheless a price). The court held that as long as there is an element or hint of bargain the law is satisfied.

Privity of Contract

Only if *you* have given consideration for the other party's promise can you bring an action if that promise is broken. If, as happened in Tweddle v. Atkinson, two fathers make reciprocal promises to give money to a young couple, only father A can sue father B if he breaks his promise (and vice versa). The young couple, for whose benefit the contract is made, are outside the contract. They are not parties to it. They are given no consideration. This point is expressed by lawyers as 'consideration must move from the promisee' or the principle of Privity of Contract.

Past consideration

If, for example, an agreement has been reached to supply something in return for a promise to pay a sum of money, the parties are bound *from that moment* even though no money has yet changed hands; *but* the promises must be exchanged at the same time. English law says that there is no contract if something is done and then, subsequently, a promise is made in respect of what has been done. The courts call this 'past consideration' and deny it any validity, as happened in the case Re McCardle, in which a father left his house to his adult children on condition that his widow should live there during her lifetime. When she died the proceeds from the sale of the house were to be split equally among all the children. One of them lived with his mother in the house and made several improvements to it. When the mother died the other children promised the one who had made the improvements an extra payment in respect of what had been done in the past. The court held that this promise was not binding. What could have been consideration for the promise, i.e. the improvements, was in the past and there was no real bargain situation.

If this all seems rather complicated, it is! As long ago as 1937 the Law Commission recommended that consideration be abolished but it still remains part of the law of contract.

False statements

A contract may be valid in the sense that there is a clear agreement (a firm offer has been unconditionally accepted) and there is consideration; but it can still be cancelled if it was made because one of the parties made a false statement to the other as an inducement to enter into the contract. We all know the kind of thing – 'only done 2000 miles', 'George III antique desk', 'planning permission granted'. These are the kinds of statement which, if false, can in law amount to misrepresentations. On the other hand statements like 'desirable residence', 'interesting neighbourhood', 'unbeatable bargain' are only statements of opinion, not statements of fact, and are not classed as misrepresentations. You cannot therefore do much about them if you subsequently discover that your idea of what is desirable or interesting is different from that of the person who made the statement.

What can you do?

If you think that someone has made a false statement to you and that you have grounds for a claim in law it is important to act quickly, otherwise you may lose the right to cancel the contract and get your money back. This, together with the right to claim damages for any loss or injury which you have suffered as a result of entering into the contract, is the main remedy available under the Misrepresentation Act 1967 (an Act which clarified and changed the common law position). In order to succeed you will have to show that:

- the misrepresentation was an untrue statement of fact; and
- the statement induced you to enter into the contract.

You do not have to cancel out the contract if you do not want to. You can keep to the contract but you can still claim damages. For example, if you bought a car because you had been told that it was suitable for pulling a caravan and you subsequently discovered it was not, you would be able to keep the car if you liked it. You would still have an action for damages to compensate you for the money you might have spent to convert the car or to buy another one suitable for pulling the caravan.

Businesspeople must be very careful therefore about their sales-talk. They may find that even though a deal has gone through it can be cancelled because their promotional literature or sales-talk contained untrue statements. They must also be aware that a false statement can be a criminal offence under the Trade Descriptions Act 1958. In R. *v*. Clarksons Holidays 1972 a number of statements made about a hotel not yet built and illustrated by an 'artist's impression' were construed by the jury as being a misrepresentation of existing facts, and the ensuing conviction was upheld as being proper by the Court of Appeal.

Breaking the contract

Why is it important to determine the two important questions of the validity of the contract, and the time of its making?

The answer is that if the contract is a valid one, the parties are bound by its terms and, if one of them breaks the contract, the other can sue for breach, either to get money compensation or, in certain circumstances, to cancel the contract.

Many contracts, of course, are properly performed and never come before the courts, but the rules of the law of contract form a backdrop to any commercial venture and a resource if things go wrong, because the injured party has a right to sue for breach. A business person will normally want agreements to be legally binding knowing that if things go wrong he or she can sue. If he or she wins the action there will be entitlement to money compensation.

Conditions and warranties

Some terms of a contract are so important that a lawyer will classify them as **conditions**. Breach of a condition entitles the injured party to cancel the contract and demand money back. Minor terms are called **warranties**. Breach of a warranty only entitles the injured party to sue for damages. The contract still stands.

Let us look at an example. You have a contract with a central heating engineer to install a central heating system in your home. The engineer installs it so badly that it is positively dangerous and completely unusable. He or she has obviously committed a breach of condition and you are therefore entitled to refuse to pay anything. You can also sue for damages to get the money to put things right. If, on the other hand, the only breach is a failure to install humidifiers on your radiators that is only a breach of warranty and you would only be entitled to sue for damages. You could not refuse to pay for the work done. In practice the best thing would be to pay the bill but deduct from it the amount needed for the humidifiers and to write explaining what you have done and why you have done it. You have then covered yourself.

Remedies for breach of contract

Remedies are ways of making things better. The best remedy in law is frequently money compensation – damages. If the court agrees with you

Damages

that you are entitled to damages, they have to decide the amount of compensation to which you are entitled. There is a clear rule in the law of contract that the defendant is only liable for loss or damage:

- that happens in the natural course of things;
- or that could have been foreseen by both parties when they made the contract.

The defendant is not therefore liable for unexpected consequences of the action or results that could not have been foreseen because the defendant was not told of their possibility at the time of making the contract.

Hadley *v.* Baxendale 1854 illustrates this point. Hadley was a miller. The crankshaft of his mill broke, so he made a contract with Baxendale, a carrier, to deliver a new one. Baxendale broke the contract by not delivering on time. The mill actually had to stop production because there was no spare crankshaft. Hadley sued Baxendale claiming compensation for the loss of profits he had suffered because of the delay. The court held that Hadley could not succeed because the natural result of the late delivery was not loss of profits. It would be normal to expect him to have a spare crankshaft. He had not told Baxendale that he had no spares, so the stoppage which resulted from the late delivery could not have been foreseen by Baxendale.

Other remedies for breach of contract

Damages are not always an appropriate remedy. The plaintiff may want the contract carried out. If someone has decided to buy a particular house, money will not put things right. The courts have a remedy which they can grant at their discretion which compels performance of the contract. It is called **specific performance**.

Another remedy which the courts can give is that of **injunction** to forbid a breach of contract. If, for example, in an employment contract you had agreed that you would not publish the results of the research you were doing and the court thought that this was a reasonable restraint on your activities, then, if it became apparent that you were about to publish your research, your employer could seek an injunction to stop you.

These are both **equitable remedies**, which means that the courts will only award them if they think it fair and just in the circumstances to do so. If you disregard an order of specific performance or an injunction then you are in contempt of court and can be fined or imprisoned.

Frustration

Supposing that the defendant can truly say, 'It wasn't my fault that I couldn't perform the contract. Something happened which was completely outside my control.' In that kind of situation the contract is said to be **frustrated**. The contract has become impossible to perform and the parties are discharged from their contractual obligations. They are 'let off'.

In the case of Taylor *v.* Caldwell, Caldwell made a contract to hire out a music hall to Taylor for some concerts. Before the concerts had taken place the music hall was accidentally burned down. Taylor sued Caldwell for his failure to provide the music hall. The court held that, as it was not Caldwell's fault that the theatre had been destroyed, and that, as it was impossible to carry out the contract, the contract was frustrated. There was no breach of contract. Taylor *v.* Caldwell was decided in 1863 when, although the courts allowed the parties to be 'let off' no provision was made for the recovery of deposits or other money paid out under a contract subsequently frustrated. The common law said, 'The loss lies where it falls'. This meant that if a deposit had been paid for the hire of that music hall it could not be recovered even though the music hall had been destroyed and could not be used.

The Law Reform (Frustrated Contracts) Act 1943 changed this by saying that any money paid out under a contract which subsequently becomes frustrated can be recovered at the discretion of the court, i.e. it can be paid back, but minus any expenses incurred by the other party. That way the consequences of the frustration are borne equally by the two parties.

xemption clauses

The doctrine of frustration, as we have seen, allows the defendant to avoid liability because he or she is not at fault, and we should all consider that fair; but exemption clauses (terms in the contract which exempt the defendant from liability) have often been used to exclude liability even when the defendant is at fault. An exemption clause would be something like this: 'The Management can accept no responsibility for loss or damage to property.' This does not seem fair, particularly in situations where the consumer is in a no-choice situation, either because of dealing with an organisation like British Rail which has a monopoly or because of dealing with a section of the business community all of whom impose the same kind of 'standard form' contract with very similar terms (including exemption clauses).

Let us look at some examples. When you buy a first class rail season ticket British Rail may accept no liability for failure to provide first class compartments on trains. This is an exemption clause. You have paid for a first class ticket but you may have to travel second class. Because of the exemption clause (if it is legally effective) you would have no remedy against British Rail here.

Business and other organisations protect themselves by inserting all kind of exemption clauses into contracts. Laundries may exclude liability for damage or loss, holiday firms may put clauses in their booking forms excluding liability for damage or loss not caused directly by the negligence of their employees. Arguably they need to protect themselves in this way. On the other hand such clauses can be very unfair on the individual consumer.

To remedy this unfairness a very important Act of Parliament was passed in 1977 called the Unfair Contract Terms Act 1977. It lays down that in relation to contracts between a consumer and a business (or other) organisation:

- no business can exclude liability for death or personal injury resulting from negligence; and
- any other exemption clause will be upheld by the courts only if it is thought to be reasonable.

Notices and clauses in contracts seeking to exclude liability will not therefore be illegal but they will frequently be ineffective, and so the plaintiff will win the action and get compensation for breach of contract – for example it is unlikely that a clause in a holiday booking form which says the firm will not be liable if the flight is overbooked and some other form of transport has to be used would be thought to be reasonable by the courts. If such a thing happened and the poor holidaymaker had to go by train rather than plane, thus losing several days of the holiday at the resort, he or she would very probably get compensation and the exemption clause would not work to protect travel agent.

What effect is this legislation going to have on business? Like much Consumer Protection legislation it will probably have the effect of raising costs and therefore of raising prices. If business and other organisations are now going to be liable for breaches of contract formerly covered by exemption clauses, they must increase their insurance cover to be ready to compensate customers to whom, before the legislation was passed, they would not have been liable. This burden will probably be passed on to the consumer in the form of higher prices. Consumer Protection can therefore be a double-edged sword. It may adversely affect the consumer, who has to pay more for goods and services.

We have looked at the basic common law rules of the law of contract and seen how legislation has been passed to give added protection to the consumer. We shall now look at two special contracts – sale of goods and hire-purchase – where the consumer is particularly at risk and where very important legislation has been passed to give protection.

Contracts for the sale of goods

One of the most important pieces of consumer legislation was in fact passed in the nineteenth century – the Sale of Goods Act 1893, now repealed and incorporated in the Sale of Goods Act 1979. The Act protects the purchaser of goods by implying in contracts for the sale of goods 4 basic promises:

a that the person selling the goods actually owns them;
b that the goods fit their description;
c that the goods are 'of merchantable quality' (roughly speaking that means 'of a reasonable standard');
d that the goods are fit for the purpose for which they are sold.

It does not matter that no reference is made to these promises at the time of the sale. The protection is there and the seller, generally speaking, cannot avoid the application of the Act. The provisions of the Supply of Goods (Implied Terms) Act 1973 now incorporated in the Unfair Contract Terms Act 1977 in general prevent the seller from contracting out of the Act. The seller cannot, for example, put up a notice in a shop saying 'No refunds given'. Indeed it will be a criminal offence to do so. If the seller does break one of these implied promises he or she is bound to give you your money back if you ask for it, and in addition may have to pay your damages.

You may say, 'But supposing the seller did not know, for example, that the goods were faulty?' This is irrelevant. The seller has a duty to check goods before putting them on sale. It may be that they are packed in such a way that they cannot be checked. It does not matter. The seller is still liable to the customer, though many, through ignorance or design, try the excuse of 'It's not my fault. This was made in Hongkong. Nothing I can do about it, is there?' Don't be fooled! The shopkeeper's liability is **strict** (that means liability whether at fault or not). This places a heavy burden on the shopkeeper. Of course the shopkeeper can sue the manufacturer or wholesaler who supplied the shoddy goods, but this may prove difficult if the manufacturer operates outside the UK.

The Supply of Goods and Services Act 1982 implies promises similar to those contained in the Sale of Goods Act into contracts for the supply of goods (e.g. commercial hire contracts) and contracts for services.

Sale goods

You often see in shops 'Sale goods not returnable'. This is not legally correct. If sale goods are not of reasonable quality (reasonable in the circumstances of the sale, that is) then there will be a breach of the implied promise of merchantable quality and the seller will have to give you your money back if you ask for it. If, however, goods are labelled 'slightly imperfect' or 'seconds', obviously they do not have to be perfect; but they must be reasonable in the circumstances. If you buy a pair of tights which are completely unwearable because there is only one leg, they are obviously not of merchantable quality and the tights are returnable.

Private sales

The Sale of Goods Act offers only limited protection to sales between private individuals. It requires that the person selling the goods should own them and that the goods should match their description; but it does not require them to be of merchantable quality or fit for the purpose for which they are sold. In this respect the buyer must generally be more careful in private sales, i.e. sales between two private individuals. This is expressed in the Latin phrase *'Caveat emptor'*, which means 'Let the buyer beware'. Remember this when you are buying a second-hand car from someone who has advertised in the local newspaper and not from a dealer.

Business sales

The terms implied in the Sale of Goods Act (the 4 basic promises which we referred to earlier) apply to contracts between businesses as they do to contracts between the individual consumer and a business. However, under the Unfair Contract Terms Act 1977 the implied promise relating to merchantable quality, while it cannot be excluded in a consumer–business contract, can be excluded from a contract between two businesses if the exemption clause is reasonable and therefore upheld by the courts.

Presents

If someone gives you, for example, an electric iron as a present and it does not work, you cannot return the iron (though the person who gave it to you could do so). Only the buyer and the seller have rights and obligations under the Sale of Goods Act. Remember also, as we said earlier, that you only have rights under a contract if you are a party to it. However it is always worth getting in touch with the manufacturer who may well do something about the iron if there is a genuine complaint. You often see slips of paper saying, 'If these goods are not in perfect condition, please return them to the manufacturer quoting XYZ.'

We shall look at duties owed by manufacturers to their customers, whether or not they themselves have bought the goods, in the next chapter.

Guarantees

Many shops give you a guarantee to induce you to buy goods. They are not legally obliged to do so. A nasty practice developed of issuing customers with a guarantee which ostensibly gave the purchaser additional rights but, in fact, removed some of the rights under the Sale of Goods Act by using a rather complicated formula like 'All conditions and warranties whether express or implied by statute or otherwise are excluded.' The word 'excluded' should give you a hint. This was in fact an exemption clause excluding the seller's liability. If you signed the guarantee you were signing away all those implied rights that we mentioned at the beginning of the section on the sale of goods.

This kind of guarantee was made ineffective by the Supply of Goods (Implied Terms) Act 1973 (now incorporated in the Unfair Contract Terms Act), and if you find clauses of that kind in a guarantee you should report the trader concerned to your local Trading Standards department.

Of course many guarantees will be perfectly legal and will give you additional rights and benefits.

Hire-purchase contracts

You cannot always buy goods outright, so you may have to buy them gradually on credit – on the 'never-never'. The most common form of 'never-never' contract is the **hire-purchase contract**. This is obviously a situation in which the consumer needs to be protected – needing, above all, to know exactly what is being undertaken when buying goods on hire-purchase. The Consumer Credit Act 1974 was passed to give the consumer much-needed protection. We shall be looking at the main provisions of this Act a little later.

What exactly is a hire-purchase contract?

It is not a contract of sale. (The Consumer Credit Act does not talk about 'seller' and 'buyer' but about 'creditor' and 'debtor'.) It is a contract of hire which also gives the hirer the option to purchase the goods. Goods on hire-purchase cannot therefore be sold by the hirer (or debtor) because they are not his or hers until all the instalments have been paid off.

It is ultimately an expensive way of buying goods because the shop will charge interest on the loan. In practice the shop frequently drops out of the deal and sells the goods to a finance house (a company which deals exclusively in lending people money). The finance house will then hire the goods to the consumer under a normal hire-purchase agreement.

Credit-sale agreements

We have to be careful to make a distinction between hire-purchase contracts and **credit-sale agreements**. With the latter the goods become the property of the buyer as soon as they come into his or her possession but time is allowed to pay for the goods by instalments.

Note that both the hire-purchase contracts and credit-sale agreements must be in writing.

The Consumer Credit Act 1974

This Act lays down that:

1 Anyone wishing to offer credit facilities must obtain a licence from the Director General of Fair Trading. Anyone who trades without a licence will be committing a criminal offence. The idea of the licensing procedure is that a constant check is kept on those persons offering credit facilities.

2 Anyone advertising a credit deal must give the true annual rate of interest and the total price for the goods bought on credit. The consumer will thus know exactly how much will be paid for the goods and so will be able to shop around for the best credit facilities.

3 If goods are faulty, this is a breach of an implied term of merchantable quality (just like the Sale of Goods Act, you remember), and they can be returned either to the finance house or to the shop.

4 If you have goods on hire-purchase you have the right to terminate the agreement at any time up to the payment of the last instalment. In that event you must of course return the goods and pay any arrears of instalments outstanding.

5 If the hirer (debtor) cannot pay off the hire-purchase payments there is some measure of protection in that, if at least one third of the total credit price has been paid, the owner can only take the goods away by getting a court order. If less than a third has been paid the dealer can take the goods away but must give notice of intention to do so.

6 Further protection is provided by a section in the Act which allows for a 'cooling-off period'. What this means is that the law allows you to have second thoughts. It applies to situations where you have signed a hire-purchase *or* a credit-sale agreement in your home (or anywhere else for that matter that is neither the shop nor the office of the finance house). You are allowed to cancel the agreement within 5 days of receiving your copy of the agreement (which should tell you about this right). The idea is to protect the consumer from fast-talking door-to-door sales people who try to persuade people to buy things they do not really want and cannot afford.

31 Negligence and consumer protection

The law of torts deals with certain situations where someone has suffered physically, mentally or, in some cases, financially because of another's action or inaction. The victim may go to court to get money (damages) to compensate for the injury or loss. For example, if you feel that your reputation has been damaged by an untrue newspaper article, you might sue in the tort of libel to get money compensation. Cases of this kind hit the headlines, so no doubt you can think of one or two interesting libel cases.

The tort that we shall be looking at is the **tort of negligence**, because it is particularly relevant to Consumer Protection. Negligence cases are often in the news either because of the dramatic nature of their facts or because of the large sums of money frequently awarded in damages.

Do not forget that we are talking here about the civil law, not the criminal law. Students often are confused because the same incident, for example a road accident caused by careless driving, may lead to a criminal prosecution in a Magistrates' Court for driving without due care and attention; but in addition, if the accident caused injury or damage, a civil action may be brought by the victim to get money compensation. No one *has* to bring a civil action and it may well not be worth the victim's while to bring an expensive action when the loss or injury is slight. In the case of a road accident, of course, there may be no need to sue because the accident is covered by insurance and the insurance company does not dispute its obligation.

Negligence covers many different kinds of harm caused by carelessness. It is the tort which underlies the relationship between manufacturer and consumer and is therefore very important in Consumer Protection. There is generally (unless the goods are bought directly from the manufacturer) *no contract* between the manufacturer and the ultimate consumer, and so if the goods are faulty no breach of contract action can be brought by the consumer. (Remember the principle of Privity of Contract discussed in the previous chapter.) Apart then from legislation like the Consumer Safety Amendment Act 1986 and the proposed Consumer Protection Bill (to be passed in response to the EEC Directive on Defective Goods), the rights of the consumer against the manufacturer are principally found in the tort of negligence. This gives, in many different situations, a right of action against a manufacturer or indeed a government department, a local health authority or a professional person whose carelessness has caused injury or loss.

Donoghue v. Stevenson 1932

We have already referred to this case of the woman who suffered severe shock and a stomach upset after finding the remains of a snail in a glass of ginger beer bought for her by a friend, and sued the manufacturer in negligence. The case, which she won, has become known to generations of law students because it was a 'test case', i.e. no case quite like it had been brought before and the judge in that case laid down for the first time 3 important points which must be dealt with in every negligence action. They are:

The duty of care

The plaintiff must show the court that he or she was the defendant's 'neighbour' and that the defendant therefore owed a duty of care. These rather technical words mean that the plaintiff has to appear as someone who would be at risk if the defendant did not take reasonable care. 'Neighbour', then in this context does not mean the person who lives next door but someone close to the defendant who might be injured if the defendant was not careful in what was being done.

If we look at a case like King *v.* Phillips we can see who might *not* be a neighbour. Mrs King was cleaning in an upstairs room. Her child was playing with a tricycle in the street. Mr Phillips, a taxi-driver, drove his cab carelessly and ran into the tricycle. The child was not injured but the beloved tricycle was and the child screamed. Mrs King heard all this but she could not see what had happened. She jumped to conclusions, thought her child had been injured, and suffered severe nervous shock followed by a long depressive illness. She sued the taxi-driver in negligence. She lost. The court held that she was not the taxi-driver's neighbour.

It seems unfair, but think about it. Is it really reasonable to expect that taxi-drivers, when they are driving along, should have in mind not only their passengers, other road-users and pedestrians, but also people cleaning in upstairs rooms? What you have probably realised is that people who are injured *indirectly* by others' carelessness will probably fail in negligence actions. This may not seem very fair from the point of view of the victim, but we also have to take into account the point of view of the person who indirectly caused the injury and decide what is reasonable in the circumstances of the case. It was obviously reasonable in Donoghue v. Stevenson to say that the manufacturer owed a duty of care to Mrs Donoghue, the ultimate consumer, because she was clearly at risk if the manufacturer failed to take reasonable care.

Breach of the duty of care

The plaintiff must then go on to show that the defendant failed to take reasonable care in the circumstances. The standard of care is not fixed – the judge must look at all the circumstances of the case, as in Paris v. Stepney Borough Council. Mr Paris, a one-eyed man working on vehicle maintenance, lost the sight of his only eye in an accident, and it was held that, while it was not normal practice to supply men doing this kind of work with goggles, nevertheless the employers were negligent in not supplying Mr Paris with them because the risks of injury to him were greater. They should therefore have taken more care of a person with only one eye.

Damage resulting from the breach

Negligence is only actionable on proof of damage. If the woman in Donoghue v. Stevenson had loved decomposing snails and had eaten hers with relish, then her action would have failed. However, the defendant will only be liable if the damage caused was reasonably foreseeable. This means that the defendant will not have to compensate the plaintiff if the consequences of the actions could not reasonably have been expected. For example, in the case of Doughty v. Turner Manufacturing, the defendant's employee negligently knocked against an asbestos lid covering a bath of very hot acid, and the asbestos reacted with the acid to cause an explosion which injured the plaintiff. No one knew before that case that there could be that kind of chemical reaction. It was unexpected. Doughty lost his action. The court held that the damage caused was not reasonably foreseeable. If such accidents began to occur with increasing regularity then of course the unexpected would become reasonably foreseeable.

Financial loss

When negligence was first developed as a tort, judges were reluctant to award compensation for injury other than physical damage to person or property. That was all very well in the law of contract where people imposed obligations on themselves by agreement for actions to be brought to recover compensation for financial loss, but not at all the same in tort, where the court *imposed* obligations on the parties and where there was no pre-existing agreement. This may not seem very logical to you, and negligence has now been developed by judges to cover cases where people have suffered financial loss resulting from negligent advice.

In the case of Hedley-Byrne v. Heller 1963, where a bank was sued for giving negligent advice as to the credit-worthiness of a client, the courts decided that in certain circumstances there could be a successful negligence action when the plaintiff suffered financial loss through acting on advice given by a professional person whose main job it is to give advice, e.g. a solicitor, an accountant, an architect or a surveyor. In Hedley-Byrne the bank was not held liable for negligent advice because they had made a waiver of liability, i.e. they had said, 'You take this advice at your own risk. We will not be liable if it is wrong.' This you will recognise as being a kind of exemption clause. In the special circumstances of banking where banks, among their many other functions, are asked to give thousands of credit references this waiver was held to be effective to 'let the bank off'.

The advice *must* be given in a professional context (i.e. not free advice given at a dinner party or a casual chat at the bus-stop). For example in Ross v. Caunters a solicitor was held liable for this kind of negligence. He prepared a will for his client but failed to warn him that where a beneficiary or spouse witnesses a will any gift to that person will be invalid. The client's wife witnessed the will and when her husband died she found to her dismay that she could not have any of the property that he had left to her because the gift was legally invalid. She needed compensation. She sued the solicitor in negligence and she won.

Have you noted something important about the facts of this case? The wife had no contract with the solicitor because her husband was the client. The only way to recover the money was to sue in negligence. Had the Hedley-Byrne v. Heller kind of liability not been developed she would have had no remedy.

Product liability

You will have realised that negligence is not a matter of merely proving that somebody was careless and getting your compensation almost automatically. It is a much more technical matter. Negligence cases may seem to be cut and dried, but the plaintiff may fail on what seems to be a technical point. The costs of bringing a negligence action can place an unbearable burden on the ordinary person, who may in the end fail to get any compensation. Individuals like the woman in Donoghue v. Stevenson are rare indeed.

It is an eye-opening experience to read the books that have been written about the trials and tribulations of the parents of deformed children when they sought to bring a negligence action against the Distillers Company which marketed the Thalidomide drug in this country. Thalidomide was a drug prescribed for pregnant women suffering from nausea. Its use resulted in many deformed births. Allegations were made that the affect of the drug had not been properly investigated. The Thalidomide tragedy is not an isolated incident. You will have read about many such consumer disasters, not just involving drugs. In a case, Lambert v. Lewis, a manufacturer was held liable for negligent design when a defective coupling caused a trailer to break loose from a vehicle, injuring other road users.

Lambert v. Lewis was a complicated judgement which caused a lot of discussion in the legal world. Because of the legal complexities of negligence it is not often that such cases are brought, let alone succeed. Because of this there has been a lot of discussion about **product liability**, which in effect would make the manufacturer of goods liable for damage caused by a defect in the goods whether knowing of the defect or not (or indeed could have known). You will remember that this kind of liability is called strict liability – liability without fault, i.e. no need to prove negligence. In this country the Pearson Commission (the Royal Commission on Civil Liability and Compensation for Personal Injuries) has recommended the introduction of a scheme of strict liability for motor accidents.

An EEC Directive on Product Liability was adopted by the Community in July 1985, allowing Member States 3 years to adopt its provisions. The UK Government has announced its intention of implementing the Directive as soon as parliamentary time allows. The UK Bill, probably to be called the Consumer Protection Bill, is likely to include a development risk defence (meaning that a manufacturer will not be held liable if at the current level of knowledge the risks of damage were not yet fully known). The Bill is not, however, likely to impose any financial limit on a manufacturer's liability. It is probable that the legislation will not cover products which have not been processed, e.g. unprocessed agricultural produce.

Widespread fears have been expressed that the introduction of this new law will result in a tremendous increase in litigation and that it will place a very heavy insurance burden on business. In the USA where similar legislation is already in force, Ford Motors currently faces product liability actions for an estimated 4bn dollars. The same scale of actions faces Johnson and Johnson currently defending in the USA 7 wrongful death actions stemming from the intentional but random poisoning in 1982 of Tylenol capsules (a widely-used pain killer).

A case often quoted to illustrate the high cost of product liability is Share v. Sears. Share, an overweight man who suffered a heart attack while trying to start his Sears lawnmower was awarded 1m dollars by a sympathetic US jury. However if we look at that case we find that even in a fault-based system Sears would have been held liable because the lawnmower's valve did not meet manufacturing specifications. Moreover the damages would probably have still been high because Share was a 32-year-old doctor earning 300 000 dollars a year who, after the attack, had to take a job at 60 000 dollars a year.

It is argued that product liability in the USA has had some unwelcome effects. Not only has the high cost of insurance been passed on to the consumer in the form of higher prices but sometimes products have actually been withdrawn from the market, giving the consumer a very restricted choice. In the USA, for example, the Searle corporation has stopped the production of 'Copper Seven' and 'Tatum T' IUDs (intra-uterine devices), apparently because of the cost of defending unwarranted actions together with the high cost of insurance. There is therefore only one US manufacturer of IUDs whose product in 1985 accounted for 3 per cent of the market. It may be that product liability legislation will have an unwelcome backlash effect on the consumer by raising prices and reducing choice. On the other hand it can be argued that manufacturers will only spend money on making products safe if they have to.

The *safety* of products was the prime concern of the Consumer Safety Act 1978 which went some way towards protecting the consumer against dangerous products (though it is interesting to note that drugs were excluded from the operation of the Act). Now we have the Consumer Safety (Amendment) Act 1986 which has produced major changes in the way the consumer safety law operates and is enforced. New powers of seizure are given, suspension notices may be served, and the courts have the power to issue forfeiture and disposal orders. The Act was passed following widespread unease about the safety of products, e.g. toys, electrical goods, pharmaceutical products – particularly imported goods. The government published a White Paper in 1984 called 'The Safety of Goods', and several of the proposals in that White Paper are contained in the Consumer Safety (Amendment) Act 1986. A major problem has been to identify and hold on to potentially dangerous imported goods before they pass through ports of entry. Sections 1 and 2 of the Act enable customs officers to provide information to other enforcement agencies, and to seize and detain goods for up to 48 hours while examinations can be made.

The price of consumer protection

We have concentrated on the rights of the consumer. We must not forget that these rights impose corresponding burdens on manufacturers and traders generally. Consumer protection costs money both in terms of the improvement in the quality and safety of the product and in terms of the insurance which any prudent trader will take out in case of having to pay out compensation when things go wrong. (Do not forget, however, that you cannot insure against criminal liability.)

Some business people would argue that the mass of consumer protection law works against the consumer, who in effect pays for protection through higher prices. Small businesses are at a particular disadvantage. They may not be able to afford either to improve their product or to pay increased insurance premiums. They may also, not having a legal department at their disposal, find it impossible to keep informed of the vast mass of legislation and delegated legislation which relates to consumer protection. If the small businessperson is put out of business the consumer will have less choice.

We have to ask ourselves, 'Consumer protection – can we afford it?' What do you think?

32 The importance of marketing

You may remember that the purpose of marketing is to establish, influence and meet customer needs, and anticipate changes in them. That latter function is carried out by **market research**, the methods and aims of which will be discussed in this chapter.

In Chapter 26 we described the marketing mix and its significance, and illustrated by referring to Buyerpad Building Society. We shall now look at features of marketing more fully. You will find that we have already referred to a number of these features, such as pricing policy and channels of distribution, but we shall look at marketing functions more cohesively. Some readers might study a marketing unit as part of their course. This section will serve as a useful introduction.

Consumer behaviour

A basic question that the Marketing Department of an organisation must confront is 'Why do people or organisations buy or refuse to buy our products?' Consideration of, and possibly research into, this issue are crucial to the development of the appropriate marketing mix.

For example, research into the manner in which consumers decide to buy has led to the distinction between high involvement and low involvement products. High involvement goods or services are those to which consumers devote much time and thought when buying, whereas low involvement products are bought with less care. Examples and influences on high and low involvement products are summarised in Table 32.1

Table 32.1
High and Low Consumer Involvement

		High involvement	Low involvement
Products		cars micro-computers perfume designer jeans house repairs	petrol adhesive tape biscuits light bulbs detergents
Influences		personal relevance complex features of the product much product differentiation between brands high price	little or no ego or personal esteem involved little product differentiation low price

Consideration of the degree of consumer involvement is important for the Marketing Department since it can, for example, strongly influence the extent and mode of advertising and sales promotion. High involvement products could necessitate personal sales contact and detailed sales literature, whereas low involvement products much the opposite.

Market segmentation

Market segmentation is the provision of goods or services with benefits designed to satisfy the needs of individual groups of consumers (rather than consumers in general), and the packaging, promoting and distributing of these goods or services in most suitable ways to reach these groups of consumers.

This is a common marketing ploy. For example, companies manufacture not just shampoo, but shampoo variants for dry, greasy or normal hair. The Rolls Royce and Mini, though both cars, are clearly aimed at different groups of consumers.

The essence of the policy is to identify in the minds of consumers that the product is different (usually with a brand name) and thus to separate a sub-section of a broad market for which the product has distinct appeal.

Can you think of other examples of market segmentation?

The main bases upon which market segmentation are founded are as follows:

Geographic

In different parts of a country or between countries there may be distinct tastes. For example car manufacturers in the USA market more cars fitted with air conditioning in the warmer Southern States of the USA, but fewer in the cooler North of the continent.

Demographic and social differences

Many products are geared to different groups according to factors like age, sex, class and status, occupation or educational background. In the holiday market, for instance, there has been a growth of organisations like Saga which specialise in holidays for the growing numbers of old people. You might likewise be aware of other companies which offer holidays exclusively for the young, like Club 18–30.

Lifestyles

While some products are aimed at the family lifestyle, e.g. the hatchback car, others might have a more 'jet set' image, e.g. designer clothes or perfume.

It is important for an organisation to identify exactly what market it is aiming at in order to tailor its product and methods of promotion and distribution most appropriately. Furthermore, by considering market segmentation, it might help an organisation to identify gaps in a market and fill them with new products.

Anticipating customer needs – market research

The more an organisation knows about its market, the better is it able to satisfy consumer needs and adapt to change. The fuller appreciation it has of market trends, of the actions and attitudes of buyers, both at the trade level and final consumers, the better equipped it is to operate more efficiently at the present and plan for the future. Market research (or marketing research as it is sometimes known) involves a range of techniques by which fuller appraisal of the market can be gleaned.

Market research can be defined as the collection and analysis of information about a firm's market or potential market in order to determine who buys the firm's products, when, why, and under what circumstances.

The larger the organisation, the more sophisticated and extensive its market research is likely to be. The small shopkeeper cannot afford to employ a market research department or commission a survey by an independent marketing research unit. Yet the small retailer or producer is still likely to undertake simple market research, even if it merely involves predictions on the basis of past trends in sales.

It could be important for an organisation to gather a wide range of information about its market.

- Is product design acceptable to consumers?
- Are prices acceptable?
- Is the distribution network appropriate?
- Could more attractive, different colour packaging induce greater sales?
- Which are the most suitable methods of advertising and sales promotion?

Various methods of gathering this information are open to firms.

Methods of market research

Desk research

This involves the analysis of already existing data. For example, sales figures in the organisation can be investigated and future trends extrapolated. Data on the firm's market share may be studied.

Additional information on the market environment may be found from government statistical publications or forecasts for the economy. *Economic Trends*, for example, provides a wide range of data on the economy, such as changes in consumer expenditure or economic growth. If anticipation of population change is important, the *Annual Abstract of Statistics* or *Population Trends* can be likely sources. Essentially, desk research involves the utilisation of **secondary data**, that which already exists and has not been derived first-hand for use in market research work.

Field research

Field research encompasses the gathering of **primary data** – information gathered fresh for that particular piece of research.

Field research is likely to be more costly than desk research, but has the advantage of providing data directly related to the case in point. There are various techniques which can be used to gather primary data.

Interview

Interviews conducted in the street by telephone or in people's homes help to formulate a picture of consumer attitudes to a product. Equally, if a manufacturer conducts interviews with firms it supplies, information can be gathered about methods of distribution, trade discounts, etc.

Interviewing is a labour-intensive activity, and hence can be costly per subject interviewed. Apt design and comprehensive coverage of questions are vital for the success of such a venture.

Postal questionnaire

Questionnaires can be sent to a selection of people, actual or possible buyers of the product, to gather consumer reaction in a similar way to personal interview. As with some questionnaires used in personal interview, postal questionnaires may well be precoded, having boxes in which the respondent would indicate the answer, e.g.

How much more X would you buy per week if the price were cut by 2p?	0	1	2	3	Over 3

The response to large-scale surveys may be collated by computer.

Postal questionnaires are cheaper per subject investigated than interviews. They are lighter on labour costs, but do incur postal charges. The main drawback with postal questionnaires is lack of response. People often cannot be bothered to complete a form and return it. Inducements, e.g. a voucher for a free or cut-price purchase of the firm's product may help, but interviews are far more likely to provide a full response.

Observation

In some situations, observation can be an appropriate technique. Local authorities sometimes count the volume of traffic to help decisions about road schemes. Important in observation is that the data are recorded uniformly by all researchers. It helps if the subjects are homogeneous, as is traffic in the above example, so avoiding ambiguous classification.

Test panels

Some market research units use test panels of consumers to gauge reaction to new products. For example, a new variety of beer might be tasted by panellists who would be given existing brands of beer to taste as well. Relative preferences could be gauged. Panel reaction to various flavours of crisps has been important in decision making in that industry. Preferences of panel members are thus important in product design. The technique can also be used to measure reaction to colour or type of packaging.

One important form of panel research is that carried out by BARB (the Broadcasters' Audience Research Bureau). Approximately 3000 households have meters fitted to their television sets which record minute-by-minute viewing. The meter readings are combined with information that members of the households provide about their viewing habits, and audience viewing figures are compiled weekly on the basis of the sample.

Such information is important to firms when contemplating advertising on commercial television. It gives a strong indication of the size of the viewing audience at different times each evening, and hence the likely number of people who might watch an advertisement. The data also give a guide to the planners at the BBC about programme popularity.

Sampling

Many of these methods are based on the statistical technique of **sampling**. When a sample is taken only a portion of the people who could be relevant to the survey are investigated. On the basis of the research derived from the sample, estimates of the views or actions of the whole are made. All those relevant to the particular survey are known statistically as the **population**.

It is crucial that the sample selected should portray an accurate representation of the relevant characteristics of the population. Otherwise statistical bias might occur, and estimates of the population might be inaccurate. If an organisation acted upon highly inaccurate market research work, the consequences would be wasteful and costly.

The representative nature of a sample is important, for example, in opinion polls. Such polls are particularly common in periods near a General Election. Newspapers and television commission polls from research organisations like Marplan or the Opinion Research Centre. Generally they choose a sample of only about one or two thousand people, and from the results attempt to estimate the intentions of some 40 million voters. The samples are carefully selected, trying to embrace in correct proportions the pertinent characteristics of the voting population – age, sex, geographical area and previous voting allegiance.

Types of market research

We have discussed methods by which market research might be conducted. Let us now venture more deeply into areas in which such research might be carried out.

Product research

This involves research into the design of the product, the development and testing of new products and improvements in existing ones. Comparative studies can be conducted whereby consumer response is gauged in relation to competitive brands. How does our product fare on design, packaging, quality, style, ease of use or price compared with that of rivals? Answers to such questions are highly important to planning in organisations.

However, the results of such sample research may not always be accurate when a new product is actually marketed. The synthetic, non-tobacco cigarette failed to attract the sales that manufacturers had expected.

More precisely, product research can involve testing prototypes of possible new products. Alternative methods of packaging or colour of the product can be tested. Research can be carried out to estimate the need for sales back-up, e.g. after-sales service, repairs and availability of spare parts. Such after-sales support is especially important in the market for durable consumer goods, e.g. TVs, freezers, washing machines.

Sales research

Research can also be conducted into the selling activities of the company. Statistics internal to the organisation are helpful here, in analysing sales performance in different geographical areas, for example.

Comparisons of the sales performance of the firm can be made in relation to growth or contraction in the industry as a whole and between leading competitors.

If our organisation faces a declining market share, its sales techniques may be at fault. Should alternative means of distribution be considered? The role of the wholesaler in the distribution network of the product could be appraised. Is the training of sales staff effective? Should alternative selling methods be considered? Should minimum order sizes be changed?

Sales research can be conducted not only in the home market but also in overseas markets if the organisation is export-orientated. There are likely to be differences in institutions, sales methods and practice between countries. Japan, for example, has far more links in its wholesale chain than are present in the UK. Awareness of the overseas market environment is vitally important for the successful exporter.

Consumer (or user) research

This involves the investigation of buyer behaviour at both final consumer level and also at trade level. Depending on the products sold by an organisation, user research can be conducted into behaviour in buying capital or consumer goods.

Surveys can be conducted to discover the reasons why consumers buy (or do not buy) particular products. Which factors are especially significant? How important is brand image compared with packaging or price? Are the consumers of a product in a particular income group or of a particular social status?

At the trade level, reliable deliveries and attractive pricing or discounts could be among the major reasons for wholesalers and retailers stocking and selling a product. User research can explore such motivations more deeply.

Once again, distinctions may need to be made between export markets and the home market. Differences in culture, habit and income level need to be investigated in overseas markets to gain a fuller awareness of the psychology of the foreign consumer. A firm can adapt packaging, design, size and price accordingly on the basis of such knowledge.

Promotion research

Organisations need to test and evaluate the effectiveness of various methods of promoting their goods or services. Especially important is mode and area of advertising: which of the media is most effective? Television viewing figures as produced by BARB can influence the timing of TV advertising. The choice of newspapers or magazines in which organisations advertise relates closely to circulation figures, but also to the type of readership the publication commands. If your product, e.g. corn flakes, is aimed at a wide cross-section of consumers, then it would be wise to advertise in popular national newspapers with a large circulation. However, if your product was more specialised, e.g. horse-riding equipment, then a more likely medium would be magazines about equestrianism.

Promotion research is not only confined to the advertising media, but also to other means of bringing the product to the customers' attention. Are exhibitions an effective means? They could be especially important to manufacturers of machinery or motor cars (e.g. the Motor Show).

Should cut-price promotional offers be made? How valuable are trading stamps in attracting customers? In recent years, some large companies have sponsored sporting and cultural events. In cricket, for example, there are the John Player Sunday League and the Cornhill Insurance Test Matches. Marks and Spencer have sponsored some classical music concerts. Evidently these firms regard sponsorship as an effective means of bringing their name to the public eye. Such sponsorship is regarded as especially important by cigarette companies, which are prohibited from advertising on television for health reasons. Furthermore, the costs of sponsorship can be offset against taxation.

Larger organisations are better equipped financially to conduct marketing research of the types discussed. This research is regarded as a very important part of organisational activity and planning. For smaller firms extensive market research is prohibitive on cost grounds. Nevertheless small-scale research is often carried out. Any organisation which fails to consider its position in the market or react to market changes is doomed to stagnation or failure.

Forecasting

Data from market research can assist organisations to plan and forecast the future. Statistical techniques such as moving averages and the derivation of a trend could be used to predict the expected path of sales. Forecasts could be adjusted to incorporate, say, potential increases in sales due to the anticipated success of an advertising campaign. Production planning can thus be undertaken to meet expected sales.

Sales force and sales promotion

To bring the product to the notice of retailers and customers an effective sales force and sales promotion strategy are important.

The role of the sales force staff would be to visit, say, retailers or large industrial buyers, to explain the benefit and potential of the product and thus to drum up orders.

Sales promotion involves bringing the product to the attention of buyers by temporarily offering better value for money. Temporary cut-price offers are a major sales promotion practice, done in the hope that having once been attracted to the product, the consumer will continue to buy it in the future. A visit to a supermarket or shop is likely to illustrate a number of sales promotion offers.

Besides temporary price cuts can you think of other sales promotion tactics?

You will doubtless have come across coupons or vouchers entitling you to discounts on a future purchase of a product. Sometimes such vouchers might be exchanged for cash or for a gift. Alternatively a gift might be directly given on purchase of the product, such as a glass if you buy sufficient petrol. Popular newspapers in recent years have competitively run bingo games as a form of sales promotion to boost circulation.

Advertising

If sales promotion offers a temporary benefit for customers of the product, the role of advertising is to create a more permanent awareness and image for the product in the eyes and mind of the customer.

Advertising is big business. It contributes 1½ per cent of the Gross National Product (GNP) of the UK. Sixty per cent of the revenue of newspapers comes from advertising. Considering individual organisations, the biggest spenders on advertising of all types in 1985 were MFI (£18.75m), followed by National Westminster Bank (£16.37m) and Persil Automatic (£13.69m). Ariel Automatic was the heaviest spender on radio advertising. Figure 32.2 shows an example of National Westminster advertising.

The bulk of advertising expenditure goes on press advertising (63.5 per cent of the total in 1982), with TV advertising accounting for 29.7 per cent. Figure 32.1 shows the sectors of the economy which spend most heavily on advertising.

It is crucial for an organisation to advertise in an appropriate medium. Thus it must have ascertained the major characteristics of its customers in order to judge, for example, in which newspapers to advertise. Here market research will have helped.

It could show into which social grade(s) or socio-economic group(s) buyers of a good or service fall. The classification in Table 32.1 was devised by the Institute of Practitioners in Advertising.

Different newspapers attract different readerships. Clearly the readership of the *Sun* and *The Times* would differ markedly between social grades. Newspapers themselves commission surveys of their readership by social grade, which aid potential advertisers when considering the most appropriate newspaper in which to place their advertising.

Depending on the nature of the product, organisations might consider groups delineated by, e.g. age, sex or ethnic background, and thus choose an appropriate medium for advertising.

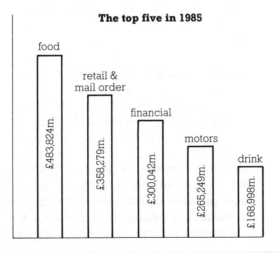

The top five in 1985

food — £483,824m.
retail & mail order — £358,279m.
financial — £300,042m.
motors — £265,249m.
drink — £168,998m.

Fig. 32.1
What advertisers spend their money on
Source: Media Expenditure Analysis Ltd (published in *Today* 2 April 1986)

Table 32.1

Socio-economic group	Social status	Examples by occupation
A	upper middle classs	doctors, solicitors, chartered accountants, bank managers
B	middle class	college lecturers, farmers, middle management
C1	lower middle class	young teachers, Civil Service clerical officers
C2	skilled working class	supervisors, miners, heavy goods vehicle drivers, printing workers.
D	working class	agricultural labourers, shop assistants, unskilled workers
E	those on State subsistence income	unemployed, OAPs

The mode of advertising will reflect the size of the advertising budget of an organisation. A large firm could afford TV or newspaper advertising. A full page advertisement in the *Sunday Times* cost about £26 000 in 1986, for example. However, a small firm may only be able to afford a few lines in the classified advertisements section of a local newspaper, or its advertising may be confined to the printing of handbills that are distributed through local letterboxes. Some organisations may advertise in specialist magazines if they serve a specific market. For example, firms selling golf equipment will advertise in golfing magazines. Larger organisations with a big advertising budget will commission an advertising agency to coin a slogan or create a brand image.

Above all an advertisement must stick in the consumer mind and be identified with the product.

What advertising jingles or images of TV commercials can you recall?

New product development

As tastes and incomes change, as fashion and styles alter, as competitors innovate, so an organisation must consider modifying its product or developing a new one. Even longstanding popular cars like the Volkswagen Beetle or the Mini were phased out and new models introduced in their place.

Developing a new product can be costly. There are research and development costs, and test marketing might be needed to investigate whether the product has a future.

For example, in the late 1970s Van den Burghs introduced Krona margarine to exploit a gap in the market caused by the rising price of butter and to offer a product with the taste and texture of butter. Rather than market the product nationally from the outset, Van den Burghs initially test marketed it in the Harlech and Westward television areas (Wales and the West and South-west of England) using TV advertising. In the first year sales exceeded expectations so that the company subsequently felt confident to market the product throughout the UK.

Compare Krona's experience with the introduction of 'match pots' by

SECOND GENERATION SAVING

ON LINE is the 'Second Generation Saving System', designed to meet the needs of modern, sophisticated young people under the age of 19.

ON LINE helps you to save by giving you interest on your money.

And when you want to spend some of your hard-earned savings, ON LINE gives you a special purchasing facility over a wide range of goods.

These items have been specially selected with you in mind – and range from sports goods to a home computer, from cameras to a personal stereo.

ON LINE SAVING

£5 is enough to open an ON LINE account. Of this, £3 is credited to your account to start you off, and the remaining £2 goes towards your stylish ON LINE wallet.

The wallet contains your slim ON LINE calculator. The memory function stores information even when the unit is switched off, allowing you to recall your current balance at the touch of a key.

Also included in the wallet is a pen, your ON LINE card, which carries your signature and personal Codeholder Number, and a space for your paying-in book (posted separately).

ON LINE savers also receive the Codeholders' Manual and a file for six-monthly account statements issued every July and January.

Interest at the applicable rate and calculated on a daily basis is normally credited to the account in June and December automatically. Rates available in branches.

All ON LINE account holders will regularly receive a glossy ON LINE magazine containing lots of interesting articles, advice on money matters, news and competitions.

ON LINE SPENDING

When you open your ON LINE account, you will receive the exclusive ON LINE Handbook containing details of the specially selected items available to Codeholders.

You can dial a special telephone number and order a particular item using the Codeholder Number from your ON LINE card.

Providing there are sufficient funds in the account, the item will automatically be despatched to you.

RUNNING YOUR ACCOUNT

You can pay into your ON LINE account at any of the 3,200 NatWest branches across the country. Of course, should you wish, you may withdraw cash from your branch and, provided seven day's notice is given, interest will not be lost on the sum withdrawn.

May we remind you that cash credited to your account earns interest from the day it reaches the account. This will generally be three working days later if paid in at a branch other than the account holding branch.

If cheques are paid in, interest starts to accrue on the new balance from the day the cheques are 'cleared'. This too is generally three working days after being paid in.

You can become an ON LINE Codeholder at the stroke of a pen. Simply fill in the form on the reverse of this leaflet and take it to the branch of NatWest where you would like to have the account held.

Fig. 32.2
Source: National Westminster Bank

Crown Paints. Crown did not engage in test marketing because they feared that other companies might copy their idea, and they felt convinced the product would be successful. Match pots were small pots of paint sold cheaply (25p) which a customer could try at home in a restricted area to check colour match. If the customer then decided to purchase a large can of paint, he or she would get 25p back by redeeming the match pot, and would have bought the larger tin knowing that the colour was appropriate. Crown's share of the paint market grew noticeably as a result of the match pot idea.

Has the organisation in which you may work recently launched a new product or service? Why do you think it did so? How successful do you think it will be?

Marketing – a conclusion

The areas of consumer behaviour, market segmentation, market research, sales force and sales promotion, advertising and new product development (along with the previously discussed channels of distribution and pricing) give a flavour of major features of marketing.

Organisations large or small, in the public and the private sectors, should give strong consideration to the effective marketing of their product or service. However, the mode and effectiveness of their marketing strategy will be influenced by marketing costs and the size of the marketing budget. It is beyond the capacity of the small firm to buy advertising slots on ITV at peak viewing time, besides facing the costs of producing an attractive advertisement. Likewise the cost of a full page advertisement in a national newspaper is penal to small organisations. Their marketing strategy is of necessity more low key.

In some industries marketing becomes competitive. For example in the washing powder and detergents areas, almost one-fifth of the price of the product is attributable to advertising and other marketing costs. The need to create a differentiated brand image is regarded as crucial to enhance sales.

Consider the organisation in which you may work, or choose one where you regularly shop. How effective do you think is the marketing approach it adopts?

33 Meeting social needs

Private sector organisations could argue that they meet society's needs in the provision of.a variety of goods and services. In so doing, of course they would expect to earn a profit, their fundamental objective.

There are, too, public sector organisations both at central and local government level which are not profit orientated but aim to meet social needs by making services or goods available to those that require them. For some we pay a price for use, e.g. National Health Service prescriptions, council houses. Others, such as roads and schools, are provided without direct charge. Often, though, we do not pay the full cost of services even when a price is charged; subsidies paid for by taxation help to reduce the price. Similarly, the services that are provided free of charge are financed through taxation or rates paid to local authorities.

What services does the public sector provide for our use? How much is spent on them? Study Table 33.1.

What is the distinction between the categories of public expenditure separated in the table?

Social services and social security

The social services are provided by the community to maintain or improve individual well-being. Their availability enables people to interact to a fuller extent, to achieve a greater awareness of their society, and to have access to accommodation and medical facilities.

The scope of the Welfare State includes social services like:

Table 33.1
UK public expenditure 1986/7 (£bn estimated outturn)

Social services and social security	
Education and science, arts and libraries	16.0
Health and personal social services	18.0
Social security	44.5
Housing and environmental services	
Housing and environment	6.8
Roads and transport	4.9
Protective services	
Defence	18.6
Law and order	5.9
Other	31.2

The National Health Service: Provision of general hospitals and specialised hospitals, e.g. for children or the mentally ill; services of general practitioners; preventative medicine.

Personal social services: Social workers, home help for the disabled and elderly, old people's homes.

Education: Provision of nursery schools (in some areas), primary and secondary schools, colleges, polytechnics and universities.

Social security: Financial payments to attempt to ensure that people do not fall into poverty, e.g.

- Unemployment benefits – payments made to persons registered as unemployed;
- Sickness benefits – payments made to workers while they are absent from work because of illness or injury;
- Retirement pensions – payments made by the State to women over 60 and men over 65 years old who have retired from work;
- Supplementary benefits – payments additional to other benefits which can be made to people in need according to their circumstances;
- Housing benefit – payment by the State of a portion of the local authority rates or rents of needy people.

Note that social security is not a service that people consume. It is a set of financial payments providing income from which people can attempt to fulfil their material needs.

Housing and environmental services
These are services designed to enhance the physical environment in which we live, e.g.

- Council housing (housing built or purchased by local authorities to provide accommodation for local inhabitants, rents being paid to the local authority by the tenants);
- Roads;
- Street lighting;
- Refuse disposal;

- Parks;
- Facilities for recreation.

Payment for many of these services is made indirectly through local authority rates rather than as a market price for their use.

Protective services

Services designed for the provision of law and order and defence against foreign antagonists, through the law courts, police and armed forces.

Other public expenditure

* For a fuller discussion of public expenditure, see Chapter 35, pp. 30–31.

Items of expenditure which are not directly aimed at improving quality of life but are to achieve other targets, e.g. grants to industry and agriculture, payments to the EEC, etc. This expenditure is not primarily set to meet social needs.*

Thus a major proportion of public expenditure is geared to meeting our social, collective needs. In some cases private sector alternatives are available, e.g. health care and education. Private hospitals and schools require payment by consumers for the services they provide and aim to make a profit. They are thus likely to market and advertise their services in a persuasive way to attract users.

Public sector provision of such services involves less of a persuasive marketing push but rather more of informative approach so that people should be aware of facilities available to them.

Do you think people should pay a full cost covering charge for public sector services (as they would if they used private sector alternatives), or do you think such services should be made available without direct charge and be financed through the tax system?

Summary, Part F

1 The term 'market' can refer to:
   a the interaction between buyers and sellers;
   b demand for the product;
   c the market mechanism, which demonstrates the interplay between demand and supply and transmits the effects of changes in those forces.
2 A perfect market is one in which:
   a there is a homogeneous product;
   b there are many buyers and sellers with free entry to the market;
   c there is close contact between buyers and sellers so that perfect knowledge of market conditions exists;
   d there is no consumer loyalty.
3 More common are imperfect markets, where one or more of the conditions of a perfect market do not hold.
4 Markets can be local, national or international, with possible overlaps between each type for some organisations.
5 In commodity markets and the foreign exchange markets, spot prices (the current prices) and forward prices (agreed prices for acquiring the commodity at a future date) are quoted.
6 In some markets, goods or services are consumed without a market price being paid directly, e.g. police, State schooling.
7 Effective marketing enables organisations to tap market potential fully

and meet customer needs. The marketing mix involves consideration of product, place, price and promotion.

8 The price of a product is determined by the forces of demand and supply. Demand is the amount of a product consumers are willing and able to buy at particular prices over a period of time. Supply means the amount of a product that organisations are prepared to put on the market at particular prices over a period of time.

9 Generally, the higher the price of a product, the less consumers will buy. Conversely, the lower the price, the greater will demand be.

10 A demand curve is a visual representation of the relationship between demand and price. Movements along a demand curve are called extensions or contractions of demand.

11 The demand for a product is influenced by the price and conditions of demand. These conditions of demand include income, population size, availability of credit facilities, prices of substitutes and complementary goods, tastes and seasonal factors.

12 Changes in the conditions of demand cause an increase or decrease in demand, leading to a shift in the location of the demand curve.

13 In general, the higher the price of a product, the greater will be the amount supplied. The lower the price, the less will be the supply.

14 A supply curve shows the relationship between supply and price. Movements along the supply curve are called extensions or contractions of supply.

15 Supply is influenced by price and the conditions of supply. The latter include costs and availability of factors of production, technological change, objectives of organisations, price changes by competitors, government activity in a market, weather and seasonal factors.

16 Changes in the conditions of supply cause an increase or decrease in supply, leading to a shift in the location of the supply curve.

17 The equilibrium price is that at which demand and supply are equal: there is neither excess demand nor excess supply.

18 Organisations may expand by merger or takeover. Such integration could be vertical, horizontal or conglomerate. The Monopolies and Mergers Commission investigates monopolies or possible monopolies referred to it by The Director of General Fair Trading

19 Pricing strategies could include pricing at the going rate, penetration pricing and market skimming.

20 Price elasticity of demand is the responsiveness of demand to changes in price. It can be measured by this formula:

$$\text{Price elasticity of demand} = \frac{\% \text{ change in demand}}{\% \text{ change in price}}$$

21 Price elasticity of demand is affected by the degree of necessity for the product, habit, the level of income, the proportion of income spent on the good, the availability of substitutes and the size of the price change.

22 The traditional method of distributing goods to the final consumer involves the manufacturer, wholesaler and retailer. The wholesaler is of especial benefit to small retailers and to manufacturers, by enabling administrative, production and storage costs to be cut.

23 In recent years, a number of large, nationwide retailers have by-passed the wholesaler by buying in bulk direct from manufacturers.

24 Other developments in distribution in recent decades include the growth of supermarkets, hypermarkets, superstores, mail order and franchises.

25 The law of contract underlies many business situations. Most contracts do not have to be in writing. They can be oral or can be implied from conduct.

26 Not all agreements are contracts. There must be an intention to create legal relations.

27 Minors (people under the age of 18) can only make a limited range of contracts.

28 Every contract requires that there be **agreement** (i.e. a firm offer has been unconditionally accepted) and an element of bargain or price (**consideration**).

29 Untrue statements which induce contracts are called *misrepresentations*. They can invalidate a contract.

30 Breach of **condition** (serious breach) entitles the injured party to repudiate and/or sue for damages.

Breach of **warranty** (minor breach) entitles the injured party to sue for damages *only*. The contract still stands.

31 The defendant in a breach of contract action is only liable to pay damages for loss that could reasonably have been expected to happen. **Damages** are the main remedy for breach of contract. Other remedies are **specific performance** and **injunction**.

32 The defendant does not have to compensate the plaintiff if
    a unable to carry out his or her side of the bargain because the contract has been frustrated, or
    b the breach is covered by an exemption clause which is reasonable and unlikely to be overturned by the Unfair Contract Terms Act 1977.

33 The Sale of Goods Act 1979 implies certain promises, e.g. that the goods sold are of merchantable quality, into contracts of sale. Such promises cannot generally be excluded. The shopkeeper's liability is **strict**, i.e. liability without fault, generally speaking.

34 However, the Act has only limited application to private sales.

35 Guarantees which try to exclude the Sale of Goods Act 1979 are ineffective.

36 The Consumer Credit Act is a very complicated piece of legislation and although it was passed in 1974, not all its provisions are yet in force. However one of its main aims was to establish 'truth in lending' so that people who buy on credit know exactly what they are getting. The Act ensures:
    a licensing procedures,
    b that the debtor knows the true rate of interest,
    c that faulty goods can be returned,
    d that even if the debtor fails to keep up with the instalments the owner cannot summarily take back the goods,
    e that the debtor has a right of cancellation.

37 Negligence is a tort which underlies the manufacturer–consumer relationship by making the manufacturer liable to the consumer if negligently causing injury or loss.

38 The three essential elements of negligence, originally laid down in Donoghue *v.* Stevenson are:

    a Duty of Care (owed to the 'neighbour'),

    b breach of the Duty of Care,

    c damage resulting from the breach.

39 There can now be liability, in certain circumstances, for financial loss resulting from negligent advice.

40 The Consumer Protection Bill will introduce the notion of Product Liability to English law in order to implement an EEC Directive.

41 Whether a product involves high or low consumer involvement can influence the extent and mode of advertising and sales promotion.

42 Market segmentation is the provision of goods or services for certain groups of consumers. Markets may be segmented according to geography, demography and social differences or lifestyles.

43 Market research is important to give an organisation fuller insight into the nature and composition of its market. This better enables the organisation to adapt and respond to market conditions. Main methods involved are desk and field research.

44 Market research can be conducted in a number of areas. These are:

    a product research, which involves research into product design, development, testing and improvement;

    b sales research, by which analysis of the selling activities of an organisation is carried out;

    c consumer (or user) research, i.e. research into buyer behaviour;

    d promotion research, involving the evaluation of sales promotion methods.

45 Suitable sales force staff and sales promotion techniques could be needed to boost sales.

46 Consideration of the mode of advertising could involve analysis by socio-economic group, as reflected in newspaper readership.

47 To accommodate changes in patterns of consumer purchase new product development is important.

48 The State provides social, environmental and protective services to meet social, collective needs.

Assignments, Part F

1

Chocopac plc

You are a trainee in the Marketing Department of Chocopac plc, a confectionery manufacturer. You are asked to advise on the marketing strategy for a new chocolate bar.

Decide on the type of chocolate bar to be produced, perhaps seeking a gap in the market. Determine the market research methods you would use, considering test marketing if appropriate. Decide on a name for the chocolate bar and design suitable packaging. Consider advertising and sales promotion methods.

Bearing in mind the nature of the product you have selected and the competition in the market, suggest a suitable price for the chocolate bar, justifying your decision.

Skills

Learning and studying, communicating, information gathering, design and visual discrimination, identifying and tackling problems.

2

Advertising and sales promotion

You are an assistant in the Marketing Department of the organisation in which you work. A new Marketing Manager has been appointed and asks for information on, and an appraisal of, existing advertising and sales promotion methods. The Marketing Manager wants to be informed as to current approaches and to get some ideas for change. Your comments should be in the form of a brief report.

a You should highlight the methods of advertising and sales promotion used by your organisation.

b You should give a brief survey of the law which might be relevant to your advertising and sales.

c You should collect advertising and promotion literature your organisation publishes and any advertisements it places in newspapers and magazines. Explain why the organisation selects those particular newspapers, journals or magazines as a medium for advertising.

d You should evaluate the effectiveness of the organisation's advertising and sales promotion.

e Can you think of any improvements in existing techniques or any alternative forms of advertising and promotion that the organisation might adopt?

Skills

Identifying and tackling problems, information gathering, design and visual discrimination, communicating

3

A.L. Things

a You are a management trainee at A.L. Things. Some self-assembly book cases have been bought from a manufacturer at £12 each. Advise the Purchasing Manager on the factors which should be taken into account in setting the retail price.

b As part of your training you are posted to the Customer Relations section. In your in-tray you find the following letter. Reply in the appropriate tone and language, explaining the legal position.

Dear Sir,

I recently purchased a self-assembly bookcase from your firm. When I got home I found that a piece of board and some screws were missing. I immediately took the kit back to my local branch of A.L. Things and asked for a refund. The salesman refused and would only give me a credit note. He said that even that was generous and the shop really had no responsibility at all for the bookcase since it was manufactured in Taiwan.

This is a very unsatisfactory position. I am sure that legally I am entitled to a refund and I expect to hear from you in the very near future.

Yours faithfully,

J Brown

---

c Later in the day an irate customer storms up to you, furious because a bookcase in the showroom had been mistakenly priced at £5 and the assistant had refused to sell it at that price because the correct price was £25. The customer is insisting that he or she should be able to buy at the stated price. In a role-play exercise with a fellow student, deal with this complaint, explaining the legal position and endeavouring to calm the angry customer.

Skills
Communication, working with others, identifying and tackling problems, information gathering

4 New organisations

Compile a list of new organisations which have been established in your locality in recent months.
a Classify them according to the nature of their activity, e.g. manufacturer, retailer, government department, etc. If there are new retailers, are they small independent shops, multiple stores, supermarkets, hypermarkets, superstores, etc?
b Visit at least 4 of the new organisations which produce or sell goods. By discussing with staff, discover the distribution network in which each organisation is involved. For example, if the organisation is a manufacturer, are goods sold directly to retailers or through wholesalers, or both?
   In a retail organisation enquire whether goods are bought directly from manufacturers or from wholesalers.
c How appropriate do you think the distribution system is in each case?

Skills
Learning and studying, information gathering, identifying and tackling problems

PART G

NATIONAL FACTORS

When you have read this part you should be able to
• Understand the nature, causes of and influences on inflation, economic growth, balance of payments problems and unemployment.
• Appreciate the formulation and implementation of government policies.
• Describe major economic policy approaches and appraise their effects and effectiveness.

34 The social context

In this part we shall be looking at the organisation in its national context and then in Part H we shall look at the international factors which have an impact on the organisation. We have seen earlier how political, legal and economic changes affect organisations. Bound up with these are the social factors which have an impact either directly or indirectly on organisations and individuals. Changes in society – for example the changing role of women – can result in changes in government policy and thus lead to legislation.

It may be useful to take two examples of social agencies set up by legislation and to assess their impact. Let us look at the Equal Opportunities Commission and the Commission for Racial Equality.

The Equal Opportunities Commission, set up in 1975 by the Sex Discrimination Act, is a quango with the general aim of promoting equality of opportunity and ending discrimination. The EOC is able in some cases to help individuals bring cases under the Sex Discrimination and Equal Pay Acts; to issue non-discrimination notices against employers or other organisations who continue to discriminate unlawfully; to organise or finance education or research projects; to keep under review the protective legislation; to make investigations into, for example, a particular company or industry or area of government policy where discrimination is suspected.

Some would argue that the EOC has been more effective in its educative and promotional role rather than in its law enforcement role, either in supporting claimants (details of cases are given in the EOC's Annual Reports) or conducting formal investigations of unlawful practices. The EOC's record of success in the latter role is not encouraging.

However this may be partly because it has been hamstrung by the limited scope of the legislation. You will have read about this earlier in the book in the section on employment. The Equal Pay Act, for example, only allowed women to claim equal pay in situations where their job was directly comparable with that of a male colleague.

The more recent (1984) Regulations on Equal Pay may be more successful in achieving equal pay in the work-place. These regulations were forced on the government by the EEC which argued that the existing law did not fully comply with the provisions of Article 119 of the Treaty of Rome on equality of treatment. They strengthen the law by allowing women in solely or mainly female work to claim equal pay with men in different but equally responsible jobs. In the past when women had to compare themselves with men doing the same jobs, the situation was very difficult for women doing traditionally 'female' work such as typing or cooking.

A case based on these regulations which went to the Court of Appeal is that of Mrs Julie Hayward who won her initial tribunal case, claiming that her job as a cook was equivalent to that of higher paid male workers at the Cammell Laird shipyard where she worked. But she lost her case in the High Court on a technical argument that, while her basic pay was significantly lower, she got better sick pay and a daily free meal. She again lost on appeal to the Court of Appeal. This new law and the work of the EOC obviously have an impact on the organisation since they must revise recruitment policies and job structures and, as far as the Equal Pay Regulations are concerned, employers can no longer avoid the equal pay legislation by recategorising jobs or employing a largely female workforce as cheap labour. This may of course have a back-lash effect by employers cutting down on the number of women employed.

It is easy to draw an analogy between the *Commission for Racial Equality* and the Equal Opportunities Commission. The Race Relations Act 1976 which set up the Commission is almost identical to the Sex Discrimination Act in its scheme and remedies. Like the EOC, the CRE has arguably had more success in its educative rather than in its law enforcement role. The legislation on sex and racial discrimination has also had limited effect in changing attitudes and indeed is a prime example of the inability of law to change people's attitudes and perceptions.

It is also clear that, in a period of economic decline, women and racial minorities can become the first victims of unemployment. The 80s have seen racially motivated violence in London and other major cities like Bristol and Birmingham where there are concentrations of ethnic minorities. Legislation can be ineffective in the face of hard economic realities.

Social costs

We analysed the cost structure of organisations in Chapter 25. Clearly, to organisations, the costs they incur in production are the money amounts they must pay to acquire the resources needed. Such costs to the organisation are sometimes called *private costs*.

However, there might be costs that derive from the activities of an organisation which it does not bear itself. These costs might not be easily measurable, but they nevertheless exist. For example, if you live near an airport, aircraft noise can be disturbing. That is a cost that you bear. The airport authority is unlikely to compensate you for the inconvenience. Likewise, if a river is polluted by industrial effluent from a factory, the pleasure for users of the river is diminished, but the organisation need bear no cost provided that the level of pollution is inside any legal requirements.

Such costs faced by others as a result of an organisation's activities are called **social costs**.

However, if a government believes that social costs are unfairly borne by those who suffer them, it could introduce legislation to remove the source of the problem or to compensate those that suffer. Sometimes a government might be influenced by a campaign mounted by pressure groups.

Pressure groups like Greenpeace, for example, have been urging the UK and indeed governments throughout the world to change their policies on the pollution of the sea and rivers. So far the UK has been slow to respond to surveys done by Greenpeace and another organisation, headed by Dr David Bellamy, called The Marine Conservation Society. These pressure groups point out that in 1976 the EEC issued a bathing water Directive which ordered member countries to designate widely used bathing sites, to monitor them and to clean up those sites which did not meet health standards. The UK was slow to designate sites and even slower to take effective action to clean them up. It is estimated that the cost of cleaning up Blackpool Beach and the sea area would be £25m. The economic cost is great but the social cost in terms of damage to health is greater and, of course, as the insanitary nature of Britain's beaches becomes more widely publicised through the activities of pressure groups, there will be a considerable economic cost because of the loss of revenue generated by tourism.

The UK government has also been slow to act on the damage done by petrol fumes. Leadfree petrol is more expensive but the damage done to the environment and to children from the lead in petrol fumes is conclusively proven. The UK government has been slow to react to an EEC Directive on exhaust emissions. However by 1988 the use of leadfree petrol should be compulsory if this Directive is implemented.

International disasters, particularly the Chernobyl nuclear disaster and the major pollution of the Rhine by chemicals in 1986 which has undone 10 years of effort to clean up the river, have concentrated the minds of ordinary people on the horrors of pollution. It is expensive to introduce new manufacturing procedures to prevent pollution but it may be even more expensive in terms of social cost and the damage to non-renewable natural resources not to act.

Cost-benefit analysis

Bearing in mind the existence of social costs as well as the more obvious private costs, government bodies sometimes carry out a cost-benefit analysis of a project to gain a wider view of costs and gains to society.

For example in the early 1980s the Greater London Council, which then controlled London Transport, operated a policy of lower fares on buses and the Underground. The fare subsidy was financed by higher rates paid by London residents and businesses. The prime aims of the policy were to reduce road congestion by increasing the use of public transport and to make cheaper public transport more widely available to all.

This involved a reduction in the social costs of traffic congestion (e.g. time lost in traffic jams, frustration), and led to greater social benefit. In addition lower income groups had greater opportunity to travel on the cheaper buses and Underground links. The Greater London Council evidently believed that the extra social benefit and reduction in social costs outweighed the greater financial loss that London Transport faced due to less fare revenue. This deficit, of course, was met by higher rates for London residents.

Do you think the benefits of such a policy are greater than the costs? Consider the effects of subsidised public transport in the area which you live.

Social accounting

National Income statistics measure the total value of output, income and expenditure in the economy each year (see pp. 343–351 for fuller explanation). Thus if more is produced, earned and spent, National Income will increase. Seemingly, therefore, our standard of living will increase. But will it necessarily?

As more people have smoked this century the National Income has risen with the growth of the tobacco industry. However, more people have also contracted lung cancer as a result of smoking. This means more expenditure has been carried out on research and training of doctors who specialise in the treatment of this illness. Such expenditure, income and output in the National Health Service pushes up National Income even further. Does this mean the nation is much better off?

The growth of the motor industry and the greater demand for cars has also boosted National Income. In their wake, though, we have more traffic jams, exhaust fumes and frustrated drivers.

There may be disadvantages to some of the extra output which our technologically advanced society has brought. As far as National Income statistics go, there is no discrimination between extra output which might be regarded as 'good' and that which is 'bad' and less beneficial to society. This is an important point if we treat changes in National Income as an accurate indicator of living standards.

The concept of social accounting involves the subtraction of the social costs of extra output from the National Income statistics (and possibly adding in the value of any social benefits that may accrue). The precise valuation of social costs is not always easy (for example, how much is the cost of traffic delay?). However, attempts by economists to engage in social accounting are aimed at getting a truer valuation of the social worth of the output the economy produces.

J.K. Galbraith's *Affluent Society* (Penguin) and E.J. Mishan's *The Costs of Economic Growth* (Staples Press) develop this theme more fully. Refer to them if you are interested.

35 Government

In looking at the impact of government policy on the economy we shall be looking at a relatively recent development. In the nineteenth century the sphere of the government was much more limited than it is today. It was the growth of industry in the early nineteenth century, with the resultant growth in towns and the movement away from the countryside, which contributed to the kind of government we know today and the division of power between central and local government with which we are familiar.

Let us first look at what we mean by **government**. It is a difficult word to define because it means different things in different contexts. However, when we speak of 'the Government' we generally mean the **Executive**, i.e. the body which formulates and carries out policy. That is different from the law-making body – the **Legislature** – which makes law (though there are circumstances in which the government makes law under powers given by Parliament. This, you will remember, is called *delegated legislation*).

In the UK the Executive means basically the Prime Minister and the other Ministers, government Departments and the Civil Servants who work in them, and the Armed Forces. We have already outlined at the beginning of the book the nature of government as an organisation. We shall now look more specifically at how a government is formed and at how central government is made accountable.

The formation of the government

After a General Election a government is formed by the political party which commands a majority of votes in the House of Commons. This normally means that the party which wins most seats forms the government, but where no single party has an overall majority it is theoretically possible for a coalition of parties to form the government. At the time of writing the present Conservative Government has a large majority in Parliament. By convention (i.e. accepted constitutional practice) the Prime Minister and the other Ministers will all be Members of Parliament. The Prime Minister is always a member of the House of Commons; a few of the other Ministers may sit in the House of Lords.

The Cabinet, i.e. the group made up of the Prime Minister and senior Ministers, is involved both in the law-making process and in making and carrying out policy. The Cabinet is *in* Parliament (the chief law-making body) and answerable to it (e.g. at Question Time). This practice is different from that of many other countries. In the USA, for example, the President may choose his advisers from anywhere he pleases. They do not have to be members of Congress. They may be people like prominent bankers who have no previous experience of government.

Government policy

A government will be elected on the basis of its policies and ideas. These will be set out in the manifesto of the party. Many people will never read the manifesto, but through the press, radio and television they will have a general idea of the party's policies. A party that is elected and forms a government will try to translate many of those policies into action. This will often mean the introduction of legislation. For example a Labour Government might be elected on a programme of nationalisation. Thus its policy would be to nationalise several important industries. This would be done by passing an Act of Parliament, a piece of legislation. You may remember (see Chapter 2) that an Act starts its parliamentary life as a Bill, which is a legislative proposal frequently formulated by a Cabinet Committee.

Influences on government policy

There are many influences at work on the formulation of government policy. We mentioned, for example, the activities of pressure groups in Chapter 34, and we shall refer to them again later. They are a very important influence on the formation of policy. Leading pressure groups like the TUC will usually be consulted by the government about proposed legislation which will directly affect them. Pressure groups can also influence public opinion to put pressure on the government to change or amend the law. Publicity about battered children, for example, might lead the NSPCC to pressure the government for a change in the law about parental rights over children or the activities of social workers.

Public opinion, of course, must always have considerable influence on the formation and implementation of policy. The general public may turn against a government which fails to carry out a large number of its election promises and at a General Election may vote that party out of office. Any democratic government rules by consensus and therefore must keep its finger on the pulse of the electorate, the people who are entitled to vote at a parliamentary election.

Public opinion polls, reports in the press and on radio and television, the views of constituents channelled through Members of Parliament, and the results of by-elections are some of the indicators of the electorate's views and are ignored at the government's peril.

Translation of government policy into law

As we said earlier much government policy will become law. A legislative proposal – a Bill – will be introduced usually in the House of Commons by a Minister. We mentioned the legislative process, and you will remember that a Bill will be debated in the House of Commons and in the House of Lords. We must note that the House of Lords is not an elected body but is composed of hereditary peers, life peers, bishops and archbishops of the Church of England, and senior judges. It can only delay the passing of legislation (up to a year for an ordinary Bill but only one month for a money Bill, which is one certified by the Speaker of the House of Commons as containing only financial clauses). The House of Lords has no power of veto.

When the Bill has passed through both Houses it automatically receives the Royal Assent. This is no longer given by the Monarch herself but by a Committee on her behalf. The Queen is a constitutional monarch, which means that power is exercised on her behalf by her Ministers. She takes no active part, generally speaking, in the running of the country. Her role is a formal one. When we talk about 'the Crown' we usually mean the Government, not the person of the Monarch. When the Queen opens Parliament every year, the 'Queen's Speech' which she reads is not in fact her speech at all but the Prime Minister's speech, setting out government policy and the legislative programme for the forthcoming year.

Government influence on the legislative process

You may wonder how the government can be sure that its proposals will successfully pass through the House of Commons. The answer is, of course, that it will command a majority of votes in the House of Commons and can thus be confident that its proposals will be passed. Members are reluctant to vote against their party. If they do so they may find their political careers damaged. If the worst happens and the government is defeated on an important issue, then, by convention, the Prime Minister resigns and a General Election is called. In an election MPs might lose their seats and thus be out of a job. Party discipline may be enforced by the Whips – senior members of a party whose job it is to ensure that members are aware of the importance of certain Bills, will attend the Parliamentary sitting and, above all, will vote the right way.

Swings in policy – the nature of the British Constitution

We mentioned earlier that the current two main parties, Labour and Conservative, are traditionally associated with certain kinds of economic policy. To take an example, the Labour Party is associated with a policy of nationalisation and the Conservative party with 'privatisation', i.e. selling off publicly owned enterprises to the private sector. Such policies, as we have seen, may well be made law in Acts of Parliament.

But any Act of Parliament can be repealed, i.e. set aside by a subsequent Act of Parliament. The reason for this lies in the nature of the British Constitution. Our Constitution is said to be 'unwritten'. This means that the rules relating to the organisation of the government, the Constitution, are not contained in one written document, but are largely derived from a mixture of Acts of Parliament and conventions (accepted customary practice). There are no 'entrenched provisions' in the British Constitution, which means that there is no rule that certain laws about economic policy can only be repealed in a special way, e.g. by a two-thirds majority of Members of Parliament voting. Indeed, there are no entrenched rules in the Constitution itself. This is unusual. Most States have written constitutions with especially important provisions entrenched in them. However, as far as the British Constitution is concerned as long as an Act of Parliament is properly passed it is valid. A repealing Act of Parliament can thus reverse completely the economic policy laws of a previous government. Given that the maximum life of any government in our system is 5 years this means that there can be major swings in economic policy. Long-term economic planning can thus be very difficult.

Additional reading

In your library find a book on British Constitutional History and find out the origins of 'Cabinet' government and the 'Whips' system. Look up the theory of the Separation of Powers and compare our system of government with that of the USA.

Implementation of government policy

We have seen that government policy is usually translated into legislation and that the Queen's Speech read at the Opening of Parliament is, in effect, a programme for legislation reflecting the policy of the current government which in its turn has been influenced by public opinion, by national and economic factors and by its ideological base as stated in the Party Manifesto. But we have to realise that legislation does not carry out itself – it has to be understood and implemented. An Act of Parliament may look very far-reaching on the Statute book but it will only succeed if it is enforced.

We mentioned in Chapter 34 in the section on the Equal Opportunities Commission how difficult it is for legislation which makes changes in social policy, for example, to work, if it restrictively interpreted by judges and if the organisations set up to monitor and enforce the legislation, in this case the EOC, are not given adequate powers or funding. The EOC is an example of a quango (a quasi-governmental body) set up to implement government policy. The Office of Fair Trading, the Monopolies and Mergers Commission and the Manpower Services Commission are other examples.

The MSC (Manpower Services Commission) was set up to implement government policy on employment and training. You are probably all familiar with the YOPS (Youth Opportunity Programme) and the YTS (Youth Training Scheme) which succeeded it. These and many other schemes have been the MSC's contribution to tackling unemployment. Following the publication of a White Paper called 'Training for Jobs' the MSC has now become a very important element in the funding of work-related education and training, thus eroding the power of local education authorities. The MSC has now an exclusively training role and will no longer have any connection with the Job Centres.

What all quangos have in common is that each was set up to take a specific governmental function away from the direct control of a Minister and his other department. The Minister is therefore not answerable to Parliament for the day-to-day activities of the quango. In one sense, therefore, quangos 'get things done', allowing government departments to look at broader issues of policy. They are not subject to political interference. In another sense they are dangerous because they are not accountable to Parliament and are thus outside direct democratic control.

Public expenditure

As described previously, the public sector includes the central government, the local authorities and the nationalised industries. The public sector was responsible for just under a half of the total expenditure in the UK in recent years.

Major forms of public expenditure

1 **Current expenditure** – covering variable costs, e.g. wages, stationery, heating.

2 **Capital expenditure** – the acquisition of fixed capital assets like buildings and roads.

3 **Transfer payments** – from the revenues it receives, the government will reallocate (transfer) money, e.g. to retirement pensioners, to the unemployed, for student grants and as interest to holders of government securities.

4 **Grants or subsidies to industry** – this category includes regional development grants and employment subsidies.

To illustrate, Fig. 35.1 includes these types of public expenditure but is categorised according to major programmes. These plans (and the corresponding intentions for raising revenue) were laid at the time of the March 1986 Budget. Consider the table, noting which sectors command most public sector resources.

By far the most public expenditure is made by central government. Of the planned total, 73 per cent was central government expenditure, 25 per cent by local authorities whilst the remainder included borrowing by the nationalised industries.

Government revenue

Figure 35.1 gives details of planned income for 1986/87. The bulk of central government revenue comes from various forms of taxation and national

Fig. 35.1
Public Money, 1986–7
Source: *Economic Progress Report*
Supplement
March–April 1986

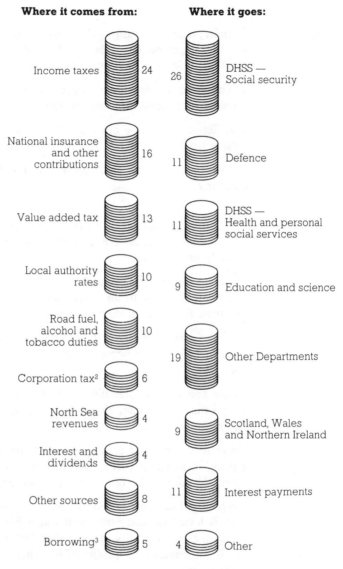

Pence in every pound[1]

Where it comes from: **Where it goes:**

Income taxes — 24	26 — DHSS — Social security
National insurance and other contributions — 16	11 — Defence
Value added tax — 13	11 — DHSS — Health and personal social services
Local authority rates — 10	9 — Education and science
Road fuel, alcohol and tobacco duties — 10	19 — Other Departments
Corporation tax[2] — 6	
North Sea revenues — 4	9 — Scotland, Wales and Northern Ireland
Interest and dividends — 4	
Other sources — 8	11 — Interest payments
Borrowing[3] — 5	4 — Other

Cash totals of revenue and expenditure £163 billion

[1] Rounded to the nearest penny
[2] Excluding North Sea
[3] By central and local government

Source: *Derived from Financial Statement and Budget Report 1986-87*, table 1.2.

insurance contributions. You will also note the significance of local authority rates, and the last item shows the extent of State sector borrowing, known as Public Sector Borrowing Requirement (PSBR). In this chapter we will consider all these sources of income, beginning with taxation.

Taxation

All modern governments require money, if they are to operate in any meaningful way. The normal way to obtain such finance is to force the members

of society to contribute towards governmental funds. These contribution
are called **taxes**.

The purpose of taxation

Initially, taxes were imposed to finance the defence of the nation and to pay
for the maintenance of law and order. In this century the reasons for
taxation, however, have increased to include:

1 The need to provide a source of revenue for the government to go
towards its expenditure requirements.

2 A desire to create a more equitable society by redistributing income and
wealth from the richer to the poorer members of society.

3 The use of taxes as a means of regulating the performance of the
economy.

Types of tax

Taxes may be differentiated into a number of different classifications:
Taxes on income These are referred to as **direct taxes** because they are levied
directly on income.

Taxes on spending These are referred to as **indirect taxes** because they de
not relate directly to an individual's income and are paid as part of the
payment for a commodity or permit.

National insurance contributions Although not strictly regarded as a tax we
have included them because they form a part of the government's compul
sory levy.

Taxes can also be classified in terms of those that are levied as a fixed
proportion of income, those that take account of the ability to pay, and
those that do not.

Progressive taxes The principle underlying this type of tax is simply that o
equity, or in other words, after taking account of allowances, the more one
earns the higher the rate of tax paid on additional income.

Proportional taxes are levied as a fixed proportion. For example, Corporation
Tax is levied on company profits at a fixed proportion of 35 per cent for
companies with profits of over £100 000 per annum (in 1987), though for
small companies with profits of less than £100 000, there is a lower rate c
27 per cent.

Regressive taxes are so termed because they are levied without consideration
for an individual's ability to pay, e.g. excise duties, VAT. This means that
a larger proportion of income goes in tax at lower than at higher incomes

Figure 35.2 details the majority of taxes levied in the UK, and Fig. 35.
shows their relationship to income earned. All the direct progressive taxe
are set according to a progressive scale; thus the more one earns the greate
the rate of tax taken at source by the Inland Revenue. The great advantage
of this type of tax is that they are considered to be **equitable** in the sens
that the heaviest burden falls on those most able to pay.

It is argued, however, that since they fall most heavily on the last unit
of income earned (the **marginal income**) they act as a disincentive to enter

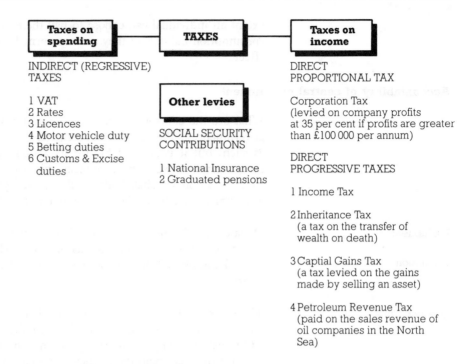

Fig. 35.2
Taxes and other levies in the UK

| Taxes on spending | TAXES | Taxes on income |

INDIRECT (REGRESSIVE)
TAXES

1 VAT
2 Rates
3 Licences
4 Motor vehicle duty
5 Betting duties
6 Customs & Excise
   duties

Other levies

SOCIAL SECURITY
CONTRIBUTIONS

1 National Insurance
2 Graduated pensions

DIRECT
PROPORTIONAL TAX

Corporation Tax
(levied on company profits
at 35 per cent if profits are greater
than £100 000 per annum)

DIRECT
PROGRESSIVE TAXES

1 Income Tax

2 Inheritance Tax
  (a tax on the transfer of
  wealth on death)

3 Captial Gains Tax
  (a tax levied on the gains
  made by selling an asset)

4 Petroleum Revenue Tax
  (paid on the sales revenue of
  oil companies in the North
  Sea)

prise. Thus, individuals may decline to increase their current earnings if the result would be to take them into a higher tax bracket.

The regressive indirect taxes, on the other hand, are levied on expenditure and therefore take no account of the consumer's level of disposable income. If one takes Vehicle Licence Duty as an example, the rate of £100 per annum (1987) obviously represents a much heavier burden to a person earning £10 000 a year than it does to somebody earning £25 000. Similarly, local rates are a far more significant item to low income earners than they are to their wealthier neighbours. Indirect taxes are also criticised for being inflationary when raised, although they do have the advantage that to some

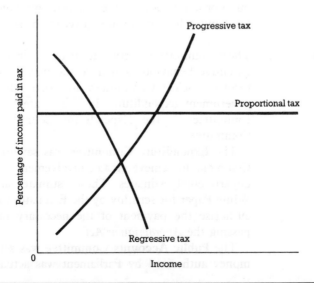

Fig. 35.3
The relationship between tax levy and income

extent an individual can choose to pay them or not by reducing or altering consumption habits and they are not normally linked with any disincentive effect.

Accountability of central government

What are the controls, if any, over central government? In a sense central government, as the ultimate authority in the State, is not subject to control as such, but it is accountable for its actions. In a democratic State when the government rules by consensus this accountability is very important. In this section we shall look briefly at examples of ways in which central government can be made to account for its actions.

Parliament

Discussion

Debates can be held on topics chosen by the Opposition, on reports of Select Committees and on motions put to the House. The legislative process – the Readings of Bills in both Houses – is of course one of review and debate.

Question Time

Time is set aside every week for members to put questions to Ministers. Notice of a question must be given to the Minister concerned, but an additional or 'supplementary' question can be asked without notice. In practice the vast majority of questions look for an oral answer – they have much better news value – but if the amount of parliamentary time reserved for such questions has run out the Member will have to be content with a written answer. The value of Question Time, as with the debating process, is that it turns a searchlight on the activities of Ministers and Government Departments. A great deal of publicity will be given to Question Time, and Ministers' answers are widely reported. It is of course possible for Ministers to give evasive replies 'in the interests of national security', but it is obviously inadvisable for a Minister to adopt this approach too often. Members of Parliament whose party is in power may not wish to risk embarrassing a Minister by putting a sensitive question and the Opposition may lack the necessary information to ask embarrassing questions; but despite these constraints Question Time can be a valuable mechanism for making the government account for its actions.

Parliamentary Select Committees

These committees carry out in depth investigation into the key areas of executive behaviour and have the power to call for 'persons, papers and records'. Select Committees are particularly important in the review of government expenditure. In this context, there are two very important committees – the Expenditure Committee and the Public Accounts Committee.

The **Expenditure Committee** was set up in 1971 to help the House of Commons to achieve greater involvement in the preparation and review of departmental estimates. These estimates are presented in the form of a White Paper for scrutiny by the Estimates Committee. Parliament will then authorise the payment of the necessary money for the departments by passing the *Appropriation Act*.

The **Public Accounts Committee** was set up in 1861 to ensure that the money authorised by Parliament was actually spent in the way that was intended. Its investigations are based on the annual reports of the Comptroller and Auditor General, whose office audits the various departments' accounts.

The Parliamentary Commissioner of Administration (PCA) – the ombudsman

In 1967 the office of the Parliamentary Commissioner for Administration was set up. The idea for this champion against bureaucracy was borrowed from Swedish legislation, and so the Parliamentary Commissioner is often called by the Swedish name of **ombudsman**. The aim of the first ombudsman was to make civil servants accountable for their actions. Although having no power to punish civil servants found guilty of some malpractice or mismanagement (e.g. failure to pay a war pension to someone who was entitled to receive one), the ombudsman does have the power to reopen questions and to give civil servants unwelcome publicity. However, complaints must be referred to the ombudsman through a Member of Parliament. Many would argue that this is a limiting device which should be abolished.

Originally there was only one ombudsman concerned with complaints against civil servants, but now there are additional ombudsmen for the National Health Service and for local government. There is, as yet, no ombudsman for the police. Complaints against the police are dealt with at the moment by a special division of the police force, though there are proposals to change this.

Annual Reports are published, giving an account of complaints investigated. These reports receive considerable publicity and this is the ombudsmen's main weapon. They cannot punish maladministration but they can give unwelcome publicity to institutions and officials.

It is interesting to note that the insurance world has borrowed the ombudsman idea and in 1981 set up the Insurance Ombudsman Bureau (financed initially by 3 major insurance companies) to deal as an independent body with complaints and grievances.

The 'big four' banks have followed suit and there is now a Banking Ombudsman.

Judicial review of government action

Delegated legislation

While Parliament is the chief law-maker in the UK we have seen (Chapter 2) that Parliament can delegate or pass on its law-making powers to other bodies. As long as those bodies legislate within the powers handed on by Parliament their legislation is valid. If the 'subordinate' body exceeds its powers (acts *ultra vires*) the delegated legislation can be set aside by the courts. A great deal of delegated legislation is made by the government itself, frequently in the form of Statutory Instruments. If this legislation is made *ultra vires* it can be set aside by the courts – if a complaint is brought by an individual. If the matter is not brought to the courts' attention it will remain in force. Parliament may grant so wide a power that it is virtually unreviewable by the courts – for example the Home Secretary's power to exclude undesirable people (e.g. members of a fanatic religious sect or terrorist organisation) from the country in the interests of national security and public policy.

Administrative action

There are other grounds on which the courts may review government actions apart from legislation, if asked to do so by a member of the public.

The courts may quash the decision of a government body on the grounds that it was taken unfairly – for example, if a Minister in conducting a Public Inquiry before making a major planning decision like opening up a coal mine in an area of great natural beauty has not consulted all the interested parties or paid heed to all the evidence. We must remember that the courts will not intervene on their own initiative. They can only question government action if called upon to do so.

Civil liability of the government

An historical oddity which remains in the English legal system is that the Monarch is still personally above the law in the sense that he or she can neither be sued nor prosecuted for any offence. However, since the Crown Proceedings Act 1947 the Crown, i.e. the government, can be sued like any private citizen for breach of contract and tort. If a government department orders 300 typewriters from a supplier and then refuses to pay for them, the supplier can sue for breach of contract. The government as employer will frequently be vicariously liable for the torts and, in some cases, for the crimes of its employees. Government departments can be sued for negligence, nuisance and a host of other torts. There are certain situations in which a government body, acting under statutory authority, might not be liable, but this would be the exception rather than the rule.

Local government organisation

Local councils are made up, like the central government, of elected representatives who decide the policy of their local area. Local council elections take place every 4 years separately from General Elections, and the council is normally led by the political party with the largest number of members or by a coallition of parties. The day-to-day administration is undertaken by employees of the council. Perhaps you will remember that we described the nature of local authority organisations in Chapter 11, where we noted their nature and functions as principally set out in the Local Government Acts of 1972 and 1985.

Councils are generally responsible for running local public services such as housing provision, social services, libraries, rubbish disposal and have planning duties as well as providing local education authorities. Do you recall that some of these services have been subject to tenders from private providers, as part of the privatisation policy of the Secretrary of State for the Environment?

Responsibilities vary between different councils, so that in London the police are controlled by the Metropolitan Police Authority while in other areas control is through Police Watch Committees (although ultimate responsibility for the police rests with the Home Secretary). It is important to appreciate that local authorities, although independently elected, do have to work within a framework set by central government, and this limits their power as you will have noticed in our discussion on the control on expenditure and rate collection.

Legal control over local government activities

You will remember from Chapter 2 that these local authorities we have just mentioned have the power to make law. Power to make this law is given or **delegated** by Parliament in an Act of Parliament – hence the name

Delegated legislation

'delegated legislation'. A local authority must, however, legislate within the powers given by Parliament. If it exceeds these powers, i.e. acts *ultra vires* (beyond the powers), that delegated legislation, which often takes the form of a by-law, can be set aside by the courts as being invalid. This happened to delegated legislation made by the then GLC in 1981. The House of Lords ruled that the GLC's cheap fares regulations made under powers given by Parliament in the Transport (London) Act 1969 were *ultra vires* and therefore void.

Mandamus

Local government not only has statutory power to make law; it also has statutory duties. If a local authority fails to carry out its statutory obligations, e.g. to collect refuse, to sell council houses, to introduce comprehensive education, then an order of **Mandamus** can be sought by an individual or a government official. Mandamus (the word comes from the Latin *mandare* – to command) is a court order which compels a local authority to do what it has failed to do. If the authority ignores the order it is in contempt of court. The elected councillors can themselves be prosecuted.

Local authority revenue and expenditure

Figure 35.1 describes patterns of public expenditure and revenue. Included in those figures are sums raised and spent by local authorities. Table 35.1 summarises the main elements of planned expenditure and revenue raising by local authorities.

Considering expenditure initially, you see from Table 35.1 that the major sectors of local authority expenditure are on education and housing. Also prominent are law and order, local environmental services (e.g. refuse collection) and personal social services (e.g. old peoples' homes, social workers).

As was explained in Chapter 18, the bulk (almost half) of the revenue to meet this expenditure comes from central government, over a third from locally levied rates, and the remainder from other income (especially council house rents) and borrowing.

As part of its overall public expenditure plans, central government sets a **Rate Support Grant** and a **Specific (Capital) Grant** for each local auth-

Table 35.1
Local authorities, England and Wales, 1983/4

Get their money from:	£bn	Spend it on:	£bn
Rates	11.9	**Current expenditure**	38.6
		of which, education	13.3
Government grants	16.9		
Rent, dividends, interest, tolls, fees	10.0	**Capital expenditure**	6.5
		of which, housing	2.2
Sales and other sources	3.5		
TOTAL RECEIPTS			
Loans	3.8		
TOTAL	46.1	**TOTAL**	46.1

Source: *Annual Abstract of Statistics 1986*, Tables 16.15 and 16.18 (adapted)

ority, determined according to central government's conception of the needs of that authority.

A local authority has some flexibility in setting the level of **rates**. In essence, rates are a tax levied on business or residential property. They are imposed on the rental or rateable value of a property (i.e. the supposed rent it would earn if let on the open market). It is the responsibility of the local authority to set the rate poundage (the actual rate levied on each pound of the rateable value) so as to raise the amount of money required, e.g.

Rateable value   = £400 per annum
Rate poundage   = 50p in the pound
Rate demand   = £200

The rates system has been criticised on a number of counts. A specific criticism is that it is not directly related to the ability of residents to pay. The incomes of the residents are not considered in setting the rateable value but only the size, type and location of the property. Although rate rebates from the government can help to offset rate payments of people with low incomes, the inherent inequities in the rating system have been criticised, for example by the Layfield Report in 1976 and in a government Green Paper on alternatives to rates in 1981.

Another inconsistency of rates has been the setting of the rateable value. Revaluations of the rental value of each property are expensive and time-consuming. Thus governments have shied away from carrying them out. Therefore, for many years, rateable values have been based on outdated figures.

The Layfield Report, echoed in the 1981 Green Paper, considered the introduction of a local income tax or a local sales tax. A poll tax (i.e. a set money amount to be paid by each resident of an area) was also mooted in the Green Paper. Firmer plans for its introduction were laid by the government in 1986. A major argument for the poll tax was that it would widen the tax net, being levied on every individual over the age of 18. However the criticism that the tax would be regressive was voiced by opponents.

Control of local government expenditure

From the late 1970s and early 1980s the Conservative Government restricted central government grants to local authorities as a part of its policy of reducing public expenditure. Under the Local Government and Planning Act 1981, central government was given powers to reduce grants to a local authority if that authority spent more than the figure deemed necessary by central government. Furthermore, tighter controls on the levying of supplementary rates by local authorities were also enforced.

This was regarded by some critics as a reduction in the freedom of local authorities to provide the level of services they considered necessary for their particular areas. This issue involved political as well as economic considerations.

To what extent should a local authority have the powers to determine its own level of expenditure, even if this conflicts with central government policy? To what extent is local democracy superior or subordinate to national democracy?

From your reading of the press or television viewing you will doubtless be aware of major economic problems which governments try to alleviate. In this and the following chapters we study the nature and causes of these problems and then consider policies to remedy them.

Economic objectives

Since World War 2, most British governments have sought to achieve the following macro-economic objectives (i.e. those relating to the economy as a whole):

a stable prices, i.e. little or no inflation;
b sturdy economic growth and an improvement in the general standard of living;
c a healthy Balance of Payments;
d the maintenance of a high level of employment.

It has proved impossible for any government to meet all of these objectives simultaneously despite the application of a variety of economic policies. This is principally due to the fact that policies aimed at achieving one objective often have undesirable effects upon others.

We shall consider the nature, characteristics and possible influences on these objectives, starting with one which has a direct effect on all of us and on all organisations – inflation.

Inflation occurs when there is a general rise in prices. A few prices may be stable or even fall, but if the prices of the vast bulk of commodities are rising the economy is suffering from inflation. The value of money falls as prices rise. A £5 note buys you fewer commodities as inflation runs on.

Inflation was far more rapid in the 1970s and early 1980s than was common in the 1950s and 1960s. A 2 per cent or 3 per cent annual rise in prices was normal in the 1950s and the 1960s, but from the late 1960s the rate of inflation rose. Between the third quarters of 1974 and 1975 annual inflation exceeded 26 per cent. However in recent years a 3 per cent or 4 per cent rate has been more typical.

Measuring inflation

Percentage changes in prices are quoted to indicate the *annual rate of inflation*. These figures are derived from a statistical measure called the General Index of Retail Prices produced by Department of Employment statisticians.

Figure 36.1 shows the percentage rate of increase in the index of retail prices on the previous year. You can see that inflation reached a peak in the middle 1970s only to set off on an upward trend again from 1978. It has tended to decline since 1981, the monthly rate stabilising around 3 per cent to 4 per cent in 1986/7.

What has been the trend of inflation lately? Consult your newspaper or a journal like *Economic Trends* if you are unsure.

What causes inflation?

Economists are not unanimous on the possible cause of inflation. There are different interpretations of the evidence and different analyses of cause and effect. There are three major explanations:

Fig. 36.1
General index of retail prices
1960–86
Source: *Economic Progress Report*,
May–June 1986

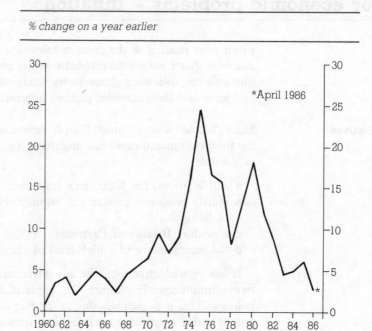

% change on a year earlier

*April 1986

Demand-pull inflation

This suggests that if incomes and expenditure are rising so that the total or aggregate demand in the economy exceeds aggregate supply, prices will be pulled up. Demand-pull inflation is unlikely to have been present in the 1970s. With the high unemployment in the economy, there existed the possibility of increasing output and supply. Demand-pull inflation is more likely to be present when the economy is at full employment, when increasing the supply of goods is difficult.

Cost-push inflation

Proponents of this view claim that firms raise prices because they face rising costs of production. In the 1970s wage costs rose noticeably, often a reaction to inflation and intensified by the desire to keep ahead of anticipated price rises.

The increase in prices of primary products, especially oil, also added to costs of production. In Britain's case the price of imports was further aggravated by the depreciation of the foreign exchange rate of the pound in the 1970s.

In the mid-1980s the Chancellor of the Exchequer, amongst others, voiced concern about the trend of wage rises aggravating the rate of inflation.

Thus there seems to be evidence to suggest that cost-push inflation had occurred. However the monetarists would disagree.

The monetarist view – an introduction

Monetarists like Professor Milton Friedman of the University of Chicago believe that inflation can only occur if the rate of growth of the money supply exceeds the rate of growth in production.

To appreciate this view we need to understand what the money supply is, how it grows and thus its possible impact on inflation.

The money supply is the total amount of money existing in the economy at one particular time.

In recent years more attention has been paid to measuring changes in the money supply since governments have set targets for the rate of its growth. These targets have been part of the anti-inflation strategy of the governments led by Mr Callaghan and Mrs Thatcher. Some economists believe that inflation is caused by too rapid growth in the money supply. The publication of money supply figures indicates whether policy is on course or not when compared with the growth the government was anticipating.

The money supply is composed of more than simply Bank of England notes and coins in circulation. The bulk of the money supply is in bank deposits of various kinds. Economists disagree on how best to measure the money supply. Thus the Bank of England* publishes money supply statistics which include M0, M1 and M2 ('narrow' definitions) and sterling M3 ('broad' definition). Most heed has been paid to movements in M0 and sterling M3 in recent years (see Table 36.1).

* The Bank of England is the UK's central bank, operating on behalf of the State. Note that it has different roles and objectives to commercial banks such as you see in your High Street.

Table 36.1

UK money supply December 1986 (£m)

Notes and coins in circulation outside the Bank of England	15 706
Bank's operational deposits with the Bank of England	250
M0 =	15 956
Notes and coins in circulation with the public	13 400
Sight deposits	61 633
Time deposits	76 532
Sterling M3 =	151 565

Source: *Bank of England Quarterly Bulletin*, February 1987.

M0 contains the most obvious elements of money, bank notes and coins in circulation, plus the deposits of the commercial banks held at the Bank of England.

Sterling M3 contains both more liquid and less liquid elements of the money supply. Liquidity means nearness to cash, so that ready cash or money easily withdrawn or transferred from a bank account (known as sight deposits) are clearly liquid assets readily usable for transactions purposes. Current accounts with banks are a major example of sight deposits.

Sterling M3 also contains the less liquid elements of money, time deposits, which are not so quickly convertible into cash but might be held as savings. Deposit accounts or fixed term deposits in banks are instances of time deposits.

It is evident from Table 36.1 that bank deposits constitute the lion's share of the money supply. When banks lend to individuals or organisations they are creating new bank deposits. If your bank lends to you, it credits an amount of money to your bank account. When you withdraw the loan and spend it at, say, a shop, the funds will reappear in the banking system as the shop's bank deposit when its takings are banked at the end of the day. This means that when banks lend, they create more money by creating more bank deposits. This is the main way in which the money supply grows.

How does this tie in with inflation? Monetarists cite evidence which they claim shows a link between growth in the money supply and changes in inflation.

Other economists known as Keynesians (basing their views on the ideas of a British economist J.M. Keynes) dispute the monetarist interpretation. The crux of the argument is whether rises in costs of production and incomes bring forth a growth in the money supply, or whether it is only with a rise in the money supply that incomes are able to rise. Which factor is the most causal?

The effects of inflation

The effects of inflation are felt more harshly the more sudden and rapid is the rise in prices.

Loss of economic confidence

If inflation occurs rapidly and unexpectedly, organisations which have signed a medium- or long-term contract for a fixed fee could find themselves in difficulties. For example, in the early and mid-1970s, some construction firms undertaking long-period work, e.g. building a motorway or housing estate, found that costs of materials and labour rose more rapidly than anticipated in their budgeting. Their profit margins were thus eroded, and in a few cases the contracts were revised to allow a larger fee.

Inflation clauses are not uncommon in long-period contracts now. An element of control is thus created in the amount of expenditure that will be required and the amount of revenue to be received.

Artificial redistribution of income

Inflation can redistribute real income. Those who earn a fixed income will suffer since their set money return declines in real terms. People with a fixed occupational pension, savers with fixed interest securities or landlords whose tenants have a long lease will all suffer.

Also, borrowers gain and lenders lose relatively. For example, if you borrow £1000 from a friend for one year at 10 per cent interest, you will repay £1100. However, if the rate of inflation was 20 per cent during that year, your friend would need £1200 to preserve the real value of the money.

Similarly, savers lose in real terms if the rate of return they receive is less than the rate of inflation. It is possible that saving might be discouraged if the real value of money saved continuously falls.

Workers with weak trade unions or no union representation at all might find it difficult to negotiate pay rises which keep apace or ahead of inflation.

Export prices

If inflation in the UK is more rapid than in other countries, as has often been the case in recent years, British exports become relatively dearer and less competitive. However, a decline in the exchange rate could help to restore export price competitiveness.

Fiscal drag

Money incomes are likely to rise in a period of inflation, but you are likely to need the extra money income to offset the rising prices. However, as one's income rises, this could mean paying income tax for the first time or additional income, or paying the tax at a higher rate. Thus, real take-home pay could decrease. This effect of a rigid tax structure on rising incomes during inflationary times is known as 'fiscal drag'. Since 1977 the Chancellor of the Exchequer has usually raised the thresholds of income tax brackets in line with the rate of inflation in order to counter the effects of fiscal drag. Thus we can earn more income before income tax applies.

oss of political and social :onfidence

A period of rapidly rising prices can cause dissatisfaction and despair amongst people. Grumbles about rising prices and the inability of governments to do much to prevent inflation could lead to people thinking in terms of radical political parties or even a different political system. Hilter's rise to power in Germany was made easier by the dislocation that the very rapid inflation (known as hyperin flation) of 1922 and 1923 caused.

37 Economic growth

Economic growth involves expansion in output, incomes and expenditure in the economy. It brings improvements in average living standards and a higher general level of income.

To measure economic growth reference is made to changes in national income statistics like the Gross Domestic Product (GDP) or Gross National Product (GNP).

In order to understand the measuring of economic growth more fully we need to explore the components and compilation of national income statistics.

The national income

The *national income* is the total money value of the economic activity going on in an economy over a period of time. In 1984 the national income for the UK stood at £239 506m.

This figure represents the total of what is earned, spent and produced by people and organisations. Extra output by the organisation in which you may work means a bigger national income. An increase in your wage and in your expenditure likewise means an expansion in the national income. As will be explained, if the value of national income rises faster than the level of prices, then the country as a whole is likely to be better off.

The measurement of the national income can be approached from 3 important and interlocking angles of economic behaviour:

   a the income approach,
   b the output approach,
   c the expenditure approach.

More precisely, we can say that the national income
      = the total of *incomes* earned by factors of production in the economy
      = the total value of net *output* in the economy
      = the total *expenditure* on finished goods and services in the economy over a period of time.

Fig. 37.1
The three approaches to National
Income

Output = £180   **Income = £180**   **Expenditure = £180**

We shall soon explore more precisely the meaning of these terms. For the
moment, let us establish the logic of the equality of the 3 approaches.

As shown in 37.1, a customer buys a new table at a furniture retailer's
for £180. What has happened? The customer has made *expenditure* of £180.
The value of the *output*, the table, is £180. *Income* of £180 has been received
by the factors of production involved in the making and selling of the table.
In every such transaction, there is this 3-way mirror image.

Consider that transaction in more detail in relation to the threefold
definition of national income stated above. The £180 income will be split
between the various factors of production involved in the making and
selling as wages, profits and rent.

The value of output of £180 does not simply represent the value of the
service provided by the furniture retailer, but it also includes, for example,
the value of output of the furniture manufacturer. This is why the total
value of *net* output is measured. Net output means the value added at a
particular stage of production or distribution, i.e. the value of output sold
by a firm minus the value of output it buys from other organisations. As
shown in Fig. 37.2, this enables the value of output to be allocated amongst
industries associated in making and selling a product, rather than attri-
buting the value of output only to the retailer at the final stage.

Correspondingly, the expenditure on the finished goods is the same as
the total *net* expenditures made during the production and selling process,
i.e. the expenditure made when buying minus the expenditure previously
made in buying components.

Fig. 37.2

Stages in calculating National
Income

	Forester sells wood to saw mill for £50		**Saw mill** cuts wood and sells it to furniture maker for £80		**Furniture maker** makes a table and sells it to a retailer for £140		**Retailer** sells table to a customer for £180	
Income	50	+	30	+	60	+	40 = £180	Total income earned
Net output	50	+	30	+	60	+	40 = £180	Total value of net output = value of finished goods
Net expenditure	50	+	30	+	60	+	40 = £180	Total value of net expenditure = expenditure on the finished goods

These explanations can best be understood by studying the simplified breakdown of the process of making and selling the table. Assume that these are all the stages involved as illustrated in Fig. 37.2.

At each stage of production the income earned, the value of net output produced, and the net expenditure undertaken are all calculated by a subtraction from the corresponding value at the previous stage.

For example, the furniture manufacturer sold the table to the retailer for £140. The manufacturer had already paid £80 to buy the wood. Thus the furniture manufacturer's income is £60, to be distributed as wages, profits and rent for premises. Similarly the value of the net output of the manufacturer is £60. The firm has produced a table worth £140, but £80 of that value includes the output of the forester and the saw mill. The retailer made expenditure of £140 to buy the table from the manufacturer, who had already spent £80 on the sawn wood. The net expenditure is £60, once again.

The total of the net output at all stages equals the value of the finished table, just as the total net expenditure corresponds to the final expenditure by the consumer. There would be double counting if the value of the tree (£50) + the value of the sawn wood (£80) + the value of the produced table (£140) + the value of the sold table (£180) were included. That would give an erroneous figure of £450 as the total value of output, income and expenditure. Hence we see the importance of aggregating *net* output.

The equality of the 3 approaches is true in the making and selling of this one product as it is for all transactions in the economy. By amassing all appropriate data, statisticians of the Central Statistical Office compile national income statistics for the whole economy. We shall next look at a breakdown of the flow of income in the economy before studying the National Income Accounts prepared by the statisticians.

The circular flow of income

You will no doubt have realised from the previous section that one person's expenditure in buying the table became income for the factors of production involved in the making and selling the table. The more expenditure made in the economy, the greater the income earned. Figures 37.3 and 37.4 show a breakdown of the economy into basic economic units, showing the movements of income and expenditure on the output of goods and services.

Figure 37.3 identifies the basic relationship between households and firms. Individuals supply to firms the services of factors of production such as labour and enterprise. Therefore they receive rewards in the form of wages, profits and rent. The total of such income is thus the national income. With this income, households are able to buy goods and services, and are thus undertaking consumer expenditure. So there is a circular flow of income.

However, in reality households do more with their income than utilise it towards consumer expenditure on domestically produced goods and services, as shown in Fig. 37.3. Some income may be saved, some will go in taxes, whilst some will be used to buy imports. Such income which is not directly spent on home-produced goods and services is called a **leakage** or **withdrawal** from the circular flow of income.

Conversely there are other sources of expenditure besides consumption

Fig. 37.3
Simple circular flow of income

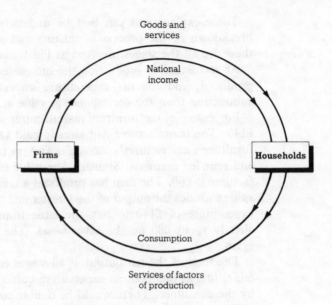

which create more income. Investment by firms in capital assets like machines and buildings, expenditure by the government on goods and services, and expenditure by other countries on UK exports all add to the UK national income. These are **injections** into the circular flow of income. They stimulate further growth in income.

J.M. Keynes, a prominent British economist, demonstrated in 1936, in his famous book *General Theory of Employment, Interest and Money*, the significance of such injections to the growth of national income and the level of employment. He showed that extra investment expenditure will add more to national income than the initial amount invested. If £5m worth of new machines are bought, engineering firms receive extra income of £5m initially, which will be paid as wages or profits both to their own workers and shareholders, and also to those of organisations from which the engin

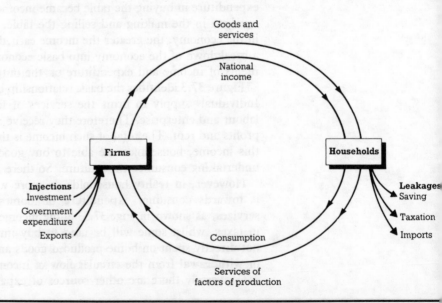

Fig. 37.4
Circular flow of income

eering firms buy components and raw materials. Hence households have additional income, some of which they will spend on goods and services. This creates extra income for the shops where their consumption takes place. These shops need to order more output from factories, so providing them with extra income. These organisations receive additional profit and the workforce additional wages. Thus there will be more income for other organisations because of the greater consumption generated. And so this cycle will go on.

Note that at each stage income is earned, not all of it will be spent on consumer goods; some will leak out of the circular flow by way of saving, taxation and spending on imports. Therefore, smaller and smaller amounts of income will be passed on as consumption at each stage.

The overall effect of that original £5m investment will be to increase the level of national income by more than £5m. Keynes described the extent to which an injection increases national income above the size of that injection as the **multiplier effect**. If that £5m investment increased national income by £20m, than the value of the multiplier would be 4.

$$\text{multiplier} = \frac{\text{increase in national income}}{\text{increase in injections}}$$
$$= \frac{£20m}{£5m} = 4$$

Keynes wrote in the 1930s, a period of severe depression when the level of unemployment exceeded 3 million people. To relieve the depression, Keynes advocated the need for more expenditure. Since there was insufficient extra investment expenditure in the private sector to reduce unemployment and stimulate growth in national income, Keynes urged the government to increase its expenditure.

Thus, government expenditure could act as the injection, just as investment did in the example above. Extra government expenditure would trigger off the multiplier effect, so creating greater national income. By the same token, lower taxes would enable people to increase consumption. This would also increase activity in firms, so increasing the level of national income. The use of government expenditure or taxation in order to influence the amount of expenditure and national income is known as *fiscal policy*. There will be a fuller discussion of this and other economic policies in Chapter 42.

So far, we have discussed the multiplier effect as a means of stimulating growth in the level of national income. However, the process can work in reverse to cause a fall in national income. This would come about if the level of expenditure in the economy was reduced.

Possible causes would be greater leakages, e.g. more saving, higher taxes or more spending on imports. Also, a lower level of injections would have the same effect with less investment, government spending or export earnings. Greater leakages or a smaller level of injections lead to less income for others, and so they can make only a lower level of consumer expenditure. In turn, this means less income for others. The cumulative effect will be a reduction of national income of a greater magnitude than the initial change in the leakage or injection. The multiplier effect would have operated in reverse, causing a decline in the level of national income.

UK National Income Accounts

The government statistical service publishes National Income Accounts, presented for each of the 3 methods, income, output and expenditure. You will see that all 3 methods arrive at totals for Gross Domestic Product (GDP), Gross National Product (GNP) and National Income or Net National Product (NNP). There are statistical differences between the meaning of these terms, which we shall explain in due course. Be aware, though, that each of them gives a measure of the total money value of economic activity in the country.

You will also note that the income and output accounts include a residual error item, whereas the expenditure account does not. Differences occur in the totalling of national income by these methods because a mammoth amount of statistical data is needed. The data are not 100 per cent complete and accurate. The expenditure data are generally regarded as being more reliable. Therefore, residual error items are inserted into the income and output accounts in order to bring all 3 into balance, which of course logically should happen.

The income method

From Table 37.1 you can see that the whole range of incomes resulting from economic activity is listed. Income from employment covers by far the largest portion. The profits, or surpluses in the case of public sector organisations, and rent income are also totalled. Note that unemployment benefits, old age pensions and other such State benefits are not listed. They are known as **transfer payments**, meaning that money is being transferred between members of the community. Such income is not listed because it does not result directly from the creation of goods or services. In fact, it involves a redistribution through taxation of part of the gross income

Table 37.1
UK National Income 1984 (£m)

Income from employment	180 34?
Income from self-employment	26 88?
Gross trading profits of companies	47 90?
Gross trading surplus of public corporations	8 73?
Gross trading surplus of general government enterprise	− 25?
Rent	18 93?
Imputed charge for consumption of non-traded capital	2 52?
less Stock appreciation	− 5 16?
Residual error	− 5 33?
Gross Domestic Product at factor cost	274 57?
Net property income from abroad	3 30?
Gross National Product at factor cost	277 87?
less Capital consumption	− 38 37?
National Income	239 50?

Source: *Annual Abstract of Statistics* 1986 Table 14.1

which are recorded in the account. If you are receiving a student grant, that is another example of a transfer payment.

'Stock appreciation' is deducted from the total of incomes. Owing to inflation, the value of stock held by an organisation will rise and this will artifically increase its profit or surplus. That rise in profit does not occur as the result of greater production, and would not have occurred at all if prices were stable and there was no inflation. Therefore stock appreciation is subtracted. The residual error item is added for the reasons explained above.

The total of all these items is called the 'Gross Domestic Product at factor cost'. It measures the total income, output or net expenditure of economic resources located in the UK.

However, some of this income might well be earned by foreign organisations operating in the UK. This could lead to a flow of interest and dividends overseas, e.g. a Japanese company operating in England remitting some of its profits back to Japan. Conversely, there are British organisations with overseas interests which might also send income back to the UK. The difference between these flows is called 'Net property income from abroad'. It is normal for this to show a net inflow adding to the UK national income.

GDP + net property income from abroad = Gross National Product

Some of the newly created output of capital goods is merely to replace that which is worn out or obsolete. By taking the extent of this depreciation or 'Capital consumption' into account, the Net National Product or National Income is measured. NNP represents all the newly produced goods and services available for consumption as well as the net additions to the stock of capital goods.

Therefore, your wage increase or greater profits earned by an organisation would be recorded in this account.

The output method

Consider next the account prepared from the output angle (Table 37.2). This account totals the net output of all industries and services in the economy, public and private sectors, in the primary, secondary and tertiary sectors.

Can you recall the distinction between these sectors? Categorise the activities listed in the output account into the correct sectors.

For public sector services like defence or education, the value of output cannot be directly measured since a market price is not charged. The cost of providing such services is used instead to indicate the value of output.

After the net output of all parts of the economy is presented, there is an item called 'Adjustment for financial services'. This is subtracted in order to avoid double counting of interest paid on loans and interest received by various financial institutions. Then, when the residual error is inserted, once again we arrive at GDP at factor cost. GNP and NNP are next measured in the same way as described above under the income method.

The outputs of many of these sectors interweave. As was explained earlier, the output of one industry could well be an input for another. Thus the ability of one industry to develop (or even survive) depends on output

Table 37.2
UK National Output 1984 (£m)

Agriculture, forestry and fishing	5 96
Energy and water supply	31 54
Manufacturing	68 37
Construction	15 83
Distribution, hotels and catering, repairs	37 04
Transport	12 20
Communication	7 60
Banking, finance, insurance, business services and leasing	36 98
Ownership of dwellings	16 69
Public administration, national defence and compulsory social security	18 86
Education and health services	25 65
Other services	18 20
Total	294 97
less Adjustment for financial services	− 15 06
Residual error	− 5 33
Gross Domestic Product at factor cost	274 57
Net property income from abroad	3 30
Gross National Product at factor cost	277 87
less Capital consumption	− 38 37
National Income	239 50

Source: *Annual Abstract of Statistics* 1986, Table 14.7

from other sources. The output of the paper industry is important to every other industry, as is the output of electricity.

Many manufacturing organisations rely on financial services also. Organisations use the banking system for payment of wages and for goods and services, as well as borrowing money from banks. Some organisations may hire the services of advertising agencies or management consultants.

In some cases inputs may be imported from overseas, but much of this interlinking is purely domestic. Consider the organisation in which you may work or the college in which you study. List a few of the goods, materials or components made by other firms on which your organisation depends for continued operation.

The expenditure method

There remains the expenditure approach. As you see in Table 37.3, this method involves totalling up the expenditure on goods and services by consumers and government, along with 'Gross domestic fixed capital formation'. This item involves expenditure by the public and private sectors on investment goods like machines and buildings. The value of 'Physical increase in stocks and work in progress' must also be included, since incomes have been earned in the production of this partly finished output. The negative figure for 1984 indicates that firms were 'destocking', that is running down their level of stocks in anticipation of falling demand.

'Exports of goods and services' must be added because foreign expenditure on UK goods and services are an injection into the UK circular flow of income. By the same token, 'Imports' are a withdrawal, since expenditure within the UK leaks overseas. Import expenditure is therefore subtracted. The total of these expenditure items is known as the Gross

Table 37.3
UK National Expenditure 1984 (£m)

Consumers' expenditure	194 673
General government final consumption	69 655
Gross domestic fixed capital formation	55 319
Value of physical increase in stocks and work in progress	− 177
Total Domestic Expenditure at market price	319 470
Exports of goods and services	91 736
less Imports of goods and services	− 91 852
Gross Domestic Product at market prices	319 354
less Taxes on expenditure	− 52 578
Subsidies	7 797
Gross Domestic Product at factor cost	274 573
Net property income from abroad	3 304
Gross National Product at factor cost	277 877
less Capital consumption	− 38 371
National Income	239 506

Source: *Annual Abstract of Statistics* 1986 Table 14.1 (adapted)

Domestic Product at market prices. The data so far reflect the prices buyers actually paid, the market prices. These prices include the effect of taxes like VAT or excise duties, and also any subsidies which would reduce the price to the consumer.

Hence, there is this difference between measuring at market price and at factor cost – the existence of taxes and subsidies on goods and services. To measure GDP at factor cost, which relates to incomes actually earned by factors of production, taxes on expenditure are subtracted and subsidies added. From GDP at factor cost, GNP and NNP are found in the fashion of the other two methods.

Note that no residual error item is present in the expenditure method, suggesting that more reliability is attached to those statistics.

Consumer expenditure that you make each day will be included in these totals. Equally, if your organisation buys a new computer, that will register in the account as part of 'Gross domestic fixed capital formation'.

The totals of GDP, GNP and National Income are in balance between each of the three approaches.

Measuring economic growth

A prime use of national income statistics is to measure economic growth. In essence the percentage change in GNP or GDP from one year to the next is needed. However adjustments should be made to counter the effect inflation has on these figures. For example if the money value of GNP showed a 10 per cent rise from one year to another, but inflation also ran at 10 per cent, then in real terms the rate of economic growth would be zero.

Thus economic growth is measured by the percentage change in real GNP from period to period.

Fig. 37.5
Economic growth rates, average
1981–5

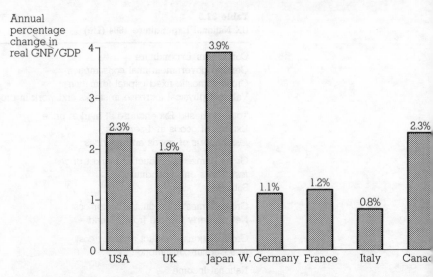

Annual percentage change in real GNP/GDP

Recent trends in economic growth

How has the UK economy fared in recent years regarding growth? The late 1970s and early 1980s saw a slowing of economic growth in the world generally, given the onset of recession in many countries. Even so, growth in the UK economy has tended to be less than in some of the major industrialised countries (see Fig. 37.5). In fact from 1979 to 1981 real GDP actually declined. The level of output shrunk rather than grew, as reflected in rapidly growing unemployment during that period.

As the 1980s advanced, though, the rate of UK growth picked up, a story also true in other major industrial countries, particularly the USA.

Factors influencing economic growth

Quantity and quality of factors of production

Modern machinery, skilled labour and management, and efficient use of these factors of production are important. This could lead to greater productivity, greater output per factor of production. Effective use of economies of large-scale production can contribute to greater efficiency.

Investment is thus crucial, for both innovative and replacement capital. Remember also that investment is an injection into the circular flow of income, so stimulating income, expenditure and growth of output by the multiplier effect.

Growing demand

Without expanding demand there will not be economic growth. However industry needs to take advantage of, and serve, this growing demand, be it domestic or overseas. Japan and West Germany have been amongst the leaders in the world growth league in post-war years. A key factor in their growth has been expansion of exports. This export-led growth has been aided by undervalued exchange rates and relatively low rates of domestic inflation. Hence their export prices have been competitive on world markets. These countries have taken advantage of expansion in the world economy and growing world demand.

Although the UK exports a high proportion of its GNP, the rate of growth of exports has not compared favourably with the likes of Japan and West Germany. Opinion is divided on the reasons for Britain's relatively slow rate of economic growth, but lack of investment and innovation is surely important.

You have doubtless heard on news broadcasts of Britain's balance of payments situation. Each month figures are published with information about trade flows, in surplus or deficit.

The balance of payments is an account which records the dealings of the UK with the rest of the world. Such transactions involve not only trade in goods and services, but also foreign capital investment or investments in securities, changes in international bank deposits, activities of the Bank of England in the foreign exchange market and transactions with overseas monetary authorities.

A balance of payments problem faces a country if there is a persistent tendency for imports to exceed exports or if investment outflows exceed inflows.

Intrinsic to these international dealings is the foreign exchange market, the market for the sale and purchase of currencies. Warning of a balance of payments problem is often signalled by fluctuations in a country's exchange rate.

The foreign exchange market

The foreign exchange market involves the foreign exchange departments of banks or foreign exchange brokers dealing on behalf of clients to buy and sell currencies. Unlike the Stock Exchange, there is no building designated where such transactions take place; deals are negotiated by telephone or telex.

For example, an organisation in the UK, Company X, intends to buy a machine from Corporation Z in the USA at a price of $150 000. X will contact its bank in the UK and arrange for Z's bank in America to be credited with $150 000. This will mean that X's bank must buy dollars on the foreign exchange market. If the going rate of the pound to the dollar is £1 = $1.50 then X's bank account will be debited by £100 000 (plus commission charged by the bank) in order to purchase the $150 000.

The determination of the exchange rate

Those of you who have been on holidays abroad will be aware that the exchange rate of the pound to the dollar, franc, peseta and other currencies does not necessarily stay constant for any length of time.

Why is this? The answer lies in changes in demand and supply for currencies. The exchange rate is determined by demand and supply. Currencies will be bought and sold for all the various transactions included in the Balance of Payments Account, such as trading or investment purposes.

If, say, there is an increased desire to import into the UK, or if there is an outflow of investment funds from the UK, there will be a greater supply of pounds ready to be sold. If others are to be induced to buy these pounds and sell their foreign currencies, what must happen to the exchange rate? It must fall. The price of pounds in terms of other currencies will decline, because of excess supply at the previous rate, for example from £1 = 1.50 to £1 = $1.40.

Conversely, if there is a growing demand for British exports or an inflow of investment funds into the UK, the greater demand for pounds will force the exchange rate up, as other currencies are sold for pounds. A rise could occur from, say, £1 = $1.50 to £1 = $1.60.

Balance of payments adjustment

Bank of England activity in the foreign exchange market

Such fluctuations in the exchange rate might be viewed with alarm by a government. Particular concern has been felt in periods when the pound has fallen too far and too fast on the foreign exchanges. This means that there is a balance of payments problem, since there is a greater tendency to sell pounds than to buy them at the prevailing exchange rate. A government could regard a falling exchange rate as damaging to the economy since it makes imports dearer, so adding to the rate of inflation. Furthermore, a decline in the exchange rate could be evidence of lack of foreign confidence in the economy, and precipitate even further capital outflow and bigger falls in the exchange rate.

There is immediate action that can be taken. The Bank of England, the UK central bank acting on behalf of the government, can arrest the fall in the rate by entering the foreign exchange market as a buyer of the surplus pounds and supplier of the desired foreign currency.

The Bank of England keeps a stock of gold and foreign currency reserves in the Exchange Equalisation Account. By using up some of the reserves, pounds can be bought and the exchange rate can be stabilised, as illustrated in Fig. 38.1 (and also see Fig. 38.2).

The above situation has been common for the UK, but countries like West Germany and Japan have been confronted with *rising* exchange rates due to expanding demand for their exports. A rising exchange rate will make a country's exports dearer on world markets and more difficult to sell, a situation ironically also facing the UK in 1979 and 1980.

The possible course of action would be for the central bank to *sell* its currency on the foreign exchanges, so forcing down the exchange rate while increasing its gold and foreign currency reserves.

Returning to the more serious dilemma of a balance of payments problem and a declining exchange rate, the Bank of England's gold and foreign currency reserves would not last for ever. The Bank could not continuously prop up the exchange rate by buying surplus pounds and running down the reserves. The reserves would soon evaporate. If the balance of payments problem is more deep-rooted and continuous, as when persistently more imports are bought than exports are sold, then other action will be

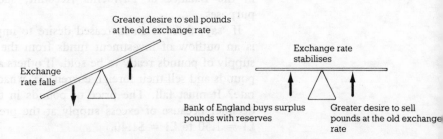

Fig. 38.1
Determination of the exchange rate

necessary by the government. As we shall see, the corrective measures taken to alleviate a balance of payments problem, though helping the balance of payments, have disadvantageous effects on other sections of the economy – including our pockets and purses.

The Balance of Payments Account

You should by now have a general conception of what the balance of payments is, and the nature of balance of payments problems. Next we shall study the Balance of Payments Account in more detail, and then explain how the account comes into balance. Table 38.1 gives the UK Balance of Payments Account for 1984. The meaning of each item will be explained. Refer also to Table 38.2 for recent trends in major items.

Visible trade

This involves the export and import of goods. We shall describe in Chapter 44 the pattern of UK trade by commodity and by geography. The difference between the value of exports and the value of imports is called the **balance of trade** or the **visible balance**. Exports are regarded as a plus item since pounds are bought by foreigners to pay for them. Imports are a minus for the opposite reason, that pounds are sold to buy other currencies. Visible trade showed a deficit in 1984 of £4101m, not an unusual occurrence for Britain. Over the last century or more, a balance of trade surplus has been a rarity. There was a visible surplus in 1971, the only one of that decade, though from 1980 to 1982 the UK recorded a surplus, boosted by North Sea oil.

Concern has been voiced in recent years about the growing deficit on manufactured goods. Britain imported in 1983 more manufactures than it exported, the first year for centuries. This gap on non-oil visible trade has

Table 38.1
UK balance of payments 1984 (£m)

Visible trade		
Exports	70 409	
Imports	74 510	
Balance of trade		−4101
Invisibles		
Credits	75 879	
Debits	70 843	
Invisible balance		+5036
Current balance		+ 935
Total investment and other capital transactions		−3291
Balancing item		+1040
Total currency flow		−1316
Official financing		
Net transactions with overseas monetary authorities		—
Other foreign currency borrowing (net)		+ 408
Drawings on (+) or additions to (−) official reserves		+ 908
Total		+1316

Source: *Annual Abstract of Statistics* 1986, Table 13.1.

Table 38.2

UK balance of payments (£m)

Year	Balance of trade	Invisible balance	Current Balance	Total investment and other capital transactions
1975	−3333	+1751	−1582	+ 154
1976	−3929	+3016	− 913	−2977
1977	−2284	+2156	− 128	+4169
1978	−1542	+2154	+ 972	−4137
1979	−3449	+2713	− 736	+1865
1980	+1361	+1739	+3100	−1503
1981	+3360	+3168	+6528	−6972
1982	+2331	+2332	+4663	−3199
1983	− 835	+4003	+3168	−4865
1984	−4101	+5036	+ 935	−3291

Source: *Annual Abstract of Statistics* 1986, Table 13.1.

subsequently widened and reflects the decline of the UK manufacturing sector.

Invisibles

That picture is totally different when the UK's invisible performance is considered. Invisibles involve 3 elements of Britain's relationship with other countries: services; interest, profits and dividends; and transfers. Britain has had a long-standing invisible surplus, of increasing size since 1982.

Services include expenditure by foreign tourists in the UK (a credit) and the corresponding debit of British holidaymakers' spending abroad. Earnings from financial services like insurance and banking involving overseas customers and from transporting passengers and freight by sea and air also contribute. For example, if you fly on a Pan American aeroplane, that causes an invisible debit. If an American flies with British Airways, an invisible credit is created. Government services overseas, including the upkeep of embassies and the cost of troops abroad are also categorised as invisibles.

Interest, profits and dividends involve earnings from overseas investment returning to the UK (a credit) or their foreign converse. For example if a foreign oil company like Texaco makes a profit from its North Sea oil activities and transmits some of that profit to the parent company in the USA or to non-UK shareholders, an invisible debit has occurred. If a British resident has bought securities issued by, say, the West German Government, and earns interest on them, an invisible credit is created.

Note that the act of making the investment is *not* an invisible. Investments are counted under a later item in the Balance of Payments Account namely Total investment and capital flows. It is only the earnings emanating from foreign investments that are an invisible.

Transfers of money between countries include UK payments and receipts to and from the EEC, such as the contribution to the EEC Budget and migrants' remittances. If, for example, a British expatriate now living in Australia sends money back to his family in the UK, an invisible plus item has been created.

Table 38.3 states recent trends in invisibles.

Table 38.3
UK invisibles (credits − debits) (£m)

Year	Services	Interest, profits and dividends	Transfers
1980	+4036	− 219	−2078
1981	+4170	+ 950	−1952
1982	+3215	+1115	−1998
1983	+3701	+2440	−2138
1984	+3985	+3304	−2253

Source: *Annual Abstract of Statistics* 1986, Table 13.1

What can you deduce from these figures?

Interest, profits and dividends have become a larger credit through the 1980s. At first this item was strongly influenced by the remitting of dividends and profits by foreign oil companies out of the UK, consequent on their North Sea activities. However that has been more than offset by large inflows into the UK from British investments abroad. In 1979 the government abolished foreign exchange controls which meant that British individuals and organisations were freer to invest overseas if they pleased. There was a substantial exodus of funds in the ensuing years. As a result, though, income on such investments has been earned, boosting the interest, profits and dividends item on the invisible account.

Services have shown consistent surplus while the deficit on transfers is largely attributable to Britain's net contributions to the EEC Budget.

The current balance

This is the overall position concerning visibles and invisibles. It is the sum of the balance of trade and the invisible balance, and is also known as the Balance of Payments on Current Account.

In 1984 there was a surplus on current account of £935m. From Table 38.2 you can see that UK tends to oscillate between surplus and deficit on the current balance. It really depends on whether the invisible surplus is sufficient to offset the visible deficit. Despite the boon of North Sea oil as an import saver and export earner, the current account surplus showed signs of decline as the 1980s elapsed.

Total investment and other capital transactions

This grouping includes investment in capital goods in another country, e.g. a Japanese company developing a new factory in the UK. This would be a plus item, since pounds would have been bought by foreigners for use in this country.

In addition, investment and other capital transactions involves investment in securities (portfolio investment), as would occur if a British resident bought shares in an American company. Here we have a debit item, since pounds are sold to acquire foreign currency.

Other components include changes in overseas bank deposits in UK banks, and in the amounts of money British residents hold in banks abroad.

The figures listed in column 5 of Table 38.2 represent the total of all such inflows against the total of outflows for each year.

Total investment and other capital transactions have varied over the years from debit to credit. In the late 1970s, though, North Sea oil exploration by foreign companies contributed to sizeable net credits, whereas the abolition of exchange controls in 1979 led to large net outflows in subsequent years.

Balancing item

In an ideal statistical world, all statistics would be gathered promptly and accurately. In reality, there are problems in gathering the mammoth amount of information needed in compiling the Balance of Payments Account. Often, for example, there are differences between the times when an international transaction is agreed, when the goods are delivered and when they are paid for.

This causes problems in gathering the data. Hence the government statistical service inserts a balancing item if there is a variation between the accurate information supplied by the Bank of England concerning official financing and the available statistics for the current account and investments and capital flows.

Total currency flow

This is the total of all items so far included – the visible and invisible balances making up the current balance, the total investment and capital flows, and the balancing item. The total currency flow effectively represents the total of one side of the Balance of Payments Account. Its size varies, depending on the fluctuating fortunes of the current balance and investments and capital flows. In 1984 there was an overall deficit on total currency flow of £1316m.

Thus we have described one side of the account. For 1984, the UK had deficit on its total currency flow. The means by which that deficit is offset in accounting terms is by official financing.

Official financing

This involves the government and the Bank of England in the raising and repayment of loans in foreign currency, and Bank of England activity in the foreign exchange market.

Net transactions with overseas monetary authorities

These transactions include the borrowing (+) or repayment (−) of loans by the UK Government and the Bank of England as a result of deals made with bodies like the IMF or the central banks of major countries. The borrowing is used to buttress the gold and foreign currency reserves. There was no activity on this front in 1984.

Other foreign currency borrowing

In recent years the UK Government has arranged loans on financial markets from major commercial banks overseas, and has issued fixed interest securities denominated in dollars. The +£408m in 1984 indicates that there was net borrowing in foreign currency to value of £408m.

Drawings on or additions to official reserves

Earlier in this chapter we described Bank of England activities in the foreign exchange market in order to stabilise the exchange rate of the pound against other currencies. The extent of such support is measured in this item. The 1984 figure is +£908m. This means that overall, the Bank of England bought pounds and sold foreign currency to the extent of £908m. Without this action the exchange rate of the pound would have been lower.

The Bank of England increased the demand for pounds on the foreign exchanges, suppressing the fall that would otherwise have happened.

On many occasions the Bank of England has done the opposite. In 1980 the change in the reserves was −£291m. Evidently, the Bank was more generaly selling pounds and buying foreign currency so supplementing the reserves. This action prevented a rise in the exchange rate which would have otherwise occurred.

The combined effect of the components of official financing in 1984 was +£1316m. This offsets the −£1316m which was the balance for official financing. Thus the two sides of the Balance of Payment Account offset each other. The balance of payments balances.

Why does the balance of payments balance?

The simple answer to this question is that every time a pound is sold on the foreign exchanges, someone else must have bought it. Every sale of pounds is matched by an offsetting purchase of pounds. For every debit there is a credit.

If pounds are sold to buy imports, the suppliers of the foreign currency now have pounds which they may, perhaps, use to buy UK Government securities or put on deposit in British banks.

However, if there is a greater desire to sell pounds at the going exchange rate than to buy them, the exchange rate will fall in order to enable the pounds to be sold and foreign currency purchased. The lower exchange rate, and a cheaper deal for the buyer of the pounds, is the inducement for such a transaction to take place. Thus pounds are bought and sold. There is a debit and a credit transaction, though in this case it requires a movement in the exchange rate to equilibrate the balance of payments by enabling the deal to take place.

As you have learned, the Bank of England may be concerned about too rapid and too large a movement in the exchange rate. Therefore, as the UK central bank, it can act as a buyer or seller of pounds, being one of the parties to a transaction on the balance of payments. If there is a larger desire to sell pounds to buy imports, the exchange rate of the pound will fall to encourage others to buy those pounds. To prevent such a fall, the Bank

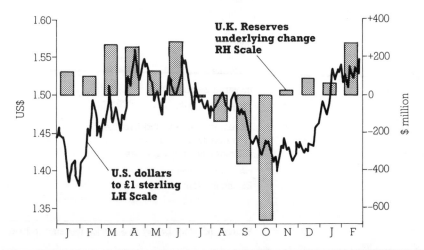

The Pound and the Reserves

U.K. Reserves underlying change RH Scale

US$

$ million

U.S. dollars to £1 sterling LH Scale

J F M A M J J A S O N D J F

Fig. 38.2
Reserves are used to stabilise the exchange rate

of England may itself supply the required foreign currency from the reserves and buy the pounds.

Thus, as far as the Balance of Payments Account would look, there would be a balance of trade deficit counterbalanced by a plus value under official financing. Therefore the size of the figure under official financing represents the extent to which the exchange rate was supported (upwards or downwards). The Balance of Payments Account would still balance if the Bank of England did not act, but movements in the exchange rate would be far greater.

If the balance of payments must balance overall, how is there so much talk of balance of payments deficits and surpluses? There is no guarantee that pounds sold to pay for imports will necessarily be used to buy imports. Those pounds might be used for investment in the UK or even bought up by the Bank of England to support the pound on the foreign exchanges. Thus there might well be deficits or surpluses on individual sections of the account, like the UK's perennial balance of trade deficit and invisible surplus, only to be offset elsewhere. Overall, though, the account must balance.

The balance of payments – alternative presentation

In recent years the Central Statistical Office, the body responsible for the presentation of official statistics, has revised the format of the balance of payments.

Rather than have the total currency flow offset by official financing, the alternative presentation involves the current account being mirrored by an amalgam of investments and capital flows plus official financing, along with the balancing item. The amalgamated section is entitled 'Net transactions in UK external assets and liabilities.' For example, the 1985 balance of payments presented in this manner is shown in Table 38.4.

Table 38.4
UK balance of payments 1985 (£m)

Visible trade		
Exports	78 051	
Imports	80 162	
Balance of trade		−2111
Invisibles		
Credits	80 611	
Debits	74 951	
Invisible balance		+5660
Current balance		+3549
UK external assets and liabilities		
Transactions in assets	50 235	
Transactions in liabilities	42 612	
Net transactions		−7623
Balancing item		+4074
		−3549

Source: *Monthly Digest of Statistics* December 1986, Table 16.1

Transactions in assets are debit items, e.g. UK investment overseas, lending to overseas residents by UK banks or the sale of pounds on the foreign exchange market by the Bank of England. Transactions in liabilities involve inflows into the UK such as foreign investment, government borrowing from abroad or the purchase of pounds on the foreign exchanges by the Bank of England, leading to a fall in the volume of official reserves.

The logic of balance in the Balance of Payments Account still holds under this alternative presentation, namely that if pounds are bought so must they have been sold. Thus a credit item has to be offset by a corresponding debit item.

39 Unemployment

We shall now look at the second major economic problem faced by governments, **unemployment**.

The word 'unemployed' is used for a person who is willing and able to work but cannot find suitable employment. This excludes people who are not eligible for work, like school children, full-time students, retired people and those not seeking paid employment, especially housewives.

In the UK we measure unemployment by the number of people who register as unemployed, and are able to claim State benefit. For example, in October 1986 the total was 3 237 200. Figures are also published excluding school leavers. That level stood at 3 119 700, or 11.5 per cent of the working population (those in or seeking work).

The groups of people who are worst affected, i.e. who have a larger percentage of unemployed of their type, are: male unskilled manual workers; the young, especially black young people; those nearing retiring age; those in regions of high unemployment, e.g. Northern Ireland and the North of England.

Throughout the 1970s the general trend of unemployment was upward, but it accelerated at the very end of that decade and in the early 1980s, echoing the depression of the inter-war years. Rapid increases in unemployment took place in 1980 and 1981, though the rate of growth slowed by the mid-1980s. Figure 39.1 shows the path of unemployment and job vacancies notified to employment offices since the early 1970s.

Although the UK in general has suffered from rising unemployment, some areas of the country have been affected more severely than others, as shown in Table 39.1.

The areas of highest unemployment, like Scotland, Wales, the North and North-west, have been affected by and large from the long-standing decline of basic industries, notably coal, iron and steel, shipbuilding and textiles. This is the root of the regional problems affecting the UK. However, note also the level of unemployment in the West Midlands. This area felt a net job loss of 301 000 between 1979 and 1986, more than any other region. The contraction of the motor and other engineering industries was the prime cause.

Fig. 39.1
Unemployed and vacancies: UK
1973–86
Source: *Employment Gazette*
Reproduced by permission of the
Controller of her Majesty's
Stationery Office

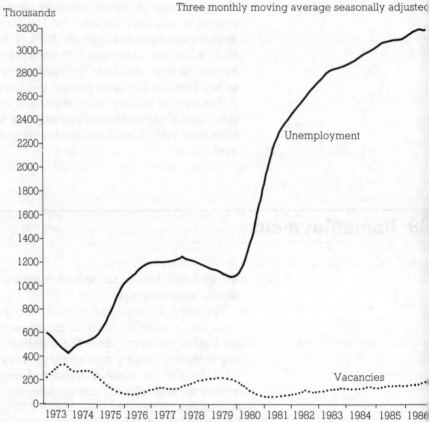

Thousands

Three monthly moving average seasonally adjusted

* Vacancies at employment offices are only about a third of total vacancies

Table 39.1
Regional unemployment rates, November 1986

Areas	Unemployed (%)
North	16.6
Yorkshire and Humberside	13.5
East Midlands	11.0
East Anglia	8.8
South-east	8.4
South-west	10.0
West Midlands	13.6
North-west	14.1
Wales	14.1
Scotland	14.3
Northern Ireland	18.9

Source: *Monthly Digest of Statistics December 1986, Table 3.1*

Job vacancies

In spite of the high unemployment, there have still been job vacancies of over 100 000 to 200 000 notified to Job Centres, employment exchanges and careers offices. Additionally, there are other job vacancies for which figures are not recorded, e.g. those only advertised at private employment agencies or in newspapers and journals.

How can the disparity between unemployment and vacant jobs be explained?

geographical immobility of labour

Unemployed people are not all in the right places to do the vacant jobs. The areas of most job vacancies tend to be in the South-east of England, whereas the areas of highest unemployment are the declining industrial areas further North or West.

Many people are not inclined to move because of the costs of moving home and the possibility of having to pay higher rents or mortgage repayments. Also, if one's family and friends are rooted in an area, these social bonds can be difficult to relinquish. If your children are settled at a school, moving to another area could disrupt their education.

occupational immobility of labour

People do not have the required skills or qualifications to do all the vacant jobs. There are job vacancies for skilled engineering workers in some areas, for example, but insufficient people to fill the vacant posts.

lack of attraction of certain jobs

Some vacant jobs do not require much skill or qualifications but still remain unfilled, such as jobs on transport systems. It would appear that wages and/or conditions of work are not sufficient to attract enough unemployed people.

causes of unemployment

frictional, search or transitional unemployment

Titled differently by various economists, this is not a very serious cause of unemployment. It is the short time-lag involved between leaving one job and starting the next one, given that the new job is on the near horizon. For example, you may have successfully applied for a new job which requires you to start work in 6 week's time. You might leave your current job in one month. Therefore, you would be transitionally unemployed for 2 weeks. Actors between engagements are also unemployed under this category. The search element is the time-lag until a vacant and suitable job is discovered.

seasonal unemployment

The jobs of some workers are only done during a part of the year rather than all year round. Thus some might be unemployed in the down period, e.g. some cricketers, building workers, hotel staff. In all these activities the winter period is quieter.

This is not an especially widespread problem in the UK, but is more serious in Third World countries which have a high dependence on seasonal crops.

structural unemployment

This is a more important cause of unemployment in the UK. Structural unemployment occurs where there is a fall in demand or supply of the particular good or service produced, or a substitution of other factors of production for labour.

If industries are superseded by the development of new techniques, e.g. synthetic fibres affecting the demand for natural textiles; if import penetration causes decline in an industry as with cars or motorcycles; if the supply of a raw material is exhausted, e.g. some coal mines; these are all cases of structural unemployment, reflecting the decline of traditional industries.

The march of technology causes a type of structural unemployment sometimes called *technological unemployment*. In this case, the industry itself is not facing decline. The mix of factors of production changes, which usually means machines replacing labour.

The widespread use of computers and word processors could well mean a loss of much clerical and secretarial employment. The introduction of robots and greater mechanisation on production lines could also mean sizeable reductions in employment.

There are differing views of the net effect of silicon-chip technology on employment. A report drawn up for the Department of Employment[*] claims that in the long run there will not be widespread unemployment: the more efficient use of resources that micro-electronics will bring will create opportunities for growth and employment elsewhere in the economy.

However, Clive Jenkins and Barrie Sherman[†] argue that if we adopt the new technology there are likely to be 5 million unemployed by the turn of the century. Worse, they maintain that if we do not develop in this field but other countries do, British industry will lose ground relative to competitors and there will be 5.5 million unemployed.

Later studies suggest that the picture is not likely to be as severe as painted by Jenkins and Sherman. For example, 'Chips and Jobs', a report produced by the Policy Studies Institute, attributed only 1 job loss in 20 in manufacturing industry to factory automation. However the report suggested that the rate of technological change was stepping up, particularly in terms of computerisation of office and factory systems. The study predicted noticeable job losses in the clerical field.

This view was echoed in a report by the Institute of Manpower Studies[*] which also emphasised job growth in the services and small business sector. A summary of employment changes predicted by this report was shown in Fig. 1.3.

By the time you read this book, there may be clearer indications of the net effects of micro-chip technology in creating or replacing employment than are available at the time of writing. The rate of technological change is speedy. Much may have occurred between the time of our writing and your reading this book. Be sure to keep abreast of any changes.

Demand-deficient (cyclical) unemployment

This is another factor contributing to the unemployment total of the UK and many other countries. Whereas structural unemployment is confined to particular industries rather than the economy as a whole, demand-deficient unemployment implies a general decline in real expenditure in the economy, so affecting a wide spectrum of activities.

The cyclical element reflects patterns of economic growth, which tend to go in waves or cycles of expansion, depression and eventual expansion again. In the late 1970s and early 1980s the world economy was in downswing, with many countries operating contractionary economic policies to combat inflation and rectify balance of payments deficits. Such policies stifle growing demand, and in so doing create more unemployment.

---

[*] Dept. of Employment: *The Manpower Implications of Microelectronic Technology* (HMSO 1979)

[†] C. Jenkins and B. Sherman: *The Collapse of Work* (Eyre Methuen 1979)

[*] The Institute of Manpower Studies: *UK Occupations and employment Trends to 1990* (Butterworths 1986).

We have reviewed the nature, size and influences on the major macro-economic problems: inflation, unemployment, growth and the balance of payments.

What is their impact on the organisation in which you work or study?

One UK industry which has been particularly affected by these problems in recent years has been the textile industry.

The cotton and wool industries had expanded on a large scale during the industrial revolution in the late eighteenth and early nineteenth centuries. Lancashire and Yorkshire became the focal points of the UK textile industry. The industry suffered a jolt during the depression of the inter-war period, when demand fell. This was exacerbated by loss of export markets when other countries, e.g. India, began to develop their own textile industries, serving their home markets and beginning to penetrate overseas.

If the natural textile industry suffered during that period, these was a brighter side – the growth of synthetic fibres. Research and developments in the inter-war and post-war periods led to the proliferation of synthetic fibres such as nylon, terylene and polyester. This became the growth area of the revived textile industry. Consider the clothing you are wearing. No doubt some of it is made from synthetic fibres.

However, since the mid-1970s, the UK textile industry has gone into further decline, both in the natural textile sector and in synthetic fibres. In 1980, an average of 1800 jobs were lost each month in the industry. Of the remaining 100 000 work-force, 1 in 8 were on short-time working. Imports supplied 58 per cent of the home market. This decline occurred in spite of a good industrial relations record and improved productivity (up 25 per cent for textiles and clothing between 1970 and 1979), and the fact that exports held up reasonably well. The problems were more associated with the home market.

In the much-vaunted fibres sector, 1980 output fell by a quarter on the previous year, to reach its lowest level since 1967. Half of the labour force lost their jobs in 1979 and 1980. Profit margins were down, and UK production capacity was reduced by a quarter between 1979 and 1981 (compared with only a 4 per cent drop in the rest of Europe).

Severe social as well as economic problems resulted in areas where there was little alternative employment. In Northern Ireland for example, a number of companies had been attracted to develop in the province by government grants. However, the decline bit hard. From a peak of 10 000 workers in synthetic fibres, employment had dropped to 2000 in 1981. The closure of the British Enkalon plant alone led to the loss of 1000 jobs. With little other likelihood of jobs, the effects of unemployment described earlier in Chapter 39 were sorely felt.

Why did the decline in the UK textile industry from the mid-1970s take place? There were 3 major reasons.

The recession

The slowdown in economic growth in the economy as a whole, and the concomitant rise in unemployment and pressure on living standards, affected demand for UK textile products.

Low-cost imports

The UK rate of inflation, higher than in many other countries, helped to make domestic output uncompetitively priced. Production costs per unit of output were lower in many competitor countries. Low wage costs in Asian countries and government-subsidised energy costs in the USA meant that such imports could consistently outsell UK competitors on grounds of price.

It should be noted that it is not simply the less developed countries which have been the source of bigger import penetration in textiles. In recent years the USA has become a major competitor. From 1976 to 1979 US fibre imports into the UK grew by 65 per cent, whereas those from Hong Kong, for example, rose only 7.3 per cent. In those 3 years the US cornered 4 per cent of the bedlinen market.

The strong pound

In the late 1970s and early 1980s the pound rose on the foreign exchange markets and the dollar fell. This made US imports even cheaper, accentuating the low-cost import point made above.

How has the British textile industry reacted to the decline?

There has been pressure on governments from industrialists and trade unions to impose tighter quotas on imports, which has been done to some extent. In fact, the textile industry was the most protected of all UK industries in the early 1980s. For example, quotas were introduced on the import of polyester yarn and nylon carpet yarn, but were relaxed under the threat of US retaliation which would have harmed UK exports. In 1982, however, quotas were imposed on dresses and underwear from South Korea. The UK was also party to negotiations of the Multi-Fibre Arrangement which pressured low-cost less developed countries to control the growth of their exports into industrialised countries. There has also been lobbying for the EEC countries to take a united view and exert more pressure to secure tighter restrictions on imports.

But quotas can be a dangerous game. As well as the counter-pressure by the USA mentioned above, a more forthright reaction came from 'little' Indonesia. When the UK Government imposed a quota on clothing imports from Indonesia worth around £10m, the Indonesian Government reacted by blocking orders for various UK goods (including aero-engines) worth up to £500m. It took much diplomatic soothing before both sides backed down.

Although quotas might help the textile industry, the Consumers' Association was quick to point out that UK consumers would lose some access to cheaper textile goods and their choice would be restricted.

As well as pushing for import quotas the UK textile industry has been forced to adapt to the changing economic environment. Some UK firms like Coats Paton invested abroad to set up manufacturing plants, importing the finished goods into the UK. By the mid-1980s about half their workforce was overseas. Coats Paton, like Courtaulds, planned to diversify into other fields. They announced plans to open an eel farm and also to produce medical equipment.

Facing foreign competition, existing companies have further stepped up investment and increased productivity. Management has attempted to adapt to rapidly fluctuating trends and tastes in the home market as typified by stores like Next. Styles and designs have been revised and changed more speedily. As a consequence, the position of the (now slimmer) UK textile industry was more stable by the mid-1980s.

However in 1986, a stronger pound in the foreign exchange markets led to a new surge of imports, particularly from the Far East. In the second quarter of 1986 2500 jobs were lost in the UK textile industry. The TUC in particular called for tighter import quotas.

The merger boom, to which reference was made in Chapter 28, was apparent in the textile industry too. By the mid-1980s, the Vantona group had taken over Carrington Viyella and Nottingham Manufacture, with the hope of being stronger to thwart foreign competition. Vantona followed this up in 1986 with a merger with Coats Paton to create a new company, Coats Viyella, to become the largest UK-based textiles company.

The benefits of the merger were proclaimed as marrying Coats's international network (70 per cent of its sales were abroad) with Vantona's strong UK brands like Viyella, Van Heusen and Dorma. One-third of Vantona's sales were to Marks and Spencer. The merger could open export doors for Vantona's products.

41 The government and the economy

Economic policies operated by governments are usually aimed at alleviating one or more of those macro-economic problems described in previous chapters, to achieve little inflation, a healthy balance of payments, solid economic growth and less unemployment. In addition some policies might be geared to reducing inequalities in income and wealth between citizens. Social policy is usually aimed at improving the quality of life, particularly for those on the lower rungs of the income and wealth ladder.

In Chapter 18 we have already described government policies relating to information technology, specific employment measures and regional aid when discussing their impact on the finances of organisations. In this chapter we describe other major policy weapons like fiscal, monetary and monetarist policies, discuss further the issue of privatisation and consider key themes in social policy. Importantly, also, we shall consider the basic reasons for governments operating such policies and appraise their effectiveness, as well as discussing the policy approaches adopted by the major political parties in recent years.

The free market *versus* economic policies

If governments adopted a totally free market approach, they would allow the price mechanism (see page 252) a free rein in determining prices and allocating resources. However, no modern government has totally abstained in the policy field. There have been differences in the extent of policy intervention and in the type of policy employed by different governments. As we shall see, such differences have often reflected the political hue of the ruling party.

The fact that all political parties advocate the use of some economic policies means that they are dissatisfied with the outcome if the market mechanism was left to take its course, or they may feel that the market mechanism would achieve the desired objective too slowly without the spur of policy.

Thus governments attempt, to a lesser or greater degree, to regulate the economy by using policy weapons. Some policies have been widely applied over the years, some modified as new thinking and understanding emerge or as prevailing economic conditions change. New approaches are sometimes heralded.

Unfortunately, as we shall see, although it would be relatively simple for a government to achieve any one of its objectives in isolation from the rest, to obtain them all simultaneously has so far proved to be an extremely difficult task. This is principally due to the fact that policies aimed at achieving one objective often have undesirable effects upon others. Thus, for example, a reduction in taxation might stimulate aggregate demand and therefore increase the level of employment, but it could also generate a rapid rate of inflation and stimulate the level of imports into moving the balance of payments towards a deficit.

The economic tactics employed by a government can be seen to operate on both a macro- and a micro-economic level.

Macro-economic policy relates to attempts to control the overall direction and performance of the economy.

Micro-economic policy focuses on the operation of particular markets and sectors of the economy.

Macro-economic policy

In their essentials the tools available for the attainment of macro-economic objectives can be presented in terms of 5 approaches:

- fiscal (or budgetary) policies
- monetary policies
- monetarist policies
- balance of payments policies
- direct intervention

Fiscal policy

This policy technique involves the government manipulating levels of public expenditure and taxation in order to influence the total expenditure (or aggregate demand) in the economy. (This is aside from considerations of the need to spend on particular programmes and to raise revenue to finance that expenditure.)

It was not until the writings of J.M. Keynes had become generally accepted that British Governments began to deviate from the precepts laid down in the nineteenth century. These precepts were based on the belief that all governments had a duty to balance their accounts, or in other words that the yield gleaned from taxation should equal government expenditure.

When Keynes's *General Theory of Employment* was published in 1936 it was realised that fiscal policies could be used to regulate the economy as a whole. Figure 41.1 shows the 3 possible budgetary options open to the Chancellor, each of which is obtainable through the manipulation of taxation and expenditure levels.

The effect of fiscal policy is designed to operate via the multiplier process through the circular flow of income.

Fig. 41.1
Budgetary policy options

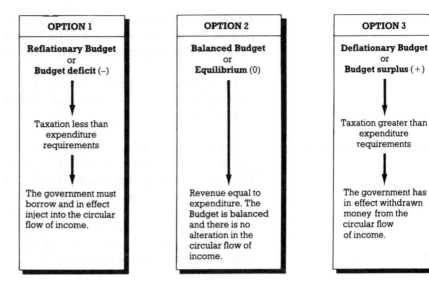

OPTION 1	OPTION 2	OPTION 3
Reflationary Budget or **Budget deficit** (–)	**Balanced Budget** or **Equilibrium** (0)	**Deflationary Budget** or **Budget surplus** (+)
↓	↓	↓
Taxation less than expenditure requirements		Taxation greater than expenditure requirements
↓		↓
The government must borrow and in effect inject into the circular flow of income.	Revenue equal to expenditure. The Budget is balanced and there is no alteration in the circular flow of income.	The government has in effect withdrawn money from the circular flow of income.

1 A **reflationary Budget** (or **Budget deficit**) is sometimes referred to as **deficit financing** and is obtained by deliberately setting the level of taxation *lower* than that necessary to meet estimated expenditure needs.

2 A **balanced Budget** is obtained by matching taxation yields to expenditure requirements.

3 A **deflationary Budget** (or **Budget surplus**) is sometime referred to as **surplus financing** and is obtained by setting the level of taxation *higher* than that required to meet current expenditure targets.

The implications of budgetary policy

In Chapter 37 we examined the ideas that are implicit in fiscal policy by introducing the idea of the circular flow of income and the possibility of inducing **injections** to and **withdrawals/leakage** from this flow. Taxation and government expenditure constitute an important aspect of this process, since by altering the volume of either the government is able to expand or contract the level of economic activity within the system. A reflationary budget is, therefore, the equivalent of an injection into the circular flow whereas a deflationary budget is in effect a withdrawal from the system.

It is also important to remember that the size of injections or withdrawals that are induced by the government depends upon the size of the multiplier (see Chapter 38, p. 346) operating within the economy.

When public expenditure exceeds tax, national insurance and other revenues, the residue has to be borrowed. This amount is known as the **Public Sector Borrowing Requirement** (**PSBR**). Therefore a bigger or smaller PSBR indicates an easier or tighter fiscal policy.

Expansionary fiscal policy

The aim of increasing the size of the PSBR (by less taxation and/or more government spending) would be to resurrect a depressed economy. With more spending being generated in the economy, unemployment should fall and economic growth be stimulated.

However, monetarist critics of Keynesian economics suggest that large fiscal stimulation could breed more inflation by increasing the money supply. (A comparison of Keynesian and monetarist viewpoints appears later in this chapter – see p. 372.) Furthermore, some of the extra income earned would be spent on imports, with an adverse effect on the balance of payments.

These conflicting effects illustrate the point made earlier in this chapter of the difficulty of achieving all 4 major macro-economic objectives simultaneously.

Contractionary fiscal policy

A tighter fiscal policy, involving higher taxation and/or less government expenditure will reduce the PSBR. Such a policy could be aimed against inflation. By reducing aggregate demand, inflationary pressures should be reduced. A contractionary fiscal policy could be directed towards combating a balance of payments deficit. Less expenditure overall in the economy implies less spending on imports, so improving the balance of payments.

However, the side effects of tighter fiscal policy will be to hamper employment and economic growth since the level of aggregate demand is reduced.

The effects of fiscal policy on organisations

How might organisations react to fiscal policy changes? The effects can seriously influence the prices that can be charged and the level of sales. If a contractionary fiscal policy is employed, some organisations will face reduced orders because public expenditure is cut: construction firms would be affected if expenditure on council housing were cut back.

Higher taxation would likewise have an impact. Consider A.L. Things, the general store in Sunhampton High Street. Higher VAT would lead to the firm raising its prices. A fall in demand would be likely to follow, and the firm would reduce its orders from manufacturers. That effect could also occur if higher income tax were introduced, so reducing take-home pay. Unemployment would be highly likely to result from all such contractionary fiscal measures.

Monetary policy

Monetary policy is concerned with the manipulation of the money supply and the rate of interest. Responsibility for the operation of monetary policy rests with the Bank of England, but the Treasury influences the overall stance of the policy and its relationship with other economic policies.

In Chapter 36 we described the composition of the money supply, and how more bank lending increases it. If necessary, refresh your memory on these topics before reading on, because monetary policy is a key influence on their behaviour.

The instruments of monetary policy

There are 4 main techniques that are used to influence the financial markets:

- reserve requirements
- open market operations
- lender of last resort
- direct controls

Reserve requirements

The Bank of England requires banks to hold a proportion of their deposits in the form of liquid assets so that customer withdrawals of funds may be met. The size of this reserve requirement varies from bank to bank, depending on the nature and spread of their customers. The reserve is agreed in discussions between each bank and the Bank of England.

The very existence of a reserve places a basic constraint on the ability of banks to lend to an unlimited extent. A proportion of deposits must be retained as a reserve, so that banks face a barrier beyond which their lending from existing deposits cannot go.

A reserve requirement is also an important adjunct to other monetary policy measures like open market operations which is described below.

Open market operations

This technique involves the sale or purchase of bills of exchange and government securities by the Bank of England so as to influence the reserves of the commercial banks.

If the bank wishes to curtail the growth of bank lending and thus the money supply, it can sell bills or government securities. This will have the effect of reducing the level of bank deposits and reserves, forcing the banks to cut back on lending and raise interest rates.

The opposite, a purchase of gilts or bills by the Bank will feed funds into the banking system. Banks can lend more and reduce interest rates as funds become more plentiful.

Lender of last resort

* Discount houses are financial institutions which specialise in the discounting of bills of exchange, (see p. 162).

Another way in which the Bank of England can influence interest rates is by its actions as the 'lender of last resort'. When banks are short of funds they may call back loans to discount houses* to replenish reserves. The discount houses, in turn, will now be tight on funds and would request the Bank of England to buy bills of exchange from them. The price at which the Bank of England is prepared to buy the bills (and in so doing provide funds for the discount houses) indicates the Bank of England's view on desired changes in interest rates.

For example, if the Bank of England was prepared to buy bills of exchange only at a lower price than that previously prevailing, then the Bank of England would be indicating that interest rates should rise. This has the effect of raising short-term rates of interest in general. Organisations and individuals borrow less because of the higher rates of interest. Thus the money supply should grow less rapidly.

Direct controls

The Bank of England Act of 1946 gave the Bank of England a general supervisory role in relation to the rest of the banking system. The Bank exercises its authority by means of informal requests or recommendations, but because the commercial banks fear the application of the other monetary controls they usually view these requests as mandatory requirements.

It is through this process that the Bank of England is able to obtain co-operation from the rest of the banking system in relation to both the volume and direction of its loan strategies. On many occasions the Bank has implemented qualitative controls, which state priorities in the pattern of lending, e.g. exporters should have priority for loans, or banks should restrain the volume of funds lent for house purchase. Less frequently quantitative controls have been introduced, e.g. limits on the growth of deposits or loans, or restrictions on HP finance (which were removed in July 1982). Such controls have not been used in recent years.

Fig. 41.2
Monetary policy options

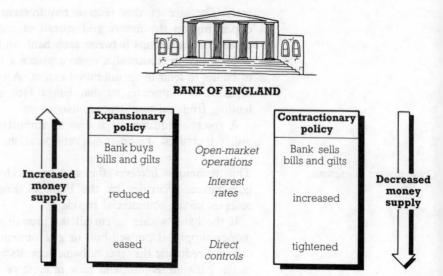

BANK OF ENGLAND

	Expansionary policy			Contractionary policy	
Increased money supply	Bank buys bills and gilts	*Open-market operations*	Bank sells bills and gilts		**Decreased money supply**
	reduced	*Interest rates*	increased		
	eased	*Direct controls*	tightened		

Monetary policy in operation

Figure 41.2 summarises the policy options available to the Bank of England which can be used either collectively or individually as part of the overall macro-economic strategy of the government.

A contractionary monetary policy could be aimed at reducing inflation. Restricted bank lending or higher interest rates will inhibit growth in the money supply, so reducing that possible fuel for inflation.

The weapon of high interest rates could be used if the balance of payments is too far in deficit. If there is an outflow of currency and the exchange rate is falling, higher interest rates could attract an inflow of foreign speculative funds, so helping to moderate those difficulties.

An expansionary monetary policy means that banks have more to lend and at cheaper rates of interest. This should encourage borrowing and spending so stimulating growth and employment (which of course a tight policy would harm).

However, there is the converse danger that freer growth in the money supply could breed inflation, and that lower interest rates could lead to an exodus of investment funds, causing a run on the pound.

The effect of monetary policy on organisations

Evidently those organisations most immediately affected will be in the financial sector. In Sunhampton, the Banksure Bank will change its interest rates and experience changes in its ability to lend. Other financial institutions such as the Buyerpad Building Society will also change their interest rates because they compete with the banks for funds.

Inevitably the customers of banks will be affected. If interest rates are higher, firms will find that their overdrafts cost more, further eating into profitability. The government will also have to pay more for the funds it needs to finance the PSBR.

The monetarists and the Keynesians

For much of the post-war period, fiscal policy was the prime means of attacking the major economic problems. However by the mid-1970s the climate of economic opinion was changing, primarily because of:

- the apparent failure of fiscal policy to combat the more rapid inflation and high unemployment of the 1970s, and
- the growing regard for the monetarist ideas of the economist Milton Friedman, that inflation was essentially a monetary phenomenon.

Thus both the Labour Government of the late 1970s and the Conservative Government from 1979 adopted forms of monetarist policies. Labour's adoption of these policies was somewhat reluctant, as part of the conditions for loans from the International Monetary Fund to combat the prevailing balance of payments deficit. However, the Conservative Government based their economic strategy around monetarism.

In the next section we shall describe the nature of monetarist policies.

Monetarist policies

These policies are based on the belief that control of the money supply is fundamental to the control of inflation. Therefore monetarist policies have set targets of two main types:

- a target for the rate of growth of the money supply (e.g. between 11 and 15 per cent rowth of Sterling M3 and 2 to 6 per cent growth of MO for 1986/87);
- a target for the PSBR (e.g. £7bn for 1986/7, equivalent to $1\frac{3}{4}$ per cent of GDP).

Concern about the PSBR is based on the link that when the government sells gilts or treasury bills to the banking system in order to fund its borrowing, this inevitably increases the money supply. That can fuel inflation. Therefore, recent governments have attempted to cut public expenditure (and have also increased taxes) in order to reduce the size of the PSBR, and hence to reduce the extent of government borrowing from the banking system.

The monetary policy weapons described earlier are also used as additional means for attempting to control the money supply within the target range.

Monetarists argue that in order to achieve economic growth long term, inflation must first be combated. However a strong side-effect of a tight monetarist policy has been high unemployment, due to the constraints on government expenditure and the higher interest rates which the policy involves. Some firms have faced shrinking order books whilst others have faced bankruptcy. Workers have been laid off as a result. Also, the quality and extent of services provided by the State sector have been trimmed, e.g. capital expenditure on roads and hospitals has been curtailed.

The Budget

The Budget has traditionally been the occasion when the Chancellor of the Exchequer has stated the government's revenue and expenditure intentions for the coming financial year, and announced major economic policy changes. The main Budget is presented to Parliament near the start of the financial year (1 April), though there may be 'mini-Budgets' at other times of the year if more immediate expenditure, revenue or policy changes have to be made. In the months preceding the Budget, the spending departments, in consultation with the Treasury, will have completed their estimates of financial requirements. These data are published in a White Paper on Public Expenditure.

In preparing a Budget a government will have to consider the relative needs of different programmes of expenditure, its priorities for revenue raising (e.g. more from direct than indirect taxes), and the economic policy mix it will adopt in relation to forecasts of the progress of the economy.

Advice will be sought from senior civil servants and government economic advisors. A government might also heed the views of pressure groups like the CBI, the TUC and the Child Poverty Action Group.

Thus a government formulates its plans. The Budget, in the form of the Finance Bill, is then presented to Parliament, to become the Finance Act after the parliamentary process has undergone its course.

For much of the post-war period, the focus of economic policy in the Budget was on fiscal policy. In recent years, a wider range of policy weapons, both macro- and micro-economic, have been blended into the Budget package. As well as the monetarist policies already described, prices and incomes controls and employment policies have also been.

Incomes policies

Broadly speaking this type of policy initiative can be separated into two classifications:

- voluntary policies
- statutory policies

The rationale of incomes policy is relatively straight forward in that it assumes that greater price stability (less inflation) can be obtained if the rise in incomes is controlled. However, the prime difficulty has been to get consensus for the continued operation of incomes policies.

Voluntary policies

These have been set through a combination of exhortation by the government of the day and negotiations with the TUC. At best they can be said to have achieved only a very limited and short-lived success. The initiative introduced in 1965 was rapidly replaced by statutory controls, and the same fate was shared by the 1971–2 measures. There were two relatively successful years of restraint between 1975 and 1977, but the policy failed to gain agreement from the trade unions thereafter.

Statutory policies

These were utilised between 1967 and 1970 and again in 1973–4. Although the policies differed in terms of the timing and percentage increases allowed, they both suffered from the same weakness that is implicit in voluntary policies, namely, that to be successful they require a genuine consensus about the equity of their application, their efficiency as a policy instrument and their validity as a legitimate governmental activity. This consensus of opinion was never really obtained, and as a result the policies were often challenged by individual trade unions, as in the miners' strike of 1973, which challenged Phase 3 of the government's statutory policy.

When successful, incomes policies have enabled organisations to curtail growth in their wage bill. However, such policies have hampered those firms which were short of labour. They were prevented from offering significantly higher wages to attract the labour they needed.

In 1979, the government decided against using an incomes policy in favour of monetarist controls, and in general left the determination of wage settlements to free collective bargaining and the price mechanism, although it attempted to give a lead to the rest of the economy by limiting pay settlements in the State sector.

Prices policies

Government price controls have generally sought to reinforce incomes policies. The National Board for Prices and Incomes (1965–70) was set up to investigate changes in prices and incomes, and until the middle of 1966 control was conducted on a voluntary basis. In 1966, however, a price freeze was introduced for 6 months and a similar expedient was adopted in November 1972. The Prices Commission operated by the Labour Government in the late 1970s had only a minor effect on controlling prices.

All such tactics failed in their basic objective of limiting price increases, for the same reasons that bedevilled incomes initiatives, namely a lack of consensus and validity, given the profit-orientated nature of the private sector. Organisations facing cost increases beyond their control because of rising import prices suffered especially from price controls.

Balance of payments policies

A government can introduce economic policy measures in order to affect overseas transactions and thus reduce the desire to sell pounds or encourage others overseas to buy them.

Measures to influence items in the balance of payments account

A government might reluctantly have to accept that its exchange rate was over-valued and a more permanent fall was necessary. Thus the government might allow the exchange rate to fall. A devaluation or depreciation of the currency would have taken place.

Devaluation (depreciation) of the currency

This occurred in 1967 when the pound was devalued from £1 = $2.80 to £1 = $2.40. Also, in the 1970s the pound depreciated considerably. The aim of the policy was to make imports dearer and exports cheaper, so stimulating demand for exports but reducing demand for imports. The 1967 devaluation helped to correct the UK balance of payments problem by 1971, by which time export earnings exceeded import expenditure.

However, there is a cost to such a policy. Rising import prices add to the rate of inflation, so aggravating that economic problem.

Fiscal policy

As explained earlier in this chapter, fiscal policy involves changing taxes or amounts of government expenditure so as to influence the level of demand in the economy as a whole.

When used to combat a balance of payments problem, higher taxes on income or higher taxes on goods and services in the shops cut down people's spending power and the amount of commodities they can buy. Thus, if there is a fall in demand in the economy, there must be a decline in demand for imports, cutting the import bill.

The drawback to this policy is that if demand and expenditure are reduced in the economy this will reduce output and cause more unemployment.

Monetary policy

You may recall that monetary policy involves policies which influence interest rates, bank lending and the supply of money in the economy.

Higher interest rates and restrictions on bank lending will reduce the amount of money that can be borrowed, and thus restrict additional expenditure made on credit. Once again, by cutting back on expenditure in the economy, demand for imports will be reduced.

Higher interest rates will also attract overseas funds into the UK by offering a better rate of return on bank deposits or securities. This will increase the demand for pounds.

The disadvantage of monetary policy is similar to that of fiscal policy – the damage done to the domestic economy. Borrowing by both individuals and firms becomes tighter and more expensive, hampering economic growth.

Import controls

A government could consider using tariffs or quotas to combat a balance of payments problem since these measures restrict the demand for imports. This reduces the need to sell pounds and takes pressure off the exchange rate. A tariff is a duty imposed on imports, so raising their prices, whilst quotas restrict the quantities of imports that may enter the country.

Although such measures will certainly cut the import bill, they have disadvantages. They will cause higher prices and, in the case of quotas, will directly restrict consumer choice. Furthermore, there is the possibility that other countries would retaliate if Britain used such controls extensively, and erect trade barriers themselves. This would then be to the disadvantage of UK exporters.

Some economists, especially those of the Cambridge University Applied Economics Group, have advocated devaluation and import controls not only as a means of balance of payments adjustment, but also an engine for expansion in the UK economy. Deterring and restricting the demand for imports, they argue, would induce British consumers to switch to the home market for substitutes. This would promote growth and employment in ailing British industry, it is claimed.

The disadvantages mentioned above would still be apparent, however. Also, given British obligations to free trade within the Common Market, it would be impossible for a government to erect such import controls without actually leaving the EEC. Almost 50 per cent of UK imports derive from EEC countries.

The introduction of these various policies will help to remove downward pressure on the pound on the foreign exchanges and to adjust the balance of payments. But, as with the operation of any economic policies, draw backs occur elsewhere in the economy. The way that the person in the street is affected by a balance of payments problem is the wounds that are inflicted as a result of corrective action – such as higher prices, higher taxes, higher interest rates and higher unemployment.

Borrowing from overseas to supplement the reserves

As well as introducing some of the policies above to remedy a serious balance of payments problem, the government could also seek to borrow from overseas monetary institutions. Such foreign currency borrowing will add to the gold and foreign currency reserves and enable greater Bank of England support of the pound on the foreign exchanges, so stabilising its rate. Likely sources of borrowing are overseas central banks or the International Monetary Fund (IMF), a body which lends to countries experiencing severe balance of payments problems.

Such lending generally has strings attached. A government would need to undertake policies to attack the reasons for its balance of payments difficulties. For example, when the UK borrowed from the IMF in 1976, cuts in government expenditure and a tighter monetary policy were introduced, in order to reduce inflation.

Employment policies

In the face of rising unemployment through the 1970s and early 1980s, governments have put greater emphasis on employment policies. These are of 3 types:

- employment subsidies
- training schemes
- job creation schemes

Employment subsidies

Reference was made in Chapter 18 to the New Workers Scheme, a subsidy to employers who take on young workers below certain wage levels. This policy is aimed at encouraging employment of young people, but at wage levels the government sees as realistic.

Also the government introduced the Job Start Scheme, whereby the long-term unemployed may receive an additional £20 a week for 6 months if they take a job paying less than £80 per week.

Training schemes

Under the aegis of the Manpower Services Commission (MSC), a number of schemes have been developed to train or retrain unemployed youths and adults in order to give them a better chance of finding a vacant job.

The MSC has set up retraining centres for unemployed adult workers to learn new skills, e.g. hairdressing, painting and decorating. Training Opportunities Schemes (TOPS) courses have also been run at colleges in, for example, the secretarial and clerical fields. TOPS has now been replaced by the Job Training Scheme.

For the young unemployed there is the Youth Training Scheme. Partly based on colleges or training centres but mainly involving work experience, these courses are intended to give young people a taste of working life as well as developing basic skills more fully.

Job creation schemes

On a smaller scale, governments in recent years have introduced a few schemes to create jobs, e.g. the Community Programme and the Community Industry Scheme. Both were intended to create jobs in the environmental or voluntary work fields.

As far as organisations are concerned, these schemes can help to lower wage costs, and provide a better trained, more adaptable workforce.

Macro-economic policies – an evaluation

One of the most important tasks facing a modern British Government is the determination of its macro-economic priorities. The choice of policy priority is determined by a desire to achieve the optimum balance between the macro-economic objectives.

The matrix in Table 41.1 outlines the various problems that can be given priority by the government and details various tactics that can be employed in seeking to establish priorities in policy. Unfortunately, as we have already pointed out, the attainment of a harmonious balance between the performance of the main macro-economic variables (employment, prices,

Table 41.1
Macro-economic problems and tactics

Problem	General strategy	Fiscal tactics	Monetary tactics	Exchange rate tactics	Direct intervention	Adverse consequences
Unemployment	Expand	1. Reduce taxation 2. Increase public expenditure (deficit financing)	1. Increase money supply (easy money) 2. Reduce interest rates (cheap money)		Employment policies	1. Tends to accelerate or trigger off inflation 2. Can push the balance of payments towards a deficit
Demand-pull inflation or monetarist inflation	Contract	1. Increase taxation 2. Decrease public expenditure (reduce PSBR)	2. Decrease money supply 2. Increase interest rates			1. Generates unemployment 2. Reduces rate of economic growth
Cost-push inflation					Prices and incomes policies	1. Threat to governmental legitimacy
Need for economic growth	Expand	1. Reduce taxation 2. Increase public expenditure (deficit financing)	1. Increase money supply 2. Reduce interest rates	Devaluation/ depreciation (export-led growth)	1. Government investment Government incentives for private investment	1. Stimulates inflation 2. Could worsen the balance of payments
Balance of payments deficit	Contract or devalue	1. Increase taxation 2. Reduce public expenditure	Increase interest rates	Devaluation/ depreciation	Import controls	1. Generates unemployment 2. Reduces rate of economic growth

growth and trade) is by no means an easy affair. For example, attempts to reduce the level of inflation by controlling the money supply will have the undesired effects of increasing unemployment and stagnating the rate of economic growth. Similarly policies aimed at 'fine tuning' (adjusting) the performance of the economy so as to reduce the unemployment rate will be likely to have adverse consequences for the rate of inflation and the balance of payments.

In addition to the above it is also valid to point out that policies must be selected with some consideration for their political popularity. This not only influences the electoral future of the government, but it is also vital to the policy's chances of success. An unpopular policy such as a prices and incomes freeze is unlikely to succeed, because it would lack the necessary co-operation from powerful pressure groups such as the TUC and the CBI and would also be likely to be unpopular with the rest of the community.

Micro-economic policy

As we have seen, macro-economic policy is aimed at stabilising the behaviour of aggregated, or total, forces and variables within the economy.

Consequently its focus is on such phenomena as total output, total employment and total domestic consumption. Micro-economic policies, on the other hand, centre on the behaviour of such variables within specific industries, sectors and regions of the economy.

The major aims of micro-economic policy are:

- to combat problems in the workings of the market mechanism,
- to supplement macro-economic policy.

Instruments of micro-economic policy

The government has a number of different instruments which it can employ to achieve its micro-economic policy objectives. These can be summarised into distinct tactical approaches:

- legal regulations
- financial inducements and deterrents
- competition policy
- public ownership

Legal regulations

As we have seen in the legal parts of this text, British Governments employ a host of legal rules, regulations and restraints to influence micro-economic behaviour. Figure 41.3 illustrates the main areas of such controls, and details of the laws cited are contained within the relevant legal sections of this book.

However, the approach of the Conservative Government led by Mrs Thatcher has been to deregulate where possible and where appropriate, e.g. as with the trimming of planning procedures in enterprise zones, the deregulation of the financial markets, and also the deregulation of bus services, enabling private sector organisations to compete with existing operators.

Financial inducements and deterrents

These take the form of taxes, tax relief, subsidies and grants to induce desired changes in the activities of various micro-elements of the economy. Prominent in this field are grants for micro-chip technology and regional policy, both described in Part D as a source of finance for business.

In addition there are the various schemes for encouraging the growth of

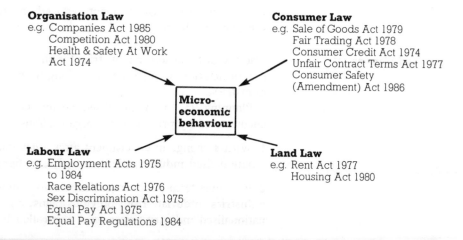

Organisation Law
e.g. Companies Act 1985
Competition Act 1980
Health & Safety At Work
Act 1974

Consumer Law
e.g. Sale of Goods Act 1979
Fair Trading Act 1978
Consumer Credit Act 1974
Unfair Contract Terms Act 1977
Consumer Safety
(Amendment) Act 1986

Micro-
economic
behaviour

Labour Law
e.g. Employment Acts 1975
to 1984
Race Relations Act 1976
Sex Discrimination Act 1975
Equal Pay Act 1975
Equal Pay Regulations 1984

Land Law
e.g. Rent Act 1977
Housing Act 1980

Fig. 41.3

small businesses, such as the Enterprise Allowance Scheme, which proffers £40 per week for one year to unemployed people starting up in business.

Competition policy

As described in Chapter 28 the Monopolies and Mergers Commission has been set up to investigate whether actual or potential 'monopolies' are acting against the public interest. By the Fair Trading Act of 1973, a monopoly exists where an organisation controls at least 25 per cent of the market. On the initiative of the Secretary of State for Trade and Industry or the Director General of Fair Trading, the Commission is asked to investigate whether abuse of monopoly power exists. It is up to the Secretary of State to reject or implement the Commission's findings.

For example, the Commission's report in 1981 condemning the practice adopted by some garages of surcharging customers buying petrol by credit card was accepted by the government.

Another aspect of competition policy is the Restrictive Trade Practices Act 1956. Collusion between firms in restraint of competition could lead to prosecution.

Public ownership

This tactic involves the use of the direct provision by the State of a range of goods and services. The local authorities provide such services as education and council housing, and the central government itself owns and controls the nationalised industries. The State authorities are thus able to exercise a degree of control over the supply of certain key commodities and also over investment and employment policies operating within those industries.

A policy adopted by the Conservative Government led by Mrs Thatcher is to sell off sections of the public sector – 'privatisation' as it has come to be known. Reference was made to this policy in Chapter 9 (see p. 86), and shortly we shall examine the reasons for it.

A variation on the tactic of direct ownership was introduced by the Industry Act of 1975 which created the National Enterprise Board (NEB). The initial motive behind the NEB was to provide risk capital for technologically orientated private firms, and in so doing maintain State involvement in their development. However, the NEB tended to become more involved in rescuing endangered companies such as British Leyland. Many people have criticised the NEB as a form of covert nationalisation, and the 1979 Conservative Government reduced the funds at its disposal. It has subsequently been absorbed into the British Technology Group.

Policy and planning

The use of State sector industries for short-term policy purposes highlights the difficulties of medium- and long-term planning of the nationalised industries.

Planning in the nationalised sector faces a number of pitfalls not encountered by private sector organisations. The main difficulties are:

1 With a change in government after a general election, different aims for a nationalised industry might unfold, e.g. tighter financial objectives.

2 For short-term policy expediency a government might cause nationalised industries to deviate from previous plans, e.g., in the early and mid-1970s nationalised industry prices were controlled by the government as part

an anti-inflation strategy. This upset the financial planning of those industries.

3 A drive for greater efficiency by closing plants or updating technology could cause unemployment. Governments might therefore hedge on whether such streamlining is necessary in the face of the social, financial and political costs of unemployment. This was a particular problem facing the steel industry in the 1960s and 1970s. Recommendations by successive British Steel chairmen for trimming capacity and manpower were not acted upon fully by governments. The crunch came for British Steel with the depression of the late 1970s and early 1980s. Orders fell. Steel could be imported more cheaply. The government accepted the need (belatedly, according to some critics) for closures of plants in many parts of the UK, e.g. Shotton, Corby and Consett.

Should the government have further increased subsidies to the steel industry (as was being done in the USA and West Germany, for example), so maintaining employment and enabling steel to be sold more cheaply? Or was the government right to cut costs by closing plants, operating reduced staffing levels and aiming for a more streamlined steel industry? What would you have done if you had been the Secretary of State for Trade and Industry?

Privatisation

As you may recall from Chapter 9 an important plank of the policies on which the Conservative Government was elected in 1979 was to denation- alise parts of the public sector and encourage private sector competition with State industries.

The main reasons for these moves were:

- The government believed in the value of market forces.
- It was claimed that tighter financial discipline and more competition would increase the efficiency and profitability of State sector organisations.
- The funds raised by selling State assets to the private sector would replenish Exchequer coffers and help to reduce the PSBR, as part of the government's monetarist strategy.
- To widen share ownership amongst the general public.

To these ends the government sold off parts of its shareholding in British Petroleum and sold shares in British Aerospace, Cable and Wireless and the National Freight Company. Subsequently Britoil was privatised, followed by British Telecom in 1984 and British Gas in 1986. In 1987 plans were being laid for the privatisation of British Airways and the British Airports Authority.

Some economists have suggested that the government's attitude to the sale of more profitable sections of the public sector is short-sighted. They claim that although the government receives more revenue in the short term, flows of revenue in the longer term are reduced. This could put a strain on government finances in the future.

Some critics have also argued that the privatisation of giants like British Telecom and British Gas does not increase competition but creates private monopolies with questionable degrees of control on their actions.

To increase competiton between public and private sector organisations,

the government permitted private sector coach operators to compete wit
the National Bus Company on long-distance coach routes. The immediat
effect was a bout of price-cutting competition, though it seems unlikely tha
the increased level of services will continue as a result. The monopol
enjoyed by British Telecom in the provision of telephone and tele
communications equipment has been removed.

The government has given local authorities the power to engage i
privatisation. For example, council houses may be bought by tenants, an
some local councils have contracted services like refuse collection to privat
operators.

Economic policies – an evaluation

As was indicated earlier success in meeting all macro-economic objective
simultaneously has eluded governments. The innate conflict of objective
has meant that success has been confined to some objectives whilst succes
in others have not been achieved. It is at the behest of a government t
prioritise which objectives it perceives as most important and gear polic
in those directions.

Different political parties have varying views on the appropriate polic
mix. The variation in view has centred on:

- the extent of State involvement in the market mechanism;
- the Keynesian *versus* monetarist debate;
- private *versus* public ownership of industries.

Let us consider the approaches advocated by the major political parties i
recent years. You might ponder on the policy mix you think is mo
appropriate.

Conservative Party

The major policy lines followed by the Conservative Government in powe
since 1979 have been to:

1 Reduce inflation by reliance on a monetarist package of curbing growt
in money supply primarily by use of high interest rates and reduction
the PSBR.

2 Encourage growth in the economy by:

a reductions in the higher rates of direct personal taxation and redu
Corporation Tax, with the aim of increasing incentives;

b easing legal constraints and regulations, as in enterprise zones and tl
abolition of Wages Councils;

c stimulatory measures to encourage the growth of small businesses an
by employment schemes.

3 Reduce the size and scope of the public sector and corresponding
increase the private sector, in order to widen private ownership, increa
competition and encourage economic growth.

The government can point to lower inflation and an upturn in econom
growth from 1981 as key indicators of the success of their policies. The
has been net growth in the number of small businesses and a substanti

increase in the number of individual shareholders consequent upon the privatisation of British Telecom and British Gas.

Critics of the government cite the large growth in unemployment between 1979 and 1981 particularly and the continued decline of UK manufacturing industry as the costs of the anti-inflation strategy. The tactic also involved some cuts in capital expenditure on public sector services like roads and housing with resultant reduction in provision and quality.

The Labour Party

The strategy proposed by the Labour Party focuses upon increased public expenditure, particularly on capital projects which are job creating and will extend provision of public sector services.

Additionally the Party proposes the introduction of a State investment bank which could acquire shares and inject funds into major private sector organisations, so that the State has a role in policy direction and funds are made available for expansion. These measures are designed to stimulate employment and economic growth.

The Labour Party would also intend to bring organisations like British Telecom back into the public sector domain by issuing interest-bearing debentures to replace shares, arguing that important major industries should be in State rather than private hands.

The plans of the Labour Party have been criticised in that the increased volume of public expenditure would mean higher taxation and a larger PSBR. It is argued that the former reduces people's choice in how to dispose of their income, whilst the latter could stimulate inflation, according to the monetarist argument.

Proponents of a non-interventionist line criticise more State involvement in the private sector, arguing that it restricts the freer operation of market forces and reduces competition.

The Liberal/SDP Alliance

Like the Labour Party, the Alliance favours a greater degree of public expenditure on capital projects to improve public services and to stimulate jobs.

It also favours schemes to encourage greater share ownership by employees in the organisation in which they work.

To combat inflation, the Alliance proposes an incomes policy whereby employers would be taxed if they allowed their workers' incomes to grow by more than a stated norm.

Criticisms of the Alliance's policy to increase public expenditure are similar to those levied at the Labour Party – concerning the manner and effects of financing the increase. There is also scepticism about the political popularity of the incomes policy scheme if extra pay is deducted at the income tax source.

Parties do change policies as the magnitude and severity of problems vary and as new ideas and opinions emerge. Keep abreast of the plans of the major parties. Consider the bases upon which policies are determined and consider their likely impact.

How might they affect you as an individual? How would they affect the organisation in which you may work? What impact would they have on the economy and society in general?

42 Social policy

We considered in Chapter 33 a range of services provided by the public sector to meet our social, collective needs. These included financial benefits such as social security plus the availability of services like health and personal social services and the police, with no direct price charged or pricing occurring at a subsidised rate.

Over many centuries such social policies have evolved. This chapter tracks the development of social policy and considers recent approaches utilised by governments, particularly the White Paper on Social Security of November 1985.

Development of social and environmental services

Whilst consumer expenditure to meet material needs has been a feature of human activity for many centuries, the consumption of State-provided services is a far more recent development. In many ways, this growth coincides with and relates to greater State involvement in the economic sphere, the emergence of the mixed economy. There had been little State provision of social or environmental services before the final decades of the nineteenth century. The Elizabethan Poor Law and the Speenhamland System of the late eighteenth and early nineteenth centuries provided small financial payments to the very needy. However, such schemes were extremely limited in their coverage of the poor and were operated only in parts of the country.

The workhouses which replaced the Speenhamland System did provide some food and shelter for the poor, but were stark, inhumane places, as Charles Dickens showed in *Oliver Twist*. It was not until this century that the conventional wisdom changed towards the acceptance of more civilised State support for those in need.

The latter half of the last century saw steps in providing improved environmental services, such as the Public Health Act of 1875. The 1870 and 1902 Education Acts saw the beginnings of State Primary and then Secondary schooling.

Prime Minister Asquith's Liberal Government accepted the duty of the State to provide financial payments for the aged, sick and unemployed. Acts of 1908 and 1911 saw the introduction of old age pensions and national insurance respectively.

In the inter-war years, there was much building of council houses and some improvement in road communications, necessitated by the increase in motor vehicles. The Poor Law was revised by the introduction of Public Assistance in 1929, in the form of small money benefits for needy individuals. The Education Act of 1918 provided for compulsory school attendance between the ages of 5 and 14.

Social attitudes were changing during and soon after World War 2, largely as a reaction to the hardships suffered during the inter-war depression with its heavy unemployment. Sir William Beveridge chaired a Royal Commission, producing the Beveridge Report on Social Insurance and Allied Services in 1942. The Report diagnosed four 'social evils' - disease, squalor, idleness and ignorance, all emanating from the problem of 'want', when families have insufficient funds to maintain an acceptable standard of living.

The Labour Government elected in 1945 accepted the challenge posed by the Beveridge Report. The immediate post-war years saw the establishment of the National Health Service, the reorganisation and extension of national insurance by the National Insurance Act of 1946, the expansion of council house building, and the creation of some new towns, e.g. Basildon and Harlow.

Already, the Education Act of 1944 had established the right to State education up to the age of 15. Further, post-war governments have accepted the responsibility to aim for as little unemployment as possible in the economy, to attempt to get full employment. This involves the use of macro-economies policies, those affecting the entire economy. Nevertheless, this tackling of the social evil of idleness has by no means been achieved continuously, owing to the simultaneous existence of other economic problems like inflation, which governments have needed to combat. Policies used to combat inflation have often had the effect of increasing unemployment (as was shown in Chapter 41 – see p. 378).

In post-war years there has been continued expansion of social and environmental services. The philosophy that the State has a duty to provide services available to all members of society has become widely accepted. The basic rationale is that all people, irrespective of income and wealth, have access to vital services like health and education, for which they otherwise would need to pay.

In recent years, though, there has been criticism in some quarters of the extent of welfare provisions. Some opinion favours a reduction in social service provision (including its administration), arguing that:

1 people should be more independent in providing for themselves and their families, and less reliant on State support, and

2 in an economy where there has been little economic growth in recent years, insufficient wealth has been created to finance expanding social services.

By reducing public expenditure and making resources available to the private sector, greater expansion of the economy might occur. This could lead to greater wealth being created for all.

The Conservative Government elected in 1979, for example, restrained the growth in public expenditure, including cuts in certain social services like education and health.

White Paper on Social Security

In December 1985 the Secretary of State for Social Services introduced a White Paper on Social Security, proposing reforms and revisions to be operative from April 1988. A prime objective of the measures was to overcome the 'poverty trap' whereby some families actually lose income if their earnings grow above certain levels and thus they lose their eligibility for State benefits.

Scales of payment of benefits are to be revised, though some benefits like the maternity and death grants will be abolished. Many of the changes revolve around the principle that the government feels all households should be, to some extent, self-supporting, so that every household will be expected to pay at least 20 per cent of their rent and rates bill given cuts in housing benefit.

Some critics of the proposals in the White Paper showed calculations that nearly 4 million people will be worse off under the changes whilst only 2 million will gain.

Another feature of the White Paper was a decrease in benefit entitlement under the State Earnings Related Pension Scheme (SERPS). It was suggested that this change was made to reduce the future financial burden on the State due to the growing numbers of old people, given the trend towards an ageing population.

Thus it seemed with the public expenditure cuts and revisions to social security announced in the White Paper that the frontier of social and environmental services has been rolled back.

Critics of this approach argue that low income families will particularly suffer because of the more limited availability of social services.

A study of poverty by Professor Peter Townsend indicated that according to the definition of poverty laid down by the Department of Health and Social Security, between 3 and 5 million people in the UK are in poverty – their income being no more than the minimum necessary for subsistence. Townsend himself suggests a wider definition of real poverty – where people are stopped by lack of money from taking part in the life of the community. About 12.4 million could be regarded as poor by this criterion. They are most likely to be families where the head of the household is a manual unskilled worker, single retired people and one-parent families.

A report* published in 1986 showed that the disparity in death rate between the poorer and richer sections of the community widened between 1979 and 1983, a period of rising unemployment. For example, death rate among semi-skilled and unskilled workers aged 25–44 were more than twice as high as those for professional people and managers of the same age. Women in social classes IV and V** are up to 70 per cent more likely to die younger than women in classes I and II.

Thus there is a body of opinion which opposes the contraction of social services on the grounds that even greater poverty is likely to result.

What do you think? Which line of argument do you favour?

* Occupational Mortality – The Registrar General Decennial Supplement for Great Britain.
** The Registrar General's classifications of social classes are according to occupation of the male head of the household.

Social class I   Professional occupations
              II   Intermediate occupations (managerial, senior administrative)
              III N Skilled occupations (non-manual)
              III M Skilled occupations (manual)
              IV   Partly skilled occupations
              V   Unskilled occupations

Summary, Part E

1 Costs faced by others as a result of an organisation's activities are called social costs. Legislation could be introduced to remedy the suffering, possibly influenced by the activities of pressure groups.

2 Social costs could be felt in terms of environmental damage.

3 Social accounting attempts to incorporate the social costs and social benefits, so as to obtain a truer picture of the value of national output.

4 Central government can be defined as the Executive – the body which carries out law and implements policy. The sphere of government is much more extensive today than it was in the nineteenth century.

5 The government is formed by the party or in theory the coalition which can command a majority of votes in the House of Commons. Ministers will also be Members of the House of Commons or the House of Lords.

6 Because of party discipline the government can dominate Parliament.

7 In a democratic State the government rules by consensus and must take account of public opinion. Pressure groups have an important influence on the formation of government policy.

8 Such legislation may set up quangos both to implement the legislation and to educate public opinion.

9 Central government meets it expenditure commitments by taxes, national insurance contributions and borrowing.

10 Central government delegates powers to local government. Control over local government's exercise of power can be carried out by the Judiciary on the grounds that, for example, a local authority has exceeded its powers or has failed to exercise its powers. Central government can exercise control over local government through the control of finance.

11 Local government expenditure is financed mainly by central government grants and by rates.

12 Accountability of central government:

  a to Parliament
- Debates
- Question Time
- Select Committees, particularly the Public Accounts Committee and the Expenditure Committee
  b To the Parliamentary Commissioner (ombudsman)
  c To the Judiciary
  d In contract and tort under the Crown Proceedings Act 1947.

13 Governments have sought to meet four major macro-economic objectives – stable prices, sturdy economic growth, a healthy balance of payments and a high level of employment.

14 Inflation means a general increase in prices. It is measured in the UK by the index of retail prices.

15 In the 1970s, the rate of inflation, though fluctuating, was generally higher than in the 1950s and 1960s. It declined in the 1980s.

16 Possible causes of inflation are demand-pull, cost-push and excess monetary growth.

17 Inflation can undermine economic, social and political confidence, artificially redistribute income, lead to fiscal drag unless tax allowances are adjusted, and affect export competitiveness.

18 The money supply is the total amount of money in the economy at a particular time. It is composed of notes and coins in circulation with the public plus various categories of bank deposits. Sterling M3 is the measure of money supply most commonly monitored by governments in recent years.

19 Banks can contribute to an increase in the supply of money by lending on the basis of money deposited. This lending creates new deposits which forms the base for further lending. However, banks must keep a fraction of deposits as a reserve.

20 The Bank of England is the UK central bank acting on behalf of the State.

21 The national income refers to the total money value of economic activity in an economy over a period of time.

22 It can be measured from three approaches, income, output and expenditure.

23 Total incomes earned by factors of production

= total value of net output

= total expenditure on finished goods and services.

24 Injections into the circular flow of income cause national income to rise whereas leakages from the circular flow cause it to decline. Injections are investment, government expenditure and exports. Leakages are saving taxation and imports.

25 Rises in injections trigger off a multiplier effect which will increase the national income by more than the size of the injection. Conversely a fall in injections or an increase in leakages will cause a fall in the national income.

26 In national income accounting, distinction is drawn between Gross Domestic Product, Gross National Product and National Income (Net National Product). Accounts are prepared for each of the three approaches income, output, expenditure.

27 National income statistics can be used as an indicator of economic growth to show the distribution of income between factors of production and as indicators of performance of sectors of the economy.

28 Economic growth is measured by real changes in national income, i.e money changes adjusted for inflation.

29 UK economic growth rates in recent years compare unfavourably with many other industrialised countries.

30 Major influences on economic growth are the quantity and quality of factors of production and growing demand.

31 The balance of payments chronicles the financial dealings of a country with the rest of the world. A country faces a balance of payments problem if there is a persistent tendency for imports to exceed exports, or for investment outflows to exceed inflows.

32 The foreign exchange rate is determined by the demand for and supply of a currency. Such demand and supply occurs due to the range of items listed in the balance of payments account.

33 The central bank of a country (e.g. the Bank of England) may buy or sell currency to smooth the movements in the exchange rate.

34 The balance of payments account is split into major sections. Visible trade involves the exporting and importing of goods. Invisibles include services, transfers and interest, dividends and profits.

The visible balance plus the invisible balance gives the balance of payments on current account.

The current balance plus total investment and other capital transactions, the balancing item, and any allocation of SDRs, leads to the balance for official financing.

This figure is offset by official financing, which includes transactions with overseas monetary authorities, other foreign currency borrowing by the UK public sector, and drawings on or additions to the reserves.

35 Fundamentally, the balance of payments balances overall because a sale of pounds on the foreign exchange market must imply a purchase of pounds. Deficits or surpluses occur on individual sections of the account.

36 The unemployed are those who are willing and able to work but cannot find suitable employment.

37 In the 1970s and 1980s the level of unemployment was generally on the upward trend, stabilising in the mid-1980s.

38 In spite of unemployment, job vacancies do exist. This is due for the most part to geographical or occupational immobilities.

39 Major causes of unemployment are structural change in the economy and deficiency of demand.

40 In the Budget, the Chancellor of the Exchequer announces government expenditure and revenue intentions and major economic policy changes.

41 Fiscal policy involves the manipulation of taxation and government expenditure in order to influence the level of aggregate demand.

42 Monetary policy influences the money supply and the rate of interest.

43 Monetarist policies aim to control the money supply, especially by reducing the PSBR.

44 If a country faces a serious balance of payments deficit, it will need to take measures for adjustment. Such measures include devaluation (or depreciation) of its currency, fiscal and monetary policies, import controls and overseas borrowing.

45 Such macro-economic policies, along with prices and incomes controls, balance of payments policies and manpower policies, can influence organisations' prices, demand and costs, forcing them to change their planning.

46 Micro-economic policies include legal regulations, financial inducements and deterrents, competition policy and public ownership.

47 Strategies of political parties in recent years have varied according to the extent of State involvement in ownership and control in the economy.

48 The development of the Welfare State is primarily a twentieth-century phenomenon. Views differ between political parties on the extent of welfare provision.

Assignments Part G

1

Economic Change

This assignment requires you to draw up a profile of economic change in the UK over a period of 6 months. Parts **a**, **b** and **c** should be kept in the form of a diary.

a By referring to national or possibly local newspapers each day, record details of any major new organisations established in the UK. You should, for example, note the line of business that the organisation is in, say computer manufacture, a government department, a bank, etc. How many people are likely to be employed? What were the likely reasons for the expansion?

b Also, by reference to the press, record in the same manner occurrences of expansion by *existing* organisations.

c Conversely, note from the press details of decisions by major organisations in the public and private sector to close down completely or trim the scale of their operations.

   Which organisations are involved? What are the likely reasons for their contraction? How many jobs are lost in consequence?

Such activity as you record in **a**, **b** and **c** contributes to changing the dimensions of the major macro-economic problems. The next section involves your monitoring these problems.

d By referring to suitable statistical sources for the UK over the chosen 6-month period, construct graphs or charts showing changes in:
(i) Unemployment (ii) Economic growth (iii) Inflation (iv) The size of the current account deficit or surplus on the balance of payments.
As new figures become available during the period, plot them on your graphs or charts.

e Once the 6-month period is up, summarise the patterns of change you have seen in the British economy. Do you notice any healthy or pessimistic signs for the short-term future of the economy?

Skills

Learning and studying, numeracy, information gathering, communicating, identifying and tackling problems.

2

The Budget

This assignment involves your analysing the most recent Budget announced by the government.

a Describe the parliamentary procedures by which the Budget proposals become enacted.

b What were the major aims of the Budget?

c Describe the main measures announced in the Budget.

d Do you think these measures will help to achieve the aims?

e How appropriate and effective do you think the Budget was? Consider the criteria against which you would evaluate the Budget when making your appraisal.

f Choose 4 of the organisations in Sunhampton High Street. Explain the impact of Budget measures on these organisations.

Skills

Information gathering, communication, identifying and tackling problems.

INTERNATIONAL FACTORS

When you have read this part you should be able to:
- Describe major patterns of UK trade.
- Consider influences on UK trading performance and opportunities.
- Consider the operation of major international organisations and agencies and their impact on UK organisations.

43 International trade

We have already considered the nature of the balance of payments and policies associated with it. In this part we consider major influences on Britain's trading relationships with other countries and how international bodies like the IMF, international treaties like GATT and international cartels like OPEC can have an impact upon British organisations.

As well as selling in the home market many organisations look overseas to expand their sales. Does the organisation in which you may work export any goods or services?

Certainly, as a consumer there is little doubt that you buy many goods and services which are imported into the UK. Consider the food you eat. Britain imports over a third of the food consumed in this country. What about clothes you wear, the car you may drive, your TV set? Doubtless, there will be a significant imported content amongst those items.

Why do countries trade?

Why do countries export and import? Should countries produce purely for their own needs and be self-sufficient? Think about these questions before you read on.

There are a number of reasons for international trade.

Different resource endowments

There is not an even distribution of economic resources throughout the world. Some natural resources are concentrated in only a few countries. West Germany or Japan do not have their own oil; Britain now needs to import iron ore for its iron and steel industry. Given there is a need for such vital primary products, they must be imported if they are not indigenous. However, to cover the costs of such imports, a satisfactory level of exports is necessary.

The benefits of specialisation

It would be possible for Britain to grow bananas and oranges rather than import them. This would mean creating the necessary climatic conditions artificially and could prove a costly exercise. It would involve the use of resources which would be more profitably employed in producing something for which Britain was better equipped, e.g. industrial machinery.

For Britain, it is cheaper to import such fruit. The opportunity cost to a country of attempting to be self-sufficient is the alternative output foregone, alternative output which Britain could produce more efficiently.

Some economists have developed a theory to explain this influence on international trade, known as the *Theory of Comparative Advantage*. It suggests that a country should specialise in the production of the commodity in which it has a comparative advantage over its trading rivals (i.e. it produces relatively more efficiently). Specialising and exporting quantities of that product enables other goods to be imported. This should increase the quantity of goods available to the population of that country and raise its living standards compared to the situation if the country did not trade.

In reality, countries do not specialise totally. For example, for strategic reasons, amongst others, it is regarded as worthwhile to develop an agricultural sector of some size, or an armaments industry. War could disrupt international flows, so that home-produced food and weapons could be essential. However, many countries do devote significant amounts of resources to the production of particular products: 96 per cent of Zambia's export earnings in 1983 came from copper; over 80 per cent of Cuba's export revenue is earned from sugar. The oil exporting countries of the Middle East specialise heavily in oil. Such specialisation, though, largely reflects the fact that such countries have yet to undergo fully the process of industrialisation, through which the Western countries had gone by the start of this century. It is very difficult for the less developed countries to break into the industrial circle, given the world economic dominance of the already industrialised.

Specialisation in primary products can also breed potential instability. Natural resources do not last for ever, so export earnings will eventually decline. Alternative energy or mineral resources develop. Agriculture can be severely affected by weather and by demand conditions imposed by the buying countries.

Thus although there are benefits in some degree of specialisation, putting too many eggs in one basket can also cause potential structural problems for an economy.

Varied wants of consumers

Wider variation in quality, price and range of goods can be enjoyed when the international market rather than only the domestic market is open to buyers. Exporters compete with home producers, extending the variety of goods available to consumers.

The significance of overseas trade to the UK

Exporting is crucial to the UK economy, since we must cover the costs of imports of basic products like foodstuffs and raw materials such as metal ores and timber. The exploitation of North Sea oil has reduced our dependence on the import of this vital commodity, but we need to import other primary products with which the UK is not endowed.

During the industrial revolution in the eighteenth and nineteenth centuries, Britain utilised indigenous iron ore and copper, and was less reliant on imports. However, these resources do not last for ever, and the country now needs to import these metals.

In recent years, Britain has tended to import relatively more consumer goods and machinery, putting further pressure on the need for export earnings. It has been estimated by economists that we spend on imports upwards of one-third of extra income we earn. Such import penetration has been to the detriment of UK producers, some of whom have faced a declining market share or even bankruptcy. Greater unemployment has occurred.

In Fig. 43.1 the extent of the growth in imports can be seen in a selection of industries. Given the country's level of imports, this puts a greater onus on exporters. As well as home-produced oil being a substitute for imports, earnings from the export of North Sea oil helps, adding to our traditional major export earners like machinery and road vehicles.

In 1983 UK exports of goods and services accounted for 33 per cent of the Gross National Product at factor cost (the total value of the country's output, income or expenditure). This is a higher proportion than for most

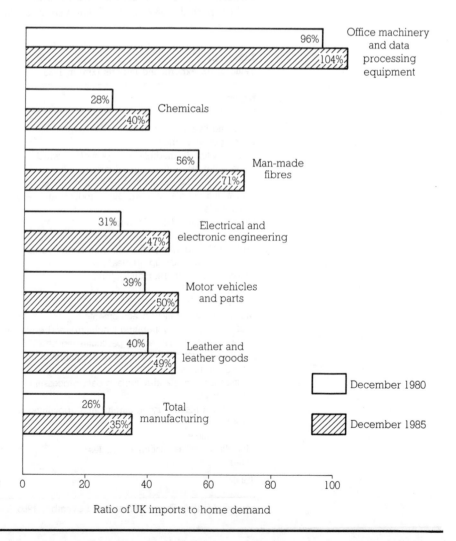

Fig. 43.1
Import Penetration into the UK-selected Industries
Source: *Monthly Digest of Statistics*
November 1986
Table 15.10

industrialised countries. The comparable figure for the USA is 8 per cent. This indicates that the USA is more self-sufficient, having greater home-produced food and natural resources.

We shall now look in more detail at the pattern of UK trade, what we import and export, which organisations are our major exporters, where are our main markets, and from which areas we import most.

As you may recall from Chapter 39 trade in actual goods or commodities is known as **visible trade**, as opposed to **invisible trade**, which includes services.

Table 43.1 lists the money value of major goods exported and imported from and to the UK. Figure 43.2 illustrates the change in volume (the change in quantities) of important imports, and Fig. 43.3 shows corresponding data exports.

From Table 43.1 you should be able to recognise which are the major export earners for the UK. The biggest category is machinery and transport equipment, which accounted for 31.5 per cent of the total in 1985. Road vehicles and office machines are prominent in this group.

The period 1982 to 1985 showed relatively more rapid growth in the

Table 43.1

Value of UK exports and imports (£m) in 1985

Exports	Exports	%	Imports	%
Food and live animals	3 252	4.1	8 107	9.5
Beverages and tobacco	1 719	2.2	1 231	1.4
Crude materials, inedible, except fuels of which	2 032	2.6	4 857	5.7
metalliferous ores and metal scrap	646	0.8	1 372	1.6
Mineral fuels, lubricants and related materials	16 796	21.4	10 664	12.5
of which petroleum, petroleum products and related materials	16 134	20.6	8 316	9.8
Chemicals and related products	9 412	12.0	6 901	8.1
Manufactured goods	10 430	13.3	14 342	16.9
of which paper, paperboard, pulp textile yarns,	768	1.0	2 532	3.0
fabrics and made up articles	1 709	2.2	3 032	3.6
non-metalic mineral manufactures	2 165	2.8	2 243	2.6
iron and steel	1 856	2.4	1 716	2.0
non ferrous metals	1 380	1.8	1 903	2.2
Machinery and transport equipment	24 668	31.5	26 938	31.7
of which power generating machinery and equipment	3 061	3.9	1 998	2.3
machinery specialised for particular industries	3 078	3.9	2 327	2.7
general industrial machinery and equipment and machine parts	2 938	3.7	2 604	3.1
office machines and automatic data processing equipment	3 747	4.8	4 510	5.3
electrical machinery, apparatus and appliances and parts	3 380	4.3	4 277	5.0
road vehicles	3 911	5.0	6 801	8.0
Miscellaneous manufactured articles	7 997	10.2	10 132	11.9
Other	2 087	2.7	1 857	2.2
Total	78 392		85 027	

Source: *Monthly Digest of Statistics* November 1986, Tables 15.2 and 15.3

Fig. 43.2
Percentage change in the volume of
UK imports 1982–5 Source: *Monthly
Digest of Statistics* November 1986
Table 15.9

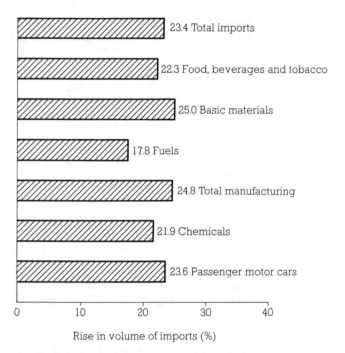

Fig. 43.2
Percentage change in the volume of
UK imports 1982–5 Source: *Monthly
Digest of Statistics* November 1986
Table 15.9

Fig. 43.3
Percentage change in the volume of
UK exports 1982–5
Source: *Monthly Digest of Statistics*
November 1986
Table 15.9

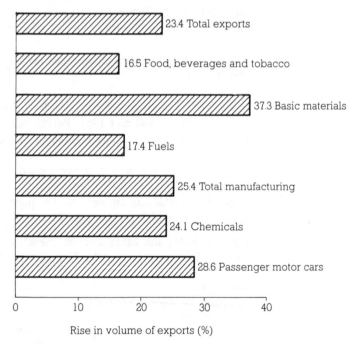

volume of exports than was evident in previous years, as economic growth
expanded and there was some recovery from recession.

Which organisations contribute most to UK export earnings?

As you might expect it is the major oil, chemicals and engineering organisations that are prominent.

Table 43.2

Largest exporters from UK (year ended March or December 1984)

		Exports (£m)
1	Shell UK	2 591
2	ICI	2 295
3	British Aerospace	1 564
4	General Electric	1 200
5	Ford	1 064
6	BL	827
7	IBM UK Holdings	745
8	Rolls Royce	519
9	BAT Industries	407
10	Johnson Mathey	299

Source: *Times 1000*

On the import front, note that machinery and transport equipment is ou[ ]
major category of imports, just as it is our most prominent export earner[ ]
Note also the significance of imported manufacturers and foodstuffs. Fron[ ]
Fig. 43.2 it can be seen that there has been continued growth in the Britisl[ ]
appetite for imported manufacturers, including motor cars. As a measur[ ]
of recovery has occurred in the economy and economic growth ha[ ]
improved, so the demand for imports has correspondingly risen. The defic[ ]
on UK non-oil visible trade is ever widening.

The geographical pattern of trade

Which are the UK's main international markets? From which countries do we import most?

Table 43.3 compares the geographical breakdown of UK visible export[ ]
and imports in 1980 and 1985. Before you read on, study the pie-charts i[ ]
Fig. 43.4 and pick out any significant changes in the pattern of trade.

What reasons do you think may have caused these changes?

Before considering answers to the questions posed, some explanation [ ]
the countries which form the geographical groupings in the charts is given[ ]

EEC includes the other current members of the European Community[ ]
namely Belgium, Denmark, France, the Irish Republic, Italy, Luxem[ ]

Table 43.3

UK exports and imports by country

	% of total exports		% of total imports	
	1980	1985	1980	1985
West Germany	10.3	11.4	11.0	14.9
USA	9.4	14.7	11.7	11.7
France	7.4	9.9	7.5	7.8
Netherlands	7.8	9.4	6.6	7.7

Sources: *Monthly Digest of Statistics*, June 1981, Table 15.9 and 15.10, and November 1986 Table 15.5 and 15.6

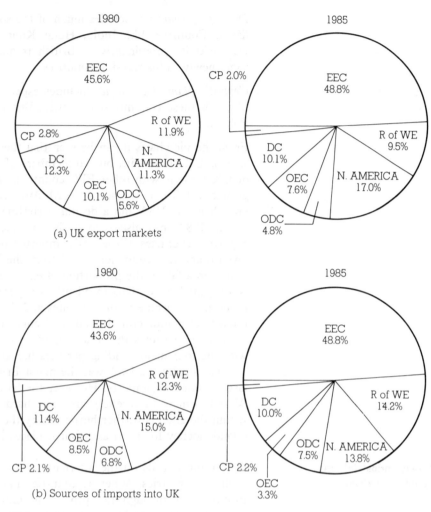

ig. 43.4
he geographical distribution of UK
isible trade, 1980 and 1985
ource: *Monthly Digest of Statistics*
ovember 1986
able 15.4

(a) UK export markets

(b) Sources of imports into UK

Key
EEC = European Economic Community
R of WE = Rest of Western Europe
ODC = Other developed countries
CP = Centrally planned economies
OEC = Oil exporting countries
DC = Developing countries

bourg, the Netherlands and West Germany. Greece is included in the 1985 figures. Spain and Portugal became members in 1986.

Rest of Western Europe includes the non-Communist countries like Switzerland, Sweden, Norway and Austria.

North America covers the USA and Canada.

Other developed countries relates primarily to Australia, Japan and South Africa.

Oil exporting countries includes particularly Saudi Arabia, Nigeria, Iran and Kuwait.

Developing countries includes much of the southern hemisphere not already listed. Countries like India, Hong Kong, Brazil, Israel and Singapore feature quite prominently in British trade, indicating the importance of some newly industrialising countries.

Centrally planned economies includes especially the countries of the Soviet bloc. Of these communist countries, Britain trades most with Russia and Poland.

From the pie charts it can be seen that there has been a noticeable expansion of UK trade with our co-members of the EEC such that nearly half of UK trade is with other EEC countries. There has also been substantial growth in UK export trade to North America, reflecting the rapid economic growth in the USA and a declining sterling exchange rate with the dollar.

The 1980s has also seen a shift in the proportion of trade with oil exporting countries. Clearly UK imports from such countries have declined given domestic production of oil from the North Sea. However there has also been a fall in the proportion of export trade with such countries. This is attributed to the falls in oil prices experienced in the 1980s which have reduced the income of the oil states and thus hampered their ability to buy imports of manufactured goods and engineering equipment.

Table 43.3 shows that the proportion of both UK exports and imports with the four major trading partners has grown through the 1980s.

Traditionally the USA was the major British export market and also the largest source of imports. However the latter mantle has been assumed by West Germany in recent years. The hardening prominence of UK trade within the EEC is further borne out by the fact that France and the Netherlands jockey for third and fourth places for both imports and exports.

Newly industrialising countries (NICs)

Significant arrivals on the international trading front are the newly industrialising countries. Whereas countries like the UK, USA, Germany and France went through the process of industrialisation in the nineteenth century, some countries are only in recent years in the process of developing as industrialised economies.

Newly industrialising countries like South Korea, Singapore, Taiwan, Brazil and Mexico tended to undergo noticeable industrial change from the 1950s or 1960s.

The following features tend to characterise their operations:

- the tendency to produce goods for the lower price range of markets e.g. cheap textile goods, cheap micro-chip based products
- the use of modern technology
- relatively cheap labour
- State investment in infra-structure, e.g. housing, transport, telecommunications to set a solid base for the growth of industry
- investment in higher education to encourage technically aware and adaptable personnel.

By attacking the cheaper end of markets, NICs have made noticeable inroads into markets in a number of industrialised countries, just as Japan did previously. In the UK, a degree of penetration has particularly occurred in the textile industry, as indicated in Chapter 41.

The response of home industry in a number of countries to such competition has been to contract and concentrate on lower volume, higher quality sections of a market, but also to raise the cries for protection against cheap imports. In the USA in particular, the protectionist lobby has urged the imposition of quotas against a number of products from newly industrialising countries, as well as from other industrial nations.

However, as far as the UK is concerned the competition from NICs should be put in perspective. As shown in Table 43.4 our major competitors are still the established industrial nations. UK imports from developing countries accounted for 11.4 per cent of the total in 1974, the same position as in 1980. Table 43.4 shows that the proportion had declined slightly by 1985. Hong Kong sells more by value to the UK than any other newly industrialising nation, but still stood only sixteenth in the league table of major sources of imports, being fifteenth in 1980. The value of imports from major industrial nations dwarfs that from the NICs. The rates of growth of value of imports through the 1980s, listed in Table 43.4 do not show significant variation between NICs and industrial nations. In fact imports from Singapore fell over the period.

Note that the data in Table 43.4 shows the percentage growth in the money value of imports. A proportion of this rise is attributable to inflation. It does not mean that imports rose in volume to the extent shown in the figures.

However, what is of concern to the UK is the greater competition that is faced in export markets given growth in the NICs, and also the concentration of imports from the Far East in products like textiles and cheaper micro-chip based goods. The effects have been felt more severely in a narrow section of UK industry.

More generally, although NICs have made a degree of penetration into UK markets, Britain's industrial survival more firmly rests in competing with the nations of Western Europe, the USA and Japan.

Table 43.4
UK imports from selected countries

Country	Value of imports (£m) 1985	% Change in money value of imports 1980–5
West Germany	12 601	+ 123
USA	9 920	+ 65
France	6 632	+ 72
Netherlands	6 551	+ 93
Japan	4 117	+ 141
Malaysia	384	+ 105
Singapore	441	− 18
Taiwan	583	+ 153
Hong Kong	1 176	+ 38
South Korea	480	+ 98
Brazil	611	+ 106

Source: *Annual Abstract of Statistics* 1987, Table 12.6

Influences on exporting and importing

In Chapter 27 we discussed the factors which influence demand and supply. These factors are just as applicable when considering goods traded on international markets. In this section we shall consider those influences which are particularly important when importing and exporting takes place, posing particular problems for firms engaging in international trade.

Price

The price of the commodity an organisation is trying to export or is considering importing is likely to have much influence on demand. The price at which an organisation sells its product will be compared by potential buyers with the price of substitutes. These alternatives could be:

* those of other intending exporters, or
* those of domestic sellers of that commodity (if any).

The price charged by an exporter for selling a quantity of its product will be dependent on the conditions of supply, like costs of production, available technology, weather, etc.* However, there is an additional factor relevant to the international market – the **foreign exchange rate**.

* See Chapter 27 to refresh your memory if need be.

The exchange rate is the rate at which a unit of one currency is exchanged for another, e.g. £1 = US$150. The workings of the foreign exchange market and the means by which the rates are determined were discussed in Chapter 39. Be clear on how changes in the exchange rate can affect prices of goods in other markets.

If a British exporter is prepared to sell goods in the USA for the dollar equivalent of £1 each, then they are likely to sell for $1.50 if the rate mentioned above holds. However, if the rate of the pound rises against the dollar, to, say £1 = $1.75 the firm's goods would become dearer to American buyers. Conversely, a decline in the exchange rate to £1 = $1.25, for example, would make its goods more attractive in price to the American consumer.

On the other hand, from the view of a British importer, a fall in the value of the pound on the foreign exchange markets is likely to make imports dearer. A rise in its value will make imports cheaper.

Trade restrictions

Trade restrictions inhibit the ability of a country to sell its goods overseas. They include **tariffs**. A tariff is a duty levied on some or all imports so increasing their price and being likely to discourage demand. Although the EEC does not have tariffs between its States, it does have a common tariff wall against the import of goods from many non-member countries. The size of the tariff varies from commodity to commodity. The intention is to promote trade between member countries but to discriminate against many imports from outside the EEC. Back in 1964 the UK Government also introduced a temporary tariff of 15 per cent on the price of imports. Here the aim was to reduce the nation's expenditure on imports because of a balance of payments problem.

Quotas

These are government restrictions on the quantities of products that can be imported. Importers have to apply to the State for licences to import limited amounts. The UK does not impose widespread quotas although they have been introduced in rare cases like the import of television tubes, polyester and nylon yarns for carpet making, and dresses and underwear from South Korea. The intention has been to protect the struggling British firms making such products.

Foreign exchange controls

A government can restrict the extent the native currency can be sold for others on the foreign exchanges. Thus there can be limits on the extent of imports that can be bought and paid for. At the time of writing, exchange controls have been removed in the UK.

Other barriers

Though not erecting tariffs or quotas on imports, some countries, e.g. Japan, make life difficult for foreign exporters. A complicated distribution network, extensive regulations and periodic changes in minimum standards of goods can all be burdensome to the intending exporter. The exporter may only need to make minute adjustments to the product, but this can be costly if production runs and mouldings have to be altered.

Marketing

Shrewd marketing techniques are especially necessary in international markets. The exporting organisation is at an innate disadvantage in being less familiar with a foreign market than with the domestic market. Effective marketing research, especially consumer and product research, can be useful tools for understanding the pattern of foreign consumer needs. Foreign markets often have different preferences for, e.g. packet size, means of packaging or special offers than the home market. A new product might need to be developed rather than the domestic version or a mere variant on it.

Furthermore, consumer research in overseas markets has emphasised the need for reliability of the product and adhering to delivery dates. Such non-price factors are very important for expanding exporters.

Government encouragement for exporters

Although giving subsidies to exporters is in breach of the General Agreement on Tariffs and Trade and is frowned upon in international circles, a government can offer more indirect assistance to exporters.

The British Overseas Trade Board, a section of the Department of Trade, provides 'export intelligence', key information on overseas markets. The Export Credit Guarantee Department (ECGD) provides an 'insurance' scheme for exporters. For a premium, it will undertake to pay an exporter in the event of default in payment by a foreign buyer. The ECGD will also provide funds to an exporter awaiting payment, to be repaid later, when the foreign buyer ultimately pays up. Banks are prepared to accept an export credit guarantee as a basis on which to lend to firms in the short term.

Economic growth in other countries

The degree of growth in real income levels in the world economy is another influence on demand for exports. The 1950s and 1960s saw significant growth in the world economy, with speedy growth in world trade. However, from the mid-1970s the rate of growth of world trade was slower, with problems of rising expenditure on oil and more rapid inflation. In these circumstances, exporting becomes even more difficult. By the early 1980s higher rates of growth were evident, particularly in the US economy.

The high exchange rate of the dollar was an encouragement to other nations to export to the expanding American market.

Multinationals

Many of the major exporters are multinational companies. These are organisations which operate in a number of countries rather than just one, having production plants or retail outlets, for example, in a variety of countries.

The largest multinationals boast a turnover bigger than the GNP of some countries. For example, the annual turnover of Exxon, the oil giant, outstrips the GNP of any African country. Table 43.5 lists the biggest multinationals according to the value of their sales.

Table 43.5
The world's largest industrial groupings: sales for year ending March or December 1984

	Country of origin	Sales (£m)
1 Exxon Corporation	USA	73 579
2 Shell Transport and Trading/Royal Dutch Shell	UK/Netherlands	72 580
3 General Motors Corporation	USA	64 382
4 Mitsui	Japan	49 815
5 Mitsubishi	Japan	48 690
6 BP	UK	44 059
7 Mobil	USA	43 014
8 Ford Motor Corporation	USA	40 189
9 C. Itoh	Japan	39 984
10 Marubeni	Japan	37 005

Source: *Times 1000*

Note the significance of the oil companies, motor manufacturers and the large, integrated Japanese corporations which produce a variety of manufactured goods. They are known as *soga shosha*.

Clearly, multinationals contribute substantially to output and employment in countries in which they operate, and exert strong influence on the markets in which they trade. They can also have an effect on foreign exchange rates since they hold and exchange large balances in a variety of currencies, reflecting the transnational nature of their business. Furthermore they can adjust their pricing and profitability by weighing up company taxation levels and investment incentives in different countries so as to minimise their worldwide tax liability and boost profits globally.

On the stage of world trade multinationals are leading players. The 100 largest multinationals account for one-third of world trade, a figure expected to rise to over a half within the next two decades.

Is the organisation in which you may work a multinational company? If not, does your organisation trade with any multinationals, such as buying stock or materials for them? Is the bank in which you may have an account a multinational?

There are a number of international institutions of great importance to the government and to business organisations in the UK. The UK Government participates in these bodies and helps to formulate policies influencing the international environment. Decisions made by these institutions can exert significant influence on policies undertaken by the British Government and can affect actions within business organisations in this country.

International institutions are usually set up by international treaties or agreements but there are certain situations in which countries enter into treaties without setting up an organisational structure, e.g. GATT (the General Agreement on Tariffs and Trade) and OPEC (the Organisation of Petroleum Exporting Countries), the second of which Britain is *not* a member.

This chapter analyses the operation and importance of some major international bodies and treaties. It is popular to criticise international treaties and organisations on the grounds of their ineffectiveness. If, however, we were to take a close look at bodies like the WHO (the World Health Organisation), the FAO (the Food and Agricultural Organisation), the various agreements on Carriage of Goods by Sea (for example the Hague–Visby rules) and Air Transport (the Warsaw Convention), we would see that these agreements are effective because it is in nations' own self-interest that they should work. The situation is more problematic when we look at, for example, GATT, the EEC (the European Economic Community) and the UN (the United Nations), where we sometimes see vested interests at war with each other.

The International Monetary Fund (IMF)

In 1944 the representatives of the Allied Nations met at Bretton Woods in the USA to discuss the post-war problems of economic recovery and the need to restore international financial stability. The Bretton Woods Agreement established two very important institutions – the International Monetary Fund (IMF) and the International Bank for Reconstruction and Development (the World Bank).

The IMF had two basic aims for encouraging the growth of world trade and promoting international monetary co-operation through a permanent institution which would provide the machinery for consultation and collaboration:

1 To establish fixed exchange rates.
2 To allow countries in balance of payments difficulties to borrow foreign exchange from the IMF.

The funds of the IMF are contributed by member States according to quotas which are revised from time to time.

Exchange rates

This increasing internationalisation of banking operations meant that capital could be shifted extremely quickly from one currency to another. This, coupled with rising inflation, had the effect of turning surpluses into deficits within a short space of time. Countries were reluctant, for political and economic reasons, to comply with the fixed exchange limits set by the IMF, and therefore the Bretton Woods system of fixed exchange rates broke down in the early 1970s and most major currencies were 'floated'. This meant that no central bank was obliged to intervene in the foreign exchange markets to preserve the value of its currency. However, on certain occasions, central banks do intervene to smooth out rapid fluctuations in exchange rates or to offset undesirable movements.

In response to these developments the IMF made an amendment to the original Bretton Woods Agreement allowing members to choose their own exchange arrangements while allowing for a possible future reinstatement of exchange rates linked to 'stable out adjustable' par values (i.e. fixed within a certain range).

Fixed exchange rates

By this term we mean that a currency has a fixed value against other currencies. In the original Bretton Woods Agreement the value of national currencies was not allowed to deviate more than one per cent up or down from a fixed 'par value'. The great advantage of a fixed exchange rate is that it removes the uncertainty associated with floating rates. This is obviously helpful as far as long-term planning is concerned. Its major disadvantage is that the burden of keeping up the rate will fall on the domestic economy and so a country with a persistent deficit will soon exhaust its currency reserves in trying to hold up the exchange value of its currency.

Conditions attached to IMF 'loans'

Countries which want to borrow from the Fund will very probably have to agree to certain conditions before the loan is granted. The greater the loan, the tighter the strings attached. The borrowing government must set out in a 'letter of intent' to the IMF the changes that it will make in its domestic economy in order to reduce the size of its balance of payments deficit. This letter of intent is written in consultation with the IMF. In 1976 the UK Government was obliged to reduce public expenditure, reduce the size of the public sector borrowing requirement and set targets for the growth in the money supply in return for an IMF loan.

The structure of the IMF

The Bretton Woods Agreement which set up the IMF was an international treaty like the Treaty of Rome which established the EEC. The Fund is administered by a Board of Directors with supervisory functions and by Executive Directors who are responsible for the actual management of the Fund. Both these bodies are elected, but the member countries which contribute most to the Fund have the most votes. There is no judicial control over the Directors – they are the interpreters of their own Treaty. However, they may refer legal questions to the International Court of Justice at The Hague, the United Nations court.

The General Agreement on Tariffs and Trade (GATT)

We discussed earlier how trade restrictions of various types inhibit the ability of a country to sell its goods overseas. It was an awareness of the need after World War 2 to encourage world trade and progressively to do away with these restrictions that led to GATT (General Agreement on

Tariffs and Trade). The agreement was drawn up in 1947 at the Havana Conference whose aim was to establish an International Trade Organisation (ITO). The 23 signatories of that 1947 agreement included the UK. This aim was never accomplished, and it is a strange fact that the GATT has never been formally ratified (i.e. accepted as binding in international law); nonetheless, negotiations aimed at abolishing tariffs and discriminatory trading practices have been carried out with some success under the auspices of GATT.

The basis of the GATT agreement is the 'most favoured nation' clause and the idea of 'reciprocity' – by this we mean that every tariff concession agreed between any country or group of countries must be extended to all member countries of GATT (i.e. if we give one country favourable treatment by cutting tariffs we must give all countries that favourable treatment and they in return will give us concessions). However, the trend in recent years has been to favour developing countries which need preferential treatment and are in no position to give concessions in return.

GATT operates on a basis of 5-year negotiation sessions.

The declared aims of the Tokyo Round of GATT negotiations 1975–80 were to expand international trade by reducing or eliminating not only tariffs but all barriers to trade and to ensure additional benefits for the trade of developing countries. For the first time negotiations were open not only to the now 80 members of GATT but to all the countries of the world. As a result 99 countries took part in the Tokyo Round negotiations and two-thirds of these were developing countries. The negotiations, in which, of course, the UK took part, achieved some measure of success in eliminating barriers to trade.

The current negotiations which started in 1986 in Uruguay are encountering major difficulties in further liberalising trade. They are encountering the same problems as before – the protectionist policies of the rich producers like the USA and the EEC and their harmful effect on the less developed countries. The USA is hostile to the EEC's common external tariff, most recently since the entry of Spain (a major USA grain importer) into the EEC and the imposition of a high grain tariff. The arguments of the USA ring somewhat hollow because of its own protectionist policies. Handing out 30 billion dollars in subsidies to its own farmers in 1985 is one example of this protectionism.

It is, of course, the less developed countries which really suffer from this kind of protectionism and, in recent years, discussions on their predicament (part of what is called the North–South dialogue, i.e. discussions between the rich countries mostly in the Northern hemisphere and poor countries mostly in the Southern hemisphere) have taken place in a different forum, separate from the GATT negotiations. This is UNCTAD (the United Nations Conference on Trade and Development).

The objective of the current GATT meeting is 'to bring about further liberalisation and expansion of world trade to benefit all countries, especially less developed parties'. The US commitment to this lofty aim may be flagging because of the domestic repercussions of its large trade deficit. The EEC's Common Agricultural Policy is a formidable obstacle to liberalisation. Unless a compromise can be reached the multilateral approach to trade conceived 40 years ago may be replaced by competitive bilateral agreements, politically damaging, disastrous for less developed countries and highly damaging to trade in richer countries like Britain by restricting the free movement of our goods, thus contributing to the down turn in the economy and resultant unemployment.

The relationship between the IMF and GATT

There is a certain amount of co-operation between the IMF and GATT Article XV of the GATT specifically refers to this, and Article XII doe allow import restrictions if a particular country is, according to the IMF in balance of payments difficulties. GATT and the IMF have frequen consultations on exchange questions and other related topics.

The European Economic Community (EEC)

History

After World War 2 the economies of the European countries were in ruins and it was apparent that there was a need to rebuild them and to foste international trust and co-operation. In 1947 a programme was drawn u (the Marshall Aid Fund) to give enormous sums of US dollars to Europ to begin this rebuilding process. General George Marshall, the US Foreig Secretary, introduced the programme by declaring: 'Our policy is n directed against any country or against any doctrine but against hunge: poverty, despair and chaos; its aim is the renewal of active econom throughout the world.' The plan was welcomed in Western Europe, b Russia and the countries of the Eastern bloc refused to participate.

The Council of Europe

There were also political initiatives in which Britain played some part i bringing the European nations together. In 1948 Winston Churchill mac a famous speech at the Congress of Europe advocating European unity. Tl Congress resulted in the formation of the Council of Europe in 1949, whic started with the UK, France, Belgium, the Netherlands and Luxembou as its original members and now includes most of the countries of Weste Europe. Its main achievement lies in the field of human rights, havir established a Commission and a Court of Human Rights before whic individuals can bring cases against member governments alleging breach of the European Convention on Human Rights. Great Britain, for exampl was brought before the court for alleged breaches of the Convention by tl security forces in Northern Ireland.

The European Coal and Steel Community

Other initiatives followed as a result of the need to develop an energ sharing programme in Western Europe. In 1950 Robert Schumann, tl French Foreign Secretary, proposed that all Franco-German production coal and steel should be placed under a common authority, and invit other countries to do the same. In 1951 the Foreign Ministers representi France, Germany, Italy, Belgium, the Netherlands and Luxembourg sign in Paris a treaty which came into force in 1952 and established the Eur pean Coal and Steel Community. (The UK was never a member.) We mig call this the first Common Market.

Euratom

The Coal and Steel Community was followed in 1957 by the creation EURATOM (the European Community of Atomic Energy), whose ma purpose is to co-ordinate atomic energy programmes, and by the creation of the European Economic Community (the EEC). Both EURATOM and the EEC were created by two separate Treaties of Rome in 1957. The separate institutions of the three bodies – the Coal and Steel Community, EURATOM, and the EEC – were merged in 1967. They can be regarded as 'facets of one basic experiment, stages in an unfinished process' towards European unity.

The UK's entry into the EEC

By the late 1950s the UK began to realise that the EEC was a force to be reckoned with and that, by staying outside it, the UK was losing economic advantages and political influence. The EEC rival organisation, EFTA (the European Free Trade Association), which had created a free trade area between Austria, Denmark, Norway, Portugal, Sweden, Switzerland and the UK, proved to be less successful than the EEC. In 1961 the UK applied for membership of the EEC, but largely because of the French veto did not become a member (together with Denmark and Eire) until 1973, when the EEC thus became the world's largest trading unit.

Greece joined the Community in 1981 and Spain and Portugal joined in 1986. We must now speak of the 12 members, therefore, and realise that it is now a Community of about 320 million people.

The organisation of the EEC and the relative powers of the Commission, the Council of Ministers, the European Parliament and the European Court of Justice are dealt with earlier in the book, in Chapter 12.

The broad economic roles of the EEC

From the economic standpoint, the EEC is a customs union. This means that there is free trade between the member countries, but common external tariffs against the imports of non-members. The aim is to promote the growth of trade between the EEC countries, and to impede imports from outside. The size of the tariff varies from commodity to commodity.

However, the economic union within the EEC goes further than simply a customs union. For example, free movement of labour between member countries is allowed. A number of institutions have, furthermore, been established to promote economic development within the EEC. We shall describe each of these in turn.

Initially, though, we must mention the form of financial measurement which is used by the EEC. Individual currencies like marks, francs or pounds are not used. The European Currency Unit (ECU) has been invented. The value of this unit of account is determined by a formula which includes differing amounts of each member's currency. Funds collected and spent by the EEC are thus denominated in ECUs.

The European Agricultural Guidance and Guarantee Fund

This body is responsible both for running the Common Agricultural Policy (CAP) and for schemes to improve the structure and efficiency of agriculture in the Community.

A fundamental aim of the CAP is stable and common food prices throughout the member States. In an attempt to achieve this objective, and to guarantee an income to farmers producing vital food commodities, the CAP operates in the following ways.

Target prices are set for each foodstuff, giving a suitable return to farmers. If non-EEC food imports can be bought below these prices on

408 International factors

world markets, then an import duty, a variable levy, is placed on them to make the import price comparable to that of EEC-produced food.

Furthermore, if EEC farmers cannot sell all their produce at the going price, they can sell the surplus to the Agricultural Fund at predetermined 'intervention' prices. These surpluses can be stored and released on the market in the event of shortages.

The CAP has the merit of encouraging farmers and providing them with a satisfactory income, so ensuring there should be no radical shortage of foodstuffs produced in the EEC.

However, the scheme has disadvantages. It means that consumers cannot benefit from cheaper, non-EEC food, because of the import levies. Also the intervention buying by the Agricultural Fund encourages wasteful overproduction, leading to 'butter mountains', 'wine lakes', etc. As previously mentioned, production quotas have been allocated to some farmers to reduce such overproduction.

The European Social Fund

This fund is intended to provide finance to member States to ease problems of unemployment, especially of migrant workers leaving declining areas and youth unemployment. Retraining programmes like the Job Training Scheme run by the MSC in the UK have been partly financed from this source.

The European Regional Fund

Set up in 1975 on British initiatives, the Regional Fund provides money to aid development in areas with a regional problem. Money from the Fund comes as an adjunct to regional policy expenditure designated by the government of the member State. Such regional policies (as more fully explained in Chapter 17) aim to create jobs and development in areas of high unemployment. For example, in 1980 Carreras Rothman received a grant of £4.5m towards a new cigarette factory at Spennymoor, County Durham.

The European Investment Bank

The European Investment Bank (EIB) provides loans usually for large high-technology projects, especially in the fields of energy and communications. For example, part of the finance for the second Dartford Tunnel came from the EIB. The UK steel industry received loans in the mid-1970s for the installation of new plant. In September 1981, British Rail borrowed £20m for the construction of new sleeping cars.

The European Development Fund

Foreign aid is the aim of the European Development Fund. Grants and loans can be made for improvements in the infrastructure (factories, roads, schools, etc.) of less developed countries. Former French colonies in Africa have been amongst the recipients.

EEC expenditure

The vast bulk of EEC expenditure goes on the CAP, as illustrated in Fig. 44.1

The pattern of EEC expenditure, and more particularly the UK's contribution to that expenditure, has been a bone of contention. Both Labour and Conservative Governments in the late 1970s felt embittered that agriculture took so large a proportion (about two-thirds) of EEC expenditure of which the UK receives a relatively small part. This reflects a more

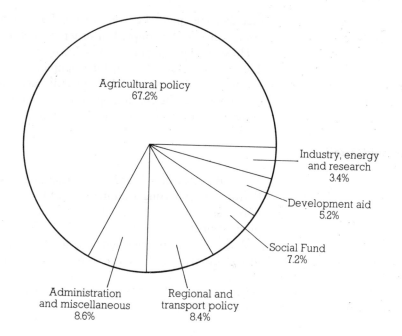

Fig. 44.1
EEC Expenditure 1985
Source: *Statesman's Year Book*
1986–7

efficient agricultural sector in the UK than in other EEC countries, where smaller farms are common, with a far larger proportion of the workforce employed in agriculture. Public opinion in Britain began to call for the country to leave the EEC.

After protracted negotiations agreement was reached on reduced net contributions for the UK. The budgetary position as affecting the UK has always caused the government to be dissatisfied. At the Fontainbleau summit meeting of EEC Ministers in 1984 a formula was worked out. As from 1985 the UK would receive a rebate from the Community equivalent to two-thirds of the difference between our contribution to EEC funds and EEC expenditure on the UK. Without this concession, the UK would have otherwise contributed up to one-fifth of the total income of the EEC and received in benefits only one-tenth of the Community's expenditure.

Although much development has taken place, the progress of the European Community has not been smooth. Entrenched national interests have often taken precedence over the European ideal. Harmonisation, or standardisation, of tax systems between member countries and the free movement of money capital have yet to be achieved. We do not yet have a 'common market' in its full sense, even though the growth of trade between EEC States has increased. Figure 43.4 shows the expansion of UK trade with EEC countries.

Another target of the founders of the EEC was European Monetary Union, with the ultimate aim of a single currency within the EEC. One step on this road began in 1979 when all EEC countries except Britain opted to join the European Monetary System (EMS). The EMS re-established fixed exchange rates between member countries in order to promote more stability in the foreign exchange market and encourage more international trade and investment.

The UK Government's decision not to participate was based on concern that damage might be done to the UK economy if balance of payments policies had to be adopted in order to preserve the exchange rate.

However, movement towards European Monetary Union has been slow. The Werner Plan of 1970, for example, envisaged the usage of a common European currency by 1980. The disparity of performance of European economies and the continuing desire for national sovereignty over economic policies are difficult obstacles to overcome.

International Cartels

You have doubtless heard of international bodies like the Organisation of Petroleum Exporting Countries (OPEC) and the International Air Transport Association (IATA). They are examples of **cartels** operating at an international level.

A cartel is a grouping together of producers of a product in order to act in concert with each other, so restricting competition.

What do you think will be the effect on price and output of a product if a cartel works effectively?

In essence a cartel operates on behalf of suppliers and against the interest of consumers. The restriction of competition will mean higher prices and the possibility of the limiting of output, such as by quota levels for different suppliers.

At the peak of its success in the 1970s OPEC restricted the quantity of oil by allocating output quotas to member states and setting higher price levels. The price of oil rose almost fourfold in only two years in the mid 1970s. These tactics increased income for the oil exporting countries and extended the life of extraction of this finite natural resource.

IATA limits the number of airlines eligible to fly on certain routes especially in Europe. This is done in order to avoid too many sparsely filled airlines competing on the same route, and thus possible bankruptcy in the airline industry. However, it does mean that consumer choice is limited and fares are higher than would be the case if there was more open competition.

The following conditions are necessary for a cartel to work effectively.

1 Demand for the product should be inelastic, so that if prices are increased demand would contract relatively little.

2 The product should not be substitutable in the short term, so that again demand would hold if prices were increased.

3 There is unity of purpose and cohesion amongst the member States in the cartel, so that individual countries would not break ranks and set price and output independently.

4 The cartel should control a substantial proportion of the market to reduce the risk of being undercut by non-members.

We shall now investigate the operations of international cartels in oil and tin, and consider how their activities have affected the British economy and British organisations.

◄ – OPEC

OPEC consists of a collection of Middle Eastern, African and South American countries which export oil. At the height of its potency in 1974, OPEC members controlled 52 per cent of world oil production. Agreements to raise oil prices and introduce output restrictions amongst member states were underpinned by Arab political unity to pressure the major Western oil importers to support the Arab side in the Arab–Israeli conflict.

In the space of less than two years prices were more than trebled by OPEC members to around $12 a barrel by the end of 1975. The end of the 1970s and early 1980s also saw substantial OPEC price rises, increasing to $34 a barrel in 1982.

What effects did this have on OPEC members? Clearly it increased their incomes, the bulk of which they invested in international banks on the financial markets. Some was invested in property, such as the acquisition of the Dorchester Hotel in London, whilst there was also some measure of spending on manufactured goods produced in industrialised countries.

What was the impact of the oil-importing countries? Many suffered aggravated balance of payments problems and opted for remedies such as those illustrated in Chapter 42. Remember that such restrictive policies can worsen unemployment and dampen economic growth. Furthermore, the oil price rises added to cost of production and distribution in a wide spectrum of industries, so pushing up the price of goods and services and adding to the rate of inflation.

The UK became an oil producer in the late 1970s with the exploitation of North Sea oil. However Britain did not join OPEC. Nor did other major producers like Mexico, the USSR and Norway.

British oil companies were content to supply oil at the prevailing high prices struck by OPEC. After all, it increased revenue and profits of the big oil companies and brought in more income for the government from Petroleum Revenue Tax. Unlike OPEC states, Britain stepped up output of oil as more North Sea fields were exploited.

However, as you may recall from Chapter 2, from late 1982 the oil price bubble began to burst. World oil prices started to fall, to $25 a barrel in 1985 and to less than $15 in 1986. The unity of OPEC wobbled as members made price cuts, and dissension broke out about which countries should bear the brunt of quota restrictions.

Why did this happen? Look back to the criteria above for the successful operation of a cartel. A number of these factors had become less secure for OPEC.

While OPEC had restricted output, non-member oil producers like the UK, Canada, Mexico and Norway had stepped up theirs. From controlling 52 per cent of world oil production in 1974, OPEC accounted for only 28 per cent by 1984.

Moreover, consequent upon the higher prices, industry in many countries had become more conscious of the need for energy conservation methods and had begun to adopt alternative techniques of production avoiding the use of oil, e.g. coal-fired or nuclear power stations rather than oil-fired.

Facing a surplus of oil in relation to a relative fall in demand, there was little option for OPEC but to cut oil prices. Clearly this reduced the incomes of member states but of course also decreased the earnings of oil companies in countries outside OPEC, and likewise cut the revenue of governments from the 'black gold' of oil. The oil price falls left Mexico in particular, in dire financial straits. However for consumers of oil th price falls brought good news – cheaper energy costs and cheaper motoring

In late 1986 OPEC tried to gather itself together under the new leader ship of Sheikh Hisham Nazer. Sheikh Yamani, the former Saudi Arabia Oil Minister who launched OPEC as a world political and economic force was sacked. Sheikh Yamani failed in his crucial attempts, particularly wit the warring states Iran and Iraq, to limit output and to take a moderate lin over pricing.

New negotiations planned for 1987 will attempt to return OPEC to fixed price system (the OPEC target price is $18 a barrel at the time c writing), but it is clear that this system can only work if OPEC can cut bac on output. This will be the difficulty as each country wants more of th available cake. The richest nations, such as Saudi Arabia and Kuwait, war to capitalise their production as much as the poorer members. They hav massive capital programmes in hand. There are levels of production belov which they simply cannot afford to drop unless power for air-conditionin and water desalination is restricted, given the drop in oil income. Th chances of success in negotiations are not assured.

Monitor future developments in OPEC negotiations and keep track of world oil prices. What are the effect of such changes on organisations in the UK?

Tin – the International Tin Council

The International Tin Council (ITC) was established in 1956 with the prim aim of stabilising world tin prices. Financed by both producer and import countries, it incorporated a buffer stock scheme to stabilise prices, bu unlike OPEC, the ITC did not allocate production quotas to countries.

A buffer stock scheme involves the purchase and storage of output supply exceeds demand, and the releasing of stored surpluses on to th market when demand exceeds supply. This brings more stability of incon for tin producers and easier planning and budgeting for tin users. Th tactic kept a reasonable degree of stability for tin prices for almost decades.

However, by the mid-1980s demand for tin had begun to fall, reflectii world industrial recession, but tin output by suppliers was sustained. Th pressure on prices was thus downward. The ITC continued to buy surpl tin to stabilise the price, but as this situation continued into 1985 fun became ever shorter for the buffer stock scheme.

Banks were reluctant to maintain lending to the ITC for fear that t value of security against the loans – namely the surplus tin – would decrea in price.

Tin prices began to drop noticeably (see Fig. 44.2) from a peak £10 300 in early 1985. To avoid a snowballing of the price fall, tin dealii on the London Metal Exchange was suspended in October 1985 pendii a solution to the dilemma. The price had dropped to £8500.

The price fall already experienced – and the potential for further cuts price – spelt gloom for tin producers. For example, tin mines in Cornw were scheduled for closure but were given a lifeline by a £15m injection funds from the government. For organisations using tin in their producti process, the fall in price was clearly good news – cheaper production cos

Fig. 44.2
Tin prices

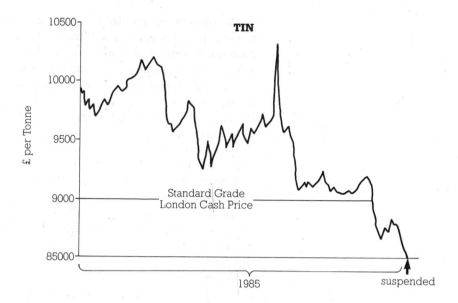

The tin market on the London Metal Exchange remained closed pending extra financing for the ITC, or a recognition that lower price levels for tin needed to be accepted.

There have been less effective attempts to form cartels for other primary products like cocoa, sugar, rubber and coffee, either on a quota allocation or buffer stock basis. None have consistently displayed the criteria necessary for the successful operation of a cartel over a continued period.

Summary, Part H

1 International trade takes place because of differing resource endowments between countries, to derive the benefits of international specialisation, and because consumers have varied wants which can be satisfied only by international transactions.
2 International trade is important to the UK because of the need to import necessary primary products, and also because of an increasing tendency to import manufactured goods. Exporting is consequently highly significant to the UK in order to cover the cost of such imports.
3 The major UK export in the mid-1980s was machinery and transport equipment, though there has been significant growth in the export of fuels.
4 Likewise, machinery and transport equipment was the UK's biggest import.
5 The proportion of British trade with other EEC countries expanded significantly through the 1970s and 1980s.
6 The countries with which Britain trades most are West Germany and the USA.
7 Newly industrialised countries have tended to produce at the cheaper end of markets, utilising modern micro-chip technology and cheap labour.
8 Factors which influence exporting and importing include price (which can be affected by movements in the exchange rate), trade restrictions (like

tariffs, quotas or regulations), foreign exchange controls, internation marketing techniques, government aid to exporters (e.g. export cred guarantees), and growth in world markets.

9 Multinational companies operate in a number of countries, and can u their global activities to adjust pricing policies to minimise tax liability ar increase profits.

10 The IMF was set up by the Bretton Woods Agreement, 1944. Its ma aims were to:

    a maintain fixed exchange rates;

    b 'lend' money to countries in balance of payments difficulties.

    A main development in the 1970s was the breakdown of the fixe exchange rates system.

    Conditions are attached to IMF loans.

11 GATT (the General Agreement on Tariffs and Trade) was drawn up the Havana Conference, 1947. Negotiations are carried out under th agreement.

12 Major landmarks in the historical background to the EEC wer Marshall Aid; the Council of Europe 1949; the European Coal and Ste Community 1954; the Treaty of Rome 1957, which brought about t formation of the EEC (and EURATOM); the UK's joining the EEC 1973.

13 Other institutions in the EEC include the Agricultural Guidance ar Guarantee Fund, the Regional Fund, the Social Fund, the Europe: Development Fund and the European Investment Bank.

14 In the economic field, the EEC is more than simply a customs unio Free movement of labour is permitted and international co-operation occu through the institutions of the Community.

15 However, some original aims of the EEC have yet to be achieved, e. European Monetary Union and harmonisation of tax systems betwee member countries.

16 An international cartel involves a grouping of countries acting togeth to restrict competition or to stabilise prices.

Assignment, Part H

1

Your organisation and international links

a To what extent does the organisation in which you may work engage in international dealings? (As an alternative choose a local organisation to investigate.) Describe recent international activities, e.g. purchase of imports, exports, investments, etc. in which your organisation may be involved.

b Explain the effects of rises or falls in the exchange rate on the volume and value of international dealings in which your organisation engages.

Skills

Learning and studying, communicating, information gathering, identifying and tackling problems, numeracy.

2

International Marketing

a The company in which you work manufactures word processors. Its sales are purely in the British market. What *additional* factors would the company have to consider if it wished to market the product in continental markets as opposed to simply the home market?

b By using the software package *Sixgam* (published by Pitmansoft) work in teams with fellow students to market competitively your company's word processor against those of other companies who will be represented by teams of other students.

c At each round in *Sixgam*, record your company's strategy and decisions, including your approach to deciding output, price and advertising. When the game is over, critically appraise the strategy adopted by your company. How successful was your company? With the benefit of hindsight would you have adopted different strategies? If so give reasons.

Skills
Numeracy, learning and studying, information gathering, working with others, communicating, information processing, identifying and tackling problems

3

International bodies

a In recent years IMF has given greater help and preferential treatment to less developed countries. Give a brief description of this aid and the likely reason for this policy.

b The most recent round of GATT negotiations is taking place in Uruguay. Maintain a diary of progress in these negotiations through analysis newspaper news items and articles. You should be able to give a presentation to the class of the background to GATT negotiations and analyse some of the political under-currents which influence the most recent round of negotiations.

Skills
Learning and studying, information gathering, communicating

4

CAP

Why was the EEC's Common Agricultural Policy introduced and what has been the effect on British farmers? Investigate the most recently fixed EEC budget and calculate the amount spent on the CAP.

Skills
Learning and studying, information gathering, communicating, numeracy

AN ORGANISATION IN ITS ENVIRONMENT – ACCOUNTABILITY

When you have read this final chapter you should be aware of:
The forces and bodies to which an organisation is directly and indirectly accountable.
The sources and impact of change on an organisation.

45 Hypersales Ltd – Sunhampton hypermarket

Throughout this book you have read of constraints within which organisations operate. The business environment restricts and influences the activities of organisations. You have read of the impact of economic, political, legal, social, technological and natural influences on the behaviour of organisations.

Amongst these environmental constraints are bodies and forces to which organisations are accountable. Accountability relates to the groups and forces to which an organisation needs to justify and explain its behaviour.

Central and local government

Central government itself is accountable to Parliament and ultimately to the electorate for its actions. Civil servants who work for central government may have their actions questioned in the courts or may have to account to the ombudsman for their decisions. Local government officers are similarly accountable to councillors at council meetings, and they in turn are ultimately accountable to the electorate at local government elections. The local government officers may also have to account to the local government ombudsman, or may have their actions questioned in the courts, e.g. on the grounds that they have exceeded the powers given to them by Parliament.

Nationalised industries

A nationalised industry with the legal personality of a public corporation has no accountability to shareholders (as has a private sector company), because it will have none. It is, however, directly accountable to the relevant government Minister. For example, British coal is directly accountable to the Secretary of State for Energy.

Additionally, a nationalised industry will have to account for its activities to Parliament, especially to the Select Committee on Nationalised Industries, and also to the relevant consumer consultative council. These councils acting on behalf of the users of the goods or services vet the quality provided and comment on prices charged.

We must remember, however, that while in the private sector the consumer may have a wide choice of supplies of the good or service, in the public sector there is probably little or no choice at all. As we said in

Chapter 30, if we want electricity in our home we must get it from the local Electricity Board.

Although the law of contract underlies the relationship between consumer and organisation, this relationship is an unequal one. The element of real subjective agreement in such a contract is small. The contract is more or less dictated to the consumer.

The private sector

By a similar token, private sector organisations are also accountable to varying groups and forces, though in some cases these are different from those that apply to the public sector. In Chapter 1 we referred to various organisations in Sunhampton High Street. To demonstrate more fully the nature of accountability we shall consider the example of a new organisation being established in Sunhampton.

* Hypermarkets were described in Chapter 29 (p. 282). Refer back if you need to refresh your memory.

Hypersales Ltd who already have 6 hypermarkets elsewhere in the UK plan to build a new hypermarket* on the fringe of Sunhampton. The site is near a major road and is sufficiently big to allow extensive car parking facilities for customers. The site is currently farmland. Hypersales Ltd have made an attractive offer for the site to Mr Smithers, the farmer, who is keen to sell.

To what forces and bodies is Hypersales accountable in this venture?

Shareholders

Hypersales is not accountable to shareholders on a day-to-day basis but principally at the Annual General Meeting of the company, directors can be voted out and replaced if enough shareholders are dissatisfied with the company's operations.

Shareholders may seek injunctions if they think that the company is about to exceed its powers laid down in the Memorandum of Association though the new venture in Sunhampton will not of course be such an instance.

Fig. 45.1
Car parking facilities at Sainsbury's, Burpham Branch, Guildford, by courtesy of J Sainsbury plc

Remember that, as yet, we have no law in the UK about industrial democracy, so that there is no legal rule compelling companies to have worker directors on the board. While Section 46 of the Companies Act 1980 says that directors should consult with employees when possible, they are not compelled to do so. There are no sanctions laid down in the Act for failure to consult. Thus in this context companies are more accountable to investors than to employees.

The law

You will realise, having read the previous chapters, that any business or other organisations must take account of legal requirements and may be subject to legal action if they fail to do so.

Once formed, the new branch of Hypersales Ltd will become part of the artificial legal person of the organisation. This will enable it to enter into contracts with suppliers of goods and services and with customers and to employ staff. In its purchase and use of premises it will have to take account of the law. All these activities, then, take place within a legal framework. The way in which Hypersales is itself set up and run will be regulated by those legal procedures laid down in the Companies Acts 1948 and 1985 which we have examined. Figure 45.2 illustrates examples of the legal accountability of Hypersales.

Creditors

Hypersales will buy stock from a number of manufacturers on trade credit, and thus will owe them money.

Fig. 45.2

To what extent is Hypersales accountable to these creditors?

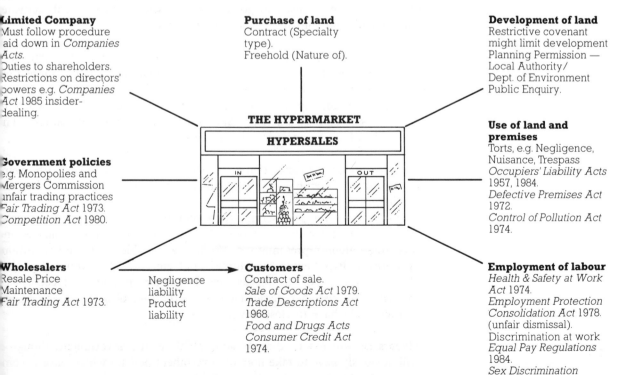

Limited Company
Must follow procedure laid down in *Companies Acts.* Duties to shareholders. Restrictions on directors' powers e.g. *Companies Act* 1985 insider-dealing.

Government policies
e.g. Monopolies and Mergers Commission unfair trading practices *Fair Trading Act* 1973. *Competition Act* 1980.

Wholesalers
Resale Price Maintenance *Fair Trading Act* 1973.

Purchase of land
Contract (Specialty type). Freehold (Nature of).

THE HYPERMARKET
HYPERSALES

Negligence liability
Product liability

Customers
Contract of sale. *Sale of Goods Act* 1979. *Trade Descriptions Act* 1968. *Food and Drugs Acts Consumer Credit Act* 1974.

Development of land
Restrictive covenant might limit development Planning Permission — Local Authority/ Dept. of Environment Public Enquiry.

Use of land and premises
Torts, e.g. Negligence, Nuisance, Trespass *Occupiers' Liability Acts* 1957, 1984. *Defective Premises Act* 1972. *Control of Pollution Act* 1974.

Employment of labour
Health & Safety at Work Act 1974. *Employment Protection Consolidation Act* 1978. (unfair dismissal). Discrimination at work *Equal Pay Regulations* 1984. *Sex Discrimination Act* 1975. Vicarious liability etc.

As we mentioned in Chapter 5, a limited company is a legal entit separate from the persons who are members of the company, i.e. share holders. This allows the shareholders to limit their liability in the event o the company being unable to pay its debts. This means that the share holders are only liable to the creditors for the unpaid amount, if any, o their shares (e.g. if a shareholder bought a newly issued £1 share for 60 the liability to the creditor would be 40p). Thus while the shareholders o Hypersales will be accountable to creditors, that accountability is limited It is quite possible, therefore, that creditors of a company like Hypersale might not recover all the money owing to them if the company were to b wound-up.

Whilst it is directly accountable to these forces and bodies, there are othe groups in the business environment of which Hypersales must take accoun in its policies and actions. Hypersales is not directly accountable to suc groupings, but failure to consider their importance and ignoring th pressure they might bear will imperil the smooth operation and growth o the organisation.

Such forces include the following.

Customers

As well as being accountable to the law in the field of consumer protection Hypersales must consider consumer response. If consumers are unhapp about the quality of products sold or of service provided, or if they conside prices to be unduly high, Hypersales will see their sales declining a customers shop elsewhere. Hypersales do not operate as a monopoly selle of foodstuffs and household goods. The market mechanism will activate and demand will shift towards other suppliers.

Suppliers

The relationship Hypersales will have with suppliers will of course be contractual one. If Hypersales fail to fulfil their contractual obligations the will render themselves liable to actions for breach of contract and will hav to compensate for any loss or damage. They themselves, by the same token wil be able to take legal action against suppliers for breach of contract. Th law is thus both a constraint and a safety net.

Employees

We have already explained that a company is accountable in law with regar to its duties to employees, e.g. unfair dismissal, hours and minimur conditions of work.

However, as well as observing these requirements, it is in the Hypersale management's interests to establish good relationships with employees an their trade union representatives. Without acceptable wages and condition of work, a discontented workforce could emerge. This would doubtles affect the quality of the service that Hypersales provide and could fee through into customer dissatisfaction. In the case of a strike, the hyper market might have to close down.

Government

Hypersales will not be directly accountable to the government, though i will obviously have to take note of government policies which have becom law.

The need to encourage competition in the economy has meant that law such as the Restrictive Trade Practices Act have been passed to make trading practices that would limit competition unlawful. If Hypersales were to attempt to buy up a large proportion of competing hypermarkets, super-stores and supermarkets, the degree of monopoly control might be investi-gated by a government body, the Monopolies and Mergers Commission. Hypersales could be prevented from pursuing the takeovers because of possible exploitation of consumers that could result.

As far as employment is concerned, policies of the 1974–9 Labour Government which were given legal force in Acts like the Employment Protection Act 1975 (now consolidated in the Employment Protection Consolidation Act 1978) control Hypersales' unrestricted power to sack employees.

Government prices and incomes policies are not usually made law because of the problems of enforcement, but the government may carry out sanc-tions against firms which do not take note of recommended guidelines by not giving contracts to those firms. As the government is a major customer of many firms this is a very important sanction.

Environmental pressure groups

Hypersales will have a duty in law concerning its responsibilities for the geographical environment. For example, the requisite planning permission must be granted before building of the hypermarket can be started.

However, additionally, Hypersales might come under fire from a local pressure group concerned about the further destruction of farmland and pleasant countryside. Such a pressure group might complain that there will be more traffic in the area as shoppers come to the hypermarket, and more litter and noise. Members of the group may write letters to the local news-paper, call local meetings to discuss the proposed hypermarket, and voice its objections to the planning authority.

Whilst Hypersales is not directly accountable to this pressure group, the company should realise that bad publicity and demonstrations about its development in Sunhampton would not be a good launching pad for success. Thus Hypersales' management may agree to meet representatives of the pressure group to attempt to allay their fears. The management may also write a letter to the local press rebutting the claims of the environmental group, and stressing the benefits the new hypermarket can bring to Sunhampton – the convenience of shopping in a large store with immediate parking facilities, and jobs to be created. To ignore the pressure group could create embarrassment and possible loss of sales for the company.

Of course, if the local pressure group is not satisfied with Hypersales' reaction, it may decide to take legal action against Hypersales, for example in nuisance (which we discussed in Chapter 17). Thus Hypersales would become legally accountable. An injunction might be issued against them to restrict their use of the premises, perhaps to limit the size of the car park. To disobey an injunction, you will remember, is to commit a criminal offence.

Business pressure

Pressure may be exerted not by people concerned about possible damage to the environment through setting up a hypermarket but by other busi-nesses who fear a drain of customers from the city centre to a hypermarket situated outside the town.

Fig. 45.3
Brent Cross large shopping precinct

An interesting case in point is the proposal by Marks and Spencer to locate a major shopping complex 10 miles outside Belfast. This proposal has caused considerable controversy and has led to a public inquiry. The result of that inquiry could have major implications for many towns and cities because M & S and other retail chains plan large-scale programmes for out-of-town developments. Opponents say that this trend could do serious damage to towns and city centres.

The M & S store in central Belfast is in the top 20 of the company's over 260 UK stores. Its food hall has recently become the busiest of them all. M & S has vanguarded the renaissance of Belfast city centre after the IRA bombing campaigns of the 70s destroyed nearly 300 shops in the city.

Their proposed move away from the centre does however make economic sense for them. The proposed site is well served by motorways and is on the main route to Belfast from the Irish Republic. There are no parking problems – it can accommodate 1 700 cars and coaches.

If M & S is a success at the new site of Springfield, the site will draw more and more firms out of Belfast, M & S will close down or curtail its own city operation and shopping in Belfast will atrophy. These arguments will be aired at a public inquiry opening in February 1987. Debates along similar lines are likely to take place in towns and cities throughout the UK as large firms forsake city centres for out-of-town sites. Even if M & S alone pursues this trend, the effect will be serious because M & S dominates local economies. With annual UK sales of £3.4bn, M & S is the country's largest and most successful retail organisation.

Internal accountability

We have described external forces to which Hypersales is accountable, and also groups that the company would be wise to take account of, so that operations run more smoothly. Note also the internal accountability which exists in an organisation like Hypersales. You will recall a description in

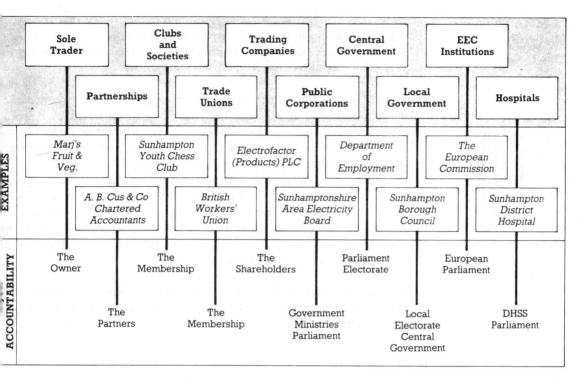

EXAMPLES

| Sole Trader | Clubs and Societies | Trading Companies | Central Government | EEC Institutions |

| Partnerships | Trade Unions | Public Corporations | Local Government | Hospitals |

| Marj's Fruit & Veg. | Sunhampton Youth Chess Club | Electrofactor (Products) PLC | Department of Employment | The European Commission |

| A. B. Cus & Co Chartered Accountants | British Workers' Union | Sunhamptonshire Area Electricity Board | Sunhampton Borough Council | Sunhampton District Hospital |

ACCOUNTABILITY

| The Owner | The Membership | The Shareholders | Parliament Electorate | European Parliament |

| The Partners | The Membership | Government Ministries Parliament | Local Electorate Central Government | DHSS Parliament |

g. 45.4
ie major accountability of
ganisations

Chapter 4 of the hierarchical structure of authority, accountability and responsibility within an organisation (see pp. 57–60).

For example, in the new hypermarket, staff are directly accountable for their actions to the manager, who in turn is responsible to the national Sales Director of Hypersales Ltd. The Sales Director is accountable to the rest of the board for the success or failure of the new enterprise.

Thus Hypersales cannot act without regard to other groups and forces. It must be mindful of its accountability both within its own organisational structure and also to the various external influences to which it is subject.

ccountability a part of the
ganisation's environment

We have concentrated on a description of accountability of one organisation to demonstrate its range and importance. Of course, all organisations are accountable to some bodies or persons. The main categories of accountability for the many types of organisations described in this book are listed in Fig. 45.

The forces and bodies to which an organisation is accountable form important parts of the environment in which each organisation operates. In this book you have read of the varying environmental constraints within which different organisations function. These environmental influences are ever changing. Failure to take account of differences in the environment or slowness to adapt or react to them spells danger for the future development of an organisation, or even its very existence.

he Hypermarket and change

A theme which runs through this book is the impact of change. We have concentrated in this chapter on the accountability of the organisation – in this case the hypermarket – but it is also interesting to see that the hypermarket is a good example of the impact of new technology on retail organisations. We might say that an important part of the total environment in which the hypermarket functions is new technology.

Bar codes

9 780272 798195

Bar codes are a good example of the use of computers in the hypermarket. Bar codes are made up of a number of dark lines, separated by 8 spaces. They give a lot of information about price, type of item and where it was made, and this information is 'read' at the check-out point when the cashier moves the bar code over a scanner.

Not only does this process avoid delays and mistakes – computers are good at doing routine jobs and don't get tired and bored like us – but it also puts a lot of information on computer. At the end of the day the manager can ask the computer for a complete list of everything that has been sold. This is vital in restocking the supermarket and in making decisions about the range of goods to be sold.

An understanding of the changing business environment is important to us as students, employees, consumers and as citizens partaking in social and political activities. Hopefully this book will have helped in such understanding.

Summary, Part I

1 An organisation is accountable to those forces or bodies to which it needs to explain and justify its actions.
2 The forces and bodies to which an organisation is accountable vary between public and private sector organisations.
3 There are chains of accountability within the hierarchical structure of an organisation.
4 Organisations must also take account of other forces in the business environment, particularly change, although there may be no direct accountability to them. Ignoring such forces could handicap the smooth operation of the organisation.

Assignment, Part I

British Rail

a Describe the bodies and forces to which British Rail is directly accountable, and how such influences affected the operation of this organisation.
b Describe also the links of accountability within the hierarchical management structure of British Rail. (You could write to British Rail Administrative Headquarters to discover this information.)
c Of which other forces and bodies does British Rail take account when planning major policies for the provision of rail services?
d Consider illustrations of technological change implemented by British Rail in recent years. What has been the impact of these changes on the provision of service and staffing levels?